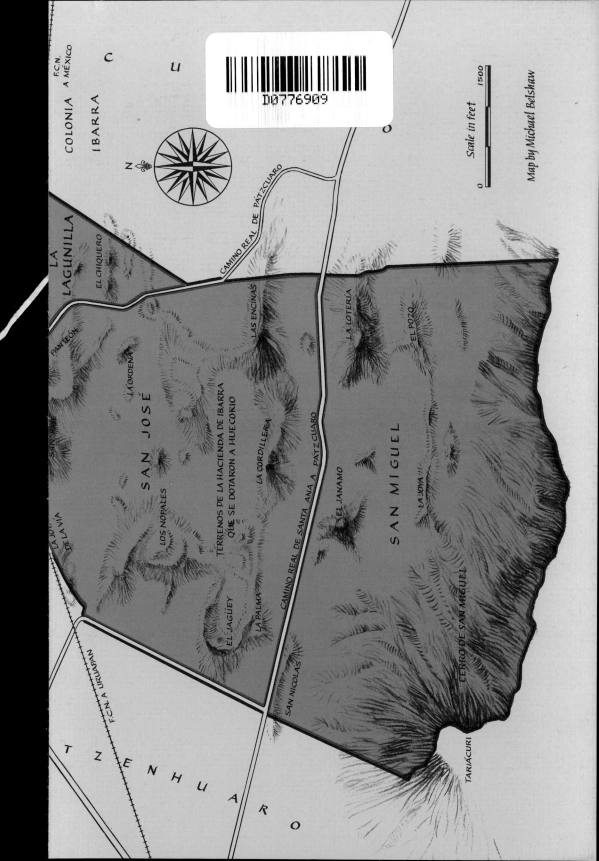

Map by Michael Belshaw

Scale in feet

0   1500

A Village Economy

LAND AND PEOPLE OF HUECORIO

MICHAEL BELSHAW

A Village Economy

LAND AND PEOPLE
OF HUECORIO

Columbia University Press
New York and London, 1967

Michael Belshaw is Associate Professor of Economics
at Hunter College,
the City University of New York.

All photographs, maps, tables, charts,
and drawings originated with and are the property
of the author.

THE INSTITUTE OF LATIN AMERICAN STUDIES OF COLUMbia University was established in 1961 in response to a national, public, and educational need for a better understanding of the contemporary problems of the Latin American nations and a more knowledgeable basis for inter-American relations. The major objectives of the Institute are to prepare a limited number of North Americans for scholarly and professional careers in the field of Latin American studies and to advance our knowledge of Latin America and its problems through an active program of research by faculty, by graduate students, and by visiting scholars.

Some of the results of the research program, as well as other research of direct interest to the program, are published in a series of the Institute of Latin American Studies. The faculty of the Institute believes that these publications will stimulate interest in and improve public and scholarly knowledge of Latin America and contribute to the advancement of inter-American relations. A VILLAGE ECONOMY: LAND AND PEOPLE OF HUECORIO is the second volume in the series.

The Institute of Latin American Studies is grateful to the Ford Foundation for financial assistance which has made this publication program possible.

To my father, Horace Belshaw,
who devoted his life to the service
of the rural folk of the world.

T H E intensive study of small communities and peasant societies has long been associated exclusively, and successfully, with the discipline of anthropology. In those studies anthropologists have focused on matters such as kinship systems, mythology, or relative cultural behavior more closely than thay have on economic phenomena. This is understandable, since few noneconomists are familiar with the host of problems that have arisen with the new-found interest in economic development, with its need for data on underemployment, types and rates of capital accumulation, new concepts of entrepreneurship, structural interrelationships in production, investment criteria, and so on. It was in search for answers to some of those problems that this study of Huecorio, a small agricultural community in the highlands of Central Mexico, was made.

There are broad, compelling reasons for studies of this kind. The bulk of the population of the world's less developed areas live in countless thousands of peasant communities, and unless their problems are understood and sympathetically analyzed, these rural folk will be condemned to an eternal netherland bereft of dignity, comfort, and happiness, and their poverty will tarnish the façade of progress elsewhere in their countries. Some will flee to cities to congregate in

the festering slums which mock the shining apartments and im-
maculate avenues. They will never have more than the cash sufficient
to buy their salt, kerosene, and cigarettes, and will thus give little
meaning to the factories whose products are outside their grasp.
Others will produce insufficient food even for their own people, and
the foreign exchange which might otherwise be used to buy machines
will go instead for basic provisions.

As I have observed Huecorio and the information its people so
generously gave, I have had three objectives constantly in mind: I
have tried to use the tools of the economist in diggings so far worked
mainly by the anthropologist; I have examined certain theoretical
problems with which postwar economists have wrestled; and I have
reflected on practical solutions and policies which might lighten or
remove the yoke under which the peasantry labor. I have had to undertake a broad yet intensive study which goes far beyond the terri-
torial limits of economics and is as complete as my limited time and
resources would allow.

HUECORIO, 1962: VIGNETTE
OF A LARGER CANVAS

The first impression one has as one approaches a village such as
Huecorio is the sight of a low covey of houses—usually with tiled
roofs—nestled for protection about the tower of the mother church.
In the fields about, men are driving their teams of oxen at a steady,
deliberate pace as they plough and cultivate their inadequate but life-
giving corn. When one comes upon the village plaza a group of
women might be waiting patiently and quietly—a certain resignation,
fortitude, and stamina is a constant among the Mexican *campesinos*
and their womenfolk—for a bus to trundle them and their burdens
to a larger market place. In the mud or cobblestone streets pigs will
be wallowing in stagnant, ugly pools while cautious, emaciated dogs
slink furtively about hoping for the pigs to die and offer an easy meal.
And above all this, the green slopes of precipitous mountains, capped

by the foam of clouds, rise like waves threatening to engulf all that man has precariously wrested from a weakening soil.

The sounds are unique and characteristic. There is, for instance, a certain inflection to the voice as a man calls his fellow across the *milpa*. Francisco would become FranSEESCOOOoo, with the heavy emphasis on the middle syllable and the last one extended and sliding down in a glissando. Men working their *yuntas* of oxen will constantly call and prod them verbally with a gasping HA! while some will whistle and others sing in the falsetto of the *ranchero* to all who will listen. Behind the adobe walls will come the blaring comfort of radios playing popular music, unfortunately little different from the kind one is exposed to in the United States.

One becomes aware, as never before, of the sense of smell. The mud is redolent with vapors of indescribable refuse, and wood fires from the ovens send an agreeable, astringent smoke filtering through the tile roofs. Or one may catch the warm, friendly aroma of *tortillas* as they are delicately picked from the griddle. The visitor is likely to carry away with him these impressions rather than the less visible ones.

Huecorio has an uncanny resemblance to an underdeveloped country in miniature. Its borders are clearly defined, and it has within it a variety of regions ranging from the precipitous volcanic shield of Tariácuri which looms in the south, to the placid waters of Lake Pátzcuaro lapping the rich lands of the northern shore. Between these extremes lies the village itself, surrounded by relatively fertile valley plains separated from each other by small sterile hills. Less than a mile to the west lies another small village-state, Tzentzenhuaro. Until an "agency of the United Nations" ended the hostility, a Tzentzen-huariano could pass through Huecorio only at the risk of a beating, and rumbles between the youths of the different peoples were commonplace.

The "agency of the United Nations" is the *Centro Regional Para la Educación Fundamental Para la América Latina* (CREFAL), which, supported by the United Nations Educational, Scientific and Cultural Organization and by the Organization of American States, has wrought many benefits among the lakeside villages, not the least of which is the softening of traditional animosities. CREFAL is situated in nearby Pátzcuaro on property donated by General Lázaro Cárdenas, and to it come students from almost all of Latin America to receive training in community development.

Pátzcuaro, and its satellite suburb Colonia Ibarra, share Huecorio's eastern frontier; and as the seat of the *municipio,* Pátzcuaro represents the locus of a powerful, external political power. Indeed, Huecorio is a colony, since its local government functions only by the grace of *políticos* in Pátzcuaro.

The rigid, traditional social structure has broken down in Huecorio, and only vestigial elements remain. Villagers, for instance, will go through the motions of deference to persons such as teachers or priests who once had a more absolute authority, but increasingly they reserve allegiance for those whose merits have been demonstrated.

Huecorianos are highly individualistic, but in a sense that is ego- rather than group-focused. As individuals they are intelligent and often witty and articulate, but these good characteristics are rarely allowed to flower for lack of educational opportunity. Physically, the Huecorianos have stamina but not energy, and the pace of life is listless.

The parallels with a typical underdeveloped country are even more clear in the economic sphere. For instance, the population is, as in most such countries, largely dedicated to primary industry (in this context, agriculture, aviculture, fishing, etc.), but there is a shift into secondary industry (manufacturing); and, characteristically, the first such industry to be established in Huecorio was in textiles. The rate of internal capital accumulation has been insufficient to maintain standards of living for a rapidly growing population, and Huecorio has had to import capital from "abroad."

Huecorianos are clearly materialistic. They know the better things that life has to offer, they dream about them and speak about them and work hard to make them come closer. But the struggle is generally a hard and a sad one, and villagers young and old wonder if perhaps the grass is not greener somewhere else, particularly in *el norte*—the United States.

In analyzing the data from Huecorio it was, of course, necessary to refer from time to time to other community studies, and I leaned most heavily on Oscar Lewis' *Life in a Mexican Village,* George Foster's *Empire's Children,* and Ralph Beal's *Cherán.*[1] These classic studies provided models and inspiration for my own work, and yet when cross references were made on any problem the differences among the four Mexican communities were striking. The more closely one examined the details, in such matters as techniques of cultivation, size of work teams, religious practices applied to agriculture, and so on, the farther apart the villages grew; yet Cherán, Tzintzuntzan, and Huecorio are all in the Tarascan culture area, and Tzintzuntzan and Huecorio are less than ten miles from each other. Considering the rich variety of detail despite the physical proximity of the villages, one must infer that until recently the villages lived as worlds (hence cultures) apart from each other in the Mexican cultural galaxy, and evolved diversely from what was once a common denominator.

But are there other reasons? As this analysis drew to a close, I came upon *The Small World of Khanh Hau* by James Hendry.[2] This is a study of a village in South Vietnam undertaken by an economist. In the comparison of Khanh Hau with Huecorio, the similarities rather than the differences were apparent, especially in the general conclusions regarding innovations and the skeptical view concerning agriculture. What could account for the apparent differences among Mexican villages and the apparent similarities between two peasant communities half a world apart? The other Mexican villages were studied before 1950, Khanh Hau in 1958 and 1959, and Huecorio in 1962. The differences in time would seem unimportant. A more likely explanation would lie with the interests of the investigators themselves. The other Mexican studies contained substantial economic data but not economic analyses, since it was at least equally important to the researchers to record information on religion, folk-

[1] Oscar Lewis, *Life in a Mexican Village: Tepoztlán Restudied* (Urbana, University of Illinois Press, 1951).

George M. Foster, *Empire's Children: The People of Tzintzuntzan* (printed in Mexico City, Imprenta Nuevo Mundo, S.A., 1948; Smithsonian Institution, Institute of Social Anthropology, Pub. No. 6).

Ralph L. Beals, *Cherán: A Sierra Tarascan Village* (Washington, USGPO, 1946; Smithsonian Institution, Institute of Social Anthropology, Pub. No. 2).

[2] James B. Hendry, *The Small World of Khanh Hau* (Chicago, Aldine Publishing Co., 1964).

lore, ceremonials, the life cycle, the quality of interpersonal relations, and so on.

The differences in the details to be found in all the studies are of real interest and demand further study and explanation, but, one wonders, would not the general outlines fuse and make the villages indistinguishable if the same approach were applied to all of them? Are there not in all peasant communities certain attributes, aspirations, reactions to change, qualities of interpersonal relations, etc., which they hold in common? If there were, and these could be clearly labeled, would not policy formulation for rural welfare be enormously facilitated?

SOME MATTERS OF METHOD

In all, the research for this study entailed four separate visits to Mexico starting with an exploratory trip in 1960. At that time an official of CREFAL, Professor Anibal Buitrón, pointed out the desirability of community studies by economists, and at his suggestion Pátzcuaro was revisited for five weeks in 1961 in order to select a community. The community had to meet two criteria, both of them dictated by the short time I would have at my disposal between academic assignments. The community would have to be open and not hostile to outsiders who would not have time for the usual "softening-up" and familiarization; and it would have to accept the intrusion of a group of people rather than the quiet insinuation of one person working by himself. Huecorio proved a happy choice. Work began within ten days of our arrival, and firm and permanent friendships were welded between Huecorianos and members of the team.

Huecorio was selected for another reason as well. Unlike some other Pátzcuaro villages with heavy specializations in, and ancient traditions of, handicrafts, Huecorio was primarily agricultural and thus it was a more useful subject for generalization.

The bulk of the field work was done in slightly less than three months during the summer of 1962, by a team of five and sometimes six persons using questionnaires, most of which I had prepared during the preceding spring.

My work included not only interviews when they could be managed, but chasing leads in Pátzcuaro and elsewhere and getting tangled in more supervisory administrative chores than I normally relish. Even for a team as small as this, a full-time secretary-administrator would free the project chief for more important duties. The task of organizing the material, grinding out the statistical data on an old Monroe calculator, drawing maps, analyzing the findings and expressing them on paper, consumed every available moment after my return to *gringoria,* as the Huecorianos sometimes good-naturedly call the United States. When, by the close of the summer in 1964, it became apparent that several small but crucial gaps existed in the data and that this information could not be elicited at long distance, a hurried drive to Pátzcuaro was undertaken and in a few days the gaps were filled.

Clearly, a group of foreigners appearing without warning in a rural community will raise nascent fears, and at the beginning it was rumored that we were *evangelistas*—undesirable Protestant missionaries. However, Miss Cuadrado and Miss Kaseta, two members of the team, began to organize a choir in the church, and given the musical propensities of the Huecorianos this was an immediate success. A minority thought perhaps we might be *comunistas,* and one old man charged, in fine confusion, that we were in league with the *yanquis,* Pancho Villa, and the pope to take his ancestral Tarascan lands away. Among some villagers there may have been a smoldering resentment of the American members of the team, since many Mexicans remember incidents in history that Americans forget or never knew.

It was, of course, extremely difficult to find people at home, since our visit coincided with the peak agricultural season. There were a few families who did not willingly open the door to us, in some cases perhaps because of indignation at the nature of our inquiry and in others perhaps because of laziness or hostility.

Including a Census of people, land, and animals, six questionnaires were used. The most important of these, the Agricultural Survey and the Social Survey, each covering some 35 households, were begun simultaneously in July. The Agricultural Survey dealt with all economic and technical facets of working the land, and the Social Survey delved into such matters as demographic attitudes, aspirations, savings, travel, and attitudes concerning the village. A fourth questionnaire was applied to two of the four storekeepers, and a fifth to the garment-making enterprise. Both of these focused on entrepreneurial histories and attitudes, capital accumulation, incomes, and so on. Finally, a sixth questionnaire was designed to be flexible enough to use in examining other occupations, such as the *comerciantes,* carpenters, or bakers, that we did not catch elsewhere.[3] It was decided not to publish the questionnaires since they are all very lengthy, are in need of modification, and would require considerable explanation.

The organization of this study is built upon an analysis of the classic factors of production—land, labor, capital, and entrepreneurship. Added to this analysis are observations on population, the social and political situation, and, finally, the level and standard of living. I have tried, in other words, to account for all the internal circumstances that impinge upon the economic condition of the people of Huecorio and to suggest some of the external factors, such as the migrant labor policies of the United States government, that play their role. Much of the work is comprised of abundant descriptive detail, and there are three reasons for this: (i) The greater the detail, the more fruitful will be the comparison of Huecorio with other communities or with itself at a later date. (ii) Huecorio is a village that holds within it a great diversity of regions, attitudes, and conditions, and at very few points is it possible to indulge in unqualified generalizations. Huecorianos are individuals of very different circumstances and outlooks, and this diversity must be acknowledged. (iii) The greater the detail, the more meaningful the analysis built upon it. We could not, for example, make predictions about the acceptability of innovations in corn cultivation unless we knew about the number and types of seeds in a *mata,* the distances between rows, the employment picture during the growing season, and so on. It is these analyses, in-

---

[3] The surveys were coded A through F. See Appendix D for designations.

tertwined with the descriptions, that suggest the policies for rural development with which the book concludes.

The various sections of the study are sufficiently autonomous so that a reader can, if he wishes, devote himself only to the subject of special interest to him. Indeed, there are some parts, for instance that describing the techniques of agricultural production, that will have only a limited interest for the general reader. These can be passed over with a free conscience. By the same token, we have frequently reused the building blocks of our observations and findings in structuring the chapters according to the different socioeconomic aspects of life in Huecorio. In the interest of completeness of presentation, this has necessitated a certain amount of recapitulation and to some extent repetition.

Although Huecorio is a real village and its people are of flesh and blood, the names of the villagers have been changed to offer them the protection of some anonymity.

MICHAEL BELSHAW

New Milford, Connecticut
April, 1966

ACKNOWLEDGMENTS

T H I S study of Huecorio is a harvest of the labors of many persons and institutions. There were, of course, the members of the team who assisted me in the field investigation, and the energy and enthusiasm with which they undertook their assignments contributed much to any merit this study might have. Two students from Hunter College—María Cuadrado and Elizabeth Kaseta—added translating and typing to their interviewing responsibilities, and they were joined in the field work by David Barkin from Columbia College. Toward the end of our visit we had the good fortune to be aided in our interviewing by the village kindergarten teacher, Señorita Rosita Hernandez. I wish to extend special tribute to Señor Richard Bolívar, who came to work for the project with neither pay nor reimbursement for air transportation from his native Venezuela. Señor Bolívar had been a student at the nearby *Centro Regional para la Educación Fundamental para la América Latina* in 1961 and had worked and lived in Huecorio, and his magnanimity was prompted by a sincere interest in the project and in the people of the village. Needless to say, his friendship with the people of Huecorio and the officials of Pátzcuaro opened many a door, and his perceptive questioning was outranked only by the long hours he worked.

From CREFAL came assistance and counsel from many persons, including the director, Professor Lucas Ortiz, the deputy director, Professor Lloyd Hughes, and the administrative officer, Señor Francisco Martínez. Much useful information on supervised credit was given to us by Ingeniero Manuel Cepeda de la Garza of the *Banco Agrícola y Ganadero* in Pátzcuaro and Ingeniero Trinidad Vegas Ríos of the *Banco Nacional de Crédito Ejidal* in Villa Escalante, while Señor Roberto Pita Carnejo, *Secretário de la Presidencia Municipal* of Pátzcuaro, filled us in on details of village-*municipio* relations. General Lázaro Cárdenas, ex-president of the Republic of Mexico, took us under his wing and amplified at length answers to many of the problems that interested us. In the village itself, we had the welcome and wholehearted support of one of the priests, Padre José Cortés Castro.

Much of the facility with which we entered Huecorio is surely due to Señora Carolina Múgica, the widow of a Revolutionary War general, whose Quinta Tzipecua is a flourishing experimental farm near Huecorio's eastern frontier. Señora Múgica has had a lengthy and warm association with the people of Huecorio, and not only did she escort us to visit some individual villagers, but she and Professor Alfredo Mendoza of CREFAL spoke on our behalf at a village meeting soon after our arrival. Although only some 65 of Huecorio's 850 inhabitants attended the meeting, we took this as a green light to begin our work. The cooperation we received from the people of Huecorio exceeded our expectations. We accepted their hospitality and gave nothing in return; we invaded their privacy and abused them with interviews lasting on the average two and a half hours; and yet, one suspects, they were aware vaguely of the broad significance of their contribution and so they gave generously.

In the United States, the sometimes tedious analysis of the data was lightened by the continuing and active interest in Huecorio manifested by the fine young ladies of Hunter College, among whom I might single out Miss Margaret Geyer, who worked with me in checking some of the statistical data. Much of the manuscript was scrutinized by Professor Charles Issawi of Columbia University, and his comments were indeed helpful. Professor Charles Wagley of Columbia took a most active interest in the project, and in many respects is responsible for guiding its successful culmination. An excellent job of typing the manuscript should be credited to Miss Ellen Moore of New Milford, Connecticut; and I cannot express sufficient praise for the firm, tactful, and thorough editing of Mrs. Marian Maury of Columbia University Press.

Clara, my wife, spent many quiet hours as a book widow, and for her forbearance I am grateful.

The Social Science Research Council contributed toward the cost of the field work undertaken in 1962, and the National Institute of Mental Health aided in the preparation of the manuscript for publication. Without such help, this study would have been most difficult.

I wish to thank Professor Everett E. Hagen, the Center for International Studies of the Massachusetts Institute of Technology, and the Dorsey Press for permission to quote from Professor Hagen's *On the Theory of Social Change*. Padre José Cortés Castro, now of Comanja, Michoacán, kindly gave permission to quote freely from his correspondence with me.

CONTENTS

A Village Economy

LAND AND PEOPLE OF HUECORIO

CHAPTER 1

THE LAND:
ITS USE AND ABUSE

As his car crests the mountain ranges halfway between Mexico City and Guadalajara, the tourist will see what seems an earthly paradise.[1] At the foot of towering, forested peaks lies a peaceful, crescent-shaped lake, shimmering in the morning sun or dark and threatened by late afternoon cumulus clouds. Several small islands pierce the surface, and canoes and launches ply their stolid commercial trails from island to island and shore to shore. Little orange-tiled knots of houses nestle into the bay line, and one larger cluster (on the southeast quadrant), dominated by a gray cathedral, is Pátzcuaro, the municipal seat for about 30,000 persons of the town and its dependent villages. One of these, some three miles distant by road, is the anonymous little community of Huecorio.[2]

Huecorio's communications are good. The one and a third miles to the Pátzcuaro railway depot are covered by a rather poorly maintained highway. Another two miles along the national highway take the villagers to the center of Pátzcuaro. Some local buses from Pátzcuaro terminate their run in the village, but more commonly the

---

[1] The distance by road to Pátzcuaro from Mexico City is 236 miles, and from Guadalajara 215 miles.

[2] Huecorio's precise location is 19°32′ North, 101°37′ West.

Huecorio, seen from the volcano Tariácuri

villagers squeeze into, or if they are men on to, the trunk line *flechas* that lumber between Pátzcuaro and Erongarícuaro on the other side of the lake.

If the buses are too crowded to take on one more—an unlikely event as anyone who knows rural Mexico will appreciate—or if a person is short of change, the distances are not great enough to discourage walking. In fact, the road is host to a constant stream of pedestrians, particularly early on Friday morning as the womenfolk carry goods to the main weekly market. On Sunday, whole families sally forth to the town for the services at the *basílica* and diversion in the squares, *cantinas,* and movie houses.

There is regular bus service to more distant points from both Pátzcuaro and Quiroga on the northern end of the lake about fourteen miles away. National Railways of Mexico offers a twice-daily run to and from Mexico City in one direction and Uruapan in the other.

Villagers will sometimes use taxis, especially to return from Pátzcuaro or the railway station when they are burdened with heavy loads. The trip from Pátzcuaro costs eight pesos, and that from the station five pesos, but since the daily cash wage of a *peón* is only six

3

or seven pesos, taxis are not a common means of transport. No villager owned a mechanically powered vehicle, although toward the end of our visit one was negotiating the purchase of an old truck.

Few persons not of the Pátzcuaro region know of, or pass through, Huecorio. The highway to Erongarícuaro is not inviting, and only rarely does a foolhardy tourist motor along it on his way to visit the handicraft shops of Lena Gordon or Vicki.[3]

The road from the Pátzcuaro railway depot skirts the lake, and Huecorio is the first of several villages through which it passes. Shortly after leaving Colonia Ibarra, in which the depot is situated, the traveler sees a castle-like structure perched on a rocky outcropping. This is the Quinta Tzipecua, owned by the active and public-spirited widow of Francisco Múgica. Near the Quinta the road curves gently southward, and the church spire and red roofs of Huecorio come into view. At the walled entrance to the church, the highway narrows and twists sharply to the left, only to turn immediately to the right at the corner where Don Juan is busy in his *taller* behind an adobe wall which is shorn short to permit buses to negotiate the bend. A few more houses, and then the road opens to allow the car to speed up and leave Huecorio behind.

To the casual passer-by, this fleeting acquaintance with Huecorio will leave no impression, since nothing apparent distinguishes it from the other Mexican pueblos that he has seen. There are the tiled-roof adobe houses, a tiny public garden hardly identifiable as such by its pathetic flowers and shriveled trees, the ancient church behind a stone entrance gate, children at play in the basketball court before the school, a lone woman merchant squatting near a public faucet, and perhaps some farmers leading cows or burros to the fields. The substance of the village is, of course, its people. Although villagers are shy, if the stranger is known even slightly he is everywhere po-

---

[3] From the station to the dock on the lake shore from which the launches leave for the island of Janitzio, the road is a divided, cobblestone avenue. The surface is uneven and full of holes so that little of it can be negotiated above low gear. Deep holes and insufficient drainage convert the section to Huecorio into a rainy-season morass. Beyond Huecorio, in the village of San Pedro, large stones in the pavement reach up to impale oil pans and transmissions on the newer American-made automobiles.

litely greeted, *"Buenos días, maestro."* But the passer-by could not know this.

Streets and alleys radiate irregularly from the center, and along them are strung clusters of houses, interspersed with garden plots. Few of the streets are negotiable by automobile, and the visitor usually walks.

To the north, a street leaves the main nucleus of houses and turns into a dirt track leading to an outlying cluster of dwellings on a knoll by the water's edge. This is Carián, once an island. In it live a group who are predominantly fisherfolk and who retain, more than the remainder of the inhabitants, elements of the original Tarascan culture. Here even young children speak Tarascan, and there is some evidence that the people are more favorably inclined toward cooperation than those of the center. Huecorio's most fertile fields line the lake shore, and in the gardens one will see a large variety of familiar vegetables.

Another street leads directly from the park to the cemetery and the *plaza de toros* just across the railroad track at the southern extremities of habitation. This ancient *Camino Real de Pátzcuaro* continues and climbs stepwise over spiny, uncultivated ridges until it reaches the precipitous walls of the extinct volcano, *Cerro de San Miguel,* from whence it turns east to enter Pátzcuaro itself. *El Camino Real* is seldom used for passage to Pátzcuaro, since the newer highway is decidedly more convenient. On it one sees only an occasional farmer and his animals on their way to work on the narrow fields where maize can be gleaned from the relatively level areas between the ridges. Little of the land to the south of the railroad tracks is very productive, and, in spite of the severe shortage of crop land, it tends to be neglected by the farmers.

An ancient map of the lake region[4] shows the village and indicates that it was in existence at the time of the Conquest. One informant with a sense of history stated that Bishop Don Vasco de Quiroga established one of his famous "hospitals" there, and that he was responsible for instilling into the people a spirit of industriousness. His coat of arms emblazons the gate to the churchyard.

Two legends persist to explain how Huecorio came to have its name. According to one, Tariácuri, a king of the Tarascans, was

[4] See Foster, Plate 1, The Beaumont map of Tzintzuntzan.

passing from Pátzcuaro to Jarácuaro when, at the site of the present village, he slipped and fell. The Tarascan word for "fall" is recorded variously as *huecorio, huecorinta, huecorincha,* or *guecorio,* and in the form *huecorio* it commemorates this event. In a somewhat less dramatic legend, a meteorite was seen to drop from the sky and the place of its discovery was thus recorded. With the Conquest, the Tarascan name was Christianized to San José Huecorio, but this full appellation is never used.[5]

THE MAIN VILLAGE REGIONS

The Village Center

The main center of habitation consists of an irregular web of streets and paths radiating from the churchyard. The large mass of the church naturally dominates the center's nucleus, but other important buildings lie close to it. Attached to the church, and sharing its court, is the public primary school and kindergarten. There is a small, cobbled public square where, in March, the villagers hold outdoor performances of Mexican and Shakespearean theater under the stimulation of CREFAL. Around the square are a community center, which houses a meeting hall, a dispensary, and a library; a public laundry; *la jefatura,* the meeting chamber for public officials; the unused jail; another small chapel; and a few retail shops selling canned goods, cookies, soft drinks, and—before our team spoiled the game—illicit alcohol.[6]

[5] Twice we were told that the *caciques* of Tzintzuntzan buried treasure near the village to prevent it from falling into the hands of the *conquistadores.* The informants offered to show us its location if we would bring along "one of those machines that can find treasure."

[6] Toward the end of our visit two male members of the team were walking through the square on their way to an interview. They were accompanied by a young Mexican veterinarian employed by the federal government and a local project of Montana State College. As they passed one of the stores the *jefe de tenencia* and some of his friends staggered out. They strongly urged our colleagues to join them. When this offer was refused, the *jefe* threatened the men with the hospitality of

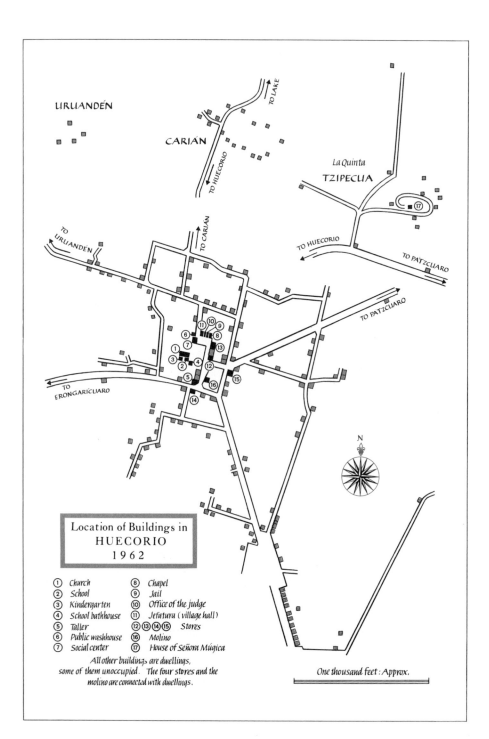

URUANDÉN

CARIÁN

TO LAKE

TO HUECORIO

La Quinta
TZIPECUA

TO CARIÁN

TO URUANDÉN

TO HUECORIO

TO PATZCUARO

TO PATZCUARO

⑪ ⑩ ⑨
⑥ ⑧
⑦ ⑬
①
③ ④
② ⑫
⑤ ⑯ ⑮
⑭

TO
ERONGARÍCUARO

N

Location of Buildings in
HUECORIO
1962

① Church   ⑧ Chapel
② School   ⑨ Jail
③ Kindergarten   ⑩ Office of the judge
④ School bathhouse   ⑪ Jefatura (village hall)
⑤ Taller   ⑫⑬⑭⑮ Stores
⑥ Public washhouse   ⑯ Molino
⑦ Social center   ⑰ House of Señora Múgica

All other buildings are dwellings,
some of them unoccupied. The four stores and the
molino are connected with dwellings.

One thousand feet : Approx.

The houses in the village are not necessarily nestled wall-to-wall, as is common elsewhere in Mexico, but tend to be detached and strung out along the streets, with the intervening spaces utilized for small orchards or garden plots. Most houses have foundations of easily worked volcanic stone, adobe walls, wooden eaves, beams, and doors, and orange clay tile roofs. Most have only two rooms, one of which is a kitchen with a clay oven. None has a chimney, and the smoke is permitted to filter lazily through the spaces between the tiles above. Usually there is a dirt-floored patio sealed off from passers-by by a high wall. Floors are of earth, cement, or tile, and few houses have glass windows.[7]

The land surrounding the center is privately held. The fields are separated by stone walls which are deliberately breached to permit the passage of animals and ploughs. These walls do not necessarily delineate ownership, however, since subdivision through sale or inheritance fragments the fields. Demarcation within the fields is usually indicated by a raised ridge of dirt, although in some cases the holdings are distinguished by the use of barbed wire.

La Orilla (*The Lake Shore*)

As recently as 1905, the waters of the lake lapped at the doors of the village itself. The waters then receded, apparently as the result of a secular decline in rainfall. Vegetables and other crops can grow here in every month except December, January, and February, when killing frosts are likely; and the high water table permits industrious farmers to irrigate this land during the dry season.

---

the jail, an invitation that could only be declined by the moderate use of force. The incident shortly reached the ears of the *presidente municipal* (an office that would correspond roughly to that of mayor), who was not pleased by the behavior of his representative in the village. As a result the *jefe* and some of his friends had an opportunity to reconsider their activities from the vantage point of the municipal jail. The store owners took the hint and ceased their unlicensed sales of *aguardiente*. Village reaction seemed largely favorable, since unrestrained public drinking was beginning to assume serious proportions.

[7] For a more complete description of housing conditions and construction see below, Chapter 8.

Fluent springs arising in the nearby mountains flow only a few feet under the surface of the *orilla,* and one of these has been tapped by a high velocity pump which lifts water to a tank on the other side of the village, from whence it flows to Huecorio and other communities.

Several small knolls rise from the level *orilla.* Two, *La Isla de Carián* and *La Isla de Urandén Morales,* are inhabited, as we have seen. These are still called islands, as indeed they were before the waters of the lake receded and left them stranded.

Ejido Lands

The *ejido* lands were passed to the village after the Revolution, when a nearby *hacienda* was repartitioned. Title to the land is held in common by the village, but a given parcel is assigned to a farmer to be worked individually.[8]

The Irrigated Ejidos of San Pedrito and La Lagunilla

These lie to the east and southeast of the Quinta Tzipecua, and border on the lands of Colonia Ibarra. The term "irrigated" is used qualifiedly, since no system of organized canals exists through which a controlled flow of water can pass to the fields. Rather, by diverting a stream known as the Río Guan, the villagers deliberately flood different sections of the land in alternate years. This stream rises in the hills behind Pátzcuaro and deposits in the fields not only automobile tires, bottles, tin cans, old boots, and other flotsam of the town, but also a rich fluvium which, some farmers claim, has raised the land's productivity. In the summer of 1962 San Pedrito north of the highway was in corn, while a part of San Pedrito south of the highway and La Lagunilla were "resting" and profiting from the combined but contrary effects of the flooding Río Guan and the village's grazing animals.

[8] A more complete description and analysis of this system is presented later in this chapter.

The Mountain Ejidos of San José and San Miguel

South of the railway line, in the foothills of the volcano San Miguel, little valleys and some relatively gentle slopes offer land which can be planted in corn and wheat. This soil is rocky and thin and most farmers do not consider its cultivation worth the effort. Nothing is done to utilize the foothills themselves, other than to graze cattle lightly, chop an occasional tree for firewood, or pick the fruit of the cactus. The walls of the volcano are covered with the light forest of pines.

Regional Distribution of Land

Table I shows the distribution of land among the various regions of the community.[9] For analytical purposes, La Quinta Tzipecua will be excluded from all calculations unless otherwise indicated. Thus, the total area available to members of the village is 1,426.2 acres. Of this, 967.3 acres (67.82%) is *ejido,* 168.9 acres (11.84%) is *federal,* and 290 acres (20.34%) is private. To arrive at the total arable area we must subtract those areas too hilly or stony to plant (448.7 acres) plus the estimated residential area of 22.9 acres, which leaves a balance of 914.6 acres, or 64.1% of the total.

Soil Qualities

There are clear differences in soil types within Huecorio, and these are prime determinants of the pattern of agricultural production.[10] The best land lies close to the shores of the lake (the *orilla*). It has

[9] For Tables I–XLI, see Appendix D.
[10] The definitions we offer in Table 1 are our own, but they derive from the descriptions of these lands given by the farmers themselves. A rumor of an existing soils analysis reached our ears, but the district agricultural agent was unable to enlighten us about it.

been enriched by deposits made by the lake waters as they have risen and fallen, and the water table lies close to the surface, where, throughout the year, it remains accessible to nourish plant life. In addition, some private and *ejido* lands were once the beneficiaries of deposits from the lake, and still others derive some advantage from the alluvium of the Río Guan. But these lands are watered only by the seasonal rains, and, as a result, take second place to those of the *orilla*.

Third in the heirarchy of quality is the bulk of the private land which surrounds the village proper. This land contains a higher proportion of clay than that nearer the shore, and it is quite stony. While it is hard to work, it responds well to conditioning by fertilizers.

The poorest lands are those of the *ejidos* of San José and San Miguel, which lie in the foothills below the massive volcano, San

TABLE 1

Classification and Location of Arable Land

Land Class	Symbol Used in Text	General Characteristics	Regional Location	Area (acres)
First class, permanently watered	1 pw	Light, loamy, "alluvial." Water table close to surface.	*Federal* lake shore (The *orilla*).	162.5
First class, seasonally watered	1 sw	Light, loamy. Some truly alluvial. Depends on seasonal rains.	*Ejidos* of San Pedrito, La Peñita, La Lagunilla. One-quarter of private holdings.	235.3
Second class	2	Clay and stones abundant. Depends on seasonal rains.	Three-quarters of private holdings.	185.6
Third class	3	Clay and stones abundant. Depends on seasonal rains. Often thin topsoil with ledge close to surface.	*Ejidos* of San José and San Miguel.	324.8

Miguel. Farmers can work only the relatively level areas in the tiny valleys. The clay and stone contents are high and the soil unproductive.

Although such considerations as accessibility, land tenure arrangements, and size of holding influence the pattern of crop production, the principal determinants are the quality of the soil and availability of moisture. The rich and permanently watered soils of the *orilla* are devoted almost exclusively to high-value cash crops—principally vegetables such as lettuce or cabbage. On land of similarly high quality elsewhere in the village, cash crops are grown where the proximity to water—a well or house supply—can overcome the shortages of the dry season. However, the balance of the land is planted in the staple crops of corn and wheat, to which the seasonal fluctuations in rainfall are more congenial. Even these crops respond in varying degrees to soil quality, and the closer their location to the lake the more bountiful are their harvests.

THE PATTERN OF LANDHOLDING

There are in Huecorio five ways in which a person can acquire the right to the use of land: by holding a private title to its ownership; by membership in the village *ejido;* by renting lands on the lake shore from the federal government; by renting *a medias;* or as security for a loan.

Private Ownership. This is similar to private ownership the world over. The land can be acquired or disposed of through inheritance, gift, or purchase, and it can be taxed, mortgaged, or attached. At the time of the Revolution, Huecorio possessed 122 hectares of private land, a situation that has not substantially changed.[11]

The Village Ejido. The *ejido* refers to the ownership of lands by the community, the usufructuary rights to the soil being held by cer-

---

[11] Our calculations indicate the area to be 117.36 hectares, the difference being accounted for by possible errors in the delineation of the various regions of the community.

tain persons in the community who are called *ejidatarios*.[12] This form of landholding grew out of the agrarian unrest of the Revolution of 1910. The Mexican Agrarian Reform was approved in a Presidential decree of 1921, and reached its final form on June 27, 1922, when it was put into effect by the National Agrarian Commission. In that year 369 hectares of land formerly belonging to the *hacienda* Ibarra on the outskirts of Pátzcuaro were ceded to Huecorio.

The *ejido* of Huecorio is individually worked, and each of the 134 persons entitled to become an *ejidatario* originally received three plots totaling 1.13 hectares.[13] Under present laws the *ejido* parcels are inalienable, intransmissible, unattachable, and thus cannot be transferred, ceded, rented, or mortgaged. The *ejidatario,* however, may designate rights of inheritance among the persons who depend on him economically even though they may not be related. The right to use *ejido* parcels is further contingent on payment of a tax to the extent of 5% of the crop, and is withdrawn if the *ejidatario* fails to work on his holdings himself for two consecutive years. The right to the parcels can be withdrawn or its harvests can be forfeited if the *ejidatario* rents them, utilizes the land in partnership with another, or employs hired labor (except in certain cases of unusual demand). Furthermore, according to the regulations of the National Agrarian Commission, a married couple may have no more than three *ejido* plots. In Huecorio all these provisions tend to be honored in the breach.

The local *ejido* is administered by a commissioner, a secretary, and a treasurer, and there is a *Consejo de Vigilancia* of three persons, the function of which is to see that the *ejido* officials carry out their responsibilities. Each of the six persons has a substitute, and the entire slate is elected by the *ejidatarios*.

[12] For a more complete and general description of the *ejido* system, see Nathan L. Whetten, *Rural Mexico* (Chicago, University of Chicago Press, 1948); Edmundo Flores, *Tratado de Economía Agrícola* (Mexico, Fondo de Cultura Económica, 1961).

[13] To be entitled to an *ejido* holding a man, if single, had to be at least 16 years old; or, if married, any age; a woman had to be supporting a family; and in all cases the individual had to have lived in the community for at least six months and to have agriculture as the principal occupation.

According to the official survey, the total *ejido* area is 369 hectares, of which 154 hectares are divided into parcels. Our own calculations give the total area as 391 hectares, of which 204 are used for cultivation. As mentioned in Table I, the 6% difference is probably due to errors resulting from our inexpert techniques of measurement as well as inaccuracies of border delineation. In addition to these reasons, a third factor would account for the difference in the areas under cultivation. As the *ejidos* have been worked, farmers have extended their lots up the sides of bordering hills and into relatively flat areas among the hills themselves. These extensions were not to be seen in the *ejido* maps which were made available to us by the *ejido* officials. Our total for the *ejido* area under cultivation is 32% higher than the official figure. If we assume that the allowance for miscalculation is 6%, then the method noted above has added 26% to the effective *ejido* area under cultivation.

Federal Land. Probably because of long-term cyclical swings in precipitation, the level of Lake Pátzcuaro rises or falls slowly over a period of years. Superimposed on the cyclical change is an annual variation of several feet in which the lake rises during the rainy season and then subsides. Many years of low rainfall seem to have occurred from the late 1930s to the late 1950s, but an upward swing may be beginning. As the lake level declined, ancient roads and stone walls came into view and islands became little hills. More important was the rich land so exposed. This land was naturally treasured by those who could till it and coveted by those who could not.[14] Since there are at least 140 households, and according to our calculations a maximum of 68 hectares in the *orilla,* the division would have given each household somewhat less than half a hectare apiece, and considerably less than half a hectare if the division had been by family or adult male. Nevertheless, the right to this land, even if the lots were small, would have been valuable. But this maximum area is available only under exceptional circumstances, and some land is under water most

[14] Among the *ejido* documents made available to us were reports of *ejido* assemblies during 1950 in which the problem was discussed and government officials were asked to help by dividing the exposed lands (presumably equally) among all the *campesinos* in the village and thus to mitigate the difficulties and disputes that had arisen.

of the time. The attempt at equality would therefore have been mean-
ingless unless the division were made in tiny plots and distributed according to location so that each claimant would have some unsub-
merged land.

The solution arrived at was that the land would be declared federal
territory. Any citizen may request a lot, and the office of *Recursos
Hidráulicos*[15] decides how much land an individual may take. A rent
at the annual rate of 10 pesos a hectare is paid and is prorated according to the size of the lot. If the payment is not met the land is re-
claimed, and for this reason individuals continue to pay for lots that
have been invaded by the encroaching tides of recent years. The
criteria for allocation are unclear, but apparently those whose lands
adjoined the lake had the first chance and could extend their holdings
as the water level fell. It was reported that "tips" had to be paid at
Recursos Hidráulicos to unstick the administrative gears.

Land Rental. The three classes of land are rented to a limited extent when the owner cannot or does not wish to use the land himself.
In the usual form of *a medias,* the owner provides the land and seed
while the labor, animals, and equipment are provided by the temporary tenant. Both the tenant and the person who claims some sort of
title to the land participate in the harvest, which is then divided
equally between them. The arrangement is informal and temporary
and covers only one agricultural season. At any one time about one-
third of the farmers are working another's land *a medias,* but in most
cases are also working their own land at the same time. In other
words, there is in Huecorio neither a class of sharecroppers nor one
of landlords living off the fruit of another's labor.

Land Used as Security for a Loan. This is a form of land use much
less common than those previously mentioned, and no farmer interviewed mentioned that he was currently using it. When a loan is made
the lender sometimes, in lieu of interest and security, assumes the
right to the use and harvests of a lot belonging to the borrower. It is
only one form of credit arrangement; the others are discussed below,
in Chapter 4.

---

[15] *Recursos Hidráulicos* is an agency of the federal government which
is responsible for water resource development.

Land Distribution

The analysis of land distribution is a morass of unknowns surrounded by a swamp clogged with the roots of hidden assumptions.
The exploration was undertaken but, we fear, the trophies survived a
little tarnished.

It is well known that tradition-bound farmers are unwilling to reveal the extent of their landholdings. Fully recognizing this, we nevertheless tried to get data on land distribution in the Census undertaken
at the beginning of our stay. The total holdings therein admitted
amounted to 155 hectares, or less than half the total arable area. Even
allowing for the fact that a few hectares are owned by people residing
outside Huecorio, this should be a lesson well learned from the point
of view of data collection.[16] At a later date, and as we were somewhat
less suspect, more accurate data were gathered. The total holdings
of the farmers interviewed came to 75.16 hectares in our Agricultural
Survey, as opposed to 50.85 hectares admitted by the same farmers
during our Census. But a more cogent point has to do with the fact
that the farmers are not accustomed to thinking of their land in terms
of precise measurements, and indeed do not know the areas they hold.
Even though the three parcels of *ejido* land total 1.13 hectares for
each *ejidatario,* most persons in stating this area gave the answer
either as *tres parcelas,* ¾ of a hectare, or 1¼ hectares. Only one
farmer described the area as being slightly less than 1¼ hectares. Indeed, one of the most progressive farmers, when asked the area of his
holding, asked us to measure his fields for him, a task we gladly undertook.

Even when given accurate measurements, per capita figures will
vary according to the assumptions one makes. What, for instance, is

[16] Not all was necessarily lost, however. It is still better to ask this
question in the census under circumstances such as ours when it is impossible to undertake a complete survey of the farmers. If one wishes to
ascertain the number of landholders it is better to ask the question "How
much land do you have?" than "Do you own land?" In the second case
a fearful or suspicious respondent is likely to say "No," whereas the
more positive question will more likely lead to a mere understatement.

a farmer? Many persons have several occupations. Do we define as farmers only those who give farming as their primary occupation? Or should we include those who list it as a secondary or tertiary occupation? What of those who call themselves *jardineros* or *granjeros*? Many casual laborers work on farms. Are they farmers? If we take the term farmer to imply only those who list farming as a primary occupation plus those who call themselves primarily gardeners but who actually work fields in Huecorio, then the number of farm households is 71. But if we include all those who list farming or gardening as their primary, secondary, or tertiary occupation, then the number of farm households rises to 104. These different assumptions lead to a confusing array of average landholding figures. Each of the various categories has some relevance, and none taken by itself is representative of the community as a whole. The various averages are presented in Table II.

The most favorable figure for the average size of farm holdings in Huecorio is 5.21 hectares, which is arrived at by dividing the total arable area by the number of households in which at least one person considers farming to be his primary occupation. But this maximum is highly misleading on several counts. It says nothing about the quality of the land held. If the land were only *ejido* the household would probably be at a great disadvantage, since the *ejido* lands are generally poor. Second, many farm households contain two or more families, each with their separate holdings. Third, the average does not allow for those who work on the land but do not call themselves farmers. Finally, it makes no allowance for those who work the land but do not consider agriculture to be their major occupation. At the other extreme the per capita average for the population as a whole is very low indeed—only 0.44 hectares or just over one acre. No matter how the pie is sliced, the shares are meager indeed.

Even the most favorable figures are below the average farm sizes of 6.5 hectares for Mexico as a whole and 5.9 hectares for Michoacán. The averages, together with the distributional data, underline the contention that modern mechanical methods of production would have only a limited applicability under the individualistic pattern of land utilization characteristic of Huecorio. Furthermore, these holdings are highly fragmented. The land of the 34 farmers subjected to intensive interviews is divided into 174 plots, or slightly over five plots for each farm. Not only does this phenomenon, which results from the egalitarian aspects of inheritance and *ejido* division, make mechanization more difficult but it is also wasteful of the farmer's time since he must employ himself in widely separated parts of the village. Furthermore, this fragmentation limits the planting of valuable crops, since it is impossible to watch all of them to prevent the stealing that takes place.

The distribution of holdings is uneven. Table 2 shows a sample

TABLE 2

Sample Distribution of Holdings by Size of Holding

Size of Holding (hectares)	Number of Households
0	1
0—1	4
1.1—2	16
2.1—3	4
3.1—4	4
4.1—5	2
5.1—6	2
9.1—10	1
Total	34

distribution as developed from the Agricultural Survey. The estimates of areas were given by the farmers themselves, except in certain of the *ejido* cases in which we interpreted their claim to three *ejido* parcels to mean that they had the standard 1.13 hectares. A household having more than the three *ejido* plots is not necessarily flouting the regulations, since it might include two separate families. The modal value is between one and two hectares, although this would undoubtedly be higher if more accurate information were forthcoming.

Some farmers have fairly adequate holdings—in one verified case, 9.25 hectares. Another, not interviewed, was reported to have twelve *ejido* plots in addition to his private holdings.

As we have seen, the *ejido* land is supposed to be divided among 134 *ejidatarios* who should have (with two minor exceptions) 1.13 hectares each distributed among three plots.[17] In addition, three parcels are for the use of the school and one large parcel for the *Liga Femenil Antialcohólica*.[18] But the *ejido* land is not, in fact, distributed equally, since many households have more than the allotted three either because the household contains more than one biological unit or because some member of the household has parcels illegally, usually in the name of a long interred or absent relative. The most recent list of *ejidatarios* was compiled on September 23, 1959. According to one informant, and verified by our study, the majority of the persons on the list were deceased or absent from the village at that time.[19] Thus is circumvented, by difficulties of administrative supervision, a noteworthy effort at providing the landless with sustenance and security.

Commentary on the Ejido

We will not pretend to offer a complete evaluation of the *ejido* system, which has played such a large role in Mexican rural life, but will confine our commentary largely to the operation of the *ejido* in Huecorio. As we conducted our investigation, proposals were being seriously considered by the government to modify the system in the light of widespread dissatisfaction with it. It is significant that the people of Huecorio were quite unaware of those proposals.

The Mexico City daily, *Excelsior,* reported on July 20, 1962:

[17] Two of the plots are *temporal,* that is, seasonally watered, while one is *riego* (irrigated), a term used advisedly in this case since no community irrigation network exists. The *riego* lands are merely near the Río Guan.

[18] The *Liga Femenil Antialcohólica* was one of several groups encouraged by President Lázaro Cárdenas in an attempt to stimulate political action by the women of Mexico. In Huecorio its activities ceased in the mid-1950s, and a non-*ejidatario* was working its *ejido* plot as virtual title holder.

[19] The list of 134 persons entitled to *ejido* plots was checked against the names derived from our census of 1962. Only 56 persons on the list were in the village in 1962 and two of these had their names listed twice. It is hard to believe that 76 persons died or left the village between 1959 and 1962.

Three Plans by Which the Ejidatario Can Benefit from the Land

The Commission in charge of formulating the draft of the new Agrarian Code, made up of members of Congress and the Department of Agriculture, is studying three land tenure proposals:

a) That it be made explicit in the Agrarian Code that the *ejidatario* has full and individual title to his land;

b) That the *ejido* be handed over as *limited* private property or, in other words, that it should be constituted as an inalienable family inheritence;

c) That the system should continue as before, since otherwise the lands which the Nation has redeemed and placed outside the market will perhaps become again the object of transactions which would lead to new latifundia unless necessary restrictions were imposed.

According to *Excelsior* of July 23, 1962, the Constitution of 1917 considered that the *ejido* was to be only a provisional stage in preparation for the establishment of private holdings. This interpretation blunts the argument that tradition demands the perpetuation of a system that has pre-Columbian roots.

The complaints against the *ejido* system are several. The Church, financially straitened as it now appears to be in Mexico, remembers bitterly that much *ejido* land once belonged to its estates and regards the system as an outrageous robbery.[20] Some informants report that, at the time of the transfer, the priest led an attack on the village *ejido* which led to factionalism within Huecorio. As far as we can judge, these wounds have healed and no opposition to the *ejido* exists on moral grounds.[21]

On a similar level, the attack on the *ejido* is made on the grounds that such a system is productively inferior to that of private property. *Excelsior* of July 23, 1962 reports that ". . . only 35% of [agricul-

[20] One person reported to us that the Church again owned lands in the region illegally through titles held by some of the faithful.

[21] The same cannot be said of some other communities in the region. Foster, pp. 170–75 examines in detail the history of land transfers in Tzintzuntzan. In that community few persons initially claimed their *ejido* rights, in large part because of the very active opposition of the priest. In nearby San Pedro and Ihautzio, factionalism is still so active that the solidarity needed for communal cooperation cannot be achieved.

tural] production comes from the *ejidos* of the country in spite of the fact that these occupy an area much greater than that of the *pequeñas propiedades agrícolas* [private holdings]." There is more substance to this criticism than to the first-mentioned, but it ignores a number of considerations. In the first place, when lands were taken from the *haciendas* the *hacendado* could select the lands to be taken, and he naturally offered the poorest for expropriation. The greater part of the Huecorio *ejido* consists of very poor land. In addition, the *ejidos* are at best small, fragmented plots, and the aggregate size of any *ejidatario*'s holding is infinitesimal when compared with the so-called "small properties." In Huecorio the average farm household at the most optimistic estimate controls no more than 2.8 hectares of *ejido,* while "small properties" range from ten to 100 hectares of irrigated lands and up to 300 hectares of seasonally watered land. No change in the legal status of the *ejido* would alter this condition, except one that would lead to the unintended result that former *ejidatarios* could accumulate land at the expense of others.

Excelsior claims, too, that "the legal uncertainty that has prevailed in the fields is one of the causes of the unfortunate migratory flow of *braceros* which has meant a disastrous exportation of the most valuable elements of Mexico's prosperity." As far as we can gather from our interviews with the *braceros,* the legal, as opposed to the economic, aspect of the *ejido* system had nothing to do with their desire or need to go north.

Nevertheless, some uncertainty as to legal rights exists. *Excelsior* argues that the *ejidatario* "considers that his rights over it [his holding] are not that of a proprietor but of a precarious and conditional usufruct, subject to vague conditions of renewal by officials that make him victim of extortion and violations by those who call themselves 'comisarios' in parody of other similar bureaucrats of Soviet Russia. . . . Experience has demonstrated that the land is fruitful only when man unites with it permanently and feels himself to be the owner." That such uncertainty exists is clear, although in view of other aspects of the *ejido* system it does not necessarily follow that the simple transfer of status will, by itself, solve very much.

The uncertainty manifests itself in Huecorio in several ways. Membership in the *ejido* does not specify the exact lots to which an *ejidatario* is entitled. Lots are assigned by the local council and are then recognized by custom. Presumably there could be some kind of upheaval in which lots were reassigned and any person who had built up the productivity of his land would be injured. It would seem that this aspect of the *ejido* system could be solved relatively easily by the assignment of titles specifying lots.

Venality on the part of *ejido* officials was reported, although the commissioner in office at the time this study was made was highly respected. The *ejido* commissioners have sometimes accumulated plots to their own account, but there is no indication that they were taken from living persons.[22] In the José Dongo case (documented in Chapter 5), one *ejidatario* who was not an *ejido* official did deprive another of his usufructuary rights, but administrative appeal prevented him from getting away with it. In other words, the complaint that the *ejido* leads to a lack of a sense of proprietorship and thence to poor utilization is not in itself a sufficient ground for doing away with the system, since administrative reform could accomplish much by preventing the abuses that give rise to insecurity.

Abuses of *ejido* title are widespread, and many *ejidatarios* hold parcels illegally. This is done in a number of ways. With the death of an *ejidatario* a title may pass, by way of a married son or daughter, to a family already in possession of the maximum number. These additional parcels should be returned to the *ejido* for general redistribution. This is probably never done. Instead, the name on the title is unchanged or is transferred to an unmarried son or daughter.

Another device is for the *ejido* commissioner to collect vacated titles for himself by the simple expedient of not transferring them to an eligible person when an *ejidatario* dies or leaves the village. Finally, titles to *ejido* plots are actually sold from one person to another. In such cases the name on the title will not change, but by mutual agreement usufructuary rights to a plot are transferred.[23]

Needless to say, all of these practices, contrary as they are to the intent of the *ejido* system, are strictly illegal and could be eliminated only by more effective, and undoubtedly expensive, administration. If

[22] The most recent case was reported in August, 1959.

[23] One farmer reported that he lost his title when another villager paid 100 pesos to an *"ingeniero* from Morelia" to make the transfer.

the *ejido* system cannot prevent such unequal accumulations, one of its main supporting columns has cracked.

All of this is symptomatic of the main complaint about the *ejido* voiced by the villagers. There is simply not enough of it. Since 1930 the villagers have been addressing themselves to officials petitioning for more land. The decree of January 6, 1915 concedes to each *ejidatario* no less than three hectares, yet in Huecorio the official average is only 1.13 hectares. The reply is that the only available *hacienda*—Ibarra—has already been reduced to *"pequeña propiedad,"* and no other *hacienda* available for redistribution exists within the seven-kilometer limit. So far, efforts to get Huecorianos to leave the village and settle elsewhere have not been successful, and the problem remains unresolved.

The complaints of insufficient land, though real enough, would have more force if the land now available were put to better use. In the words of Geronimo Roca, a man very much aware of village and *ejido* problems even though he is not himself an *ejidatario,* "The parcels are too small, and every day, with neither fertilizers nor irrigation, they go from bad to worse." With some exceptions this is an apt characterization. While farmers fertilize and irrigate their private holdings, they rarely do so on the *ejido*. Enough uncertainty about tenure exists to make investments risky, but there are other, more persuasive reasons why the *ejido* lands are not fully exploited.

We have mentioned problems associated with fragmentation, poor soils, and theft. In addition there is the need, under present techniques, to find pasture for the animals. The practice is for all to plant in a given area at the same time in order to leave another area free for the grazing animals. This reinforces the tendency for all farmers to plant in the same cycle—wheat, corn, and *descanso*—since any other pattern would get out of synchronization and subject the crops to animal damage. No time is available in this cycle to grow cover that would build up the lost soil nutrients. Only if the farmer fences off his little plot can he buck the cycle by planting different crops. This is expensive, and the weak fences that can be installed are easily broached by animals or cut by malcontents.[24] To fence all

---

[24] Some farmers have, at various times, fenced their plots with wire so that they might plant vegetables. To do this they had to pay bribes to

plots is quite inconceivable, since the only passage would then be along the raised divider, which is only about 18 inches wide—hardly enough to permit the passage of a working *yunta*. Fences in these tiny plots—59 by 400 feet and 98 by 249 feet are common dimensions —impede the animals working in them and reduce the effective culti-vable area. Consolidation of plots would be a partial answer, but since the village lands are of such varying qualities it is unlikely to gain much favor in Huecorio.

Another standard solution to this and to many other problems is cooperation. Villagers will cooperate to limited degrees in a variety of ways, and cooperative working of one *ejido* area was tried in Huecorio until disputes over division of the crops broke it down. Truly cooperative agriculture requires a mentality quite foreign to Huecorio, and it is futile to expect it to arise. A form of cooperative agriculture which employs trained administrators and in effect pays laborers to work their own land is, with its built-in contradictions, also unlikely to succeed.

Let us return to the several solutions to the *ejido* problem that were proposed in *Excelsior*. Those villagers with whom the matter was dis-cussed, and the officials of the local agricultural and *ejido* banks, unanimously agreed that the second solution—limited ownership of *ejido* plots—was the best. The first solution—unlimited private own-ership—would lead to villagers' losing their lands through sale or in-debtedness, and it is therefore inadmissible.[25] The third solution— continuance of the *ejido*—has not been satisfactory. People feel that only limited ownership, permitting transfer only by inheritance, would prevent alienation. But, as we have seen, unless a system is ef-

---

the *ejido* commissioner, but the bribes did not assuage the anger of those who wished to pasture their animals in the *ejido* during the *descanso* phase. The fences were usually broached by the owners of the animals. For this reason some farmers would prefer to see the *ejido* transferred to private ownership. The majority, faced with the need for pasture, would probably reject this change.

[25] This is an indirect admission of one of the *ejido* system's major vir-tues. In Huecorio at least, it has effectively prevented the growth of a class of landlords on the one hand and a mass of landless peasants on the other. The *ejido* cannot legally be mortgaged and thus the moneylenders who prey on villagers in other ways have not been able to deprive them of their land.

fectively administered it will be outwitted.[26] The problems of the *ejido* have little to do with its legal framework. They lie in questions of insufficiency of land, its poor quality, fragmentation, a lack of credit, and inadequate administration.

Conclusions Regarding Land Tenure

It can safely be said that the land tenure situation in Huecorio is unsatisfactory and can be summarized as follows:

There is an acute shortage of land, particularly land of good quality.

The uncertainty of *ejido* tenure leads to neglect of good soil conservation practices.

Illegal dealings have frustrated the original egalitarian intent of the *ejido* legislation.

The practice of providing animals with common pasture on the *ejido* damages the land and limits the *ejidatarios'* freedom to plant crops other than corn and wheat, with perhaps the addition of *frijoles* and squash.

The fragmentation of land into tiny parcels constitutes a major obstacle to mechanization.

Plots are widely dispersed, and this prevents the farmer from managing his holding effectively and discourages him from growing valuable crops on land that cannot be closely watched.

The distribution of land is unequal but not extremely so.

To the credit of the *ejido* has been its effectiveness in preventing the rise of classes of landlords and tenant farmers.

---

[26] Actually, limited ownership cannot possibly ensure egalitarian land ownership. It would be only a question of time before deaths and intermarriages had garbled the erstwhile ideal.

Huecorio, with Tariácuri beyond

AGRICULTURAL PRODUCTION
AND PRODUCTIVITY

Crops

Some 26 different crops were reported in the Census and in the Agricultural Survey. While this variety is not great, it nevertheless departs from the monoculture so frequently practiced under minifundia. Corn, wheat, and *frijoles* are substantially the main crops, and 11 of the 34 farmers intensively interviewed planted them exclusively. The remaining two-thirds widened their range at least to some extent by planting flowers for sale in the market, vegetables, tubers, and forage crops.[27]

Corn, wheat, and *frijoles* are essentially subsistence crops, retained for home consumption, while the others are generally sold. This emphasis on subsistence crops can be seen in Table III. The number of hectares planted in corn reported in the Agricultural Survey was 22.25, in wheat 19.47, and *frijoles* 12.42. The largest area planted in any other crop was 7.12 hectares for squash, and since squash is interplanted with corn this statement of its planted area is an exaggeration.[28]

Aggregate Production. The total corn crop for the 22 farmers whose output could be calculated came to 667.23 bushels, or an average of 30.3 bushels per farmer.[29] The total output of wheat was very much less, and amounted to 170 bushels, or about eight bushels for each farmer planting it. A cold and dry winter was to blame for this, and four farmers harvested none of the seed they planted. The total

[27] See Table III. In addition to the crops listed therein we should note small plantings, usually in household gardens, of barley, cauliflower, peas, and chili.

[28] As will be explained shortly, even the small areas dedicated to cash crops overstate the true situation.

[29] Thirty farmers responded to this question, but not all gave production data in terms of measurable output.

Comparable estimates of output were possible only for corn, wheat, and *frijoles*. To be able to make such estimates it is necessary to reduce all outputs to a common denominator for which, in this case, we chose the commonly used measures of bushels per acre and kilograms per hectare. However, farmers variously reported their outputs in *fanegas, anegas, manojos, cajas, bultos, medidas, toneladas, costales, docenas, cortes, litros, kilos, tercios,* and *unidades.* The conversion of these into bushels or kilograms was usually difficult and sometimes impossible.

In a typical case, one farmer reported his crop as two *toneladas.* We assumed this to be a metric *tonelada* weighing 1,000 kilograms. One hectolitre of corn weighs about 80 kilograms, so his crop was approximately 2,500 liters. This was converted to *fanegas,* each of which is 90.8 liters, and then to bushels, there being 2.576 U. S. bushels to the *fanega.* Finally, his total output had to be reduced to bushels per acre. In this example a misplaced decimal turned up later and necessitated adjustments in several tables. Output reported in *kilos* often could not be converted to bushels because of the differing weights of the various crops. "Handfuls," "dozens," "sacks," etc., obviously offer similar imponderables.

crops of *frijoles* was 68 bushels, or 3.5 bushels per farmer on the average. A rough approximation of the total village output of corn would be 3,272 bushels, of wheat 184 bushels, and of *frijoles* 136.5 bushels.

Productivity.[30] In 1961 the weighted average yield for corn was 1,995 kilograms per hectare, and this is nearly three times the national average of 680 kilograms per hectare for the years 1945 through 1949.[31] An official of the Pátzcuaro branch of the *Banco de Agricultura* reported that the average yields of the region are 800 kilograms per hectare for unfertilized land and 3,000 kilograms per hectare for fertilized land, and Foster[32] gives the yield in nearby Tzintzuntzan as 1,388 kilograms per hectare. Several factors account for Huecorio's relatively good showing. (i) Although half of the area under corn is in poor soils, the balance is planted on good land (for example, San Pedrito) and very good land (the *orilla*). The national average takes into account plantings in areas—deserts, for example—that are vastly inferior to the worst of Huecorio's lands. (ii) Huecorianos are beginning to use fertilizers—*gallinaza* in particular—which raise their yields three to four times above their previous harvests. (iii) The average for Huecorio is given a significant upward bias by the very high and possibly exaggerated yields reported on the best land. The

[30] The productivity of human labor is a critical determinant of a society's wealth; accordingly, it would be useful to measure per capita productivity in Huecorio. However, productivity measurement requires proper accounting procedures for all inputs and outputs, and it goes without saying that such data are not available for Huecorio. To gather information of this kind a research team would have to be in a community for at least one agricultural cycle, and some members of the team would have to dog the steps of chosen farmers to record exactly all their activities. Needless to say, this would call for extraordinary rapport. Farmers remember the various component parts of their output well enough, but cannot possibly be expected to recall how many days or hours they spent on each particular operation involved in each of the various crops they planted. Furthermore, records would have to be kept not only of their own labor but also of that of their assistants. Some data were gathered for the major crops, but the difficulty of collecting data for cash crops frustrated the calculation of an over-all index of agricultural per capita productivity.

[31] International Bank for Reconstruction and Development, *The Economic Development of Mexico* (Baltimore, Johns Hopkins Press, 1953), Table 49, p. 239.

[32] P. 74.

differential productivities of the four classes of land are extreme. For corn they range from only 451 kilograms per hectare in the mountain *ejidos* of San Miguel and San José to 5,638 kilograms in the fertile soil of the *orilla*. (iv) Huecorianos spend more man-days per hectare in the preparation and cultivation of their fields than do the Tzintzuntzeños. (v) 1961 may have been an exceptionally favorable season, but no farmer volunteered this to be the case. (vi) Huecorianos interplant their corn to a lesser extent than do the Tzintzuntzeños.

Frijoles tend to reduce the corn yields, and so Huecorianos in many cases do not interplant, but if they do they only plant a small portion of the plot in corn and *frijoles* and leave the rest for corn alone.

The wheat crop planted in 1961 and harvested in 1962 was extremely low, due to an unfavorable winter. The CREFAL team of the previous year gave the yield as about 1,000 kilograms per hectare, as opposed to only 214 in 1962. The national average for 1945–49 was 810 kilograms per hectare, and the average yield for Tzintzuntzan given by Foster[33] was 364 kilograms per hectare, but several of the outputs included in his sample were for the drought year of 1945 and the normal yield "should produce two or three times as much crop." We would infer from this that Huecorio's normal harvest would at least equal, and probably exceed, the national average. But the yield would probably not be more than twice the national average as was the case for corn, since, unlike corn, wheat is not so often grown on the better land and is not fertilized.

The average yield per hectare for *frijoles* is rather low—226 kilograms as compared with 644 kilograms per hectare in Tzintzuntzan. This was a normal crop, and the low output is explained by two factors —the tendencies in Huecorio to plant *frijoles* on poorer land and not to interplant them extensively with corn.

Comparison of Value Yields for Cash and Subsistence Crops. Value yields for the cash and subsistence crops were calculated, and the data are presented in Table III. The differential yields on lands of different qualities show up very clearly for corn, wheat, and *frijoles,* but since the other crops are planted only on better land as a rule, this productivity comparison cannot be made for them. Possible earnings per hectare vary—for corn, from 280 to 3,500 pesos; for

[33] P. 75.

wheat, from 140 to at least 502 pesos; and for *frijoles,* from 248 to 702 pesos.

Casual observation of the column for average value yields would suggest that corn is a more valuable crop than all others except coriander, onions, and lettuce. However, closer analysis of the use to which land can be put in Huecorio would suggest that, on the contrary, the value yields for the cash crops are significantly higher than for the subsistence crops.[34] To reach this conclusion it is necessary to distinguish the two cycles of land utilization found in Huecorio.

The subsistence cycle covers a two-year period beginning with the planting of wheat, followed by corn, *frijoles,* and possibly squash and lima beans together, and finally a period of fallow. The cash cycle allows for no fallowing, but two crops—or possibly three when irrigation is used—are planted each year. On first-class permanently watered land the value outputs would be 3,500 pesos for corn, 2,200 pesos for wheat,[35] and 1,400 pesos for *frijoles.*[36] This gives a total of 7,100 pesos every two years, or 3,550 pesos on an annual basis. If a crop of lettuce (1,135 pesos) and one of carrots (823 pesos) were grown on the same land, the value of the output would be variously 1,958 pesos, 3,916 pesos, 5,874 pesos, or 7,832 pesos, depending on the factor by which one multiplies the cash crop to allow for our understatements of acreage.[37] We would suspect that the factor is at least

[34] Cash crops are those which, as a rule, farmers sell in the market rather than consume at home. The division is apparent from observation of the last two columns of Table III. The subsistence crops are corn, wheat, *frijoles,* and lima beans. Potatoes might be added to this list, but since only one informant planted potatoes, generalization is difficult. The data from the table, together with our knowledge of the specific crops, indicate that all the other crops are grown with the principal intention of selling them in the market.

[35] Estimate based on four times the value of wheat grown on class l sw land during a poor year, plus 10% for stubble.

[36] Estimated, since no *frijoles* planted on class l pw land.

[37] It has been noted that cash crops tend to be planted together on the same plot of ground, much like the suburban home garden. If cabbages are reported grown in a field of one-quarter of a hectare, it is very unlikely that one-quarter of a hectare is planted in cabbages, but the vegetable will share the field with other crops. Such mixed plantings are the rule, but it was not possible to measure the areas in question since, in most cases, the crops with which we were concerned had already been harvested. Thus, if only a fourth of a quarter of a hectare was planted in

four, giving a yield of at least 7,832 pesos, in which case the rationality of the Huecoriano's preference for cash crops on 1 pw land is evident. On first-class, seasonally watered land, similar methods of estimation give an annual value for the subsistence cycle of 1,548 pesos, and a range from 1,518 to at least 6,072 pesos for the cash cycle.[38]

Farmers' Attitudes Toward Their Land. In spite of the apparently respectable yields, farmers have a rather poor impression of their lands. In the Agricultural Survey they were asked the question, "Do you believe your land to be good land?" Six replied yes, four said it was indifferent, six gave qualified answers, and 17 said that it was bad. Of those who said it was good, two held only first-class permanently watered land, and another used fertilizers extensively. The other three showed a rather fatalistic attitude, giving such replies as *"Se dan ye no se dan"* (It gives and it doesn't give), or "I am accustomed to the little I get." Those who gave qualified answers made distinctions between the good land of the *orilla* and the generally poor *ejido*. The same persons were asked, "What, if anything, is wrong with your lands?" and they gave in reply several answers tabulated as follows: The land is "thin" (8); stony (3); crowded (1); damaged by animals (1); lacks water (1); lacks fertilizer (9); too spread out to be properly attended (1).

Interestingly enough, all the causes given, except the first two, are subject to human control. Their enumeration may indicate at least a vague awareness that qualitative improvements can be made. This is particularly true of the advantages of fertilizers. One farmer reported that using natural fertilizers from his *granja* and *corral* raised his corn production in third-class land from ten *bultos* to 37 *bultos*. If such applications could become widespread, Huecorio could increase its average yields three or four times. A mechanized farmer in nearby Villa Escalante plants 120 hectares, and, using 120

cabbage, a factor of four would have to be applied to derive the productivity *as if* the entire plot had been planted in cabbage. Then, of course, the product would be multiplied again by four to get the productivity per hectare. Visual observation of the degree to which the plots were mixed would suggest that the factor of four was conservative.

[38] One cannot infer from this that farmers should dispense with the subsistence crops and devote themselves exclusively to cash crops. Soil conditions and other factors are more important than hypothetical income calculations in determining what farmers will plant.

kilograms of sulfate of ammonia per hectare, gets approximately 106 bushels per hectare. Huecorianos could exceed this without mechanization by proper fertilizer application.

Decline in the Quality of the Land. Such changes in methods cannot come too soon, for there is some evidence of a secular decline in the quality of the soil. Farmers were asked, "In your opinion, is your land producing better or worse harvests than previously?" Thirteen replied worse, nine better, nine the same, and three offered no answer. Those who said it was worse may have been indulging in the diet of "sour gripes" characteristic of farmers all over the world, but they were supported slimly by one farmer's report that certain of the best seasonally watered land which could once be used for vegetables can no longer grow those crops. On the other hand, those who claimed better harvests referred in four cases to rather specific improvements due to irrigation and more utilization of fertilizer.

When asked about the cause of the change, the farmers responded with a confusing array of often conflicting answers. Some reported that the weather had been improving, others that it had been worsening; some said that there was too much water and others said there was too little. Certainly, clear distinctions between factors that cause cyclical changes as opposed to trends were not made. Annual variations in temperature and the volume and timing of rainfall have profound effects on crops,[39] but in the absence of scientific measurements secular changes in patterns sufficiently marked to affect the soil's fertility cannot be established. One farmer mentioned "lack of care" as an explanation for the decline that he felt had occurred, and in a similar vein six others referred to a lack of fertilizer. Lacking definitive data, we can only suggest that a secular decline in fertility is a distinct possibility over most of the village terrain; and that if it has occurred its probable causes are man-made and take the form of poor methods of cultivation, erosion, and overgrazing, although we should not rule out the possibility of a secular climatic change.

Costs of Production. Estimates of costs of production involve many practical and theoretical difficulties. Land, animals, machines, equip-

---

[39] Geronimo Roca explains it in this way. Too much rain chills the ground and slows the growth of the corn. Too little rain inhibits the growth of the roots and the plants are easily uprooted by the wind.

ment, tools, seed, fertilizer, and men combine their efforts with nature to produce a harvest. In the context of Huecorio, reasonably reliable cost estimates could be made only for men, seed, and animals. Land values could not be approximated, and in some cases, as in the *ejido* and *federal* areas, they involve a social rather than a private cost. The taxes paid on these and private lands bear no relation to realistic land values, and in the absence of accurate valuation it is futile to impute interest charges.

While values were ascertained for tools and equipment, the accurate imputation of the cost of these to an operation would involve getting information on rates of depreciation, maintenance costs, and the amount of time the item was used in one operation relative to the time it was used in all other operations during a given year. Fertilizer is used to some extent in Huecorio, but it is the natural fertilizer of animals and comes mainly from *corrales* and *granjas*. In the absence of commercial transactions involving animal fertilizer, its value cannot be established.

Even labor costs involve difficulties. The wage for a *peón* in Huecorio is six or seven pesos a day plus a meal valued at three pesos. A *peón* who lives with a family (only one recorded example) receives 40 pesos a week plus room and board. What, however, should be the imputed wage or salary of a farmer or a member of a farmer's family, who works his own fields? Should this rate include an allowance for his management function? Are his food and board in the family home costs of production? We will have to avoid such issues and assume labor costs of ten pesos a day, recognizing that, in view of all the other costs that have to be ignored, we will get at best no more than a rough approximation and undervaluation of agricultural costs.

Table IV samples real costs of production for corn, and offers comparisons of the average data with those of Foster and Beals.[40] The average total cost of production in man-days per hectare in Huecorio is 52.5, as compared with 51 for Cherán and 44.6 for Tzintzuntzan. In terms of the distribution of this time among the various operations, Huecorio closely approximates Tzintzuntzan. The larger yield in Huecorio is at least partially attributable to the larger input of seed and possibly also to the greater labor input. However, one should

[40] Foster, p. 75. Beals, p. 65.

not be too positive about the importance of the greater labor input, since it might mean that the Huecorianos devote more attention to their plots than the people of the other two communities, or alternatively, that soil conditions in Huecorio are inferior and demand more effort. Within Huecorio there is considerable variation in labor input. In the preparation of the seedbed the effort required will depend very much on whether or not the ground has been softened up by an earlier harvest of wheat. As can be seen from Table V, the one farmer who did no seedbed preparation apparently made up for this by greater diligence in cultivation.[41]

Table V presents data on money costs per hectare. Two of the four farmers for whom data are reasonably complete suffered losses which remained even after the *frijol* crop was gathered. The average farm appears to make a small profit on maize, which becomes slightly higher when *frijoles* are added to the maize harvest. The profit is raised even more if squash is interplanted. Since we lack data on cases in which corn is planted exclusively, it cannot be ascertained whether the resultant increase in output would offset the decline in income from not growing *frijoles* and squash. One farmer stated that his squash sales pay for labor and seed, leaving the corn and *frijoles* as pure profit. Although he referred only to his out-of-pocket costs, he hinted at the rationale behind interplanting. Unprofitable though the planting of maize may appear to us even when only partial costs are considered, interplanting seems to raise the value of output per hectare and in some cases to provide the cash necessary for out-of-pocket expenses. But in this we are speculating somewhat. The matter should be very carefully considered by agronomists before they persuade the farmer to abandon interplanting.

Weaker statements have to be made with regard to wheat. (Table VI.) Again, the Huecorio real cost estimates are higher than for the other two communities, but these cannot be accounted for by yield differentials, since the yields for Tzintzuntzan were similarly affected by the weather in the year studied. Sampling inadequacies are probably the major cause of the difference in this case. The crop harvested in 1962 resulted in significant losses, but since data are lacking for

[41] Although it could be that in avoiding proper preparation he invited more weeds and grass, which took more effort to eradicate later.

normal years comparisons of the relative advantages of planting corn and wheat cannot be made. Even were we to make such comparisons they would have limited value, since wheat and corn are not competitive crops but complementary in the wheat-corn-fallow sequence.

Factors Determining the Allocation of Production Between Cash and Subsistence Crops. Of the subsistence crops, only corn is grown extensively on the best land—55% of the plantings on classes 1 pw and 1 sw and 45% on the remainder. Of the cash crops, only the unimportant gourd is grown extensively on poorer land, while 36% of the squash plantings are found on it.[42] All other cash crops are grown on the best land. We doubt that the value product of the various land classes determines what will be grown there, since only one or two farmers talk in terms of crop value per hectare. A more likely reason lies in the essential natural differences among the land classes. While availability of water makes the difference between class 1 pw and 1 sw land, the viability of the soil itself distinguishes these two classes from the others. The more delicate cash crops cannot be grown on the poorer land.

These natural conditions are not, of course, the only factors determining what will be planted. The matter of crop diversification is actually comprised of two questions: What determines the distribution of plantings between cash and subsistence crops, and what determines the distribution among the various cash crops?

In terms of area planted, subsistence crops are more important than cash crops, and at any given time the area under subsistence crops is five to ten times as large as that under cash crops. This preference for subsistence crops is underlined by examining the number of farmers planting the crop types. Only two farmers did not plant any subsistence crops, and in both cases their allocation was due largely to the fact that the *ejido* lands on which they would normally be growing subsistence crops were lying fallow, and under the annual *ejido* council agreement they could not plant there. Nevertheless, the fact that these two farmers did not plant their remaining land —which is of good quality—in corn is of some significance, and suggests that they are not overwhelmed by the insecurity that prevents

---

[42] A cash crop is defined for our purposes as one which is sold by more than 50% of the farmers.

some of the others from escaping the blind subsistence cycle. It is worthy of note that their crop income averaged 3,756 pesos as against a Survey average of 1,036 pesos.

Eleven farmers followed the subsistence cycle exclusively. Although these farmers have less than the average amount of land (1.65 hectares as opposed to 2.21 hectares), only two of them do not have land on which cash crops could be grown. Since one cannot conclude that either the size or the quality of their lands determines their resistance to cash crops, each case must be examined individually. In three cases the farmers were employed outside of agriculture during the season and could not afford the intensive effort necessary for cash crops. A variety of technical reasons prevented four others from growing cash crops in the year under study. One of these had no good land; one had only a small *ejido* plot and this was probably not fertile enough for cash crops anyway; in another case the best land was under water and the good land was lying fallow under the communal pattern dictated by the *ejido;* the fourth had elected to use his good land for an orchard. The remaining four we might call traditional in their outlook, since although they have good land available for cash crops they utilize it for growing corn. Because we do not know the reasons behind their choice, it would not be proper to say that they are necessarily behaving irrationally, for rationality can only be defined in terms of objectives. If their objective is security and a full *tapanco* of corn gives a feeling of security, then they are rational. If their objective is maximizing income, then they are not rational. As we have seen, the average crop income is 1,036 pesos. Those devoting themselves exclusively to cash crops exceed this significantly, earning on the average 3,746 pesos. Those mixing their cycles, and perhaps their objectives, earn slightly more than average—1,234 pesos. Those following the subsistence pattern gain on the average a mere 359 pesos.

Conscious, reasoned decision-making in terms of well-defined objectives is probably not nearly as widespread, even in sophisticated societies, as economists pretend. We asked two questions in an attempt to get farmers to verbalize their reasons for growing the various crops they had planted. One question, asked after the interviewer had examined the actual allocation was: "How did you decide to plant *n* hectares in maize, x rows in squash, y liters in wheat, and z rows in carrots, etc.?" Ten found it impossible to verbalize an answer for this admittedly sticky question. Nine gave answers ranging from the fatalistic "the land is only good for wheat and corn" to the traditional "we are using the land in the best possible manner." In other cases diversification was prevented by a lack of time (3), a lack of land (4), or a lack of pesos to buy seeds (3). Three cited market conditions, and one said he diversified for protection.

Mexican peasant farmers are frequently accused of a compulsive propensity to devote themselves exclusively to maize and other subsistence crops. The data from Huecorio do not support this. Undoubtedly some of the farmers react to their environment blindly and compulsively in this way.[43] Our conclusion would be, however, that the main determinant of the subsistence-versus-cash distribution is the availability of suitable land.[44] Were the land in some way to be improved, it is likely that the majority of the farmers would increase their acreage in cash crops.

For most farmers, the distribution between cash and subsistence crops has developed as a rational reaction to a natural and economic environment. The situation was characterized succinctly by Geronimo Roca, whose comments we paraphrase:

(1) Some land is suitable only for corn and wheat. This is due to (a) inadequate water, and (b) the need to pasture animals. If large areas of land were withdrawn from the subsistence cycle there would be a serious reduction in the availability of pasture.[45]

(2) Vegetables are planted in the only suitable terrain, the humid *orilla*.

[43] Four of the 11 planting only subsistence crops, perhaps, and possibly some of those who had difficulty answering the distribution question. This latter example may, however, be a reflection on the question rather than on those who tried to answer it.

[44] "Suitable" in this case refers not only to natural conditions such as soil qualities and humidity, but also to removal of some of the obstacles inherent in the use of land.

[45] Technically, and perhaps economically, neither of these problems is beyond a solution. The political and social organization of the community, a lack of knowledge of feasible alternatives, a lack of credit—all these prevent any significant change. Accordingly the farmer, acting as an individual, cannot change the major influences on his environment and must accept them.

(3) Corn is planted in large quantities because (a) it is a basic component of the diet, and (b) if the farmer did not plant it he would be subject to the price manipulations of the "monopolists" from whom he must buy.[46]

Salvador Gorozpe, another thoughtful informant, confirmed much of what Geronimo said. "In the *ejido* lands one can plant only wheat, corn, and *frijoles,* for there is no water for irrigation. And one knows of no alternatives because one has no experience with them. In addition, grazing animals would damage the other plants. No one has the money to encircle his plots with fences—and the owners of the animals would not respect them anyway and would destroy them. In addition, anyone who put up a fence would suffer 'inconveniences' from the *ejido* commissioner because, by law, the animals have to be pastured there." [47]

Regarding the farmers' pattern for cash-versus-subsistence planting, we again contend that these statements confirm the general rule that the farmers behave rationally in terms of the natural, economic, and social environment in which they are involved.

Factors Affecting Cash Crop Decisions. When we examine the farmers' pattern of cash crop production, rational behavior is even more evident, although, as before, some farmers tend toward established, traditional decisions rather than deliberation. The interviewer, after examining a farmer's crop pattern, selected a single product, lettuce for instance, and asked, "Why did you not plant more lettuce?" Since this was a less complicated question than the one asked just before it, only four of the 34 were unable to respond. One of the re-

---

[46] In an economy such as that of Mexico, where transportation is good, and where the government agencies act to keep the prices of basic commodities low, no single private trading group can exert any significant influence. Normal annual fluctuations may have seemed to Geronimo to be the result of deliberate manipulation rather than the result of fluctuating supplies. The term "monopolist" is widely used throughout the world to refer to any business using a practice that the speaker dislikes.

[47] Again, this is not an insoluble problem technically. Mechanization, for instance, would obviate the need for draft animals and extensive planting of pasture could vastly reduce the needed grazing area. But the organizational problems are baffling. We have mentioned the obstacles to mechanization, particularly fragmentation, and the individualism which undermines effective community action in agriculture.

maining answers we would judge to be just a spur-of-the-moment excuse since the reply (with reference to a year when the rains were late) was, "The rains came too early"! Indeed, one cannot be certain that some of the other answers were not similarly given merely to satisfy the questioner. The classification of the answers is as follows:

	Number of Farmers Giving This Reply
Insufficient demand	3
Seed expensive, outside competition lowers prices, thefts from plots (same respondent)	1
Lack of money to buy seeds	8
Land of poor quality	2
Lack of water	1
Other technical reasons	3

It is clear that the reasons are technical, economic, and to a minor extent, social. With regard to the last of these, as we have seen, the wide dispersion of plots makes it impossible for a farmer to prevent theft. High-value crops are accordingly planted only in house gardens, or in the *orilla* where production is high enough to make the losses less felt. Technical reasons refer to rainfall and land quality conditions, as well as factors related to specific crops. *Frijoles,* we were told, should only be grown on rich land since they damage the *milpa*.[48] Squash should not be planted too extensively since they spread all over the field. Chili is too delicate, as are tomatoes, which are destroyed by the frosts and dry winters.

Economic conditions have considerable weight. In some cases the eight who said they had no money to buy seeds may have been rationalizing, but it must also be remembered that cash crops are generally planted before the corn is harvested and by this time the cash available from earlier sales has evaporated. Huecorianos are very much aware of market conditions and attune their behavior accordingly. The risk factor discourages some from growing cash crops extensively, while it motivates others to diversify. One said, "Prices

[48] Nevertheless, they were also grown on the poorer land to some extent.

change from night to day and the only people who seem to gain are those carrying stuff to Apatzingán." On the other hand, Geronimo Roca represents the larger group that diversifies. He argues that "markets are limited for any given crop, and if we planted exclusively in one crop it might lead to a slump in prices. Furthermore, it is best to have crops maturing at different times since our wives could not carry all of the crop to market before it perished." When asked about a specific crop (iceberg lettuce), Geronimo replied that there was no demand for it. "It can be sold in Mexico City, but it does not pay the *comerciante* to do so. It has to be transported in boxes, otherwise it will get crushed. To make the boxes involves expenses and risks, not only because of the poor market that offers little profit, but because one can also lose the costly boxes. You can't even sell two dozen a day in the Pátzcuaro market. This type is not bought here even though we have lots of tourists." Juan Mirasol, who planted cash crops exclusively in 1961, shows an astuteness that would have delighted Adam Smith. He visits other communities to see what is being planted, and then plants other crops! This shrewdness earned him 6,330 pesos—almost six times the average crop income.

A rather progressive farmer described his fellow villagers as *tontos* (stupid) since they grow many different crops but sell their flowers, vegetables, eggs, and chickens to buy corn and a piece of meat now and then. An outsider commented that an egg worth 50 centavos would not fill the stomach but 50 centavos' worth of corn would. The cash crops are, in effect, exchanged for corn, and if this were not done Huecorianos would soon starve to death. As it is they frequently have a very lean time waiting for the corn to be harvested. Maize consumption is about eight liters for a family of nine. There are about 833 persons in the village proper, which implies a daily village consumption of about 740 liters. In 1961 the crop was about 115,316 liters, an amount which would last 156 days. Like many villages, indeed like many underdeveloped countries, Huecorio must import much of its basic food even though it grows the identical crops predominantly. The Huecoriano would not seem to be *tonto*. He has made the best adjustment to his environment that his techniques and society allow.

Tree Products

Food product trees are grown by all but four of the 34 farmers surveyed. Twenty different trees are grown, and; as in Tzintzuntzan, the peach is by far the most popular. In Huecorio it is followed at great distance by the *chayote,* which is actually a vine, and the apricot.[49] Only four of the farmers have substantial orchards of over 30 trees, although one farmer, who was not surveyed, learned something of horticulture in the United States at the turn of the century and he has over 100 good trees. Most of the orchards are rather casual operations, and this is reflected in the preference for consuming rather than selling the fruit. Those who sell large quantities, usually peaches or apricots, tend to be those with the larger plantings. The average income from food product trees is only 176 pesos, or 207 pesos for those with orchards, and the incomes range from only five pesos to 1,040 pesos.

For several reasons, only eight farmers collect firewood. One would expect the number to be higher since the cold season of January through March coincides with the slack time for agricultural tasks. Many men migrate to the *tierra caliente* to work the cotton crop or are employed in local industry. Others, however, in the words of one of them, are just plain lazy. Furthermore, little wood is available for cutting within Huecorio, and to collect a *burro* load requires a four-hour round trip to another community where it can be cut on *ejido* or private lands for a tax or charge of 50 centavos a load. Only two of the farmers interviewed collect wood for sale. One of these, who cuts throughout the year and works his land after he has returned from forests in nearby communities, had an estimated income of 2,106 pesos, of which about 200 pesos was income in kind from wood retained for home use. The other had sales of 234 pesos, and

[49] The types and quantities of food product trees grown in the village, before the large gift of nursery stock from the state of Michoacán, were as follows: peach 792, *chayote* 152, apricot 96, *tuna* 88, apple 72, fig 68, *zapote* 64, plum 44, lemon 40, avocado 37, pear 32, *cherimoya* 28, cinnamon 20, quince 20, orange 20, medlar 20, cherry 12, pomegranate 12, lime 8, walnut 4.

similarly retained about 200 pesos' worth for his family. The remaining six farmers collect only an estimated sixty pesos' worth of wood a year apiece and sell none of it. The majority of households appear to buy their wood from cutters who live outside of Huecorio and sell door-to-door within the village.

Animal Products

Income-earning animal products in Huecorio are eggs, milk, and meat. As far as could be ascertained, by-products such as skins are not subject to special transactions. Neither butter nor cheese is made, and manure is used as fertilizer by the farmers who own animals. Only 17 of the 34 farmers in the survey raise hens, but in terms of aggregate value this activity far exceeds all others in importance. While the gross income from crop production amounted to 33,306 pesos, the gross income from egg production was 141,830 pesos and the net income was 28,070 pesos. This substantial sum was almost entirely accounted for by the six *granjeros* participating in the *Asociación Avícola,* a poultry cooperative initiated by CREFAL.[50] In the remaining 11 cases, egg production can only be described as casual, and since the birds receive no special attention, costs of production can safely be said to approximate zero. (See Table VII.)

Chickens are also raised for home consumption, and in the one case in which they were marketed the sale was made within Huecorio. No attempt is made to fatten the birds, and this effort would not be justified in view of the high price of this form of meat relative to that of beef or pork, a situation which limits the local market considerably. On the other hand, there is a market for pigs in Huecorio and Pátzcuaro, and sometimes they are fattened on special feed, although this is not usually the case. The cows reported sold were actually calves and were not sold for meat but for pasturing to other Huecorianos. Nobody makes a practice of raising cattle for beef, but instead animals are hold to Pátzcuaro butchers when it is obvious that they have outlived draft or milch functions, or that they are

[50] For a description of the *Asociación Avícola,* see below, pp. 85–88.

literally on their last legs, in which case they are hurried to Pátzcuaro while they can still travel on their own power. As a result, one can only describe the local meat as being rather durable. A few turkeys are sold, but again they receive no special care. It is clear that meat production has little economic importance in Huecorio, and a significant contribution to income is made only with the rather rare sale of a large animal.

Although many cows are to be seen grazing in the fallow *ejido* fields, the importance of these rather drab looking animals is not apparent to the casual visitor. Eighteen farmers have milch cattle offering a net yield of 35,820 pesos, which slightly exceeds the gross yield from crops of the 34 farmers interviewed. (See Table VIII.) Two-thirds sell some milk either in Pátzcuaro or at a small market near the railway station.[51] Most of the cows are *corriente,* which means that they are the result of random matings and their yield—of about three liters—is low. A few farmers try to improve their stock and this is reflected in their higher yields, which reach ten liters a day—somewhat over 2.5 U. S. gallons. The labor input in producing milk is not great. Certainly milking involves no more than an hour a day, and another hour, perhaps, if the milk is to be sold. Because milking and selling are not usually done by the farmer himself but by some younger member of the family, there is practically no opportunity cost involved, and our money estimates of costs may be too high. Since little cost is usually involved in feeding the animals and since a ready market exists—many families deliver to the homes of a few fixed customers—this is again a wise utilization of resources from an individual point of view.

From a broader social point of view the issue is less clear-cut. Milk production tends to perpetuate the subsistence cyclical pattern in the use of the *ejido.* From a technical standpoint it would be desirable to utilize the *ejido* during the fallow phase of the cycle for growing fodder or a restorative crop, but this would be resisted by the milk producers who—even though they might benefit from this change—would be faced with the problem of finding a place to graze their cows while the crop is growing.

[51] The milk is neither boiled nor pasteurized before delivery.

Fishing, Hunting, Gathering

Although Huecorio is on the shores of a large lake, only 18 persons in the actively employed labor force of 241 persons consider fishing to be their primary occupation, and for another five it is a secondary or tertiary occupation. Fishing in the lake is dominated by the island folk, who have few alternative opportunities, and this way of life tends to be followed only by Huecorianos who live in the two former islands which are now hills near the water's edge. One of the two men interviewed fishes for about five hours daily—from 7:00 a.m. to noon—and works his fields in the afternoon. His principle catch is the *chavalito* and he claims his average daily catch to be between five and eight pesos. The interviewer, basing his claim on knowledge of this fisherman's spending pattern, judged that the average was the higher of the two figures and possibly more. Thus, his gross income from fishing is at least 2,912 pesos a year. His equipment consists of a canoe worth 100 pesos, a paddle worth five pesos, and a net. His annual costs would be rather modest. If the canoe and paddle are depreciated at 20% annually and the net at 100%, the costs would be:

Canoe	20 pesos
Paddle	1
Net	30
Canoe registration	5
	56 pesos

The net cash income, then, amounts to at least 2,856 pesos.

The other fisherman interviewed had annual costs of 67 pesos, which were slightly higher due to possession of a more expensive canoe.[52] With a longer day's fishing (six hours) his gross income was also more:

[52] The small canoes, known as *ichárutas,* cost between 150 and 250 pesos when new. The large canoes (*teparis*) cost some 1,500 pesos, since it is difficult to find the thirty-foot logs from which they are made. Small nets (*cherémekuas*) cost only thirty or so pesos, but the large seine nets (*chinchorros*) are complicated and extremely expensive. The price in 1964 for a new net was quoted at 3,000 pesos, which, allowing for in-

	Annual Rate (pesos)
Posing for tourist pictures—2 pesos a week	108
May, a good month—40 to 50 pesos a day (average 45 pesos)	1,350
August, September, October—bad month due to winds —2 pesos a day	180
Rest of year—5 to 10 pesos a day (average 715 pesos)	1,830
Total	3,468

The net cash income in this case amounts to 3,401 pesos annually.

No other collecting activity has any economic significance. The paucity of game restricts hunting to the rabbits, birds, and raccoons that damage crops, and the ducks which settle on the lake after the annual fall migration from the north.[53] Gathering is confined to the collection of the fruit of the prickly pear cactus, variously known as *nopal* or *tuna*. These grow largely on the small hills which rise from from the *ejidos*. Collecting is done by women and children, and the tasty ripe fruit are retained for home consumption.

Distribution of Agricultural Products

Farm products are distributed in a variety of ways. Huecorio is far from an autarchic self-sufficient economy, and, in fact, is highly dependent on external commerce to supply its basic needs. In summary, one can distinguish seven ways in which agricultural products are disposed of, but, as far as can be ascertained, there is no bartering either within or outside the village.

Home Consumption. Corn, wheat (about 60%), *frijoles,* peas, lima

---

flation, confirms the estimate of 1,000 pesos made by George Foster in 1945. Foster, pp. 101–13, describes fishing instruments and techniques in fine detail.

[53] Very few Huecorianos participate in the lake-wide duck hunt that takes place at the end of October on the eve of *Todos Santos,* and the throwing spear (*atlatl*) used on that occasion is unknown in Huecorio.

beans, potatoes, non-cooperative produced eggs and chickens, some of the milk, firewood, and most of the fruit are all produced to be consumed by the farmer and his family. Less than 50% of Huecorio's needed corn is produced within the village, and cash crops must be grown for sale to cover the deficit.

The Comerciantes. The cash produce are lentils, squash (75% sold), tomatoes, coriander, cabbage, beets, onions, lettuce, radishes, flowers, carrots, string beans, gourds, and fish. These are sold by *comerciantes,* who are usually the farmers' wives or daughters but sometimes the farmers themselves. The principal markets are the towns of Pátzcuaro, Uruapan, Apatzingán, and Morelia. Although closer than Uruapan or Apatzingán, Morelia is not an important marketing center for Huecorianos since it is easily accessible to *comerciantes* from other villages where similar products are produced. Uruapan is a large center some forty miles by train, and Apatzingán, in the *tierra caliente,* is further—55 miles by bus. Prices are much better in those towns than in Pátzcuaro. Radishes, for instance, might sell at 20 *centavos* a handful in Pátzcuaro but 40 *centavos* a handful in Apatzingán. In some cases, farmers sell their products to *comerciantes* who belong to other families.

The Cooperative. Members of the *Asociación Avícola* have no marketing problem. The eggs are delivered to the poultry cooperatives' warehouses situated on the grounds of CREFAL near the railway station. These high-quality eggs have found a ready market in Mexico City.

Merchants. Pigs and cattle are sold to butchers at the *Rastro Municipal.* Pigs, however, may sometimes be illegally slaughtered and sold within Huecorio.

Individual Clients. Chickens and firewood may be sold to individual clients within the village. Milk is carried to the homes of clients in Pátzcuaro or sold at stands at the station, where, again, the clients are generally steady customers.

Intermediate Products. Alfalfa, *cañamargo, gallinaza,* and *abono de corral* are intermediate products used by the farmers themselves to further production. Alfalfa and *cañamargo* are forage crops for the animals. *Gallinaza* and *abono de corral* are the natural fertilizer of animals.

The Acaparadores. The *acaparadores* are Pátzcuaro "monopolists" who offer a form of credit which is particularly associated with *"el trinquete del 8 de diciembre."* It is customary for villagers to buy new clothing to celebrate the important fiesta of *Nuestra Señora de la Salud,* which occurs on the 8th of December, just before the corn harvest takes place. Ready cash is not available in households in time for the fiesta, but certain Pátzcuaro merchants buy the green corn at half the normal harvest price and then receive the mature corn when it is harvested. It will, of course, be sold back to villagers for its full value later during the year, when the normal reduction in supply has forced the price to rise.[54]

With the exception of those who succumb to the *trinquete,* Huecorianos make good use of the distribution channels and markets available to them. This is not to say that the situation could not be improved, but improvement is beyond the capabilities of the Huecorianos acting by themselves. It is conceivable that the Church might be able to persuade Huecorianos not to despoil themselves by succumbing to the felt need to dress up for the fiesta, but it is unlikely that more reasonable forms of credit could be arranged unless a consumer cooperative were formed. Many towns and cities in Mexico, in particular the industrial city of Monterrey, are inadequately supplied with fresh vegetables, and the Pátzcuaro basin could be a potential source. This, however, would require processing and transportation facilities, ample credit, technical advice, and good leadership. Both a consumer cooperative and a vegetable marketing organization are potential extensions of the poultry cooperative, but the poultry aspects will be, for some time to come, sufficient to utilize all the cooperative's resources.

[54] See Señor Bolívar's fuller explanation on pp. 181–82.

CHAPTER 2

METHODS OF AGRICULTURAL PRODUCTION

T H E rhythm of life in Huecorio is dictated primarily by the timing of the rains, which begin in June and taper off in October and November. A second influence is the temperature, which sometimes reaches freezing levels during January and February. After that it becomes uncomfortably hot, even in May and early June. Were it not for the low temperatures of the winter, the lake shore lands could be cultivated continuously, and were the rainfall more evenly distributed, the remaining lands could be more fully utilized.

January, February, March, and April offer little to do agriculturally, and some farmers take advantage of the harvests of cotton, fruits, and vegetables that take place in the nearby *tierra caliente*. Others prepare their fields in anticipation of later plantings of maize and vegetables. This is also an opportunity to collect firewood and do odd jobs around home and field. Some farmers just relax at this time, but all of them—as in other months of the year—must go forth daily to attend their animals. The lack of interesting things to do in agriculture is well compensated for by important religious fiestas, which offer, as well, an occasion for secular indulgence.

The tempo begins to quicken in April, when those who have land suitable for vegetables plant cabbage and lettuce in nurseries. In

Barbechando *in San Pedrito, mid–June, 1962. Colonia Ibarra beyond hedgerow*

May, under a burning sun, wheat must be harvested and threshed, and many begin the preparation of the same fields for corn. By June, the pace has become intense as corn is planted, and vegetables are planted, cultivated and, for some, harvested. *Corpus Cristi,* on the 10th of June, is a very important break and work is often delayed for several days as the festivities and their effects taper off. During the summer farmers must work early in the day with great diligence, for the rains thunder down about four in the afternoon and outside activities are impossible. During the time available corn and vegetables are cultivated, and in August preparation for planting wheat in October will begin. The rains start to diminish in October, and precipitation is rare from December through May. Corn, *frijol,* and squash harvests begin late in November and continue through early January. December is also punctuated with the major religious festivities connected with Christmas and *Nuestra Señora de la Salud.*[1]

To what extent is it possible to improve the utilization of natural resources within Huecorio? Is the village farmer bound by tradition and his mind closed to technological change? What improvements appear feasible, what possible objections might be made to them, and

[1] See Appendix B.

how might these changes be brought about? In this chapter we direct attention to these questions, but in order to do so we must examine in close detail the techniques that are currently being used. Unless this is done and unless we fully understand the reasons for the present methods, proposed changes in technique, no matter how worth-while they seem to the outside expert, will frequently be rejected for reasons that seem perfectly valid to the local farmer.[2]

METHODS OF CORN PRODUCTION

Selection of Seed

After the December harvest, the majority of those who plan to plant corn the following June will select and store the best grains. Of the 26 farmers whose corn cultivation practices were studied, only four buy their seeds. These four have very tiny plots of less than a quarter of a hectare, and one can infer that their seeming lack of foresight is largely the result of a pressing need to consume much more than they are able to raise.

For the remainder, the practice is to select long, thin ears of corn with straight rows of large kernels. The ears with rotten or damaged kernels are rejected.

Preparation for Planting

In preparation for planting on the *ejido* lands, a meeting of the *ejidatarios* takes place at the end of April for a formal decision as to which lands will be planted and when the planting can be done. Al-

---

[2] It was recognized that our observation might have to be confined to one summer's intensive effort, and our questionnaires were designed to cover the agricultural cycle completely. We were not able to obtain the necessary support to continue the study during the full agricultural year and can offer therefore only preliminary and incomplete data. Nevertheless, there is no substitute for direct observation, since significant changes can stand or fall on small details which are very rarely picked up in questionnaires.

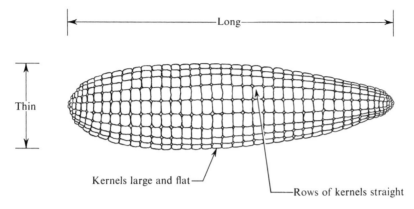

Seed Corn

though the rotation of the areas among wheat, corn, and fallow follows a regular pattern and so little, if any, decision-making takes place, this meeting has the effect of serving notice on the owners of animals of the fields available for grazing.

Corn is apparently the only agricultural product for which there is any religious observation, and even this is of diminishing significance. Offerings are made at the *Misa de Buen Temporal* held on the 17th of April to San Isidro, the patron saint of farmers, by whose grace it is hoped to bring good rains. Although Huecorio is formally Catholic, only five of the farmers interviewed said they attended this mass, and another said he did not bother any longer.

The first step in preparing the land is the removal of a thistle variously known as *chicatole* or *espina*. This is usually done with a simple yet ingenious combination of forked sticks. One, shaped like an inverted Y, holds the thistle near the base while the other, with a hook, catches the thistle a little below and yanks it out. It is not necessary to touch the spines at all with one's hands, and the sticks can be used to stack the thistles in piles, which will later be burned. The ashes are sometimes collected and spread as fertilizer.[3] Other farmers,

---

[3] In one place where this had not been done and the ashes merely scattered by the plough, the differential effect of the ash on the crop was noticeable at an early stage. While most of the plants in the *milpa* were about six inches high, those near the ash were over one foot. This was drawn to the attention of the *dueño* of the plot, but he did not find the observation interesting.

either too lazy to clear the *espina* properly or too pressed for time, merely uproot it with a plough and leave it where it lies.

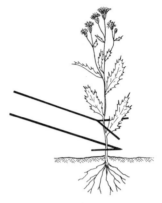

In addition to the removal of the *espina,* there are three distinct variations in land preparation. The most commonly used procedure involves a deep ploughing, done lengthwise down a plot with a steel plough. This is known as *barbechar* or *arar.* The traction is almost always a pair of *bueyes,* although one farmer used a pair of horses. A wide yoke of seven *cuartos* is bound to the horns of the *bueyes* by *aperos,* and a steel chain connects the yoke to the plough. The Oliver ploughs are highly prized, since, unlike the newer steel ploughs that have become available, they "throw" the soil cleanly.

The newer ploughs are in appearance identical to the Olivers, but, according to Geronimo Roca, the tempering of the mouldboard was done mechanically rather than by hand and the result is a more porous surface, to which the soil clings.[4] The Olivers were apparently

[4] Correspondence with the Oliver Company reveals that the plough models we observed—ASBF-706—were known as chilled-bottom ploughs. The A is a model number, SB refers to steel beams, and F-706 to a pair of metal hand grips. "[T]he plough you referred to was an A1 or A2 with fitted steel beams. The A1 had a 4½" by 8" cut and the A2 had a 4½" by 9" cut. The plow was taken out of production on March 27, 1950, due to the low volume of sales. The A series plow was a former version of our very famous number 40 used throughout the world as a two horse walking plow." The chill, as ploughmakers call the hardening process, crystallizes the metal so that the grain is edgewise to the mouldboard instead of lengthwise. With an ordinary plough, soil particles scratch the surface and these scratches catch the sod and prevent it from falling as the plough moves forward. The crystals, on the other hand, are polished by the soil and the smooth surface then "throws" the sod. Imitation Oli-

Oliver plough breaking turf

Oliver chilled-bottom steel plough

introduced in the 1930s with the encouragement of General Múgica and originally cost about 40 pesos each, but farmers now value them at 500 to 800 pesos.[5]

Barbechando is to a depth of about 20 centimeters (8 inches), and the heavy turf is broken and overturned. Even the better Oliver plough must be cleaned frequently if the soil is damp. For example, one *yuntero* took 1½ minutes to plow a *surco* of 90 paces, but another

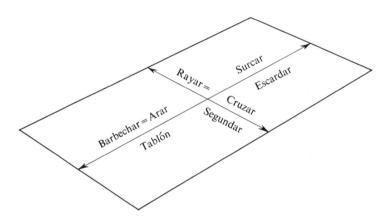

Directions of Ploughing for Corn

1½ minutes was needed to clean the plough and turn the *yunta* around. Cleaning is done with a *rejada,* which is attached to a *garocha.* On the other end of the *garocha* is a *pica* to goad the oxen. A correspondingly greater time is needed to clean the other steel ploughs, but the better Oliver needs no cleaning in dry soil, which is the usual condition under *barbechar.* Two persons commonly work together in *barbechar*—the *yuntero* to drive the *yunta* and a *peón* to clear the

vers are made in Mexico and are visually identical. The trade mark, part number, and name are copied although the "O" is sometimes left off the name Oliver. The mouldboards are not chilled and therefore they do not polish and "throw" the dirt. Huecorianos have bought these imitations and have been disappointed in them.

These imitations and the rise of the tractor-drawn plough forced the Oliver Company to end production of the Model A. However, a chilled plough is still being made by the Hamburg Plow Works of Hamburg, Pa.

[5] By contrast, the new ploughs copied from the Olivers were purchased in the 1950s for prices ranging from 110 to 150 pesos.

thistle. The work can, however, be done alone. Sometimes, particularly when time is short, two *yuntas* will work together.

The next step is to use the Oliver to plough (*rayar* or *cruzar*) across the width of the field at an angle of 90 degrees. This can be done by one person if sufficient weeds have been removed, but more commonly two are employed.

The second generally employed method eliminates the *rayar* or *cruzar*. This is done under several circumstances: the plot may be too narrow to permit it, or may be on the side of a hill, in which case erosion is to be avoided, or the rains may come unexpectedly before' the *cruzar* can be completed.

The third method, if it can be so termed, is to eliminate the preparation altogether. This is often but not always done if the land has already been leveled and the turf broken up by the wheat crop. In this case the first step involves the simultaneous preparation (*surcar*) and planting.

Other individual variations exist at this stage and suggest that the Huecorio farmer is not so circumscribed by tradition that he follows a customary pattern blindly and unquestioningly. At least 11, and probably more, of the 30 farmers use fertilizer. A minority of these spread it at this stage and use *abono de corral,* which is broadcast and then ploughed under. Geronimo Roca sometimes plants irrigated corn in February, and a primitive type of irrigation is practiced by the previously mentioned diversion of the Río Guan. In 1961 farmers with fields in the *ejido* of La Lagunilla cooperated to build three ditches to divert the stream to their fields. This is not a true irrigation system in which water is supplied to the growing crops, but instead the fields are flooded during the summer rains and the lands are benefited by the alluvial deposits. The first year's experience promised spectacular results, but these were wiped out by bad weather.[6]

---

[6] Slash-and-burn agriculture exists nowhere in Huecorio, probably due to a lack of available forest land, although hoe culture is sometimes practiced in small private plots. The preparation involves the use of a hoe to break the turf and make mounds about 45 cm. apart.

Wooden plough breaking turf

Wooden plough,
showing orejeras

Planting

The decision as to the time of planting is probably made in a similar fashion by most of the farmers, although the verbalizations of the decision vary considerably. Some gave a specific date such as the eighteenth of May or the first of June, and others in general terms such as "when the rain falls." The general characterization would appear to be as follows.

As a rule, planting takes place between mid-May and early June. Ideally the seeds should be in the ground shortly before the rains begin. The indication of the imminent torrents is the towering cumulus in the distance. Two advantages derive from planting *en seco*—that is, in the dry ground before the rains. The ground is warm from several months of uninterrupted exposure to the sun, and the corn will germinate immediately when the rains begin and will have a head start before the weeds begin to grow. Geronimo Roca experimented to prove the point, and found that a section of his *milpa* planted before the rains gave better results than that planted after the rains began. Sometimes, he says, maize planted *en seco* will germinate fewer seeds, but the plants that do grow will have larger ears. Planting cannot always be done *en seco,* however. Sometimes the rains commence earlier than usual and catch the farmers unaware. More common, however, is the plight of those who lack work animals and who must wait until those who have them are finished so that they can be borrowed or rented.

Planting is usually done by a two-man team, a *yuntero* to drive the oxen and a *sembrador* to place the seed. Since the planting itself is somewhat slower than making the furrow, two *sembradores* will sometimes be used. The *surcos* are cut lengthwise, at an average distance of 2½ feet.[7] A wooden plough is used and this is fitted with an

---

[7] The farmers are not accustomed to thinking of these distances in precise measurements. It is not necessary for them to do so, since the oxbows are more or less standardized and the yokes set the distance between the oxen and the plough which is centered between them. Customarily, one ox treads a previously made furrow and the rigid yoke sets the distance for the next furrow. In respect of the distance between the furrows,

orejera, a wooden plate which projects from either side of the plough and pushes the earth away from the center line. The *sembrador* follows, dropping seeds in the furrow. He carries the seeds in a sack and measures a distance of about 50 centimeters with a step of his right foot. Several seeds are dropped and covered with dirt by the left foot. Sometimes the seeds are covered by the plough on a second pass, and this practice is followed if the ground is wet or the field large.

Considerable variation exists in the number and types of seeds planted in each *mata.* The differences appear to be due to the carrying capacities of the soil and the individual preferences of the farmers. Typical sequences are shown below. Complete interplanting is rare, since *frijoles,* squash, and lima beans compete with the corn for nourishment and reduce the harvest.[8]

It is anticipated that seeds will sometimes not germinate, and for this reason several are planted together. With one exception no attempt is made to cut back the growing plants in a *mata* to only one. Geronimo Roca is this exception, since he believes that the size and weight of the ears from one plant will be more than the total yield from two or three plants which would have only small ears. When used, fertilizer is applied at this time, a handful being dropped in each *mata.* The fertilizer is a mixture (50/50) of *gallinaza* from the poultry *granjas* and *abono de corral* gathered from the yard. Experience has taught the farmer that *abono de corral* used alone encourages weeds while *gallinaza* alone burns the plants. Since, in addition, *gallinaza* has turned out to be a good herbicide, the combination of the two produces excellent results, raising the harvest at least threefold. After the planting, the fields are carefully watched and scarecrows are sometimes placed to discourage birds.

Cultivation begins two or three weeks after the corn has begun to grow. The first step, the *escarda,* is taken when the plants have developed three leaves. The work team almost always consists of three persons—a *yuntero* to drive the oxen, and two *peones.* The wooden

the data collected in 1962 showed wide variation. In 1964 four persons were again asked this question and the answers were "60 centimeters," "70 centimeters," "50 centimeters," and "one meter." Measurement by tape showed the distances to range from 66 to 84 cm.

[8] Squash and lima beans may be broadcast in small quantities rather than planted regularly, since they tend to spread anyway.

Interplanting Combinations (Number of Seeds)

Farmer	Corn	Frijoles	Squash	Lima Beans
		First Mata		
a	2	2	0	0
b	3	2	0	0
c	3	1	0	0
d	2	0	0	0
e	3	1	0	0
f	2	1	0	0
g	3	2	0	0
		Second Mata		
a	3	1	0	0
b	3	2	0	0
c	3	1	0	0
d	2	0	2	0
e	2	1	0	1
f	2	0	1	0
g	4	1	0	0
		Third Mata		
a	2	2	0	0
b	3	2	0	0
c	3	1	0	0
d	2	0	0	0
e	3	1	0	1
f	2	1	0	0
g	3	2	0	0

plough is attached to the oxen by a yoke of seven *cuartos,* and on one side of the plough is a *bigotera,* a plate about 30 centimeters long and ten centimeters high. The plough makes two passes down each row, and in the process throws the soil up against the *matas.* This effectively raises the plants and places furrows between them. Prior to this the *mata* is in a hollow into which the rains drain, thus encouraging a deep root system, which is necessary to hold the plant during high winds. Once the roots have developed sufficiently, the position of the furrows is reversed and water flows away from the *mata* so that the leaves do not rot.

The *peones* who follow the plough are supposed to remove the sods of grass that have begun to grow, and shake the soil from their roots to prevent regeneration. In addition, the *peones* are supposed to use their hands to scrape away dirt that the plough has thrown over the growing corn. To do this they must work constantly in a rather uncomfortable bent position, and they move as rapidly as they can to get the job over with. The result is pretty sloppy. Uprooted corn and beans are not replaced, and the dirt surrounding the plants is not especially well scraped away. One of the claimed advantages of labor-

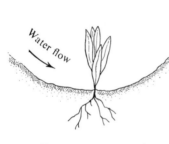

Deep roots encouraged

Position of Corn as Planted   Corn after *Escarda*

intensive agriculture is that more care can attend cultivation, raising the productivity per unit of land thereby. This is true only when the proper attention is provided the plants. Such is not the case in Huecorio, and our observations would suggest that more care at this stage of the operation would raise productivity by at least 15%.

The next step in cultivation, the *segunda* or *raya,* is done one or two weeks after the first, when the corn is about 25 centimeters high. An *orejera grande* is fastened to the wooden plough. It extends about 25 centimeters to either side of the plough, and the furrow is ploughed at right angles to the *escarda* between the plants. Two *peones* follow the plough, shaking out weeds and scraping dirt from the base of the *mata.*

A third step, called the *tablón,* is practiced by about half of the farmers. This is done when the plants have reached a height of about one meter, but no higher since they would then be damaged by the *yunta.* A *yuntero* and two *peones* work in the same direction as the *escarda.*

Little more is done until the harvest, although two farmers mentioned that they sometimes weed the *milpa* with a hoe and all visit the fields now and then to make certain that no animals have broken in to damage the plants.

Harvesting the *milpa* takes place at irregular intervals between September and January. In September small squash will be cut off the vines, sometimes by women if the men are busy. The vines are left in the hope that some of the remaining squash will grow to a substantial size, to be harvested in December. Lima beans are cut in October, but are generally left to dry and be collected later. A meeting of the *ejidatarios* is held in early November to reach agreement about the time of the harvest. To make sure that people cut only their own parcels, there is a fine for those who harvest before the stipulated time. Those who do not harvest on time lose their crops to the grazing animals. The premium thus placed on speed results in the use of larger work teams, which range in size from one to five, with the mode at four persons. Women will sometimes help if time is short.[9]

The first and most difficult task is to cut the *frijoles,* which are yanked out by the roots and then untangled from the cornstalks. They are then) collected with the beans and squash and carried home on burros, to be stored in the *tapancos.* The workers carry net-like bags called *ayates* on their backs, and are armed with *piscadores,* which resemble leather-cutting tools. The corn is harvested fully mature as a rule, although a very few persons cut and eat it green. The ears

[9] The time available for the corn harvest is further straitened by the concurrence of numerous fiestas in December. Because of the restrictions on the use of the *ejido,* farmers concentrate on harvesting those lands first and then work their private fields. Frequently the time needed for harvesting spills over into January.

When the parcel is being worked *a medias* or under contract, the proprietor will usually turn out to supervise the harvest and verify the agreed-upon repartition.

are cut off with the *piscador* and thrown in the *ayate*. From the *ayates* they are in turn emptied into sacks, in which they are carried home. The ears are then husked and strung up on poles placed between rafters or, if space is insufficient, stored temporarily in the *tapanco*.

The cornstalks are usually broken and left for the grazing animals, but some farmers cut the stubble with a scythe and store it in sacks until February and March, when there is a shortage of fodder.

Differences Within Huecorio[10]

In the sense that it is performed in a given way by a majority of the farmers, one can say that there is a standard procedure for all of the steps in the growing of corn in Huecorio. There is a size of work team, a sequence of steps, and so on, that many farmers follow; yet a great variation can be seen at every stage, and it is the fact that differences, rather than similarities, exist in Huecorio that characterizes the agricultural picture. The variations in procedures seem to stem from four factors: differences in soil qualities; differences in skills; differences in capital resources; and differences in attitude.

Differences in Soil Qualities. These affect procedures in two main ways. Poorer soils imply lower productivity of corn, and accordingly in such areas *frijoles* will be planted in lower ratios vis-à-vis corn. In addition, where land is hilly the *raya* or crosswise ploughing will be omitted to avoid erosion.

Differences in Skill. As in all societies, differences in ability are important. I recall watching two farmers simultaneously preparing adjoining plots in the *ejido* of San Pedrito. One was having no difficulty. He worked quickly and his rows were straight and true. The other was experiencing heavy weather. His furrows were crooked, he was constantly tripping over sods, he ran his plough through the boundary lines, and at the end of each lurching row he had to stop and rest. His *yunta* may well have been undisciplined, but incompetence is also a likely explanation.

Differences in Capital. These are particularly important, as they

[10] For a comparison of the different techniques used in other Mexican villages, see Appendix C.

apply to the ownership of oxen. Those who do not own *bueyes* must wait to borrow or rent them when others have finished their tasks. As a result, corn is frequently planted late and the cultivation cannot proceed on time. Other farmers own inferior steel ploughs or have to make do with wooden ones. In the former case a given task will consume more time than with one of the better Olivers, and in the latter case the soil cannot be easily and deeply overturned to destroy the weeds. Similarly, those with more resources can hire more *peones* in order to work more land or get a job done on time.

Differences in Attitude. These are difficult to pinpoint, but they manifest themselves in such things as laziness, drunkenness, or on the other hand openness toward new techniques. We could not identify the lazy farmers directly or indirectly, but even the more progressive farmers would succumb to the bottle and neglect their work for days. There are a few persons who escape rather frequently in this manner. Nevertheless, a significant number are open to new methods and crops, and several conduct experiments in an effort to produce better harvests.

THE PROSPECTS FOR IMPROVED
TECHNIQUES OF CORN PRODUCTION

Technical improvements—the steel plough and the *gallinaza* fertilizer for instance—have been applied by Huecorianos to the production of corn, and it goes without saying that there exists a potential for further changes. Nevertheless, Huecorio's output could probably reach the feasible limits of the production function only if the land were divided into a small number of family-unit farms using sophisticated capital equipment. These farms would provide employment for only a handful of men, and one cannot accept in good conscience the implications of such a change, since the majority of the farmers would be forced thereby to find other employment. Less drastic changes are, of course, feasible technically, and the Mexican Department of Agriculture publishes pamphlets advising farmers of relatively modest, yet worth-while, improvements. It is helpful to analyze the recommendations of one of those papers in terms of potential changes in Huecorio.[11]

Good Preparation of the Soil

Pamphlet Recommendation. Pulverize the top layer to at least 15 centimeters. Level the surface and drain well.

Feasibility in Huecorio. No Huecorianos attempt to level or to drain their *milpa,* even where the contours are shallow. The construction of effective drains is hampered by the small size of individual plots, and, for much of the land, the contours are too abrupt to permit leveling of the surface.

As to the recommendation that the soil be pulverized, it must be noted that there are considerable differences in the care with which individual farmers prepare their fields. These variations are due in part to the differences in temperament and attitude that exist in pre-Orwellian society, but they also arise from prior differences in income and available capital, which make some persons better farmers simply because they have better ploughs and can hire more *peones.* Conversely, others lacking resources cannot cultivate properly or on time, and, to a large extent, differences in agricultural technique and income become self-perpetuating.[12]

Preparation would be significantly improved by the use of tractors, and several farmers well understood the advantages of those machines. Said Miguel Salinas, "I can work all my lands with *peones,* but tractors would save time and could turn the soil to a greater depth than is possible with *yuntas.*" [13] Ricardo Pérez felt that a tractor would avoid

[11] *Aumente Su Producción de Maiz: Recommendaciones para el Estado de Michoacán,* Agencia de la S.A.G. en Michoacán, Delegación de Agricultura, Morelia, Michoacán, Abril de 1962.

[12] This is not inevitable, of course, since some poor farmers can elevate themselves by nonagricultural work while some of the wealthy may sometimes have large families, thus passing to their children the blessing of poverty.

[13] Miguel whimsically referred to his *yunta* as "My two-horsepower tractor."

the night work that is necessary at certain times, and that work in the fields would become less arduous and more agreeable. Although the cost of a tractor is high and many problems are associated with its use, it is not unlikely that one or two farmers who have large holdings, and can finance tractors through membership in the *Asociación Avícola,* will introduce them in the 1960s. Small, garden-type tractors might be effective in the light soils of the *orilla,* but no farmers expressed curiosity about them.[14]

[14] Tractors were not necessarily recommended in the S.A.G. pamphlet, but the nature of the problem was discussed with an official of the Pátzcuaro branch of the *Banco de Agricultura,* and in correspondence with officials of the International Harvester Company offices in Mexico. It is possible that miniature tractors, such as the Gravely, could be used in the light soils of the *orilla* where work is generally done by hand, but in the greater part of the village lands machines must be larger. In the opinion of the International Harvester Company, the McCormick International Model B-275 Diesel would be the smallest feasible machine. The price f.o.b. Pátzcuaro for this tractor with disk ploughs, cultivators, a trailer, and other equipment was quoted in 1961 at 61,949 pesos (approximately $5,000 US). A few John Deere Models 720 were seen in the region and were quoted at 84,500 pesos with equipment. Under Mexican relative cost conditions, such tractors are not practicable on less than 50 hectares, which means a cooperative purchase would be necessary to justify their utilization in Huecorio. On such an area the John Deere tractor would cost, on a five-year amortization, 16,900 pesos a year; with an additional expenditure of some 14,000 pesos a year on supplies and fertilizers, an annual produce of 150 tons' worth of corn (about 120,000 pesos) could be harvested. Monetary calculations then would seem to justify such an investment.

A primary stumbling block lies in the need for cooperation among a group of five or more to share the expenses and responsibilities. We would judge that a permanent cooperative of this kind is not feasible in this individualistic culture. Some individuals may soon be able to finance such a tractor from their *granja* earnings, but only one of the *granjeros* has holdings of even ten hectares and most have considerably less.

Even if more economical and practical tractors were developed, other problems remain. The majority of the fragmented holdings would be difficult to plough with a machine that necessarily needs a substantial area for maneuvering. Stone fences separate many plots, and these would have to be provided with gates. At present a narrow gap in the fence is merely broken down every time the animals must pass through. In the *ejido* lands there are no passageways or trails sufficiently wide for tractors and, in view of the serious shortage of land, it is unlikely that the non–tractor-owners would accept lightly the loss of even a few feet of the plots that would be entailed.

Introduction of Hybrids

Pamphlet Recommendation. The hybrids H-24, H-125, H-126 are suitable for introduction in the Pátzcuaro region and have procured "magnificent" results.

Feasibility in Huecorio. Unless they are most carefully introduced, there is little prospect that hybrid seeds will be accepted in Huecorio in the near future. In an attempt to understand local reaction to hybrids we asked the farmers, "Would you get better results if you used special seeds?" The word "special" was used deliberately to ascertain the farmers' knowledge of hybrids, without any suggestion on our part, but it proved to be unfortunate since many took "special" to be synonomous with "selected." As a result, of the 13 who replied "yes," only six really expressed even a lukewarm reaction to hybrids. No farmers in Huecorio currently use hybrids, but one of the men interviewed had used them with success for one year and stated that they were "lost" within three years. Apparently he had purchased the hybrid only once, and within three years cross-fertilization with the *criollo* strains in other plots led to its adulteration.[15]

Of those whose reaction might be construed as favorable, four said they lacked the cash to buy them, one said they had to be matched to the soil, and another said that it was necessary to experiment. The nine farmers who claimed that hybrids would not help, and several who in misinterpreting the question said "yes," were quite positive in stating that the *criollo* seed was better because it had developed in the best way possible to suit local conditions and always gave results.

Geronimo Roca is an enlightened and intelligent farmer but even he, after experiments with hybrids, mistrusted them. *"Como nuestras tierras son muy pocas no podemos arriesgas el pan de nuestras bocas. Es por eso que no sembramos hibrido."* [16] If hybrids are to be intro-

---

[15] Four other farmers stated that hybrids "do not produce," but it was not clear whether their statements were based on experience or hearsay.

[16] "With so little land we cannot risk the bread for our mouths. This is why we don't use hybrids."

duced into Huecorio, considerable educational effort will be needed to overcome this resistance. In unsophisticated agriculture throughout the world hybrids have run into difficulties, not the least of which is the flavor of the corn products made from them. Although the question of taste was not mentioned in Huecorio, it should certainly be considered by agronomists before they try to introduce new strains.

Adequate Population Density

Pamphlet Recommendation. Population density should vary with the hybrid, soil fertility, and humidity, but should range from 36 to 55 centimeters. The distance between the rows should be 92 centimeters, and two seeds should be planted in each *mata* at a depth of 6 to 8 centimeters.

Feasibility in Huecorio. Huecorianos plant their *matas* at distances of about 50 centimeters, which is within the prescribed limits. If this distance were reduced any further it would entail a substantial alteration in local techniques of cultivation. In Huecorio, the *segundo* is done at right angles to the rows of plants, and this change in direction would not be possible if the plants were closer together, since the *yunta* could not pass between them. Technically it is possible to do the *segunda* longitudinally[17] in the same direction as the *escarda,* but this is not economically feasible since a longitudinal *segunda* would destroy fewer weeds than a *segunda* at right angles, and the farmers would have to supplement the work of the *yunta* with hand weeding at the very time when vegetable cultivation in the *orilla* makes great demands upon them.

In Huecorio the rows of plants are from 66 to 84 centimeters apart —a distance just sufficient to permit the *yuntas* to pass when the *bigotera* is used on the plough. If they were widened to the 92 centimeters recommended in the pamphlet, the oxbow and *bigotera* would have to be redesigned. Although this is not an insurmountable obstacle, the farmers are most likely to question the desirability of wider spacing, since they would obviously get fewer rows of corn in their *milpa.*

Huecorianos are also likely to resist the recommendation that only

[17] It is done longitudinally in Cherán and Tepoztlán. See Appendix C.

two seeds be placed in each *mata*. As can be seen from the chart of interplanting combinations,[18] the most common number of seeds per *mata* is four, and corn seeds are mixed with *frijoles*, squash, and lima beans, while the recommendations apply only to corn planted in isolation. Agronomists claim that the total value of the output of the *milpa* is greater if their practices are followed, but to farmers who are not accustomed to selling their corn, the argument is academic. Interplanting has for them two major advantages: it offers some variety of products which can be stored in the *tapanco*, and it is a means of partially insuring themselves against the risks of failure of any one crop. Agronomists often characterize subsistence farmers as stubborn and inflexible; but when one reflects upon the agronomists' lack of interest in experimenting with interplanting, one can but wonder if the shoe is on the other foot.

Fertilizers

Pamphlet Recommendation. For the Pátzcuaro basin the Department of Agriculture recommends per hectare 600 kilos of 10–10–10 at planting and 200 kilos of ammonium sulphate at the third cultivation.

Feasibility in Huecorio. Some Huecorianos have recently begun to use natural fertilizers—the 50/50 mixture of *abono de corral* and *gallinaza*—but it does not follow that chemicals would be as readily accepted. Twenty-four farmers were asked, "Do you think you could get better crops if you used fertilizers?" With only one exception, all replies were affirmative. It is significant, however, that when they were asked what fertilizer they would use, ten spoke of the natural fertilizer, nine did not know, and only three thought chemicals would help.

While no farmers in Huecorio apply chemicals, 11 of those queried were applying the natural mixture. The reasons for this pattern were not hard to find. The natural fertilizers involve no monetary outlay, and are therefore applied by all those who have stables or *granjas*.

[18] See above, p. 59.

On the other hand, chemicals require the payment of cash but bear returns in a subsistence crop. In other words, farmers are reluctant to undertake heavy cash expenditures for which there is no proximate cash return.

There are other disadvantages to chemicals, they say. Chemicals last for only one season, while the natural fertilizers show benefits for three or more years. It is "bothersome" to apply chemicals without machinery, especially when it has to be done several times a season. It is much easier to put a handful of manure with each *mata* early in the growing season. The farmers feel too that chemicals can damage crops, especially if the rains do not come in time.

The negative reaction to chemicals is due, at least in part, to an unfortunate experience in 1954 when students from CREFAL persuaded some farmers to apply a chemical fertilizer, *"Salitre."* The experiment was neither carefully prepared nor supervised, and the crops were damaged. In the absence of skilled persuasion and supervised credit, the attitude toward chemicals is unlikely to change no matter what their virtue.

Control of Insects

Pamphlet Recommendation. The Department of Agriculture recommends several sprays and dusts specific to certain insects, DDT for the *Gusano Cogollero,* Clordane for *"La Gallina Ciega,"* and so on.

Feasibility in Huecorio. During the team's residence, an invasion of worms began to attack the growing corn. An opportunity was offered to observe communal paralysis in the face of a serious crisis. To combat the plague it was necessary to spray all the affected *milpas* with a DDT dust, and several of the farmers accompanied two members of the team to Villa Escalante and Morelia to ask government officials for help.[19] While a search was going on to find some DDT from a government agency at no charge, several dusters were dug up and a

---

[19] It is significant that none of these four farmers was affected, and in one case even likely to be affected, by the insect, but all felt a sufficient responsibility toward the community to take some initiative.

young villager repaired them. But individual activity could accomplish nothing by itself and the leaders tried, without success, to arrange a meeting of the farmers to get a cooperative attack under way.

As fortune would dictate, the plague coincided with a rash of weddings in the village, and the only communal activity was convivial in nature. Even those most affected by the worm preferred to escape from the problem by battling a bottle instead. But even had the festivities not occurred, it is unlikely that any action against the worm would have been stimulated. Five years previously the Department of Agriculture had brought in dusting equipment, but it had not been cared for and had deteriorated. Such well-meaning benevolence on the part of the government has nurtured the belief that its support will always be forthcoming in time of emergency, so why bother to do anything on one's own?

But another reason exists, too, and it is easily overlooked. Because of fragmentation, any given area affected by a plague will contain the land of as many as fifty farmers. Many of them, out of laziness or the lack of a sense of responsibility, or perhaps for some legitimate reason, will not carry their part of the work or financial burden. This naturally creates ill will, which is antithetical to the necessary cooperation. Furthermore, there are always difficult administrative and organizational problems, such as assigning work teams or collecting financial contributions. Such chores are naturally unpaid and take people away from their own labors.

Thus, because of a social system ill-adapted to cooperation, because of the ease by which the bottle provides an escape, and because of the stifling effects of fragmentation, the worm continued to munch away at food no longer destined for human mouths.

POTENTIAL CHANGES
IN CORN PRODUCTION

Although the S.A.G. pamphlet made no mention of it, irrigation of the seasonally watered fields would perhaps be second only to widespread use of fertilizers in raising agricultural productivity. Since most of the village terrain is hilly or sloping, this technique would be available only in the *ejidos* of San Pedrito, La Lagunilla, and La Peñita, and the private lands that lie between the populated area and the lake. Those areas are sufficiently separated so that several distinct systems would be called for. Alternative methods would be to tap springs or to pump from the lake. Geronimo Roca argues that a 12-inch pump and pipes would cost about 36,000 pesos, and if 30 or 40 people cooperated this could be paid for in five years. But apart from the lack of cooperation implicit in Geronimo's statement, difficulties of drainage, water utilization, and water sharing are too complicated for Huecorianos to solve without competent technical support.

In keeping with Huecorio's social structure, one or two farmers plan to purchase pumps with their *granja* earnings and use these to tap springs or a high water table under their fields. For these people, and their immediate neighbors with whom they would share the water without charge, a major problem is solved. But for the remainder of the village no economically or socially feasible solution is in sight. Villagers would have to cooperate permanently in a venture such as this, and, as will be suggested in Chapter 6, such permanent cooperation is out of the question in Huecorio's highly individualistic culture.

In general, Huecorio farmers exhibit a rather ambivalent attitude toward their harvests. When asked, "Are you satisfied with your maize harvests?" 21 out of 26 replied "yes," yet only three farmers believed that the harvests could not be improved. One of the latter clearly voiced a fatalistic attitude by his reply, *"Si Dios y la buena suerte me ayuda tengo mejor cosecha."* (If God and good fortune help me my crops will be better.) But the frequency of the "yes" answers together with a recognition that methods can be improved would seem to indicate an attitude of passivity—one stage removed from fatalism but definitely an improvement.

The impact of the recent introduction of fertilizers was quite clear when farmers replied to the question, "What could you do to improve your crop?" Nineteen mentioned fertilizers, two talked of water, and the remaining five did not know. Then we asked, "Why don't you do this?" Fourteen replied that they lacked sufficient cash and five said that they lacked the knowledge of what fertilizers to apply. Other random answers included a need for analysis and experimentation and a fear of borrowing. Clearly, Huecorio has reached the point where credit and *skillful* technical advice could bring great changes to the agricultural scene.

METHODS OF WHEAT PRODUCTION

The planting of wheat is the first stage in the subsistence cycle of wheat, corn, and fallow and is usually undertaken in October, about ten months after corn has been harvested from the field. During the interval between the corn harvest and the planting of wheat, animals have been permitted to graze on the stubble and exceedingly thin pasture that grows during this time.

Selection of Seed

The usual practice is to set aside seed after threshing the previous harvest, but poorer farmers frequently cannot keep this seed and must buy from merchants in Pátzcuaro.

Preparation of Land

Preparation involves two steps, *barbechar,* the deep longitudinal ploughing, and *cruzar,* the deep ploughing at 90 degrees to the original cut. Usually a team of oxen with a narrow yoke of four *cuartos* will be used with an Oliver plough, although horses may sometimes be used since the preparation for wheat coincides with extensive cultivation of corn and consequently there is a shortage of work animals. One farmer, who is also employed at Tzipecua, rents a tractor with disks from La Quinta.[20]

The work is usually begun when the cultivation of corn is drawing

[20] All the tasks necessary for the production of wheat, with the exception of threshing, are generally performed by farmers working alone.

to a close in the middle of August, and frequently spills over into September. An exception applies to those who have land in La Lagunilla, La Peñita, and the southern section of San Pedrito, all of which are flooded by the Río Guan. The canals are closed in September, and time is needed to permit the marshy but fertile soil to dry out. Religious practices have less importance for wheat than for corn. Some Huecorianos are content with the offerings made for corn in April, and others may attend the *Misa de San Isidro Labrador* on the 16th of October.

Decision to Plant

The 4th of October is the day of San Francisco de Assisi, and this is taken as the signal to begin planting wheat. An earlier planting would expose the maturing crop to the risk of frost damage, while if the planting is much later the rains may cease and the seeds would fail to germinate.

Planting

Planting involves four steps: *melgar, tirar, tapar,* and *arrastrar,* the last two being undertaken simultaneously. The *melga* is a rectangle from 3 to 3.5 meters wide and 7.5 to 10 meters long, within which the soil is pulverized and the boundaries of which are indicated by lines made with a wooden plough without *orejeras* or *bigoteras*. Each *melga* is separated by a distance of two meters, and its function is merely to indicate to the farmer where the seeds have been planted. The seed is then broadcast, as the term *tirar* indicates. *Tapar* is to cover the seeds with earth, and *arrastrar* is the process of leveling the *melga*. To accomplish these tasks, branches are tied to the wooden plough (without *orejeras*) and weighted down with stones or by the *yuntero* himself. This smooths and compacts the soil to lock in the moisture.[21]

[21] One can note that the farmers of Huecorio are practicing thereby a form of dry farming.

Cultivation

No attempt is made to cultivate the growing wheat, and nothing is usually done until the harvest. However, if the crop is damaged by frost it will be cut back, and in sprouting again will sometimes yield a harvest up to 75% of normal.

The Harvest

Harvesting begins in April and continues through May, and most persons work alone at it. The wheat is cut with a sickle and tied into sheaves, which are stacked until a dry, windy day presents good conditions for threshing.[22] This work takes place during the hot season, and the sharp sickle causes many injuries; as a result the pay is high when the work is contracted out. The contract is usually by the job, and because of this it is done fairly rapidly. As a consequence, *peones* can earn at least 12 pesos and sometimes up to 25 pesos a day. Usually no meals are included since the individual jobs are small, but the daily rate compares well with the standard six or seven pesos a day plus meals that are generally earned.

Threshing

Wheat may be threshed by an ancient John Deere which can be seen and heard trundling from village to village in early June. About 25% of the farmers use this machine at a charge of 10 centavos per kiloliter, but most prefer to do the work themselves if time permits. At several locations in the village, round and level platforms have

[22] An outsider criticized villagers for leaving the sheaves too long in the fields. This, it was felt, led to their drying in the sun, with a consequent loss of weight. The matter does not seem to be one of choice, however. The Huecorianos have no alternative storage areas and, in their own words, thresh the wheat as soon as it can be done, preferably on the day it is harvested.

been prepared, and the wheat is brought to them for threshing and winnowing. From three to seven animals are tied together at the neck in echelon with *burros* (known as *madrinas*) on the inside and horses (called *padrinos*) on the outside, where their longer gait keeps them in formation with the *burros*. Five animals and two men can thresh up to 100 bundles a day. One man guides the animals, which trample the wheat under foot and force the seed from the pod. Other men use wooden pitchforks and *palas* to turn the straw over. For winnowing, the animals are removed and the *basura* is thrown into the air with pitchforks. The chaff is blown away and the heavier grain falls to the ground to be collected later, placed in sacks, and carried home.

Differences Within Huecorio

Wheat practices show less variation than those for corn. In preparation the method of traction is customarily oxen, but horses or a tractor may be used.

Size of work teams will vary in harvesting and threshing, but such differences are probably functions of the varying pressures of time and the ability of a farmer to pay for *peones*. In other words, larger or smaller work teams at this time will not affect the total output of wheat, although they may facilitate work on corn by making it possible to start preparation early.

Wheat is sometimes worked *a medias,* and the procedure is slightly different from that for corn. With corn the *dueño* only provides the land and seed, and supervises but does not participate in the harvest. For wheat the *dueño* not only gives the seed and the land, but also works in the harvest. In addition, he shares half of the cost of the animals which do the threshing. The output is then divided fifty-fifty.

One can infer from this that, even though wheat operations have no great opportunity cost, sharecroppers find them less attractive because they consider a return in wheat to have less utility than a return in corn. In other words, although both wheat and corn are classed as subsistence crops in Huecorio, corn is more "basic" in the sense that it is the principal component of all meals, whereas wheat is used in a less versatile manner—indeed, exclusively in the baking of bread. When a Huecoriano thinks of food, he thinks of corn and not of wheat.[23]

POTENTIAL CHANGES
IN WHEAT PRODUCTION

Little historical change seems to have taken place with regard to wheat production, except for the very minor exception of the use of a tractor by one farmer. Another farmer claimed that because fertilizers are not applied, harvests used to be better than they are now, but there is no other evidence to support or undermine this contention.

In spite of the frequent damage to the crop by droughts and frosts, the farmers claimed to be satisfied with their harvests. Nevertheless, all but one agreed that productivity could be improved, particularly by the use of fertilizers, but a lack of money and knowledge about appropriate fertilizers were claimed to be obstacles to their use. About half of those questioned agreed that hybrid seeds would be helpful, but the same reasons were offered for neglect of them. During the summer Ricardo Pérez had arranged with the local extension agent, Ingeniero "Tacho" Morales, to experiment with a variety which would be planted in June and harvested in November. This faster growing variety would have the advantage of the rains and lead to larger yields. It was intended to fertilize half the field with manure to see the differential effects, but unfortunately the pressure of work on corn prevented this experiment.

FALLOW PRACTICES

Letting the land lie fallow is an essential stage in the subsistence cycle. In principle the alternated crops, the grass which grows under

[23] For some comments on differences in wheat growing techniques between Huecorio and Tzintzuntzan, see Appendix C.

fallow, and the manure from the grazing animals, all serve to maintain the soil's productivity. Geronimo Roca does not think that this is still the situation. "At one time, the land used to produce more because there was more stubble, and more of the residue of the corn was left to decompose and make a fine fertilizer. But today there are more cattle and less area available to pasture them, and people collect the stubble to feed their cattle during the dry season. Even the grass has little chance to grow and fertilize the soil, because the hungry cattle use their hooves to dig up the roots to eat. The land does not rest, and the manure is insufficient to maintain it."

Geronimo's characterization of the situation would seem to be correct, although we have no firm evidence that the soil's productivity has declined. Removal of stubble and overgrazing are factors that need to be counteracted. Under present techniques about 25% of the land is fallow at a given time, and its main function is seen not as an opportunity to maintain productivity but rather as a place to keep cattle. In the absence of irrigation, two alternative uses for the fallow land might be found. (i) Green manure could be grown to maintain soil productivity, but then the animals would not be provided for. If the animals are done away with, then mechanical cultivation would have to be employed; but as we have seen, this would be frustrated by the combined effects of minifundia and fragmentation. In addition, the profitable dairy operations would have to be terminated. (ii) A more beneficial alternative would be to grow fodder during this interregnum and feed it to the cattle, which could be grazed in the hills. This would require adequate fencing and community acceptance of what would seem to most to be a bothersome notion.[24]

CASH CROPS

Information was gathered on the techniques used for growing lettuce, cabbage, carrots, radishes, beets, potatoes, and *cañamargo,* a

[24] Since the fodder alone would be particularly restorative, this sequence would have to be combined with the application of fertilizers to maintain fertility.

forage crop. Enough similarities exist for lettuce, cabbage, and radishes so that their techniques can be generalized.

Most farmers collect seeds from earlier harvests by permitting some of the plants to mature and flower. On the other hand, seeds are sometimes purchased from merchants in the nearby communities of San Pedro and Cucuchucho. Two farmers, however, prefer to journey to Morelia, 40 miles distant, where imported seeds are available. One of them pointed out that he prefers the imported seeds to the domestic varieties even though their price is 50% higher, because the germination is 100% and this justifies the higher cost. Domestic seeds, he says, are adulterated and do not "take" well.

The ground is first ploughed in January, and worms and insects are killed by exposure to the frost. The ground is further pulverized twice—*barbecha* longitudinally and *en cruz* at 90 degrees—with a steel or wooden plough if the plot is large enough or with a hoe if it is small. The land is ploughed again after each harvest, if multiple cropping is practiced. For vegetables which can be sown broadcast, such as radishes, the custom is to make *melgas* similar to those used for wheat, and the land is made as level as possible to facilitate irrigation if it is used. *Abono de corral* is applied in April before the June planting.

The time of planting will vary according to the availability of moisture. Near the lake, ditches filled with stagnant water can be tapped by the laborious use of buckets, which are dropped in, hefted out with a rope, and deposited about the plot. Ricardo Arizpe used a horse-driven Persian wheel, which he loaned to his neighbors without charge, and Geronimo Roca used a two-inch gasoline-powered pump for ten years until it finally broke down. Others, despite community disapproval, tapped the water supplied through the village waterworks.

With irrigation, planting can begin in late February or March, after the frost danger is over. Geronimo Roca pointed out that the timing of irrigation should vary with the vegetable—too little or too much water can damage the plants. Lettuce should be watered every three to seven days, carrots and cabbages every two weeks. On the land which cannot be irrigated, the crops must await the rains. A first planting takes place in June and a second crop may be planted in August.

For plants such as lettuce and cabbage, which cannot be broadcast but must be sown in rows, a portion of the field or the house garden is set aside as a nursery, and after the ground has been pulverized the seeds are broadcast lightly. Soil is raked over the seeds and then pressed down and watered. One farmer reported that he covered the nursery with branches for a week until the seeds germinated and the lettuce (in this case) had sprouted. Since this was the only report of this practice, we do not know if it is general. Lettuce is retained in the nursery for one month to six weeks, by which time it has reached a height of 4 inches (10 centimeters). Cabbage requires two months in the nursery according to one respondent, and only one month according to another.

The plants are then transplanted to *matas* 30 centimeters apart. After two weeks they receive the *escarda,* at which time the earth is piled around the growing plants. This is followed by the *segunda* two weeks later. Lettuce requires one month more to mature and is harvested with a sickle or a knife. The reported growing time for cabbage from seed to harvest is four to five months, for radishes 40 to 45 days, for carrots six months, and for beets eight months. Beets are planted in August, and harvested in March of the following year if the crop is not damaged by freezing ground.[25] They are broadcast in the same fields as cabbage during the final cultivation of this vegetable.

In the irrigated lands at least two crops are harvested annually, and sometimes alfalfa is a third crop grown during the winter. Potatoes are grown in one house garden for domestic consumption. Two types were observed—large *anita,* rather like an Idaho, and the small *evendira. Cañamargo* is a commonly grown fodder. The procedures are identical to those for wheat, except that after a growing season of only five months a little is cut for seed and the animals graze the remainder.

Alternative crops were briefly discussed with Ingeniero Manuel Cepeda de la Garza of the Pátzcuaro branch of the *Banco Agrícola y*

[25] According to Geronimo Roca, the ground does not freeze frequently and only does so when there are no mists.

Ganadero Michoacano. Chili, for instance, can render a gross return of 30,000 pesos and a net profit of 15,000 pesos a hectare. Although it is grown in small amounts in other villages, Huecorio farmers feel it is too delicate to be grown on their land. Potatoes can yield a net return of 8,000 pesos, but Huecorio farmers have noted precipitous price declines in this crop, such as those which occurred in 1959 and 1961. Crops such as these could not be marketed locally in large quantities, and because their holdings are too small to make them eligible for the loans from the *Banco Agrícola* the villagers cannot avail themselves of the advice and marketing facilities that this agency has to offer.

One interesting possibility for Huecorio would be to grow "wild rice" in the *orilla*. In 1961 a person described as a "tourist" gave some seeds to the people of Chipicuaro on the other side of the lake. The harvest was excellent, but no one knew how to market the rice and it was therefore consumed by the farmers themselves.

Huecorianos have utilized those crops which their techniques, their land, and their marketing facilities make possible. In agriculture they have little advice and assistance from the outside, and until help is made more effective only minor changes can be expected.

FRUIT TREES

Although 29 of the 34 farmers interviewed have fruit trees, this activity is essentially casual except for one farmer with a large orchard.[26] Only ten of the farmers prune their trees, and still fewer (five) take the precaution of painting the trunks with lime to discourage climbing insects.

A rare instance of folklore is associated with fruit trees. It is believed that eclipses and earthquakes cause the immature fruits to fall from the trees.[27]

[26] His activities were not examined systematically.
[27] *"Temblores y eclipses influyen mucho en la pérdida de las cosechas. El año pasado hubo un eclipse y un temblor y todas las frutas pequeñas se*

This relative lack of interest in orchards is understandable, in view of the high opportunity cost of the land which would be removed from cultivation when trees were planted. Generally the trees are found in out-of-the-way portions of backyards, or, if in the gardens, they are closely crowded—a factor that partially influences their yield. This is one consideration that suggested to the team the possibility of utilizing for orchards the otherwise idle hills that intersperse the *ejido*. Since the *cerritos,* as they are called, are part of the *ejido* and are thus communally owned, the inevitable difficulties of reaching communal agreement and of work- and profit-sharing would have to be faced. Credit for the acquisition of fences, sprayers, and insecticides would be available through the *Fomento Ejidal,*[28] and the trees would be available free of charge from one of the three state nurseries in Michoacán.

There are, however, other uses for the *cerritos.* They might possibly be used as grazing areas to free the level *ejido* areas for planting, or they might offer sites for industrial or residential expansion. The development of this idle land would be of some benefit to the community, but the problems are many and the leadership and community cohesion necessary to overcome them will not arise spontaneously.

CARE AND TREATMENT OF ANIMALS

During the day small families of pigs grunt and wallow in the streets, or, squealing, try to gain entrance to their owners' houses whenever the gates are opened. Although they forage for themselves most of the time, some special care is taken when they are penned for fattening in anticipation of sale. The most common fodder is *salvao* (alterna-

---

perdieron. La esperanza es lo último que se pierde. Esperamos el otro año si Díos quiere."

[28] *Fomento Ejidal* is a reserve fund built up by the taxes paid for the privilege of working *ejido* forests. The amount credited to Huecorio is probably very little indeed, since the forested area within the village is small and difficult of access.

tively *salvado*), which consists of the husks of wheat or barley remaining after threshing. This is sometimes purchased at 70 centavos a kilogram, but it is more often obtained from the preceding wheat harvest. Corn, alfalfa, lettuce leaves, grass, and *zapotes* are also used, although five of the 14 farmers who gave information on hog raising made no effort to provide feed. Each family recognizes its own pigs, and although theft is rare the animals are brought into the patio or house *corral* at night.

By day horses, oxen, cows, and *burros* are led to fallow fields, most frequently the *ejidos* which are available for use as pasture by *ejidatarios* and non-*ejidatarios* alike. The manure that is left is felt by most persons to be useful in maintaining the soil's productivity. Yet, as has been pointed out, the large animal population is probably damaging the *ejido* by overgrazing. Some few persons graze their stock in their own fields or in the *orilla,* and although the pasture is rich on the lake shore the animals there must frequently be rescued from the mire. In the evening the most common practice is to collect the animals and return them to a *corral* attached to the house. This is simply an area of perhaps 25 by 25 meters enclosed by a stone wall. Others will use the *plaza de toros* on the outskirts of the village in the *ejido* of San José. These places are likely to get too muddy during the summer rains and the animals must be left in the open *ejido,* where they are sometimes stolen. The owner visits them every three days or so "to verify if they are present, living, and well." Branding is rare. In most cases the animals are recognized by "spots or lines," and in turn the owner is recognized by the animals, although by what identification marks we do not know. Animals which wander off are impounded by the *municipio,* and a notice is posted in Pátzcuaro for ten days. During this time the animal can be retrieved upon payment of a fine, but if it is not claimed it is then sold.

Except in the dry months of February through May, when all the animals must be provided with cut forage, few farmers provide supplemental greens or hay. In anticipation of this, some farmers collect wheat and corn stubble or plant *cañamargo,* which matures in March. At other times a few of the animals will receive alfalfa or *salvao;* in one case squash is given to milk cows. Animals receive inadequate attention, the only exception being a Holstein known as Amy who arrived during our visit.

Amy was given by the government to the Baltazar Pérez family to demonstrate the higher milk yields of superior breeds. The only condition attached was that Amy's calf, to be born in February, was to be given back to the government. Nevertheless, the Holstein was proving to be an expensive burden on the family. A special stable costing 3,000 pesos had to be built and a monthly outlay of 170 pesos in hay, alfalfa, and concentrate had to be covered somehow. Amy is expected to give 18 to 20 liters a day in contrast to the three liters from *"corriente"* animals, but since no milk could be sold for some time these unmatched expenses may have a discouraging rather than stimulating effect upon the innovators.

Jersey and Holstein studs are kept at Tzipecua by the Montana State College project, and a young resident Mexican veterinarian is performing artificial inseminations at cost throughout the region. Three farmers from Huecorio have taken advantage of the project, but without success. Several others were thinking of it, but as one put it, *"me gano la vaca."* Cows grazing in the *ejido* cannot be watched closely enough, and the Tarascan bulls have a better idea of what is going on than do the farmers. Another ten farmers know of artificial insemination but prefer to let nature take its course, while two did not know of its existence in spite of the project's location within the village.

A large number of farmers claimed that their animals never get sick, even though they talked knowledgeably about domestic remedies. Others said that their animals do not get sick very often, but we have no way of ascertaining whether this *is* the case, or whether infirmities are passed over unnoticed—or whether, as a third possibility, sickness in animals is not a worrisome condition because it is easier to kill than to cure them. Nevertheless, of the 22 farmers who responded to the question on treatment of infirmities, 16 had used veterinarians at one time or another. Some of them also use homemade remedies.

A common affliction of horsekind is *torzon* (*torozon*) *riñon* (kidney grip), which results from eating the weed *kalate yerba* while green. The animals bloat up, and to cure this a hole may be punched in the animal's side "to let out the air," or a purgative may be rendered. The purgative is sometimes a *cerveza* made from grass, apples, and *mezcal* or alcohol. At other times the purgative is simply diesel fuel. Some of the farmers prefer to call one of the several veterinarians in the region because, as one said, vaccinations are quicker than herbs.

The veterinarian in nearby Colonia Ibarra is easily accessible and charges 20 pesos for the consultation plus the prescribed medicine. At least one farmer has a hypodermic needle and undertakes the prescribed injections for animals belonging to family and friends.

Although vaccinations are common, confidence in veterinarians is not universal. In one instance, an ox developed an infected foot and could not be used in the *yunta*—a circumstance that seriously delayed the preparation of the land for corn and prevented the wheat experiment mentioned above. One veterinarian was called in and an injection was administered. Since there was no improvement by the next day another veterinarian was sent for, who ordered lemon and alcohol rubs, which, combined with rest, were successful. Veterinarians were frequently blamed for the deaths of animals they treated, but this incident suggests an expectation that veterinarians can work miracles.

One farmer reported, "Once I had 16 pigs and a person came to vaccinate them and they all died. I'll never use a veterinarian again." Another said he had little confidence in people who merely guessed. "One should be certain about these things in the first place." When a veterinarian cannot cure an animal he'll say it is old anyway and won't last." These statements underline an ambivalent attitude toward the care of animals. With few exceptions, care is offered only to the more valuable animals because of their significant economic importance. Nevertheless, the expense involved seems to be resented, and it is felt that if one spends money one should have successful results. There is, in other words, little understanding of or sympathy for the complexities and uncertainties of veterinary science. Preventive medicine is not practiced on any animals—with the exception of the chickens in the poultry cooperative—and disease is usually well advanced and therefore difficult to check by the time the veterinarian is called in.

During August, 1962 a disease attacked the pigs and many were to be seen lying on their sides breathing their last, surrounded by swarms of flies and predatory dogs. The Montana State College project veterinarian spoke at a meeting urging that the pigs be vaccinated and that the dogs be kept from eating the dead animals. He recommended that the dead animals be burned and buried, but it is doubtful if any of this advice was taken. Treatment of pigs is rare, and only one case of vaccination was reported. In point of fact many persons prefer the taste of diseased pigs—"*cerdos con granos en el cuerpo*" (pigs with granular cells in their bodies)—and it is therefore not considered advantageous to prolong the life of a sick animal.

Several rabid dogs were reported and a number of persons, including the author, were bitten. Since no treatment is possible once the animal has contracted the disease, the dogs are shot, or more likely, because of the expense of bullets, simply stoned to death. In the town of Pátzcuaro, when rabies becomes a threat or the dogs become too numerous the police distribute poisoned meat. We were assured that properly vaccinated dogs were spared this treat.

As far as we can gather, practically no attempt is made to fatten animals for market. The exception seems to involve a few farmers who pen some adult pigs and provide them with *salvao,* lettuce scraps, and grain. With chickens and most of the pigs, fattening—if it can be so described—is nothing more than the casual process of foraging. Cows are sold when they no longer produce milk and *bueyes* when they can no longer work. Horses and *burros,* on the other hand, are not sold for meat. If sickness is evident pigs will generally be sold, but useful cattle will be treated if possible.

All animals are supposed to be killed in the municipal slaughterhouse in Pátzcuaro, where an inspector is in attendance to collect a tax of 9 pesos and 60 centavos per head of cattle. This practice is hardly calculated to encourage legal slaughtering, and animals, especially pigs, are frequently killed in the villages.

The most important development in Huecorio, perhaps since the Revolution, has been the introduction of the *Asociación Avícola.* It was initiated by CREFAL in 1956, but under the guidance of a Food and Agriculture Organization expert in cooperatives, Ingeniero José Manuel Luján, has developed almost complete autonomy. The functions of the cooperative are: the sale of products of the *granjas*; the acquisition and processing of the inputs needed by the *granjeros* to develop production, not only of their *granjas* but also for their other trades; and the purchase of consumer goods for the members.[29]

An initial credit of 100,000 pesos was received from the *Banco Nacional de Comercio Exterior,* and CREFAL acted as intermediary between the bank and the individuals in the villages of the lake area who became members. Since few of the *granjeros* had assets to pledge as security, the loans were underwritten by CREFAL in principle, although in practice they rested on the strength of character of the individuals chosen. In 1960 and 1961 the loan repayment rate had reached 100%.

Eleven persons in Huecorio are members of the cooperative. Geronimo Roca was one of the first, and in 1956 received credit to construct the *granja* and to purchase the White Leghorns and the necessary nests, perches, feed troughs, and water troughs. This credit, plus the additional expenses incurred in feed and medicines, is paid for principally by the eggs which are shipped to Mexico City.

Apart from the initial construction, which can of course be contracted out, the labor demands are modest. The feed must be mixed, water put out, the birds inoculated, the *granja* cleaned, and the eggs collected. Half of the *granjeros* assign these tasks to the children. Nevertheless, a *granjero* cannot avoid his responsibilities and leave Huecorio without permission from the council of the cooperative association. In 1958 Geronimo went to the United States without permission, and was punished by the withholding of additional credit for two years.[30]

The *granjeros* are universally satisfied with the project. One of them, Juan Roca, said, "My *granja* is the best investment in years. Not only do I get all the eggs and the *gallinaza* for fertilizer, but I am also paid for the chickens that don't produce any more. I got the money practically free—8% a year. I'll be without debt in two months, with no initial investment on my part except for labor. Be-

[29] For more details see *José Manuel Luján, Breve Reseña del Programa de Crédito Avícola Supervisado* (CREFAL, Pátzcuaro, Michoacán, Mexico, 1962).

[30] A revolving fund has been built up by contributions of one peso per bag of feed and one peso per chicken purchased. From this, consumer and productive loans are made at 8% annually. This contrasts with an average rate locally of 3% a month.

sides this, the cooperative forces me to save 500 pesos a year and I like that."

The *granjeros* were asked what they had learned from the operation, and all replied that they had learned how to feed and treat the hens. We suspect, however, that they have learned a great deal more, albeit serendipitously. Ingeniero Luján says that "the fact that farmers have common interests within the association has been a great stimulus in ridding them of the traditional isolation in which they live, and the relationships among neighbors of a community and the different villages have been facilitated and reinforced even where strong rivalries existed in the past." This is undoubtedly true. The *granjeros* are among the leaders of their communities, and the initial members were chosen for the very qualities which have been reinforced by their experience. Thus stimulated, the *granjeros* have extended their positive attitudes to other aspects of their economic life. The use of *gallinaza* has demonstrated that they need not be content with traditional methods of production.

Two *granjeros* plan to use their credit to buy irrigation equipment. Another, Francisco Cruz, acquired a rubber-tired cart and a horse which he uses to transport goods, especially *granja* products, to Pátzcuaro for the other farmers. The question remains whether persons not similarly open in their thinking could profit psychologically from being *granjeros*.

One significant omission in the learning experience relates to the business aspects of *granja* management. Prices of inputs are fairly stable, and in this carefully figured operation farmers are not induced to think in terms of costs, efficiency, and profit rates. In addition, the distribution is handled entirely by the cooperative and thus the *granjeros* learn nothing of marketing. To permit the farmers to extend themselves successfully beyond the *granja,* an attempt should be made to train them in basic aspects of business management.

There are 11 *granjas* in Huecorio, but 137 households which are, at least in a first approximation, potential candidates for cooperative membership. *Banco Nacional de Comercio Exterior* had amplified available credit to 940,900 pesos by 1961, and in 1962 the cooperative was prepared to establish ten more *granjas* in Huecorio. Yet, as one *granjero* observed, no one was willing to bother himself. When asked why they did not join the cooperative, the 28 nonmembers among the farmers interviewed offered a total of 17 different reasons or excuses. Only five of the 28 had reasons of indisputable merit. Four of them did not have sufficient space for the *granja* on their land, and one did not yet have electricity. A lack of cash was cited in 11 cases and a lack of security in another. These may or may not be legitimate reasons in some cases, since *some* cash outlay is now required on the part of the *granjero*. Four persons admitted that they had not thought about the idea or did not like it, and two did not understand it. However the remainder of answers were nothing but excuses and some respondents gave more than one: "There is nobody to care for them" (4); "Nobody asked me" (2); "I have no time" (2); "It is very complicated" (1); "It doesn't give results" (1); "Lots of risk from sickness and theft" (1); "I have bad luck with animals" (1).

One can only speculate as to what prompts these reactions. In some cases it is the fear of breaking unfamiliar trails, and in others complete misinformation as to the nature of the *granja* operation. Undoubtedly these misapprehensions could be dissipated by skillful education. However, there is sufficient interest in *granjas* in other communities, and the cooperative has neither the financial nor the human resources to undertake an educational program for Huecorio, irrespective of its merits.

FISHING

Since fishing is considered a primary occupation by only 8% of the labor force, no intensive investigation was made of the techniques involved.[31] One member of the team participated in fishing one day in August, and we quote a passage from his report:

Accepting an invitation offered me during an interview with Felipe Mercado, I went fishing today. The fishing day starts at about 6:30 a.m., when they start to string the nets, actually put-

[31] Hunting and gathering are of so little importance in Huecorio, with its sparse woodlands, that no study of the techniques involved was attempted.

Cultivating vegetables in the orilla

Nets strung to dry near the pumphouse

ting them on the poles in a secure manner. Then after completing breakfast they go to the canoes (one in a canoe—I also got a separate one). We went out to the middle of the lake and there met five others, with whom they would stay all morning. They fish in groups of 6 and form a circle with the idea of scaring the fish from the center into the waiting *mariposa* nets. They fish in one area for about five minutes before moving on, and in a short period they cover a great deal of territory. However, they do not catch much in this the worst month of the year, and no one had a catch of more than one peso. However, about 9 launches came by asking to take pictures, and they earned about 2 pesos from this. This income is fairly steady."

Interesting differences exist between Huecorio and Tzintzuntzan as reported by Foster.[32] Huecorianos do not have the larger canoes owned by some Tzintzuntzeños and the use of large nets is uncommon.[33] In 1945 Foster was unable to find a true *mariposa* net, so closely associated with Lake Pátzcuaro in the mind of the tourist. This was due to the diminution of the small *thiru,* which was the primary catch of the *mariposa* net. In turn, the *thiru's* virtual disappearance was attributed to the introduction of the large-mouth bass to the lake. Apparently an ecological balance has now been established, and many *thiru* can be seen drying out on the beaches, to be sold in the Pátzcuaro market. Huecorianos catch some *thiru,* but if their success is limited with fish they are adept at catching tourists, since Huecorio is the first village to be passed on the popular trip to the island of Janitzio.

[32] Pp. 102–6.

[33] In 1964 the matter of the large canoes and their use was discussed with Geronimo Roca. He said that there were no large canoes in the village and only two small ones were left. Only minutes later, as we walked the crest of Carián, four canoes, one of them large, were seen beached near the village pump house. Geronimo did not attempt to explain this discrepancy. He himself had a large seine net (*chinchorro*) which he was trying to sell for 1,000 pesos in order to buy an irrigation pump. He did not expect any takers, because the fishing had been very poor in recent years.

LEARNING PROCEDURES

Almost all of the farmers have learned the rudiments of agricultural techniques from their fathers, although this knowledge is sometimes amplified by working at Tzipecua. Uncles, grandfathers, or brothers have occasionally been the primary source, but one farmer claimed that he relied exclusively on his own superior intelligence.

Professional technical advice and assistance is readily available to augment the basic knowledge and can be had for the asking. Veterinarians reside in Colonia Ibarra, Pátzcuaro, Morelia, and Tzipecua. The young, energetic, and dedicated veterinarian at Tzipecua, Antonio Tena, is an employee both of the Montana project and the federal government, and he has an earnest desire to help to the limits of his ability.[34] United States agronomists are in residence at Tzipecua several months of the year, and their experimental plots can be observed at any time. Huecorio is also visited by a government agronomist, whose advice could be sought. Furthermore, the *Banco Agrícola y Ganadero* and the *Banco Ejidal* are potential sources of supervised credit.

In spite of the availability of technical information, only five persons out of the 34 interviewed replied "yes" when we asked if they had ever tried to get aid from anyone, but 22 replied "yes" when asked, "Does the government have anyone who can help you?" There is, in other words, a wide gap between the rather vague comprehension that assistance is available and the actual utilization of such a service.

The question, "If you wished to know how to get a better crop, whom would you ask?" was extremely revealing, as Table 3 shows.

Only six of the 34 farmers knew a specific source of regularly available professional information. In other words, the farmers are technically self-reliant, and they rarely seek advice from others. The variety of answers confirms rather than undermines this. When asked

[34] Tena had much success in persuading regional farmers to utilize the anthrax injection. He performed 200 in 1961 and 500 in the first six months of 1962.

TABLE 3

Stated Sources of Technical Advice

	No. of Respondents Citing Sources
Official Sources	
Ing. "Tacho" Morales (the extension agent)	6
Ing. Saucedo[a]	1
An extension agent	5
An agricultural bank	2
Village Sources	
Andrés Dongo	1
Ricardo Pérez	2
Felipe León	1
César Bustamente	2
The *Ejido* commissioner	1
Other Sources	
Anyone who could help	2
Señora Múgica	1
Friends in Pátzcuaro	2
"Someone" at the station	1
Himself [b]	2
No idea who could help	3
No answer	3

[a] Ing. Saucedo was a Mexican agronomist studying at CREFAL during 1962.
[b] Two persons stated they would refer the questions to themselves. One stated that everyone in Huecorio was of equal intelligence and so such questions addressed to others would be pointless. The other said he did not need to ask others since he knew agriculture well.

about a source of technical advice they were confronted with a question that simply had not occurred to them before, and they responded by answering with a quick and easy reply. Even the naming of persons in the village does not necessarily imply that they sought the advice of those persons. This is evident from the tiny number who actually sought advice. One, in naming those respected village farmers, said he would not ask them anyway because they know more than he does and wouldn't want to reveal their knowledge to him. Again, we have a confirmation of the highly individualistic social structure of Huecorio.

There are, however, other reasons why the potentially available sources of information are not used. Although the Montana project was located within the village and many farmers had seen the splendid experimental plots, they did not relate them to their own problems, since the Tzipecua land is particularly good, and sophisticated devices such as tractors and irrigation networks were in use there. The *Banco Agrícola y Ganadero,* although geared to *"pequeñas propiedades"* and run by a dedicated agronomist, is not of much help to Huecorio since it is permitted to offer its supervised credit only to private holdings in excess of five hectares and below various large maxima which depend on the class of land.[35] Only three of the 34 farmers interviewed had total holdings of five or more hectares, and these totals include *ejido* holdings, which are not eligible for the supervised credit. Such assistance might be available if several farmers with private holdings would form an association to share the responsibility, but as we have suggested, such cooperation is unlikely in Huecorio. Similar difficulties apply to obtaining assistance from the *Banco Ejidal,* which offers supervised credit to *ejidatarios.* Five farmers said that there was a need for an agricultural society in the village, but they agreed that it could not be organized because there was nobody to take charge.

Of his extension work "Tacho" Morales said, "As usual with this type of work, it is impossible to go as fast as one would like, but it is progressing slowly. I need more cooperation. The people should help me more. Things are just beginning in Huecorio. Fertilizer 10–10–10 is needed but in varying quantities in different parts of the village."

Ingeniero Morales prefers to work with individual farmers rather than groups; for instance, he has helped the Pérez family substantially with new seeds and with Amy, the Holstein. But his preference for working with individuals is reflected in the observation that hardly anyone in the village knows of his existence.

It became evident to the team that there is a serious need to train agricultural agents not only in agriculture, veterinary medicine, and so on, but also in how to present their ideas successfully to groups of

---

[35] These maxima are 100 hectares for irrigated land; 100 to 300 hectares for seasonally watered land; 300 to 500 hectares for mountains and open range.

campesinos, who will rarely seek advice voluntarily because they do not know it is available, they do not know whom to ask, in agricultural matters they are culturally oriented toward individualism and isolation, and they often do not know what to ask for. Meetings of one sort or another are held every week in Huecorio by the villagers and offer many opportunities for persuasion and enlightenment should the technicians wish to utilize them.[36]

Farmers were asked, "What kind of aid could other persons give you?" Their answers are tabulated below.

Specific Aid	Number Replying
Seeds	6
Loan of tools	1
Loan of tractor	1
Loan of animals	2
Credit	1
Fertilizers	2
Control of plague	1
Less costly seeds and fertilizers	1
Other	
We need an association before we can ask for help	5
I don't know	5
No answer	5

Again, it would seem that the question was one to which farmers had given little prior thought, and they responded with the first thing that came to mind. We have noted that although farmers claimed to be satisfied with their crops, they generally recognized that improvements were feasible. Clearly, the role of an agronomist should be to heighten this awareness and at the same time to demonstrate that improvements lie within the capabilities of the people.

Miguel Salinas said that "if one or two people in Huecorio ex-

[36] Agronomists were accused by some persons of being *flojo* (lazy)— driving around in trucks with pretty girls or just sitting in bars. This may or may not be true. But neither the local extension agent nor the veterinarian had received his modest pay check for several months.

perimented successfully with new methods all the rest of the community will follow." Certainly Miguel is himself very open to new
ideas—he is hoping to start an apiary and is interested in the possibility of using the *cerritos* for orchards—but we have indicated
several facts which suggest that within Huecorio, small as it may be,
new concepts and techniques do not move rapidly from one person
to another in the normal course of events. Less than a third of the
farmers use fertilizers, only two or three use imported seeds, only 11
have started *granjas,* and only six have heard of the extension agent.
Experiments such as Amy the Holstein, and demonstration plots, will
be a waste of time until the communication aspects of extension work
are solved.

The agent cannot be expected to solve Mexico's agricultural problems working alone. He can and should be supported by other devices: little garden plots for primary school children; more schools
for older boys, such as *La Escuela Práctica de Agricultura 'Presidente
Ruiz Cortinez'* in the *tierra caliente,* where neophyte farmers learn
practical techniques during relatively short training periods; early
morning radio programs on which farmers can hear news of prices,
products, and techniques; country fairs where prizes are awarded for
superior products; credit for minifundia; income or crop guarantees
for farmers willing to experiment with new crops, and so on.

CHAPTER 3

THE LABOR FORCE

A WIDE variety of unskilled and specialized trades is found in Huecorio. Some few villagers—the masons, for instance—are semiskilled, but the majority sell or utilize their energy rather than their aptitudes. This is in part a function of the absence of local demand for specialized abilities, but it flows to a large extent from the inadequacy of the education received. Earnings are unexpectedly low, but there is a great deal of variation within and among trades. Unskilled *peones* average less than ten pesos a day, but some traders are on their way to relative affluence.[1]

The pressure of population upon the land has forced Huecorianos to follow new pursuits. *Comerciantes* represent the most important nonagricultural activity, numerically speaking, and they have begun to break away from the elementary pattern of selling exclusively products of their own households. Some engage in fairly complicated three-way transactions, while others sell no products produced in their own homes.

The opening of the United States border to migrant workers was enormously significant to the economy and spirit of the community

---

[1] A special kind of labor—that embodied in the entrepreneur—is so important as to warrant a chapter to itself.

Home from Pátzcuaro at the end of the day

and the *braceros* tell their story here in their own words. The border was subsequently closed again, and anyone reading the autobiographies of the *braceros* will surely have doubts as to the desirability of the closing.[2]

From a theoretical point of view, the evidence concerning underemployment is significant. It calls into question the validity of the Nurksian theory and suggests that purely seasonal underemployment is not *necessarily* a serious problem in an agricultural community ruled by the rhythm of the climate.[3]

EDUCATION AND LITERACY

One of the important determinants of the quality of a labor force is the level of education. As indicated in Table IX, the educational level in Huecorio is quite high for a rural area of its type. Of those reporting in the age group 21 and over, only about 10% of the males

[2] See below, pp. 123–33.
[3] See below, pp. 135–55.

and 20% of the females admit having no formal education. Even if all those for whom no answer could be recorded had received no schooling, the percentages would climb to a maximum of 20% for the males and 36% for the females.

Males show a slight tendency to attend school for longer periods, but nevertheless the norm for both groups is only three or four years at the primary level. Few have attended secondary school, but a number of young men are enrolled in the evening secondary school in Pátzcuaro, which they attend after working all day in their parents' fields.

Four males have gone to university or its equivalent. One of these is the veterinarian, not a native of Huecorio, who works for the Montana State College agricultural project in Tzipecua. The other three come from a remarkable Huecorio family that has succeeded in sending all its sons to the University of Morelia, from which they were graduated as teachers.

The Spanish literacy figures correspond to those for educational level and tend to confirm them. Again, literacy, as indicated by an ability to read Spanish, is high—at least 84.6% for the males and 62.9% for females.[4]

This high level of literacy is by no means fully exploited. The more alert farmers study the government pamphlets on agriculture seriously, a few persons purchase the daily tabloid, *La Voz de Michoacán,* and some use is made of a small library of light reading matter in the *Centro Social.*[5]

The social questionnaire was administered to 37 families, and some information was gathered on reading materials in the homes. Out of the 37 houses visited, 17 contained textbooks and these generally belonged to the children attending school. In two cases the

---

[4] Of the 176 males and 189 females over 20 years of age, 149 males and 119 females stated that they could read Spanish, and 143 males and 118 females stated that they could write Spanish. The actual literacy figures may be higher, since no data were collected for 13 males and 31 females on the reading question, and 17 males and 31 females on the writing question.

[5] One respondent was intently viewing a history of Mexico when two members of the team arrived for an interview, but this may have been ostentation since he knew that we were to arrive at that hour.

texts had been retained by adults from their school days. Only three houses had books of a more general nature. In the house of one farmer we found three books on agriculture: *El Hombre y la Tierra, Clubes 4 J, and Catalogo para Abejas.* Juan Barrera, who owns the *taller,* was well supplied with books on history, physics, stamp collecting, and fiction. Six persons purchased newspapers and eight magazines, although in some cases the latter were acquired by schoolchildren. Fifteen of the houses were without any reading matter at all, but in seven of them one or more of the senior members of the household was illiterate.

Bearing in mind that in the majority of the cases reading materials are introduced into the homes by the medium of school-age children, we can infer that the relatively high level of education and literacy of the adult members of the community would seem to have little momentum to invoke a profound change in the life of the community. People do *not* read. This is probably due to a combination of things. The costs of books and periodicals, the fact that villagers are occupied with their labors during most of the day, the lack of adequate light and comfortable places to sit in the home at night, many times a lack of curiosity—which is in itself a comment on the educational process—and perhaps a lack of material suited to their interests and needs.

The quality of the education is also an important factor. The faculty turnover in the grade school is quite rapid, and teachers themselves complain that they are transferred frequently and cannot therefore establish the proper rapport with their charges.[6] The number of teachers varies from one to four, and is never sufficient to teach the sixth grade. Children in this grade attend school in nearby Colonia

[6] "The *maestra* had taught here in Huecorio some time before, but then had been changed to Santa Ana. Now she is back again. She doesn't like being changed because, while all children have the same general characteristics like restlessness and the desire for activity, each group is distinct and it is necessary to get to know them. She said she likes it here, but that of course there are problems. The children who come in the morning often do not return in the afternoon. Others come only in the afternoon. She teaches the third grade—a class of 45. With such a large class of active youngsters, it is difficult to give them the attention they need and they do not learn quickly." From Elizabeth Kaseta's *Daily Report,* July 18, 1962.

Ibarra. Because they must walk and do not have adequate rainware, the trip is bad for their health during the rainy season.

Good and bad teachers are well remembered. A new kindergarten teacher was assigned during our residence, and her sympathy and enthusiasm had a marked effect on attendance. Complaints about the principal teacher were so numerous that he has since been transferred. The villagers felt that this teacher did not participate in the life of the village or exercise any leadership. His transfer was precipitated by several unpleasant incidents. In one case he refused to hand over to the *Centro Social* some sewing machines which had been given to the village by CREFAL. In another, he viciously attacked the work and members of our team at a village meeting. Rather than sway the villagers to his xenophobic point of view, he ensured their support for the rest of our stay.

Some knowledge of English exists. In the age group 21 and over, 22 claim to speak the language, 14 to read it, and 13 to write it. Those who can read and write English generally picked it up in high school. The large number with some speaking knowledge is accounted for by the extraordinary proportion of adult males (one-third) who have been to the United States.

Tarascan is by no means a dead tongue in the village. Ninety-four persons, 11% of the total population, speak the language while many others understand it or speak a few words. Children still learn Tarascan, and a musician of Carián composes some melodious songs in the language.[7]

OCCUPATIONAL STRUCTURE

The inventory of primary occupations reveals a large variety, which becomes even greater if secondary and tertiary occupations are considered.[8] In almost all cases an individual will have other occupations,

[7] Forty youngsters under the age of 21 were reported to speak this Indian tongue.

[8] In the context of Huecorio we define a primary occupation as the one which the respondent considers to be most important.

since in few cases can a person employ himself fully throughout the year in one trade alone.

Certain of the definitions used in Table 4 should be explained. *Jardinero* is ambiguous. Although literally the word means "gardener," only two of the individuals calling themselves *jardineros* are gardeners in the sense customarily implied in English, and they are employed to attend the lawns and shrubs of CREFAL. The others work in their plots of land on the lake shore, and these plots, because of their fecundity and the nature of their products (vegetables), are sometimes called *jardines* or *huertas* by the villagers. To all intents and purposes, however, these individuals are farmers. Laborers call themselves *jornaleros,* but are dubbed *peones* by others. The woodsmen have as their function the collection and distribution of firewood. Those who work in the clothing factory are the several people who cut and sew garments for Vicki in Juan Barrera's *taller*.[9] There is no chair-making shop in Huecorio, but several individuals work at home under a putting-out system, weaving plaited palm cording on furniture that is constructed and finished in Pátzcuaro. The net weavers are self-employed women who pursue this occupation for their fishermen husbands. *Comerciantes* distribute products, usually of village origin, to the markets of Pátzcuaro, Morelia, Uruapan, Apatzingán, and in one case Mexico City. The cook, nurse, mechanic, the woman public official, and most of the servants are employed outside of the village itself.

Although we include the 173 women occupied at household tasks in the labor force to show the relative importance of this activity, this is not a customary procedure and we subtract the group from the total figures to get the "Actively Employed Labor Force." Nevertheless, many of these women constitute a potential labor pool since they are often supernumeraries in the household—daughters and sisters who would join the active labor force if given opportunities for employment.

As might be expected, the major portion (68.89%) of the actively employed labor force is in primary industry, and of these 166 individuals 148 are in agriculture and 18 are fishermen. Secondary industry

---

[9] *Taller* is literally "shop," in the sense of a workshop where goods are manufactured or serviced on a small scale. See below, and Chapter 5.

TABLE 4

Primary Occupations: Males and Females 16 and Over

Sector	Male	Female	Total	Percent of Total Actively Employed Labor Force
Primary Industry				
Farmer	97	1	98	
Gardener (*jardinero*)	6	1	7	
Farm laborer (*jornalero*)	38	1	39	
Milkmaid		1	1	
Woodsman	2		2	
Fisherman	18		18	
Cowboy	1		1	
Total Primary Industry	162	4	166	68.89
Second Industry				
Clothing factory worker	4	5	9	
Palmero	3		3	
Net weaver		3	3	
Total Secondary Industry	7	8	15	6.22
Tertiary Industry				
Mason	4		4	
Chauffeur	1		1	
Comerciante	8	29	37	
Cook		1	1	
Nurse (*Inyectadora*)		1	1	
Public official	1	1	2	
Household duties		173	173	
Teacher	3		3	
Mechanic	1		1	
Baker		1	1	
Servant	1	5	6	
Shopkeeper	1	1	2	
Veterinarian	1		1	
Total Tertiary Industry	21	212	233 − 173 = 60 [a]	24.89
Total Actively Employed Labor Force			414 − 173 = 241 [a]	100.00
Other				
Invalid		2	2	
Student	8	5	13	
No reply	10	5	15	
Retired	3	2	5	
	21	14	35	

[a] See text for explanation.

is numerically insignificant in spite of Huecorio's severe shortage of land. Occupations in tertiary industry generally, but not always, involve only a slight degree of formal training. The most important of these service workers are the *comerciantes,* who, if this is their primary occupation, follow their trade very intensively.

About half of the actively employed labor force has two occupations and much smaller proportions have a third or fourth source of livelihood. Those occupations—in addition to the ones on the primary list—are chicken farmer, carpenter, dance teacher, musician, landlord, and nightwatchman. (See Table X.) Chicken-raising and music-making are ideal complementary activities in the context of the village economy, since in terms of timing they do not conflict with other activities. Although consideration of the secondary occupations widens the range of skills available in the community, none involves a high degree of formal training.

CONDITIONS OF EMPLOYMENT IN VARIOUS OCCUPATIONS

Laborer

About 60 persons work as unskilled laborers, and four distinct employment situations exist for these laborers.

Most commonly they are Huecorianos employed on a day-to-day basis by other persons in the village to assist in the various agricultural tasks. The normal wage for an eight-hour day is six or seven pesos in cash plus an afternoon meal worth three pesos.

A special situation applies to the harvesting of wheat, which is contracted by the job rather than the day. In this case the six-hour day is divided into two parts—from six to nine in the morning and four to seven in the afternoon—in order to avoid the burning heat of the dry month of May. Under those circumstances, daily rates vary from 12 to 20 pesos a day but no meals are provided.

Rather infrequently laborers are hired on a more permanent basis. In the one instance observed, a man came from the *tierra caliente* seeking work and was hired by the Ricardo Pérez family at 40 pesos a week plus room and board. Significantly, Don Ricardo said that there was enough work to keep the *peón* fully employed all year but that he was free to leave whenever he wished. Although he was apparently satisfied with working in Hueeorio, his wife came from the *tierra caliente* and successfully badgered him into leaving.

A large but undetermined number of Huecorianos practice a fourth kind of unskilled labor. When agricultural work is slow in Huecorio they migrate to the *tierra caliente,* where they work 12-hour days harvesting cotton, fruits, and vegetables. There they gross from 15 to 18 pesos a day, but have to spend as much as six pesos a day on food.

As may be expected, *peones* are either landless or have very little land. We did not, however, encounter any persons who were entirely dependent on their earnings as unskilled laborers.

Tailors and Seamstresses

Nine persons, including the *patrones* themselves, work in the *taller* of Don Juan and Guadalupe Barrera.[10] Those persons own their own heavy-duty sewing machines and shears, and they cut and sew fabrics supplied by an American who, under the trade name "Vicki," sells attractive soft goods to passing tourists and retail outlets in the United States. Payment for the piecework is made directly to the workers by Vicki, and they are not, therefore, employees of Don Juan.

The operation of the *taller* is informal. The room itself is of concrete construction, about 15 by 25 feet. Two metal windows face on a small patio, and two doors enter from the patio and kitchen respectively. Two large beds bear witness to the room's nighttime function, and frequently the beds and sewing machines are put aside and the Barreras are hosts at someone's saint's day. Festivities aside, the machines and cutting tables are busy from Monday morning to Saturday evening.

Although the *taller* is open at predictably regular hours, from 9:00 a.m. to 7:00 p.m. with a lunch break from 2:00 to 3:00, there

[10] See below, Chapter 5.

is no time clock to monitor the several "employees." Indeed, each follows a different pattern and none is typical. Juana, the 15-year-old daughter of Francisco Cruz, came to the *taller* at her father's bidding in November of 1961. She likes it, she says, for there is really nothing else to do. Juana rises each day at 7:30, and after breakfast steps into the street for the short walk to the *taller,* which is next door to her father's house. There she sews from 9:00 to 2:00 and then goes home for lunch. She returns to the *taller* at 3:00 and continues sewing until 7:00. Since the Barreras are one of the prominent families of the village, her work is frequently interrupted by professors from CREFAL, who bring students and other persons from all over the world. She returns home for dinner at 7:30, helps her mother about the house, reads a little, and goes to bed at 9:00. On Sundays while her mother sells in the Pátzcuaro market, Juana cleans house and cooks—but if there are basketball games in the schoolyard she will go to cheer for Huecorio. Juana turns most of her earnings over to her mother, but manages to save two or three pesos a week. Señora Barrera taught her to sew and now she can earn as much as 50 pesos a week. The brightly-colored finished pieces are then turned over to Vicki, who has them embroidered in attractive adaptations of Tarascan folk figures.

When Ricardo Arizpe was a *bracero* in 1960 he brought back a sewing machine. Doña Guadalupe taught him the trade, and he planned to work during the slack agricultural season. His experiences as a *bracero* impressed him with the hardness of the life of a farmer in Huecorio, and now he prefers to hire other people to work his land while he works in the *taller* all year through. The flexibility of the *taller* operation permits him to manage his farm as well. He rises at 6:00 to milk the cows, eats breakfast at 8:00, and sews from 9:00 to 2:00 and from 3:00 to 5:00. He returns home to feed the animals, eats dinner at 8:00, and goes to bed at 9:00. He claims he could make 50 pesos a day if he tended his gardens himself, but prefers the lighter work of the *taller* even though his daily earnings are only 12 pesos. Nevertheless, this is twice as much as a laborer can earn and it is supplemented by the profits from his farm and cows.

Juana's brother, Elpidio, a gentle, studious boy of 22, has been working in the *taller* for two years. Elpidio's father told him many times of the difficult and hard life of a farmer. "Would he like to study or work in the fields?" The question did not need to be answered. Although Elpidio has no clear idea of what he might follow, his life centers on attending the Pátzcuaro high school, where he has classes in Spanish, mathematics, history, geography, English, art, civics, music, and biology. He rises each day at seven, feeds the chickens, takes the animals to pasture, and studies before breakfast. He works in the *taller* from 9:30 to 2:00 and from 3:00 to 4:00. He then leaves for school and returns home to eat at 9:30. Then he must study until 11:00. As with the other persons in the *taller,* he knows that he could make more money if he worked harder or longer hours. But it is hard to do any more during the few hours he is in the *taller* because there are constant interruptions, and he cannot work longer hours for he is a conscientious boy and he worries about the pressure of his studies.

About a third of the households in Huecorio own sewing machines, used mostly for making and repairing garments for the household. Some, however, make garments to order. For instance, in the family of Alberto Dongo the husband, wife, and eldest daughter use their single, ancient machine for this purpose. Señora Dongo learned to sew in Pátzcuaro in 1942 and then taught her husband and her eldest daughter—11 years old in 1962—to use the machine. The machine is in use about six hours a day by whatever member is not engaged in gardening or selling in the Pátzcuaro market. Together the family can earn about 50 pesos a week, but they intend to purchase two more machines so that they can earn more. (See Table XI.)

Teamster

Francisco Cruz obtained credit from the *Asociación Avícola* for the purchase of a horse and a rubber-tired cart. The cart cost 1,000 pesos, and the rather good horse another 600. He makes a scheduled trip to and from Pátzcuaro each week to carry eggs, feed, and assorted cargoes for other Huecorianos. His rates vary from 50 *centavos* to one peso for a sack or a box, depending on its size. The eggs alone bring him 25 pesos a week, and assorted cargos, which may be carried

The teamster returning from Pátzcuaro

on any day of the week, bring in another 30 pesos. From this activity, then, he would earn a gross income of 2,860 pesos, from which would be deducted interest of 128 pesos, depreciation on the cart and horse at 10% or 160 pesos, leaving a net annual income of 2,572 pesos.[11] "It is good to have this cart, for it has been a great help to my economy."

[11] This net income of 2,572 pesos may be too high, depending on whether or not Francisco feeds the horse or lets it graze, and on the rate of depreciation applied to the horse. A rate of 10% is standard for brood and work horses in the United States. However, the horse in question here was about five or six years of age, in which case a higher rate of depreciation would have to be applied.

Carpenter

Carpentry is considered to be an attractive occupation, but because of the lack of demand for this skill in Huecorio no person regards it as a primary occupation, and only four regard it as a second skill to be offered when the occasion arises. (See Table X.) Francisco Cruz is relatively well endowed with tools of the trade and has a saw, a brace, several planes, a hammer, a square, a metric tape, a drill, and a chisel. Several of these tools were purchased in the United States, where he worked as a *bracero* when he was 27 years old. In 1940 he was a nightwatchman at the high school, and learned carpentry by watching the teachers at work during the day. Although he could earn 20 to 25 pesos a day as a carpenter in Pátzcuaro, he claims he cannot practice the trade there because he must stay in Huecorio to watch the *granja*. On odd jobs he grosses about 150 pesos a year, which, allowing for a 10% depreciation rate on his tools, would net him about 110 pesos.

Adolfo Pérez works occasionally as an apprentice in Colonia Ibarra. He is being taught the trade by the *patrón* of *Industrias del Lago,* Jesús Guido, who makes no charge for this. Adolfo has only a plane, a square, a saw, and a hammer, but Don Jesús lends him others as they are needed. Like Francisco he would be happy as a full-time carpenter, were it not for the insufficient demand for this skill. A number of would-be carpenters have thought of opening a *taller* in Huecorio, but nobody has the initiative and resources for such an undertaking.

Palmero

Three Huecorianos are *palmeros,* who weave reed twines on pieces of furniture. The source of employment is Jesús Guido, who teaches the necessary skills to those who wish to work for him. One *palmero* worked in Señor Guido's *taller,* while the others took the unfinished pieces to their homes where they worked on them as agricultural

Palmero *in his home. Suckling pigs in background*

obligations permitted. No tools are needed other than blocks of wood to tighten and align the warp and woof, and the required skills are not great. Working hard, a *palmero* can earn 15 pesos in an eight-hour day, but a normal return is 12 pesos.

Musician

Many persons in the village have musical talent, and two groups of men have formed bands. In Carián Geronimo Roca manages a band of about six men, who compose and play melodies with Tarascan lyrics. They are very dedicated and practice together two or three nights a week and hope to achieve semiprofessional capabilities. In the meantime they confine themselves to playing without remuneration at the various *fiestas*. Another group led by Salvador Gorozpe has more experience, and is frequently called upon to rise before dawn to play the *mañanitas* as a lively and abrupt awakening to someone's saint's day. Parties and dances keep them quite active outside of their regular working hours, and from their various sponsors each of the several may earn as much as two or three hundred pesos a year.

Librarian

Olga Pérez has the responsibility for maintaining the village *Centro Social*. She receives 100 pesos a month to keep the center open two hours a day and maintain the library of magazines and books which are lent to persons who have paid their *Centro* dues.

Inyectadora

Olga is also the only person in the village qualified to give injections, a technique that she learned from a doctor at CREFAL in 1954. For this she has a syringe, several needles, and a case. She receives 50 centavos for an injection, which—including the time necessary for sterilization of the needle—requires about 20 minutes.[12] About two are administered every week. When asked about the possibility of earning more from this occupation, she slyly suggested, "Make more people sick!" [13]

Net Weaver

Three persons regard net weaving as their primary occupation, and five consider it a secondary trade. These persons live in Carián, where fishing is generally the principal livelihood of the men of the family. Two types of net are made—the small *mariposa,* and a larger dragnet. In all cases the work is undertaken as time permits (*en ratos*), and the weaving of a large net might drag on for about six months. Income from this essentially part-time trade would be at least 200 pesos per person.

Chauffeur

One of the few persons in Huecorio who can drive, Joaquín Galíndez, learned at Tzipecua where he is employed. This is virtually a full-time job, six days a week from 7:00 a.m. to 3:00 p.m., and from time to time at other hours. Not only does he drive a car but also operates the Quinta's Ferguson tractor and helps at odd jobs about the property.

Mason

Four Huecorianos regard masonry as their primary occupation, while five consider it a secondary occupation. As we use it here,

[12] The patient supplies the antibiotics. The most commonly treated complaint is described as *gripe,* which is either grippe or influenza.

[13] On another occasion, when Olga was about to administer an injection to a young man, I wished him "¡Buena suerte!" (Good luck!) to which she quickly quipped, "¡Buena muerte!" (Good death!).

masonry is a collective, encompassing a number of skills, in particular construction with stone, brick, and adobe, tile setting, and plastering. A great deal of stone is found within the town, most of it black or gray and volcanic in origin. Although face stones are rare, this volcanic stone is easily cut and is used in footings, foundations, and walls.

Quantitatively speaking, the masons have more tools per worker than any of the other Huecorio artisans, and the value of their tools is only exceeded by that of the sewing machines of the tailors. Salvador Gorozpe, for instance, has a saw, mattock, two brushes, two hammers, two pinch bars, two squares, a large plane, six punches, seven cold chisels, two levels, two knives, and two stone hammers, one of 18 pounds and the other of eight pounds. He values these tools at 323 pesos. Leonardo Muñoz has a similar investment, which he values at 279 pesos. Both learned their trade as apprentices in Morelia —Salvador in 1946 and Leonardo in 1950.

The customary working hours for the construction trades are from 7:00 a.m. until 3:00 p.m., with a few minutes' break for lunch at about 10 o'clock. Salvador works at Tzipecua ten months a year and grosses about 6,740 pesos, from which a modest 10% depreciation on his tools would net him 6,708 pesos. Some of this time is devoted to carpentry, however. Salvador likes his work and takes a justifiable pride in it. Leonardo works as a mason during the slack agricultural season of February through April and grosses about 2,500 pesos. A 10% depreciation on his tools nets him 2,472 pesos. As we shall see below,[14] the skills required of masons lead to hourly earnings significantly higher than those of other trades.

Barber

Leonardo Muñoz, Huecorio's only barber, learned his trade in 1940 from another Huecoriano who is now in Mexico City. The tools of his trade are five hand clippers, two combs, an electric clipper, scissors, a razor, a brush, a honing stone, and a leather strop, most of which he purchased in the United States. He has ten or twelve

[14] P. 133.

customers a week and charges one peso each. Thus his gross is about 600 pesos. His equipment is about 670 pesos total, so that allowing for a 10% depreciation his net income from this occupation would be 537 pesos a year. He claims he could make more from this trade by getting a government contract to cut the hair of school children or by opening a barber shop, but he would have to pay taxes and would need to hire assistants, and so he is content to follow this trade only in his spare time.

Comerciante

The *comerciantes* are itinerant traders who operate singly and who wholesale or retail small amounts of goods. In other respects—types of goods sold, market location, astuteness and energy, income, attitudes to their occupation—*comerciantes* will vary considerably.

In the census, eight men and 29 women regarded trading as their primary occupation and 31 persons considered it a secondary occupation. At this secondary level we would consider the true number to be twice as high, however. In nearly all farm households at least one female member will travel to nearby Pátzcuaro to market household produce several times during the season. Apparently this was considered to be so much in their normal line of duty as housewives that they did not distinguish their mercantile activity from the other chores such as cooking, washing, and looking after children. An American housewife would not consider the visit to the supermarket as a form of employment distinct from other household management. By the same token, for a housewife in Huecorio, selling household products is often not distinct from buying for the household, since the two activities are concurrent. The housewife will take some produce to the Pátzcuaro market to sell, and the cash received will be spent, usually the same day, to buy something for the house.

Among the important farm products sold by *comerciantes* are corn, milk, and milk derivatives. One or two also sell fish, prepared food such as *tortillas,* and pottery. Nevertheless, the bulk of the products sold consists of fruit and vegetables grown in Huecorio, although products will be sold that have been acquired in markets elsewhere, particularly in the *tierra caliente*. Sixteen *comerciantes* were interviewed; four of them sold products exclusively of their own household and two sold only products purchased from others. The remaining ten sold both home-produced and purchased products.

Supply considerations seem to be most important, in the sense that the *comerciantes* sell what their husbands have harvested, or, in their own words, "what is available." The *comerciantes* did not volunteer that they tried to influence their husbands' decisions, although this might have become apparent on further questioning. Only three verbalized demand considerations as influencing what they carried to market. Two of them said they sell those things that are "most purchased," and one specialized in selling lemons from the *tierra caliente* because they are "most profitable."

It would appear that a type of general equilibrium has been resolved in the markets in which the *comerciantes* sell, in that the *comerciantes* can dispose of agricultural products which have become established in the region, and customers have come to expect a predictable range at any given season. These are the limits within which the *comerciante* operates. Two things she cannot generally do. She cannot establish an output mix based on the best cost-price ratios, because in a situation where there are many small, independent producers and where there is a significant time lag between the decision to plant and the time of sale, prices on any given day are no guide to their structure a growing season hence. Thus one does not speculate, but trades in established and safe commodities.

Neither can the trader innovate. There is no scope for new commodities, partly because of the limitations on the input-mix in agricultural output and partly because, in the open-air markets in which the *comerciante* operates, there would be few customers for an innovated product. The one exception to this characterization does not fundamentally change it. One girl specializes in lemons, which are purchased in Apatzingán by her mother. On the supply side she is not constrained by the family's farm product mix because the lemons are purchased from packers and she does not buy unless price differentials warrant. On the demand side she has built up a reputation as a specialist, and thus has no difficulty in finding customers.

Two-thirds of the *comerciantes* trade throughout the year. For

Comerciantes *in Pátzcuaro on a quiet day*

some this is possible because their product—milk or fish in particular —is produced every day. Others whose farm products are seasonal will manage to trade throughout the year by buying at wholesale from other *comerciantes* in the Pátzcuaro market, or they will sell Pátzcuaro products in the *tierra caliente* or vice versa. The remaining third sell only as products from their own household become available. One exception is a farmer who becomes a *comerciante* in the *tierra caliente* when his lands are idle during the dry season.

Huecorianos sell in widely scattered markets. In the village itself a solitary woman sits outside the churchyard with a small collection of vegetables. During *fiestas* the square outside the *Centro Social* is active with women and girls selling cake, fruit, and fruit-flavored cold drinks. The most frequented market is of course in Pátzcuaro, in the main square opposite the municipal offices. Traditional market days used to be Friday and Sunday, but Sunday is now very quiet and has been eclipsed by Thursday. A few permanent stands are placed in the porticos of the surrounding buildings. In the square itself, under the shade of giant fresnos, are several merchants who sell soft goods such as *rebozos, gabanes,* and blankets to unwary tourists at inflated prices. On market days several thousand *comerciantes* will spread their ground sheets on every available piece of pavement and will usually spill out into the narrow street. The *comerciante* will sit with her wares displayed in the midst of a throng, and buyers must step gingerly over piles of merchandise to get from one place to another. People, carts, dogs, *burros,* automobiles, and trucks fight for the right of passage through narrow byways. Everything is animated but —contrary to the casual impression—quite orderly.

Huecorianos also trade at a secondary market in Colonia Ibarra, near the Pátzcuaro railway station. Here the stands are semipermanent, and several villagers attend these posts every day.

Next in descending importance are the markets of Uruapan, which is reached by a 40-mile train journey, and Apatzingán, 55 miles beyond in the *tierra caliente.* Quiroga, Morelia, and Mexico City are trading points for several Huecorianos, but only a handful of villagers have permanent or semipermanent trading posts in any of those places. Most of the time they squat wherever room is available, although a minority try, by getting to the market early or with the cooperation of the *plazero,* to get a location at a corner where there is more traffic.

As Chart 1 indicates, trading patterns are diverse.

The Pátzcuaro market absorbs the bulk of Huecorio's produce, and the *comerciante* activities associated with it are relatively straightforward. Señora Gómez is from one of the poorer families, and the few vegetables from the unkempt plot surrounding her house are sufficient for only one trip a week during the rainy season. While most *comerciantes* have more to sell and take the bus, she leaves the house on foot about seven o'clock and trudges for almost an hour. By the time she reaches the market with her coriander or squash, the best places are taken. She settles down on a ground cloth made from old sacks, and arranges what she has into convenient piles. Being shy, she sits quietly waiting for customers and does not feel the high

CHART 1

Trading Patterns of *Comerciantes*

	Source of Produce or Merchandise	*Point of Sale*
One-way Trade	Huecorio ⟶	Pátzcuaro Market
	Huecorio ⟶	Market at Railway Station in Colonia Ibarra
	Huecorio ⟶	House-to-house in Pátzcuaro and Colonia Ibarra
	Huecorio ⟶	{ Apatzingán and/or Uruapan }
	Huecorio and Pátzcuaro ⟶	{ Apatzingán and/or Uruapan }
	Pátzcuaro ⟶	Mexico
	Pátzcuaro ⟶	Pátzcuaro and Quiroga
	Pátzcuaro and Morelia ⟶	Station Market
	Pátzcuaro ⟶	Pátzcuaro
	Pátzcuaro ⟶	Morelia
Two-way Trading Trips	Huecorio and/or Pátzcuaro ⟶	Apatzingán
	Apatzingán ⟶	Pátzcuaro
	Huecorio ⟶	Pátzcuaro
	Pátzcuaro ⟶	Mexico

spirits that animate many of the more aggressive women. Her modest display does not catch the eye of the customer, but the *plazero* comes anyway to collect the 40-centavos tax. Some *comerciantes* can persuade the *plazero* to let them off more lightly, but not Señora Gómez. She is even timid with the customers, and they can get a handful of coriander from her for only 10 centavos when others might manage to get 30 centavos on the very same day. She does not like to sell, and does it out of necessity to buy a little salt or meat for the house. She is glad when her *manta de costal* is clear in the early afternoon and she has two or three pesos, which must last her through the week while her husband is away in *el norte*. She conserves her centavos carefully and frowns on some of the *indias* from Carián who drink all they earn and bring nothing back for their houses except maybe some firewood.

Most women do better at market, however. Señora Casagrande is more typical. Each Friday she has something to sell. Her son brings vegetables in from the *orilla* the afternoon of the previous day, and in the dry season there is always some squash or garlic that can be sold. She gets up at 6:00, and by the time the *flecha* is ready to leave at 7:00 all her produce is packed into sacks or canisters. The market will be busy by the time she gets there because people from distant villages will have arrived the previous night and slept under the portico. From them she may buy some carrots or lettuce, and she always can get 20% and sometimes 50% more than she paid. She may sell to them too if she feels she is overstocked with some particular item. To her the market *"es bonito."* "There is no better way to earn money." And besides, all her friends are there and they have no difficulty in finding something to talk about.

Life in the household of Don Ricardo Pérez centers on trading, and, at least for the elders, the members are involved in it every day of the week. Don Ricardo is mainly concerned with growing vegetables in the *orilla,* and his wife will often help him there when she is not away trading. On Monday and Tuesday mornings, produce is brought in by the son Baltazar and stored in a rather substantial second house that the Pérez family owns. Other farmers will wholesale their goods to the Pérez family, and these are also brought to the house. The whole family is usually occupied packing the goods on Tuesday morning, although the eldest daughter Luisa will also go to Pátzcuaro to make more purchases for resale at higher prices in Apatzingán.

Most of the vegetables are washed either in the *orilla,* where a convenient ditch leads in from the lake, or in a large tub in the patio of the house. All hands will be busy washing and tying handfuls of radishes, flowers, mint, parsley, lettuce, and so on, and visiting outsiders may be called in to help so that Luisa and her mother can catch the bus connecting with the noon train to Uruapan.

Baltazar will help carry the bundles from the house to the plaza where the bus is met, but from there on the women must carry enormous sacks and packages on their backs—staggering weights several times heavier than anything the less robust women north of the border would touch. Luisa and her mother will spend 50 centavos for the bus to Colonia Ibarra, 3 pesos 80 centavos for the train to Uruapan, and 5 pesos at least for their bundles which must go in the express car. In Uruapan they pick up a bus which goes to Apatzingán. This will cost them 5 pesos apiece and another 7 pesos or so for the bundles. If connections are bad they may not arrive until 10:00 p.m. Then the produce is sorted out for display, and perhaps a few minutes' sleep can be snatched before the market becomes active at 6:00 a.m. By 9:30 most of the retail trade is over, and they work to wholesale the remainder of their goods. Some tropical fruits, particularly lemons, will be purchased to sell in Pátzcuaro. If the bus which leaves Uruapan at 9:00 p.m. is not late, they can catch the night train to Pátzcuaro and can sleep at home, but frequently they must sleep over in Uruapan in a room Luisa has rented.

The grind continues, for the menfolk have collected another quantity of vegetables and Luisa goes to Pátzcuaro to make more acquisitions. The process is repeated. The women catch the noon train to Uruapan on Thursday and are back in Huecorio on Friday night. Weekends occupy them again in the *orilla,* and on Sundays they are up early to bake bread for the entire community. Meanwhile Olga, a very attractive and vivacious girl, has taken the lemons from Apatzingán to the Friday market in Pátzcuaro. Things are very *alegre* at the Friday market by the time Olga arrives with a case of 1,000 lemons. These she sells wholesale to other *comerciantes,* keeping 100 or so for herself. Then she will have something to eat before finding a place to retail whatever lemons are left.

No other trading appears to be as complex as that of the Pérez family. One other person reported a more elementary form of two-way trade, in which the household products from Huecorio were sold in Pátzcuaro to purchase fish and pottery for resale in Mexico City.

In most cases, even when a trader visits several towns or distant places, full advantage of possibilities are not exploited. Nevertheless, one Huecorio family has built up its trading to a very high level. Señor Diego Quintero has a post in La Industrial Corona in Mexico City, which is licensed to sell milk products. To retain this license he must attend the post five days a week, and thus he is in Huecorio only during the daytime on Tuesdays and Fridays. Even then he is extremely busy from the time he steps off the train in the morning until he boards it again in the evening, for he must be home to receive the goods people bring him direct to avoid the taxes and inspection in the Pátzcuaro market. He acquired the post in October 1961, and was still paying it off when he was interviewed in August 1962. The investment is a good one, for his net weekly sales amount to 400 pesos. Amortization of the post, transportation, taxes, and food reduce this to about 300 pesos a week, which yields a substantial annual income of about 16,000 pesos. His wife has no stall but sells at a post close to him. Her fish products net a further 2,600 pesos a year after expenses. In addition, one son maintains the family farm in Huecorio. From the family income it was possible to save about 2,000 pesos in the previous year, and this was then lent to another Huecoriano. Two other sons who have families of their own each net about 50 pesos a week. While this family was exceptional, it can be seen from Table XII that other *comerciantes* often make a significant contribution to the incomes of their families.

The capital used by a *comerciante* is modest. One reported having three *canastas* worth 4.5 pesos each, three sacks worth six pesos each, and three ground cloths worth 1.5 pesos each. Most have even less equipment than this, although several have sets of scales, each valued at about 15 pesos. These equipment expenses are not large enough to justify calculating depreciation rates.

Table XII shows the contributions of a number of *comerciantes* to their family incomes. It must, however, be interpreted with care. Where the *comerciante* sells no products of her own household, the income figure of the last line is a reasonable approximation of her contribution as a *comerciante*. At the other extreme, where a *comerciante* sells only products of her own household, her contribution is more difficult to assess, since other members of the household have contributed to the production of the product she sells. To each must be imputed a share of the income from the output. Thus, not only must one follow the product through each of its stages of production and account for *all* the factors of production that have entered, but one must also establish product values at each stage to ascertain values added. If there were in the market such a thing as a standard percentage markup, 33% for instance, one could attribute to the *comerciante*'s activities that proportion of the retail price. However, the ratio of "wholesale" to retail prices varies from trader to trader, from season to season, and from market to market.

All the above-mentioned influences affect the price structure. In August of 1962 the price of lettuce, for instance, varied from 10 to 30 centavos a head in Pátzcuaro and 50 to 60 centavos in Uruapan. Prices will be high early in the morning in all markets, and will drop as retail customers thin out and the best heads have been purchased. Modal values are those most commonly reported, and these were used to establish output values for agricultural production. Markups varied from zero for lemons in February and negative values for tomatoes in August, to 150% for lemons in August. The most common markups appear to be about 30%.

For the women *comerciantes,* this activity is largely determined by a division of labor in which the men work in the fields while women tend to household chores and trade farm products as they become available. Men *comerciantes* who are not engaged full time take to trading as a supplemental activity during the dry season. Full-time trading is unusual for men. While one man was away working in St. Louis, Missouri, his wife started trading in Mexico City on her own initiative. She was so successful that he followed her lead and has built up a very profitable business there. Almost all the women *comerciantes* enjoy the activity. When this point was examined, the replies were universally related to money. "Yes, I like to earn money." "Yes. It is very *bonito*. The best way to earn money." "Yes, I like to earn a lot of money," "Yes, I get money fast." "*Bastante. Me deja centavos.*" Although most women go to the market alone, when they are there they are among friends—and the bustle of activity, the different people who pass, the challenge of bargaining, all add to a sense of excitement. Yet the replies clearly indicate that to the women from Huecorio trading is attractive for economic rather than social reasons. A minority dislike the activity and do it out of necessity. One girl was quite emphatic about it and called it a form of slavery.

Baker

The women of the family of Ricardo Pérez are the village bakers. A large adobe oven dominates the kitchen shed in the patio, and late on Saturday evenings the mother and two or three adult daughters prepare dough for 300 loaves of various shapes, sizes, and types. The three most popular kinds are *de blanco*,[15] *de azúcar,* and *piloncillo*.[16] The women are up at 5:00 the next morning, and as the oven is being prepared they mold the loaves, which are baked to be ready for customers, who start arriving at about nine o'clock. The family keeps about 100 loaves for its own use, and any balance is sold to customers in Colonia Ibarra.

Whether or not the family makes a profit from this operation is debatable. Table XIII shows a net return of 2.50 pesos on weekly gross sales of 60 pesos. But this includes the value of the bread consumed at home, and the cost data may be understated due to the difficulty of establishing a true hourly wage rate. But the family does not consider bread-making in terms of money cost accounting. The women do not rise much earlier than they would on any other day, and since they are busy with household chores most of the day their labor input in bread-making is not thought of as having an opportunity cost. Although the family is well aware of the nature of profits, bread-making is viewed in different terms. If they had to buy their bread in the market it would cost them 20 pesos, but by baking their own and selling part of it, their out-of-pocket cost is only 7.50 pesos.

[15] Known alternatively as *con sal.*

[16] The *de blanco* is a white bread, the *de azúcar* is coated with white sugar, and the *piloncillo* with brown sugar. All are unleavened and are generally shaped like squat, round rolls. The loaves are made in three sizes, the largest of which—*el grande*—sells for one peso and weighs ½ kilo. The *regular* sells for 50 centavos and weighs proportionately less. The same is true for the *pequeño,* which costs 20 centavos.

Bracero

One-third of the adult males in Huecorio have been to the United States as *braceros*. All members of the team were busy with structured interviews during the entire three months, and no formal interviews had been prepared to administer to *braceros*. Indeed, the significance of this activity did not strike us until the research was well under way. Since time did not permit interviewing the *braceros*, we resorted to the expedient of passing out a list of questions and asked that replies be written out for us.

Each informant was handed a paper on which important questions were listed. It read:

Can you write me a report about your experiences as a *bracero* in the United States? I would like to know all that you can remember about your visit to the North. For example, the following facts would interest me very much.

Your name.
Your age.
When did you go to *el norte?*
How many times did you go?
In what way did you go to the border?
Did you travel alone or with friends?
Did you have any difficulties with the trip? For example, did you have to pay bribes to get your papers? If so, to whom?
Why did you go to work as a *bracero?*
Where did you work?
What kind of work did you do?
What wages did you receive?
What favorable impressions did you have of the United States?
What things did you not like about *el norte?*
Did you learn anything useful for your life here?
Do you now think anything different about your life here?
Do you think that your visit to *el norte* was worth the effort?
Would you like to live in *el norte?* Why?

Twelve candidates were selected and six of them replied. Most wrote out quite lengthy reports in longhand, but one discovered the typewriter we had left with a family in the village and he banged out a very creditable job. The replies are reported here verbatim in the hope that, even though they are subjected to translation, some of their spirit can be conveyed. To protect the informants we shall withhold their names.

The first reply was in the form of a letter to a member of the team after we had left:

(1) My age is 24 years. I went to *el norte* in April of 1961. I went not more than one time. When I left Huecorio, I traveled alone until I reached Empalme, Sonora, where there are the contracting places, and I waited ten days to get a contract. After getting the contract I went to the border at Mexicali. The government paid my fare on the train. I went together with a friend who already had been before and he knew how to go around and arrange the papers. I had no difficulties in my trip because my friend knew how to solve them.

Yes, I had to pay money to arrange the contract since otherwise I would lose more time. There are people who devote themselves, upon payment of money, to find the permits to get a contract.

I was a *bracero* because, in truth, one sees that the majority of the results are good and one can earn more and save a little.

I worked in the state of California. I worked harvesting oranges and lemons—nothing more. The wage was according to the work I did; for example there were fortnights with a higher salary but the average I believe was 90 to 100 dollars a fortnight. My impressions of the United States are good. For example the work that I did was very pleasant since even though I had not done it [before] I learned it quickly. Also the towns I visited seemed to me very *bonitos*. Truly I encountered nothing unpleasant in the time I was there.

In the United States one earns a great deal, but here many things are impossible because of a lack of economic resources. I have always thought that life could be different here, but what one thinks about a little cannot be resolved in the same way. It takes time and there are times when one cannot even hope or change the course of one's decisions. My trip to *el norte* was very important since in a large degree I improved my economic situation. But I could not become accustomed to living only in the United States. I would like to return and work for a while but would always return to my country.

(11) I am 28 years of age, and went once in 1955 for three months and for 17 months in 1961 and 1962.

I traveled from Huecorio by bus to Waimas [Guaymas], Sonora, and then took the train to Mexicali. From there I took another bus to California where I had a contract.

I went with friends from Zacatecas. These fellows knew the road.

I had no difficulties because I paid 1,100 pesos as a *mordida* [bribe] to a lawyer in Guaymas to arrange the papers. According to him this wasn't much money to pay for getting in quickly.

I became a *bracero* to get a little more money so I could live better. I worked in Oxinar [possibly Oxnard] for three months harvesting lemons for $15 a day. Then I worked in Fimor [Fillmore] for eight months and in Ojai for three months harvesting oranges. I got $20 to $25 a day *limpio* [net] and worked all week except Sunday and half of Saturday.

Most of all I liked the steady work, and earning a lot of money. I also liked the buildings and the traffic—so many cars—in the state. There were lots of cute Mexican girls that worked in things such as packing fruit.

In the United States there are many crooks. If one is stupid they'll easily steal your money. And there are many vicious women who'll get your money with their pretty faces.

Here you can be happy with only five pesos. There, at times, $40.00 or $100.00 is not enough.

What a man needs is work, booze, women, and to know many things.

I wouldn't marry an American woman and live in the United States because there the woman rules.

Here, the man is the boss.

In the United States, if the husband does not earn enough money, the wife goes looking for more money with other men.

I had to come back to Tijuana in Mexico to have a good time.[17]

[17] A reference to the lack of hospitality in the form of "bawdy houses" in *el norte*.

In the United States I learned how to save money and prune fruit trees. For the people here life is very difficult, but not up there. The trip was worth the trouble because I brought back 35,000 pesos ($2,800). That's the only reason why one goes to the United States—money.

I would not like to live in *el norte*. There's plenty of work but one is not free because one is a slave of work, and I'm nobody's slave. There are rents and taxes on everything. Not only are the women swindlers but there is also the government with its taxes. I am a Mexican and I will not change my country for anything.

(1 1 1) I am 29 years old and I went to *el norte* twice. Once in 1955 I had a contract and went by myself. I did pay a *mordida* to get my papers, but to whom I cannot say because they were people unknown to me.[18] I went because of an interest in the dollars and for necessity. I worked in Arkansas[19] where I picked cotton and earned $70 every two weeks, free of board.

I did not have any good impressions of the United States for the simple reason here in Mexico I was born and have grown up and here I taught myself to work. My single impression is only working with all. A man can live well in his country. For this reason it was not worth while to work in the United States. I will only work for Mexico. What I did not like about *el norte* is the bad treatment they give Mexicans after they go to work.[20] I didn't learn anything good because I picked cotton and I have done that before here.

[18] It may be of interest to quote part of this passage directly as an example of the phonetic spelling frequently found. "*¿A quien? eso no lo puedo disir por motibo que son jentes desconosidas.*"

[19] This was spelled "*arquenso*" and illustrates delightfully the lack of a logical relationship between English as spelled and as heard.

[20] In 1964 I questioned this man further about the treatment he received. His resentment stemmed from what he thought to be the excessive discipline to which he was subjected on a farm in California owned by a Japanese. The Mexicans were not allowed to talk, whistle, or smoke while they were in the field, and the wages were only 75 cents an hour. Several *braceros,* including this man, pointed out that the 45-day contracts they received were not long enough for them to cover the costs of their passage. When the men entered the United States illegally some ranchers would take advantage of their status by promising work (at low wages) and then calling in the immigration authorities before the wages came due.

[Do you now think anything different about your life here?] Well no, for the simple reason that always my impression has been of working as a farmer, which doesn't seem useful for another career.

[Do you think your visit to *el norte* was worth the effort?] For me no, because I will not go [there] for any business. I would not like to live [there] because I would be a slave all the time.

(I V) I am 39 years old and have been to *el norte* five times. The first time was in the year 1943 in the month of January. The first time I went to the border I was contracted in the City of Mexico. At this time they begged the people to go and work in the United States. Very few people moved themselves to go as *braceros*. The first time I went alone. I invited several friends but no one accompanied me from this village of Huecorio.

The only difficulty that presented itself was a lack of money. I used it all up two days before leaving for the United States. These two days seemed to me like two years, because I sacrificed eating and to this day these days are present as if they just happened. I had the luck never to know the need to pay a *mordida* to anybody.

I went to work as *bracero* in the United States of the North by necessity of our poverty, for there was no father in our house. He died in 1935. Without the presence of our *papacito* and seeing how my mother was so afflicted by the need to sustain and clothe us, I had to leave school and help her.

The first time I went to *el norte* I took a job with the Southern Pacific Company in the state of New Mexico in a place called Tres Ríos. The first work that I undertook was on the track, that is to say on the right-of-way of the railroad. The second time I tried the cultivation of sugar in the state of Colorado. Later I changed to peas in the state of Illinois [spelled *Rilinayes*], and from there they sent me to Wisconsin to pick string beans, and later in the same state in the harvesting of cherries, or *capulin* as we call it here. The following time I stayed over in California and went to work in the San Joaquin Valley and worked harvesting asparagus. Well then, for me this was a fantastic time—like the best days of my life.

Well my wages in the United States were all different but all were very good. Every two weeks my check came to about $70, but on some of the best fortnights came to $180. And all this to aid my little sisters, who were still little girls, and for my mother. And now I feel happy because all my family lived well.

Even though I saw mainly agriculture, my impressions of *el norte* were much more [vivid] of the industry so advanced. I would give great thinks if I could see all this in our own Mexico. In the United States of the North there was nothing disagreeable. I found myself enchanted with all that I saw. Well, my trips *al norte* served as a security for my life—above all in the work that I have undertaken. It was very helpful, as much in the way of life as in an experience of a manner of working. Now all that they tell me does not make me angry, for now I know it for myself. And now I think how different my life is from before, because there have been great changes in my way of life. I have even had time to travel to the capital of Mexico or Guadalajara, when before I did not have enough even to eat *frijoles*. My visit to *el norte* was great to such an extent that I said good-by to my ignorance, and I gave thanks for my effort from which I reaped such a great advantage. Now I feel proud and have had complete dignity.

Now I say if there should be some person able to help me to settle and live in *Estados Unidos del Norte* I would go do it with such pleasure, and would reward him with my repeated thanks because I would like to live in *el norte,* with a government so considerate in its behavior. And life is convenient. Above all there is sufficient work. Only those who do not like to work do not work.

Again I give repeated thanks. Pardon me for my way of writing, for I have had little education. Nothing more than the third year of primary school.

This *bracero's* report was tape-recorded, and extraneous details have been edited:

(v) My age is 40 years, and I was born on the 21st of December 1921. I have been to *el norte* six times, once legally with a contract and the other times illegally. I first went to Montana in 1947, and each year from 1951 to 1955 I went to Texas by way of Tamaulipas and Reynosa.

I crossed the border with other fellows, and we had the help of people who specialized in helping people to make the illegal crossings. Twice I walked—once across the bridge at Reynosa and once through Capotes. One other time I went by way of Alacranes and twice through Joyita to the east of Reynosa. The federal officials treated the *braceros* well when the ranchers needed them, and the immigration people only made pretenses of looking. They had *la vista gorda*,[21] but when we returned the ranchers sent us with the "feds." The officers were courteous, but if somebody lied then they would hit him. If you didn't lie and said the truth all went well. Every time we went they took our fingerprints.

The people who took us across were Mexican. We hid in the woods on the Mexican side during the day and went across in launches hidden by night. Fifty, sixty, or seventy people went across together and it cost 10 pesos each. The police were not waiting for us on the other side because according to the *lancheros* they did not realize we were coming, or if they did know, the ranchers paid them off to simulate. After stepping on North American land we walked and kept asking the ranchers if there was work, and on finding it we stayed. We walked at night or in the morning before sunrise, and during the day waited at a ranch where there were fellow Mexicans. Even women came along to pick cotton and many brought children—their whole family—to live with them. Some people passed over swimming with boxes or automobile tubes, but nobody crossed the river during the day. We sometimes hid in orchards and waited all day until nightfall, and then passed on to another ranch. Our countrymen offered us their food. We always helped each other.

In 1947 I crossed the frontier legally because I had a contract. The government set up an office in Uruapan for contracting *braceros* because there was an agreement between the two governments. The *braceros* from all the state of Michoacán went there. The American government gave us our food and all our expenses, and later took us to another office in Irapuato where they made the medical exams. From there we went to our place of work. I went to the state of Montana to harvest sugar beet. I never gave one peso in *mordidas*.

When I went contraband I traveled with many fellows from

[21] Literally, "fat view." They looked but did not see.

here. Four or five of us would go to the border, but we would not always cross together. Sometimes yes, but at others we would cross alone while other fellows would wait three or four days. Later in the United States we did not know where the others were. We didn't see each other.

There we were busy one or two months or only twenty days, depending on how long the work lasted. Then the same ranchers told us to return to Mexico and called the "feds," and they came with trucks and returned us to Mexico. In Texas we picked string beans, tomatoes, onions, fruit, etc., etc. Sometimes a rancher would grab as many as 200 men. The same ones would throw us out when they had no more work and could no longer support us. At times the federals would drive around and see us, but as long as we were working in the fields they did nothing to us and it wasn't necessary to hide.

I went to Montana because I needed money to fix my house, and the other times I went because I was out of work and needed money. In Montana I worked with sugar beet and later as a *peón* on the railway track. There I earned 94 cents an hour plus social security. Working in contraband I weeded and picked cotton and harvested tomatoes. The work in Texas did not seem very hard in spite of the sun. I earned $2 a day, and many times they kept a day's wages to pay it later and then they didn't pay it. They took advantage of my illegal status and exploited me by not paying me.

The favorable impressions I had were the good wages I could make, the things I could buy, the way of life, the low cost of living, and the clothes. In the United States I could buy a shirt for 99 cents which would cost more than 20 pesos ($1.60) here. I like everything about *el norte*. All was good and to my liking. Nobody treated me badly and I was always happy.

The rancher in Montana was a good man. Not only did he give me everything I needed but in the mornings he helped me milk the cows and later went out to work himself. Besides the rancher, his wife and two children, there were six *peones*. The rancher kept the money for us and I didn't even drink because booze is pretty expensive in the United States. When I came back I had saved $500 and they gave me $30 more as a gift. And there I learned that one can live better and I learned something about cultivation, but one can't do anything because there they have *facilidades*[22] and here one has nothing. In the United States the government helps with all the work instruments. On the other hand, *here* if one goes to them dying of hunger it is better for them and they want you to get it over with right away!

Already much has changed here. Little by little we have had the *facilidades* to have everything—better beds, better food. There one sees that to live one must be better. If one goes one sees, and if one doesn't go anywhere one sees nothing and everything stays the same.

Yes, I would like to live in *el norte,* because I could live with less concern than here. And if I should have my family here, even what little money I earned there would increase greatly here, and I would be able to send it here for them to live better. There one can more easily earn more money, and with more money one could advance—to buy many things, to live better—better foods, clothes, books, and I could study another language. The food is different and I like it.

Two factors influenced the *braceros'* reactions to their experiences —their individual personality and the treatment they received. All were courageous individuals. They had to be to shake off the routine of village life and travel far into the unknown. All were industrious, and when given the chance to demonstrate this quality they would accept responsibility. On the other hand, those who ventured into certain states felt themselves abused, and their reaction to this abuse varied with their temperament. The more extroverted had the resources to shed their mistreatment, while others became bitter.

Most of them admired the United States, but at the same time they evidenced pride in and devotion to Mexico. Many would migrate if given the opportunity. Gentle hints along these lines were sometimes directed at members of the team.

Economic motivations were the only overt reason given for the trip, and several were able to bring back substantial sums of money. These savings were sometimes needed to sustain life in Huecorio. However, more frequently they flowed into improvements for the home or acquisition of productive equipment such as sewing machines or carpenter's tools.

---

[22] In this context the best translation would be "resources."

The *braceros* learned little that might be of direct economic value. The techniques of production on the large ranches and orchards in the United States are quite different than those that can be applied in Huecorio's minifundia. For this reason, the accumulated savings were rarely applied to agricultural operations. Tools were acquired for other occupations, and in one case the savings enabled a *bracero* to open a store. In spite of the fact that the *braceros* acquired little useful specific knowledge, the experience made a real contribution to their outlook on life. They became new men. They acquired a new dignity and self-respect, sloughed off their fatalism, and began to realize it was in their power to change things.[23] Such changes in self-appraisal are more important than any other factor in bringing about economic development.[24]

Although those who worked in some areas may frequently have found the experience disagreeable, most seemed to have found it pleasant, the ofttimes hard work notwithstanding. Fair and considerate treatment was fondly recalled. One *bracero* who was not interviewed commented, "Why! I even ate at the boss's table and ate meat and eggs and fruit!"

At the time the replies were given and subsequently, opposition to the *bracero* program was rising in the United States. The program was, unfortunately, terminated in December 1964. The opposition was based in part on the fact that domestic migrant farm labor frequently works under conditions inferior to those of *braceros*. This situation is, of course, unfair and undesirable. Nevertheless, prohibiting the entry of *braceros* will, by itself, do little to overcome the injustice.

We must emphasize that this does not constitute an argument against improving the lot of the domestic migrant, but rather that his lot should be improved in a program that continues to permit the *bracero* to enter. The discontinuance of the *bracero* program is bound

[23] The men may well have had this outlook before they left. Certainly if they had no incipient spirit of adventure, the trip would not have been undertaken in the first place. A change in outlook is clearly evident in I, IV and V. At the very least, the experience of being a *bracero* usually released attitudes that had previously been suppressed by a traditional environment; at best, a virtually new human being emerged.

[24] The author accepts the general propositions of Everett Hagen's *On the Theory of Social Change* (Homewood, Ill., Dorsey Press, 1962).

to bring unfortunate results. There will be a resurgence of illegal and uncontrolled immigration that will lead to abuses. Mexicans will not be able to take advantage of this unique and virtually costless form of foreign aid. The United States will be denying itself a badly needed device to stem the tide of anti-American sentiment, more easily created than dissipated.

EARNING RATES

Earning rates[25] for some occupations are sufficiently predictable to permit their presentation. Nevertheless, in most cases there is some variation in the rates applied to any given skill. Tailors, seamstresses, and *palmeros* are piece workers whose hourly rates are functions not only of the worker's skill and application but also of the piece rates for the different items. A seamstress gets only 50 centavos to make up a potholder, which takes an hour and a half. On the other hand, in the same time she can make up an apron which is worth three times as much to her. Whereas a seamstress may gain as little as 4 cents U.S. an hour at the present rate of exchange, masons in Huecorio constitute an elite of manual labor and can get up to 2 pesos and 92 centavos an hour (about 24 cents U.S.). If the masons travel to Morelia where there is a greater demand for construction skills, the rate rises to about 35 cents U.S. an hour.

Daily rates will vary similarly, but they cannot be derived directly from hourly rates because of variations in the number of hours worked per day. Some garment workers may apply themselves to this trade only three hours a day, whereas *comerciantes* may work for twelve hours. Agricultural laborers earn as a rule six or seven pesos a day, plus a midday meal valued at three pesos. On the other hand, during the harvest of wheat they will get at least 12 and possibly 20 pesos a day but do not receive meals. This difference is accounted for not by an increase in demand at harvest time, but by the unpleasant and quite dangerous nature of the work during the hot month of May.

[25] We use the term earning rates as a collective to cover wage rates, salaries, and income from self-employment.

Workers frequently cut themselves with their sharp scythes. In addition, the work is contracted by the job and an effort is therefore made to work rapidly. *Comerciantes* can earn substantial amounts per day (up to 40 pesos) or very little (2 pesos and 50 centavos). Most commonly the net profits are between ten and fifteen pesos. One *comerciante* regularly receives net profits of 300 pesos a week, but in this exceptional case he trades in Mexico City.

The wide variation in weekly rates for tailors and seamstresses can also be seen in Tables XIV and XV. In only one case is a *peón* employed by the week, and he receives 40 pesos plus room and board of an undeterminated value. Those who receive wage payments on a weekly basis are the masons, the chauffeur, and the one *peón* who boarded.

Monthly payments are made only to servants and the librarian. The librarian is employed by the government to maintain the Social Center. Servants are employed in several Huecorio households, and receive 50 pesos a month in addition to food. If a girl can work at one of the bungalows at Tzipecua or for a household in Pátzcuaro, the rate will be higher.

In the frictionless world of classical economics, these variations in earning rates for a given occupation would not exist. Labor is assumed to be perfectly mobile; higher rates existing in one place would attract labor from low income areas, and the shift would tend to equalize the rates. Mexicans are indeed highly mobile. Low transportation rates combined with a desire to see new places lead to a great deal of travel. Nevertheless, frictions of various kinds exist to perpetuate differences. Servants who work outside of Huecorio must either commute to work several times a day and return home after dark, sometimes in the heavy rain, or they must live in, which is lonely and keeps them from their friends and families. In addition, a further assumption of classical economics is not met, in that labor in Huecorio is not homogeneous. For instance, carpenters can earn more if they work in Pátzcuaro, but the proficiency demanded there is higher than in Huecorio and the laborer must supply his own basic tools.

Then, of course, we must mention knowledge and motivation, for these clearly affect how much one can earn. *Comerciantes* can do exceptionally well if they trade in Mexico and quite well if they go to Apatzingán. But those places require "know how" and organization. One does not simply go there and sit and sell, as in the Pátzcuaro market. One has to know where to go, how to get licenses, what things to sell, how to buy those things in Pátzcuaro, and so on. Those few who trade between Pátzcuaro and distant points have organized their whole lives around trading, and they have very little time for anything else. Traders who are more casual will be occupied in other activities, and for them the switch to full-time trading usually cannot be made.

Ralph Gray, who with his wife Vicki employs many people in the area to make garments for sale in the United States, believes that workers respond to higher prices by producing more. Vicki does not agree—but neither can produce any evidence. Vicki, however, is probably correct.[26] Work is done for the *taller,* "Vicki," only when workers are released from other tasks. It is complementary rather than competitive, and except for a few persons it has not replaced farming as a primary activity. Ricardo Arizpe is the only person encountered who made the shift, although Elpidio Cruz consciously chose garment work in preference to agriculture. In neither case was the choice made in response to price differentials, but in reaction to the difficulties associated with hard agricultural work. Huecorianos often demonstrate an economic calculus in organizing their lives, but psychological and other factors make the "economic man" less than complete.

UNDEREMPLOYMENT

Economists concerned with economic development have paid a great deal of attention to a phenomenon known as underemployment, which presents itself in a variety of forms but essentially involves a situation in which an individual is working but below his capacity. Underemployment is not unique to underdeveloped countries, of

[26] Although Ralph may be wrong, his rates have led to a high quality of work and an enduring loyalty to him. See Chapter 5.

course, but it is supposed to exist in them to a greater degree than elsewhere. A number of distinct types can be identified, and an effort was made to study them in Huecorio.

Zero or Negative Marginal Productivity Underemployment

The first and most difficult type of underemployment to understand is generally associated with the name of Ragnar Nurkse,[27] who gave the idea its most powerful impetus. The source of this underemployment is the diminishing returns which occur in agriculture under certain conditions. In a conceptual analysis certain assumptions must be made, and the most important of these will be listed to keep them easily in mind.

On (i) a fixed amount of land of given quality, (ii) a homogeneous labor force (iii) produces a single product with (iv) unchanging techniques of production. There are, then, three inputs—land, labor, and capital. Two of them are fixed. There is a given area of land of a uniform quality that is retained through time. The capital input in the form of seeds, ploughs, and animals does not change, and there are no changes in techniques. Furthermore, the variable labor input is homogeneous—all workers are equally able and apply themselves with equal diligence. If this were not the case, changes in the rate of change of output[28] could be caused by changes in the quality of the labor input. The nth laborer hired might add less to the total output than the second or third, simply because the employer had begun to scrape the barrel and was beginning to get some incompetents. The assumption of a single product is one of convenience. With mathematical techniques one could analyze a multiproduct situation, but that would merely complicate the situation.

Here, then, is what happens. Let us suppose we have an acre of land on which we grow corn. We hold our techniques of production constant, and our capital is a *yunta* of oxen and a wooden plough.

[27] Ragnar Nurkse, *Problems of Capital Formation in Underdeveloped Countries* (Oxford, Blackwell, 1953), Chapter 2.

[28] We momentarily avoid the technical term "marginal output."

At first only one man works the field, and he can produce, let us say, five bushels of corn. If he is joined by a second man, they can co-operate in various tasks and perhaps finish some on time. Together the two men produce 11 bushels, and thus the increase which resulted from employing the second man is an additional six bushels. This increment is known as the marginal output.

For a while marginal outputs rise as new workers are added and cooperate in the division of labor with other men. But as more men are added, the marginal outputs begin to decline. Because the field is limited in extent and because techniques of production do not change, there is a maximum amount of corn that the land can produce. As this maximum is approached it becomes more and more difficult for additional workers to add to the total output. Their *marginal* contributions begin to fall even though the *total* output continues to rise. For instance, the 18th man may add 12 bushels to total production while the 19th man, who is just as hard-working and competent, may only add 11 bushels.

By the time the nth man is employed, the total output has reached the technically feasible maximum and his marginal contribution is zero. He is working but producing nothing. If we add man n plus 1, his marginal contribution is also zero, or even negative if he impedes the other workers or tramples the plants. In other words, total output may now remain constant or even decline as more workers are added.

Those workers whose marginal outputs are zero or negative are underemployed. They appear to all concerned to be working, yet they are, in fact, producing nothing. This kind of underemployment is believed to have an important practical implication. Underdeveloped countries are, by definition, short of capital. Capital accumulation normally requires saving—the abstention from consumption. Consumption levels in underdeveloped countries are too low to facilitate capital accumulation, but the kind of underemployment just mentioned is unique in that it permits capital accumulation without abstinence from consumption. The underemployed agricultural workers can be removed from the fields and put to work on needed community projects such as drains and roads. They can continue to be fed as before by their families, but no sacrifice is involved in this capital accumulation. Since production does not decline, and may even rise if the marginal productivity of the workers had been negative, no one has to consume less to make capital accumulation possible.

Thus we have a rather sophisticated argument for a kind of community development. There are some obvious practical difficulties in this approach, but there are also conceptual aspects to Nurkse's theory that give rise to doubts. This is not the place to discuss these matters, however, and we are concerned here only with attempting to establish the existence of this kind of underemployment in Huecorio.

We must emphasize that the principle of diminishing returns is no more than a very reasonable proposition. It is not easy to test it in reality, since there are too many variables that cannot be controlled— soil quality, wind conditions, light and shade, drainage, incidence of insects, and variations in labor quality, to name only a few. In the Western world of the 19th century techniques were changing and the area under cultivation was expanding sufficiently rapidly to offset diminishing returns. In many parts of the world today, however, land areas are constricted and technologies are not changing enough to offset rising populations, and Nurkse's concern appears legitimate.

What, then, is the situation in Huecorio? How closely are the assumptions being met?

A Fixed Area of Land of a Given Quality. There has been a slight *increase* in the area under cultivation. This is true even if we concern ourselves only with the major crop, corn. The area under corn has increased for two reasons. First, farmers have gradually extended their plots up the sides of the hills that border the *ejido* parcels. Second, it appears that one area, La Lagunilla, switched from vegetables to corn production as the quality of land there deteriorated. The change in land quality is more difficult to assess. Now that the Río Guan is being diverted, the land in La Lagunilla, La Peñita, and part of San Pedrito has improved greatly. On the other hand, most of the *ejido* has probably deteriorated due to overgrazing. These two contrary trends may have offset each other, and it is probably safe to assume that, over all, the land quality has remained static. Thus, the slight increase in area may have led to a similarly slight increase in total corn output, although not in output per hectare—and it is with the latter that we are concerned.

A Homogeneous Labor Force. The agricultural labor force in Huecorio is not, by any means, homogeneous. We have noted that some farmers are more skillful and some apply themselves with greater diligence than others. We have also noted that hired *peones* are inclined to work in a rather sloppy fashion. Yet there is nothing to suggest that as the population of the village grows, the mix of skillful and unskillful workers will deteriorate. Thus the qualitative factor would not, by itself, lead to a decline in marginal returns.[29]

A Single Product. Quantitatively, corn is the most important crop in Huecorio, covering as it does the largest part of the cultivated area during a growing season. It is therefore reasonable to select it as the single product to be examined. Other crops could also be chosen, but their annual outputs generally vary as changing acreages are planted. No qualitative change in corn has occurred. Hybrids have not been successfully introduced to raise the output, and the *criollo* variety has been used for generations. Farmers merely maintain the quality of the *criollo* by selecting the best grains from each year's crop.

Unchanging Techniques of Production. This assumption is also reasonably well approximated in Huecorio, even though two important improvements in corn production techniques have taken place. The first was the introduction of the Oliver plough in the early 1930s, and the second was the introduction of the *gallinaza* fertilizer in the early 1960s. For the thirty years between the two dates the innovation horizon was barren, and we can safely use these years as a continuum of unchanging techniques within which to observe our "experiment."

The assumptions necessary for the classical principle of diminishing returns to take effect have been reasonably well met in Huecorio over this 30-year period. What happened to the variable input? Did it increase sufficiently to make the principle evident? The three decades saw the population of Huecorio double in size—from 400 in

---

[29] Indeed if, as we shall shortly argue, the population grows more rapidly than the demand for agricultural labor, the quality of the marginal workers could rise, since employers would have a larger pool from which to make their selection.

1930 to 844 in 1962. This does not, however, imply necessarily that the total actively employed labor force or the agricultural labor force increased in the same proportion, as these would be affected by such things as age and sex distributions, occupational structure, and mores. The agricultural labor force in 1930 was of the order of 134 persons, for in 1922, when Huecorio established its *ejido,* there were 134 successful applicants. To become an *ejidatario* an individual, among other requirements, had to have agriculture as his principal occupation. Persons who had substantial private holdings[30] or were not farmers could not apply, and so the number of successful applicants is an accurate indicator of the number of farmers in Huecorio in 1922. We should add that it is not legitimate to add to this total a figure for landless *peones,* since the distribution effectively, if temporarily, eliminated this class. The number of farmers may have fallen slightly by 1930, because Huecorio's population fell from 429 to 400 between 1921 and 1930. This is a decline of 9.32%, which if applied to 134 would reduce the agricultural work force to 122 persons in 1930.[31] By 1963 there were 144 persons (farmers, "gardeners," and *jornaleros*) who regarded agriculture as their primary occupation. (Table 4.) In addition 60 such persons regarded agriculture as a secondary occupation and eight considered it a tertiary or quartic trade. (Table X.) However, the size of the agricultural labor force is not arrived at by the simple addition of these figures, since double counting would be involved in almost all cases. For instance, a person who calls himself a *campesino* owns land but may call his secondary trade *jardinero* because he cultivates vegetables in some of his land. Furthermore, he may also work someone else's land as a *peón.* To get the net number of persons employed in agriculture in some degree, we should subtract from the totals for primary through quartic occupations (212) the 40 persons who list themselves more than once as *campesinos, jardineros,* or *jornaleros.* The total number of persons who work in agriculture in some way,

[30] Huecorio had no large landholders and so none were excluded on this count.

[31] A decrease of this magnitude is unlikely, since it would imply that some persons had given up their agricultural holdings—a most unlikely situation in a community of this kind.

then, amounts to 172. This represents an increase of 28% over 1922 and possibly 41% over 1930. In other words, while Huecorio's population more than doubled from 1930 to 1962, its agricultural labor force increased only by 28% or possibly by 41%.[32]

What has happened to the output of corn? No accurate historical data answer this question, and the farmers themselves are unclear about it. We noted above that when farmers were asked about changes in their harvests of corn, 13 said they were worse, nine said they were better, nine said they were the same, and three did not answer. In at least four of the cases where the reports were of better harvests, the farmers were referring to situations in which the crops had been improved by means of irrigation or fertilizers. It is possible, then, that there has been some decrease in the output of corn per hectare in the *ejido* lands except where the alluvium from the Río Guan, or fertilizers, have had beneficial effects. In other words, productivity seems to have declined in those village areas where techniques have remained constant. If this is the case one might argue, if one did not look more deeply, that the increase in the size of the agricultural labor force had pushed the production function all the way through diminishing returns to negative returns.

What has happened as more persons have worked in agriculture? One effect might be a move in the direction of more labor-intensive methods of production, either in the form of larger work teams or smaller farms, and to understand this we must clear up a minor muddle.

When analysts talk about a given "area of land" in the context of this kind of underemployment, to what are they actually referring? Is it a whole country? A region? A village? Or just a given field? In Huecorio the reference could be either to a given field or to the village area as a whole. The effects of the increasing labor force will be different in each case. Analytically we have two possibilities which could give rise to diminishing returns. As the population increases, the number of farms could remain constant but each farm would employ more persons. In other words, the sizes of the various work teams

[32] Since 38 of these workers are part-time farmers, the full-time equivalent of the agricultural labor force would have grown by a much smaller percentage.

would rise. Alternatively, the work team sizes could remain constant and the number of farms would then have to increase. In the latter case, the total area would be worked by a larger number of teams, and hence persons.

Where we consider a given field owned by one man, the conventional theory would have us believe that he would use more and more people to work that land as the population increased. This has not taken place in Huecorio. At the various stages in the production of corn different sized work teams are used—two men and a *yunta* prepare the ground, three men and a *yunta* do the cultivating, and so on, and variations from these norms are mainly functions of time. If a farmer is pressed for time and can afford it, he will hire more *peones;* but because cash outlays are generally involved when more *peones* are used, farmers do not increase the size of work teams simply because the population of the village has grown. *Historically, there has been no tendency for work teams to increase in size.*

Since the work team sizes have remained the same during the period we are considering, the only way in which a greater number of persons could work the land would be for the number of farms to increase. Surprisingly, this seems not to have taken place. The analysis of this is quite difficult, and we must call upon some rather indirect evidence.

The number of farms cannot be measured directly, because of the distinction between land ownership and land management. In one household, for instance, the father, mother, and daughter each holds title of a sort to a distinct and separate piece of land. Three farms? The land is worked by the father and son. One or two farms? Do they work the land together as a team (one farm), or do they work separately and independently, each in a different area (two farms)?

Let us try another approach. If, assuming a constant arable area, the average size of farms had decreased, then it would follow that the number of farms had increased. There are several difficulties here, pertaining to the need to deal with a single crop, calculation of the area under cultivation, and a semantic confusion between "farmer" and "landowner."

When we speak of farms we refer to fragmented holdings scattered over the village and planted in several different crops according to the region, but our analysis of diminishing returns must deal with only a single crop—corn in this case. The area under general cultivation has increased since 1930, but by how much we cannot say since it cannot be ascertained where the shore line of the lake was at that time. The area under corn has also increased, perhaps as much as 10%, as farmers have ploughed further up the sides of hills and have planted corn in parts of the *ejido* that were once in vegetables. The number of full-time farmers has also increased, from 134 to 144— a rise of 7.4%. But "farmer" is not synonymous with "landowner." Representatives of the landowning group can be found among full-time farmers, part-time farmers, and non-farmers alike. Obviously, the average size of a farm cannot be calculated in this way.

An increase in fragmentation might also be an indication that average farm size has decreased, although it is a poor one since—conceptually at least—increasing fragmentation could be the result of a redistribution of a given number of farms among an unchanging number of persons. Fragmentation already existed in Huecorio in 1930. When the *ejido* was set up fragmentation was built into it as each *ejidatario* was given three tiny and widely separated plots. Among the 34 farmers questioned in our survey, only two have less than the three plots allowed by law. On the other hand, five had more than three plots. This results from intermarriages among families of *ejidatarios,* and this consolidation more than offsets the tendency toward fragmentation in the *ejido.* Fragmentation may also have taken place in the private lands, but the net situation is not clear. Huecorianos are reluctant to sell agricultural land, and do so only under duress. Some private fields have been divided into smaller parcels, but this may have been partly offset by some others who have been able to buy land. If there has been an increase in fragmentation during the 30-year period under study, it has not been extensive, and it does not appear that the number of farms has increased.[33]

[33] Fragmentation is associated with another form of underemployment which is wasteful of human labor. Huecorio is a nuclear village, and all farmers have their lands scattered at different points of the compass. The closest fields are about five minutes' walk from the houses, and the most distant are a good half hour away. These times are longer if the farmer is taking a slow-moving *yunta* to work. In any case, the total time involved in going from field to field every day is between half an hour and

Since such a shift in the direction of increasing labor intensity did not take place, we must look elsewhere for the cause of the declining yields reported by a significant number of farmers. One is the secular decline in rainfall reported to have occurred over the first twenty or so years of the period in question. A more likely cause, however, is the extent of overgrazing which has reduced soil productivities over the larger part of the area under corn.

There is one other piece of evidence of dubious validity concerning Nurksian underemployment which we might add here. Conventional analysis argues that wage rates equal the marginal productivity of labor. If the marginal productivity is zero wages would be zero, and if it is negative, as would be the case when overpopulation results in a declining total output, we would have the preposterous situation in which workers would pay employers rather than vice versa. Leibenstein[34] developed an ingenious argument to demonstrate that zero or negative marginal productivity could occur simultaneously with positive wage rates, but this is completely unconvincing—it is quite out of touch with reality in its postulate of enlightened self-interest on the part of landlords and it contains serious logical flaws.[35]

In Huecorio, wage rates are positive and there is no evidence to support the case for the zero or negative marginal productivity type of underemployment. We are left, nevertheless, with the obligation to explain what has happened in Huecorio as the admittedly small increase in the agricultural labor force has made itself felt. One effect has been the development of a small class of landless agricultural workers. The size and significance of this class are difficult to determine. We have established that there are 172 persons who work in agriculture even though for some it is not a primary occupation.

---

an hour. While this is wasteful, it is not a time loss of serious proportions. Fragmentation involves inefficiencies on two other counts, however. Most fields in Huecorio are too small to permit mechanization; and most, being distant from the house, cannot be carefully watched and this means that on the better lands there is some reluctance to plant high-value crops which are subject to theft.

[34] Harvey Leibenstein, *Economic Backwardness and Economic Growth* (New York, Wiley, 1957), Chapter 6.

[35] The analysis of the flaws requires a close reference to Leibenstein's original statement, and would consume more space than can be justified here.

The number of landholders seems to have remained stable over the 30-year period. In the census 124 persons admitted to the ownership of land other than their household plot. However, in some families two or three persons own land and the respondents answering to the questionnaire did not always separate the ownership shares. In other words, the number of persons owning land is slightly greater than 124 and is probably only one or two more than the 134 landholders who existed in 1922. The maximum number of landless agricultural laborers would be the difference between the total number of agricultural workers and the number of landholders—in other words 35 or so persons.

This, however, is misleading and still too high. Take the case, for instance, of a farmer who owns a hectare or two of land and has two sons living with him who are in their late teens or early twenties and who work the family farm. Are these boys landless laborers? If they are, then peonage has been growing at the rate of less than 1% per year. But eventually this property will be divided in some way, and unless they leave agriculture the boys will become landholders.

It is much more meaningful to define a landless laborer as one who works in agriculture and has no access to land, other than perhaps a small garden plot in his household. If this definition is accepted, then there are only seven landless agricultural laborers in Huecorio. And even this is less serious than it might appear, since for all these persons agriculture is a secondary rather than a primary source of income.

The agricultural labor force has been absorbed in other ways which have avoided the Nurksian underemployment trap. While the increase in this sector of the labor force has been between 28% and 41%, the area under corn has grown by about 10%. During the same period there was a much larger but indeterminable increase in the land available for cash crops as the waters of the lake receded. Together, these factors were sufficient to absorb the increase. Furthermore, since much of the total agricultural labor force is only part-time, the full-time labor equivalent is less than the 172 persons who claim to work in agriculture. Indeed, at busy times of the year Huecorianos must call in labor from other villages to help with their agricultural tasks.

This leads to consideration of the most important means that Huecorianos have chosen to offset the effects of population pressure on the land. They have left agriculture for other occupations, and even within the village there has been a change in occupational structure away from agriculture.

As we have seen, during the three decades of constant technique the population of Huecorio grew from 400 persons to 844. Such an increase in population implies also an increase in the labor force. However, the labor force cannot have doubled, even assuming that sex ratios and cultural attitudes remained the same, since the high rate of annual increase in population during the ultimate 12 years implies a changing of the age structure in favor of minors. Since we have no data on either the age structure of the population or the size of the labor force in 1930, no direct comparison can be made. The total actively employed labor force was 241 persons in 1962—about 28% of the total population. In 1930 the absolute size of the labor force was less than in 1960, although its proportion to the total population was undoubtedly higher.

Although this lack of historical data prevents us from making statements with absolute certainty, it is clear that there has been a shift in the structure of the labor force, with certain new occupations entering the village since 1930. If we concern ourselves only with primary occupations, these new activities would include the garment workers, the *palmeros,* the masons who received their training in the late 1930s at the earliest, the chauffeur, the nurse, the full-time public officials, the mechanic, and the veterinarian. This is a total of 22 persons. In addition, certain other occupations existed in the 1930s but the number of persons in them has increased. A conservative estimate of the number of persons shifting their primary activity to an established occupation would be the eight male *comerciantes,*[36] two of the teachers[37] and two of the shopkeepers.[38] In other words, a

[36] The male *comerciantes* were singled out since they generally trade at distant points and this would have been very much more difficult in 1930.

[37] A smaller absolute population in 1930, together with a lower proportion of children and a less active education program on the part of the government would suggest the presence of only one teacher.

[38] All the shops at present in Huecorio were opened relatively recently.

total of 34 persons in Huecorio, or 14.1% of the total actively employed labor force, would now be employed in primary industry if the percentage of persons in primary industry had remained constant over the three decades. Although we do not know, and have no adequate basis for calculating, the size of the actively employed labor force in 1930, it is clear that the proportion employed in primary industry was higher than today—at least 83% as opposed to 69% today.

This, then, is what happened in Huecorio: The techniques employed in agriculture did not fruitfully allow a change in the production function toward the greater use of labor. Because land is so fundamental to the historical way of life of Huecorianos, it is rarely sold and such fragmentation as may occur is likely to originate through inheritance rather than the market. But fragmentation has increased slowly if at all. Nurksian underemployment is avoided in Huecorio. As population pressures intensify, individuals transfer out of agriculture into secondary and tertiary industry. Some leave for employment elsewhere. The kind of escape that Huecorio has been able to take advantage of has been made possible largely by the economic expansion taking place throughout Mexico, which has provided both employment and markets. Of some importance has been the relative proximity to the United States. *Braceros* have found temporary employment there, and goods originating in Don Juan's *taller* find their way to northern markets.

Seasonal Underemployment

Agriculture, because of the changing seasons, almost always carries with it fluctuations in the intensity of work and Huecorio is no exception, but the manifestations of the agricultural cycle were quite unexpected. A dry season extends from October or early December until late in May or June. December through March is cold, and one would naturally expect that the farmers of Huecorio would be idle

---

Undoubtedly there was at least one shop in Huecorio in 1930 but it may not have been open all day as are the present shops.

from the termination of the corn harvest in December to the harvest of wheat in May. Statements by some Huecorianos would even seem to support this when they say that "during the dry season the more ambitious do such things as collecting firewood but the less ambitious sit back with crossed arms." The overwhelming majority appear to feel differently. In the words of Lorenzo Villanueva, "There is never a lack of work for those who wish to work. In the dry season I go to Apatzingán as a *comerciante*." Ricardo Zavala says, "I work every day from dawn to dusk. There's not really enough work on the land from January to April so I go out and collect firewood." César Bustamente told us, "Even though I am old I work every day from January to December from eight in the morning until four in the afternoon." Gregorio O'Donojú goes to the *tierra caliente* to work as a laborer from January to April. In May he returns to Huecorio to harvest wheat. In June and July he plants and cultivates corn. Then in August, September, and October he returns to Apatzingán to sell vegetables. In the middle of October he must come home to Huecorio to plant wheat, and in November and December there is corn to be harvested.

Farmers and workers in other fields were asked to recount in some detail the daily activities and hours worked month by month throughout the year. At the risk of overemphasizing a point, it is worth while to report two typical responses. Although we offer only the barest details, there is sufficient evidence to demonstrate the way in which farmers manage to fill the voids in the agricultural seasons and perhaps to dispel the notion frequently held that people in "tropical" countries are inherently lazy.[39]

Sebastian Martínez

January	Goes after firewood and sells it, leaves at 6:00 a.m.
February	and returns at 2:00 p.m. From 3:00 p.m. to 7:00
March	p.m. prepares the field in the *orilla* for vegetables, or sells firewood.

[39] See also Appendix B.

April Plants cabbage and lettuce in nurseries and irrigates them with buckets of water drawn from drainage ditches. When the rains come the seedlings are transplanted. 7:00 a.m. to 7:00 p.m.

May Harvests own wheat and then cuts for others under contract. From 7:00 a.m. to between 4:00 and 7:00 p.m., depending on onset of rains.

June Cultivates vegetables and continues preparation to plant carrots, radishes, and saltwort in nurseries. Prepares his own land for corn and works as a laborer for others. 7:00 a.m. to 4:00 p.m.

July Cultivates corn with a borrowed wooden plough and works at the same task for others.

August Continues cultivating corn, and about the 20th begins to prepare land for wheat.

September Works at various agricultural tasks for himself and
October others. If nothing to do he will go after firewood.
November

December Harvests corn from 7:00 to 7:00.

Geronimo Roca

January Harvests corn and makes nurseries for vegetables. Once a week he goes after firewood for the house. Every day he works from 6:00 a.m. to 6:00 p.m. (Geronimo reported that he usually gets up at 4:00 a.m. to look after animals and *granja*.)

February Prepares land for vegetables. 6:00 a.m. to 4:00 p.m.

March Plants or transplants vegetables. 6:00 a.m. to 4:00 p.m.

April Harvests wheat and cultivates vegetables. 6:00 a.m. to 9:00 p.m.

May Prepares for and plants corn. 8:00 a.m. to 5:00 p.m.

June   Cultivates corn. Never works for others as a laborer because he is too busy with his own fields.

July   Cultivates corn. 6:00 a.m. to 6:00 p.m. if the rains permit.

August   Prepares for wheat.
September

October   Harvests wheat and cultivates vegetables. Cuts fod-
November   der, plants wheat, and harvests *frijoles.*

December   Harvests *frijoles* and corn.

Detailed information on work patterns to permit calculation of hours worked was collected from fourteen farmers. The norm was based on a six-day week for the calendar year 1962, and the total number of work days for any given month was reduced by the number of Sundays and fiestas that fell within it. An eight-hour day was assumed for every month with the exception of the especially busy period of June, July, and August, during which a nine-hour work day was assumed.[40] The result was a norm of 2,487 hours per year. Seven farmers reported working more than this, and seven less. However, several farmers who have animals did not include the time necessary for their care.

Only four farmers interviewed reacted more or less passively to the seasonal fluctuations, and the majority kept themselves fully employed on their own land, as agricultural workers in the *tierra caliente,* as *comerciantes,* as semi-industrial workers, or by collecting firewood.[41] The climatological differences within Mexico and the existence of handicraft industries make it possible for farmers to offset the effects of the seasons, and effectively mitigate seasonal unemployment. Those who are seasonally underemployed are, in a sense, voluntarily unemployed for part of the year.

Although not of direct relevance for seasonal unemployment, similar data on hours worked were gathered for other occupations. Only

[40] See Appendix B.
[41] Adolfo Pérez offers an example of this pattern. His primary activity is that of *palmero* which keeps him busy for 1,107 hours. He works his own land for 1,060 hours and as a *peón* for others 876 hours. In addition he goes off for firewood every three weeks.

three *comerciantes* can be considered as being full-time,[42] and two of those did housework as well. Daily hour schedules indicate that housewives, whether *comerciantes* or not, also manage to fill their waking hours with work. Several of them are picked at random from the social questionnaire:

(I) Rises at 6:00. Sweeps out the house, brings in water and starts the fire. Then she goes to milk the cows and later to the *molino*. When she brings back the *nixtamal* she prepares *tortillas* for breakfast and lunch. In this household breakfast is at 8:00 a.m., lunch at 2:00 p.m. and dinner at 8:00 p.m. Around noon on Mondays and Tuesdays she goes to wash clothes, or she might cut some grass to take to the cows. Later she will remove grains of corn from the cob to be taken to the *molino* the next day and will prepare *tacos* for the evening. After dinner the family goes to bed at 9:00 or 10:00. Sundays she goes to Mass and prepares the meals but never does washing. During the week she will frequently help her husband by weeding or harvesting vegetables.

(II) Rises at 7:00. Feeds chickens in the *granja* and cleans the coops. Prepares breakfast at 8:00 for the children who go to school and at 9:00 for those who do not. Then she takes food to her husband where he is working. When she returns the house is swept and things are straightened up. If she has time, she will sew a little before collecting eggs. She begins to prepare lunch at one o'clock and it is eaten some time between 2:00 and 3:30. Again it is cleaning house, attending the chickens, and collecting eggs. Then she might iron before preparing dinner at eight or nine. After dinner there might be a little time to listen to the radio before retiring at 10:00 or 11:00. The older daughters will help in the household tasks.

(III) Rises at 6:00. On Tuesdays, Thursday, Fridays, and Sundays she cleans and packs vegetables to take to the market in Pátzcuaro. She goes to Pátzcuaro on the seven o'clock bus and eats breakfast there. She will sell until 2:00 p.m. and then return home to prepare lunch. Then she will wash the dishes,

---

[42] See Table XVI, code nos. F5, F9, and F12.

clean the house, wash clothes and work in the garden. Dinner is at 7:00 p.m., and she goes to bed at 9:00. On the other days including fiestas she will work about the house, and her daughter-in-law helps in all these tasks except trading. When she was asked whether she has any free time she replied, *"¡Pues! ¿Para que?"* (What for?) "We don't go to the movies."

These examples could be continued indefinitely with little significant variation. The time of the women is as fully consumed with productive labor as is that of the men. Households clearly work as a unit, although there is a broad division of labor in that the men are employed in field or shop while the women attend the house. Men do not usually cross over into household tasks, but they will bring in firewood or make repairs or additions to the house. Women will nevertheless frequently help with light field work such as weeding, harvesting, or looking after the *granja* and animals, and it is more usual for the women, rather than the men, to sell the products of the farm. More often than not there is more than one woman in the household. While the older women sell farm products, daughters-in-law or older daughters will cook and younger children may clean the house. Other than the *molino de nixtamal* for grinding corn, and the sewing machine, labor-saving devices are not found. Tools and equipment consist of brooms, charcoal stoves, buckets, and so on, and household tasks are laborious and time consuming.

Little time is left for leisure, and this may consist only of a Sunday walk to Pátzcuaro or attendance at a *fiesta,* although families sometimes take in a movie at Pátzcuaro. To describe life in Huecorio as uninteresting may be reading alien cultural values into it, but it seems to offer little in stimulation and excitement. Pleasure stems from quiet things such as those involved in family life.

We can offer some data on employment in other occupations, for example, that of the tailors and seamstresses. (Table XVII.) Other than Don Juan and his wife Guadalupe, only one person working in the *taller* is fully employed in the trade, and so the data have little value as a measure of the level of employment. Nevertheless, in each of the other cases the persons involved are fully occupied in farming, attending school, or trading. Don Juan and Guadalupe work very long hours, and if orders pile up they must frequently work on Sundays.

They rise at 6:30, clean the house, and prepare the shop by clearing furniture away from the work area. The workday begins at 9:30, and Luisa, the daughter-in-law, prepares lunch for the break between 2:00 and 3:00. Work then continues until 7:00 but may go on far into the night if necessary. Guadalupe must also travel to Pátzcuaro twice a week to buy household supplies.

Similarly, the two shopkeepers bear a heavy burden of responsibility. The store of Carlos Gorozpe is open from 6:30 a.m. to 9:00 p.m., and may be closed only once or twice a month when there are fiestas. Carlos himself usually leaves his wife to attend the store while he is busy elsewhere trading or working as a *palmero,* carpenter, mason, mechanic, or truck driver, as opportunity offers. The store of Antonio Iturbide is also open from 6:00 a.m. to 9:00 p.m., and had not been closed for a full day during the 11 months it had been in operation. Antonio's time revolves entirely around the store, and he is either behind the counter or away from Huecorio making wholesale purchases.

All the information presented so far could be amplified with data from masons, *palmeros,* and others, but the employment picture would change only to the degree that one would need to show how the different individuals filled their waking hours. One *palmero,* for instance, works his lands as the occasion demands and shifts to weaving chairs only as the agricultural pace slackens.

In reviewing the employment situation as it extends through the seasons, one can then make a generalization, subject to exceptions, that Huecorianos—perhaps like mankind as a whole—see idle time as a vacuum that must be filled, and as long as opportunities exist to fill it they will do so. Most farmers fill the slack season void quite successfully, while a few do not take advantage of opportunities which become apparent upon the application of just a little effort. To advance satisfactory explanations for these differences would require a very close examination of individual cases, and would call for skills beyond the competence of the economist.

There is one exception of some importance. Two of the men interviewed are full-time employees of Tzipecua, who work there eight hours a day for six days a week and finish regularly at 3:00 in the afternoon. Both have farmlands, but one contracts out the work and the other leaves it to a brother. Unlike other persons who must fill their daylight hours with labor, these two do not. Except perhaps for an occasional minor chore, 3 o'clock sees the end of the working day. One can postulate that the security associated with their jobs does not act as a drive, as does the insecurity of other Huecorianos. Since only two persons are involved in this exception, it would not be wise to speculate further.

Voluntary Underemployment

In its purest form, voluntary underemployment exists whenever an individual who has a productive task available which he can perform, knowingly and by free choice elects not to do it. It will be expressed in various ways, of course. An industrial worker may work only long enough to become eligible for unemployment insurance and then subsist on the benefits until they cease. A college professor may go to a concert instead of staying home to write that book. But what about the villager who goes to a *fiesta* instead of working in his fields? Obviously, there are cultural limits to voluntary unemployment.

A society designates certain times when people are expected not to engage in work, although, of course, they are not generally constrained from doing so. We might take the example of Thanksgiving Day in the United States. One is expected to relax at a turkey dinner, and this would not be an example of voluntary unemployment. In Huecorio one is not expected to work on Sundays or at such times as Mexican Independence Day or the *fiesta* of the Virgin of Guadalupe. In other words, the number of culturally determined workdays is about 300, and the number of working hours about 2,500 a year.

Many persons will work more than these norms, and others less. But one who works less is voluntarily underemployed only if there is something available for him to do which he knowingly and voluntarily ignores. In order to assess the magnitude of voluntary underemployment one must know a good deal about an individual, and for this reason a measure of its magnitude in Huecorio cannot be attempted in this study. Take, for instance, some of the farmers who work only short hours during the dry season. Is their underemployment voluntary? Do they know they can work as *comerciantes, palmeros,* or laborers in the *tierra caliente*? Probably they do. But can they work at those trades? Do they have the necessary skills? Does some legitimate reason restrain them from leaving Huecorio? Most of these individuals would probably be found to be voluntarily underemployed, but without personal study they cannot be sorted out.

Voluntary underemployment in two other manifestations can be identified but not measured. Individuals will sometimes quit their daily tasks to leave Huecorio to perform functions of social importance for the community. On one occasion four farmers accompanied the investigator on a trip to Villa Escalante and Morelia to search for insecticides. At another time several helped in a search for a good basketball for the village team. Again, several leaders felt obliged to represent Huecorio when the President of Mexico was dedicating a dam in the *tierra caliente*.

Of a more serious nature and of greater magnitude is voluntary underemployment stemming from drunkenness. This is usually associated with the village *fiestas*, weddings, deaths, and saints' days, but some persons need no such excuse. Several weddings took place during one week in July, and possibly half the farmers were quite unable to work for three or four consecutive days. A *fiesta* or a wedding can start a chain reaction of communal conviviality that cannot be broken until ready cash runs out or the cumulative effects of *aguardiente* incapacitate the individual for everything but sleep. We felt it prudent not to bother our acquaintances during these binges even as participant observers. Thus our observations on voluntary unemployment must remain couched in generalities.

CHAPTER 4

CAPITAL AND
ITS ACCUMULATION

ECONOMISTS usually define capital as man-made means of production. This conception stems from a concern with analyzing
the constituent elements of the creation of wealth; accordingly, the
usual categories of capital are construction, equipment, and inventories. More recently, recognition of the less tangible aspects of economics has led some to accept human knowledge as an important
category. For analytical purposes it is sometimes advantageous to include animals and agricultural land to the list, as we have done, for
they, like construction, equipment, and inventories, give rise to a
positive flow of benefits,[1] and their acquisition and accumulation
usually involve the individual in the practice of abstinence from consumption. Consumer durables such as beds, radios, or automobiles,
also constitute a form of capital even though they do not directly, or
of necessity, further production. Their inclusion is justified largely on
the basis that, in principle, one does not consume the item itself but
rather the flow of services that the good produces. With these distinctions in mind, noneconomists can observe the wide variety of guises
assumed by capital in a community such as Huecorio.

[1] Conveniently dubbed "profits."

Chicken granja; *white Leghorns feeding*

Capital accumulation does not cause economic development in any sense, but it is of course associated with it. Societies which are progressing will create capital at high rates, and unless this creation is offset by rapid population growth or unfavorable capital-output ratios, per capita incomes and usually levels of living will rise. Calculations of rates of capital accumulation require the collection of aggregate data at various points in time so that comparisons can be made. Base-line data were, of course, not available for Huecorio for any year prior to 1962, and it was our duty therefore to prepare the initial inventory so that later comparisons could be made. As the reader will soon appreciate, such inventories are complicated and laborious to compile and involve the researcher in many hazardous speculations.

Despite the lack of a base line, an attempt was made to calculate the rate of capital accumulation. The results were not encouraging, for even with the presence of CREFAL and the activities of the *granjeros* and *braceros,* it would seem that insufficient capital is being created to counter the depressing effects of population growth.

It is also apparent that capital in Huecorio is unevenly distributed.

157

Some few persons have sufficient animals, tools, sewing machines, or *granjas* to better their position materially. The others are merely treading water or, in some cases, sinking ever lower.

CAPITAL INVENTORY

Construction

Table XVIII offers an inventory of public and private buildings. No estimate of the value of the public buildings could be devised. The value of nonresidential buildings was derived from the Agricultural Survey, while information on house values, shown in Table XIX, was derived from the Social Survey. In the latter case a number of owner-estimated valuations had to be rejected as being clearly out-of-line in light of the researcher's knowledge of the house in question. It was hoped that tax payments would confirm the estimated values, but this was not the case since such payments are based on assessments made by the government in 1958 and many houses have been improved since that time or have not yet been registered. In addition, the assessment is for house and lot while our evaluations are for house alone.[2]

Some confirmation of the evaluations came from the fact that the one house recently changing hands sold for 10,000 pesos. This figure provided a comparative evaluation for the other houses, since its quality and location were known.

The private nonresidential construction had a value of at least 45,408 pesos, the most important category being the chicken houses, which are of recent acquisition.[3]

The total valuation for private houses amounts to 545,790 pesos. The individual house values vary considerably—from 350 to 15,000

[2] Our data were not extracted directly from the tax records themselves, because although the records were freely opened up to us they were in a form that did not accord with an efficient use of the team's limited time.

[3] Where the houses are for both residential and nonresidential use, the valuation was included in the residential category.

pesos, and they range from dirt hovels, partially buried in the ground, to quite comfortable structures of two stories with glass windows, tile floors, electricity, and running water. Naturally, the quality of the house itself will be a prime determinant of value. However, the villagers pointed out that value was also a function of location—particularly in terms of proximity to the center and availability of electricity and water. The significant rise in values in recent years is largely due to inflation, especially as represented by the rising costs of materials. Most villagers recognized this, but one was sophisticated enough to see that the increasing demand for housing had something to do with it.

Agricultural Capital

The limits to a definition of agricultural capital are somewhat debatable. If capital is defined in its most widely accepted fashion— that is as man-made means of production—it would include only construction (covered above), equipment, and inventories. In agriculture the inventories would be crops in the field and in storage. Both would vary considerably during the year, and therefore no attempt was made at their calculation.

Data on equipment were gathered, however. We chose to expand the definition of capital for purposes of this inventory, on the grounds that draft and other animals, fruit trees and land, represent an investment on the part of the farmer even though they are not man-made. With the logic of accounting they should probably have been included in the inventory of natural resources, yet except where animals breed randomly their acquisition has involved some effort on the part of the farmer or the community.

Equipment. The total estimated value of the agricultural equipment held in the village is 42,617 pesos, or $3,409 U.S. (See Table **XX**.) This is less than the cost of one small farm tractor without equipment, and partially explains why no tractors are found in Huecorio. The only machine-driven device is a small irrigation pump purchased by one farmer from his earnings as a *bracero*.

The most important piece of equipment is the Oliver steel plough.

These ploughs cannot be replaced by others of the same quality, a fact which is reflected in their steady increment in value. Two, for instance, were purchased in 1932, one for 42 pesos and the other for 50 pesos. Today they are valued as high as 800 pesos each. Thirty-three—or less than half—of the farm households own this essential device.

Wooden ploughs used for cultivation are less numerous, even though they could be made in the village. Less than half the farm households own the yokes for ploughing and cultivating. Two farmers have irrigation equipment installed near the lake. One is the above-mentioned 2-inch pump, and the other is a chain-and-bucket device driven by a horse. Both effectively raise the productivity of the farmers involved, but their efforts have not yet been emulated by others.

Tools. The total estimated value of small agricultural tools is 8,113 pesos for the village as a whole, of which 5,374 pesos is for the agricultural households. (See Table XXI.) It was necessary to use mildly speculative procedures to estimate the total figures for the village. While the number of any given tool could readily be ascertained for the farm households, the tools owned by the remaining half of the households—many of whose members own garden plots or engage in part-time farming—had to be estimated by means of a calculation that reflected the likely use of the tool by nonfarm households. The sickle, for instance, is fairly specialized and is used mainly for harvesting wheat. Some nonfarm households will own the sickle, especially if one member is a *peón* who depends on employment in such harvests, but its ownership is likely to be less widespread than that of the *machete*. Accordingly, a correction factor of 100% was applied to the omnipresent *machetes* and only 50% was applied to sickles.

The range of tools is narrow, and in variety and quality is likely to be outdone by the toolshed of the suburban middle class of the wealthier countries. The most valuable of the tools is the ax, the price of which ranges up to 50 pesos. The instrument is large, and although of a single bit is very awkward for one used to the light New England type of instrument. Most of the tools are handmade and rather crude, but usually serve their purpose effectively.[4] Ownership is uneven, and

[4] The curved *machete* is made from automobile springs, and while not

no one tool is found in more than two-thirds of the farm households. Not all farmers own these vital means of livelihood, poor in quality though they may be.

Work Animals. In the absence of machinery, the village farmer must rely on animals to ease the burden of his work. *Bueyes* are used to plough, and occasionally to pull carts. They are expensive animals, valued at 3,000 pesos a pair, and 39 of the 71 farm households do not have them. The 89 adult animals are sufficient for 44 work teams, clearly an inadequate number. Those who do not have teams can rent or borrow them, but the general shortage means that important activities cannot always be done on time and the effect on production is unfortunate. (See Tables XXII, XXIII, and XXVI.)

Burros, of which there are 60, carry tools to the field, crops from the harvest, or produce to the market. Every farm household should have one for these tasks, but 47 do not. Horses to some extent meet this lack, and while not as sturdy as the *burro* they can do much the same duty. Like the *burro,* they can also thresh wheat and be ridden. At least two are used for ploughing, and, as we have seen, one somewhat better than average animal costing 600 pesos pulls a cart hauling goods between Huecorio and Pátzcuaro.

Other Animals. Chickens abound in Huecorio, largely due to the establishment of the 11 poultry farms (*granjas*) under the auspices of the *Asociación Avícola* founded by CREFAL. In most cases households have a few birds that scratch impartially in house and patio alike.[5]

The large number of skinny cows—170—supply milk which is

---

fully tempered and thus fragile, is ideally suited to cutting brush. Nothing comparable can be found in the United States.

[5] Hereby we recount a typical pitfall of international data accumulation. During the Census it would frequently happen that in a household obviously graced by a dozen or so birds the answer to our question about the number of chickens present was "two" or "three." There was neither the batting of the eye nor the furtive glance away to indicate an attempt to deceive. We felt it impolite to mention the seemingly obvious discrepancy. During the Agricultural Survey the matter cleared up. In English the word "chicken" is a universal but inexact collective for *gallus gallus,* and our questionnaire translated this *gallina.* The Huecorianos made nice distinctions however between *pollos, gallinas,* and *gallos,* and had we asked about chickens, hens, and roosters we would probably have gotten the right answer to begin with.

both consumed at home and sold, untreated, in Pátzcuaro. Pigs are frequently plagued by disease and, if weakened, attacked by dogs. When stricken they are rushed off to be sold while they can still walk. Six sheep worth perhaps 100 pesos apiece and 20 turkeys at about 15 pesos each can also be found. Surprisingly, no goats are owned by village families.

Fruit Trees. Even the poorest Huecoriano has some of the approximately 1,500 fruit trees in his garden. To determine the value of a mature tree would probably defy an accountant, but, bearing in mind the quality of the trees, relative prices in the United States, as well as the exchange rate factor, we would judge that 25 pesos would be a conservative average value, giving a total value of 40,725 pesos, including an allowance for the seedlings distributed by an agricultural agent during our visit.

Land as Capital. Land, of course, can be considered capital only in the strictly limited sense that it is something one buys when investing *ab initio* in a farm and requires abstinence from consumption in order to make the acquisition possible. Given adequate data on land values, some comparison of agricultural investments might be made. Unfortunately, we were unable to gather enough information on prices and values of agricultural land to be able to estimate current values with much confidence. Apparently, sales of nonresidential property are infrequent and only three of the 34 farmers interviewed had purchased agricultural land. The data from this tiny sample of land values are generally inconsistent, although, even allowing for the natural tendency of property owners to monetize their affection for their land, it is clear that land values have risen rapidly in recent years.

Comments on Agricultural Capital. Table 5 summarizes agricultural capital values. Work animals, corresponding in significance to the tractors and trucks of more sophisticated agriculture, are the most important items. Other animals are, relatively speaking, of less value than they would be on modern farms. Together, animals comprise 74.3% of the total value that could be established and fruit trees another 8.1%. In other words, only 17.6% of the capital was in a form conventionally described as such.[6]

[6] In his informative study of small farming in Jamaica, David Edwards

Table 5

Summary of Agricultural Capital Values

	Value	
Category	*Pesos*	*Percent*
Equipment	42,617	8.4
Tools	8,113	1.6
Work animals	202,290	40.3
Other animals	159,040	34.0
Fruit trees	40,725	8.1
Agricultural buildings	38,408	7.6
Land	?[a]	?[a]
	491,193	100.0

[a] Not possible to calculate.

Within Huecorio itself considerable variation exists. One of the wealthier farmers lists his assets as given in Table XXV. Those for which we can account amount to over 26,000 pesos plus 3¾ hectares (9.27 acres) of land, while the poor farmer, whose assets are tabulated in Table XXVI has a total of 526 pesos and ¼ hectare (.62 acres) of land.

offers similar comparative data based on 87 small farms in that country. The composition of farm capital was: land, 41%; crops, 48%; buildings, installations, tools, and stores, 4%; and livestock, 7%. David Edwards, *An Economic Study of Small Farming in Jamaica* (Jamaica, Institute of Social and Economic Research, University College of the West Indies, 1961), p. 125.

Were we to find it possible to include crops and land values in our estimations, the buildings, installation, tools, and stores component would decline proportionately in importance but would probably remain above the relative level of Jamaica. In other words, Huecorianos are more richly endowed in conventionally defined capital than are rural Jamaicans. Among the families surveyed on the island, all implements were hand tools with the exception of two steer-drawn ploughs and a spike harrow. In part, this is accounted for by the different nature of the crops. In Jamaica over 70% of the food crops are tree-borne, whereas short-term food crops characterize Huecorio.

Capital Employed in Manufacturing and Other Occupations

Capital employed in other occupations is noted in Table XXVII. The capital input per capita varies considerably among the occupations. The nine tailors working in Don Juan's *taller* each invested 1,663 pesos on the average in a heavy duty sewing machine and a pair of good scissors. The *comerciantes,* on the other hand, need only invest a few pesos in sacks and containers to carry their goods to market, an *ayate* on which to display their wares, and perhaps a pair of scales.

Apart from their inventory, and some expenditure for shelving and a counter, the storekeepers have little capital. It is usually confined to scales, various measures, and baskets for storage. Carpenters and masons will have the hammers, chisels, trowels, saws, levels, etc., of their trade. One has only a jack plane, and he borrows or buys the other instruments as needed. The investment of a fisherman is confined to a canoe, a paddle, and a net or two. The barber, on the other hand, lists various electric and hand clippers, razors, and a stropper, all purchased, like many of the tools of the artisans, in the United States during a sojourn as a *bracero*.

Two *molinos de nixtamal* should also be included. The price of cooperation from the owner of the mills was *"una botella de whisky,"* and payment of this we deemed would have been unfair to the remainder of our informants, who received no such consideration. Five hundred pesos each would probably be a conservative valuation of the mills.[7]

---

[7] An informant wrote in 1963 *"Otra noticia que me supongo le sea de interés; la sociedad de avicultores de Huecorio han comprado un molino para nixtamal y ya está travajando instalado en el anexo a la tienda de Don Antonio Iturbide. El motor no es de electrisidad sino de Diesel así ya Don José Dongo ya no está muy contento y empiesa a mover sus influencias a su modo digo yo."* In this we are told that the uncooperative gentleman of whom we spoke in Chapter 1 has received his just deserts. The community, annoyed by the high prices he charged, moved to install a competitive mill for grinding corn. Señor Dongo was apparently not pleased by this development.

Inventories

For the reasons we have stated, an attempt to gather inventories of agricultural commodities would have little significance. Two of the four stores in Huecorio were studied, and a list of their combined inventories is given in Table XXVIII. Basic commodities such as rice, flour, cigarets, and soft drinks are common to both. Bearing in mind that the unstarred items are found only in one or the other of the two stores, one sees that the variety is not great. There are 22 commodities common to both and 23 which are unique. This limited range is accounted for by the proximity of Pátzcuaro where a large variety of goods is available, and by the smallness of the local market. Soft drinks are by far the largest selling item, with a continuing demand for them by the schoolchildren. The sale of alcohol is strictly illegal and may now be abandoned as the result of complaints of the rising tide of drunkenness in the village.

If we assume that inventories are twice the weekly gross sales of a store, the inventory would be about 3,000 pesos for the most active store and perhaps 1,000 for each of the other three, or a total inventory of 6,000 pesos.

Inventory of Consumer Durables

The social questionnaire was administered in 36 of the 142 households, and household goods were inventoried. From this, an estimate of the total inventory of consumer durables was made and is presented in Table XXIX. The method of estimation was as follows. The total number of households relevant to the survey is 140, since two of the 142 are in Tzipecua. Of the 36 households surveyed, one was exceptionally affluent in consumer durables and was temporarily excluded in the estimation to avoid an upward bias. In calculating the number of beds, for instance, we subtracted from the total (54) the seven in household B36. The 47 thus arrived at was multiplied by four and the seven beds in household B36 were added back to get the total of 195 for the village.

Some inadequacies in the estimates must be admitted. No allowance in the questionnaire was made for bicycles and musical instruments, and those listed were mentioned incidentally by the informants. Certainly there are several trumpets, a trombone, and a *guitarrón* that are missing. Clothing and the number and value of kitchen utensils had to be omitted because of insufficient time for such an investigation.

Bearing these shortcomings in mind, we cay say that the total value of consumer durables amounts at least to 155,506 pesos, to give a household average of 1,111 pesos ($89 U.S.). Although this is not the place to discuss levels of living, it is clear that considerable variation exists within the community. One dismally poor household contains assets of 53 pesos ($4.24 U.S.) while another, enormously wealthy by village standards, has assets of 14,045 pesos ($1,124 U.S.). That the average level of living is not extraordinary low in terms of comparable underdeveloped countries is indicated by the relatively small percentage of households without beds. It is worth noting that the movement away from the use of the *petate* is such that 11.4% of the households do not own them. The modern convenience of the sewing machine and the semiluxury of the radio are quite widely distributed.

Public Capital, Other Than Buildings

Public capital, other than buildings, owned by the community or by some government agency, consists of the network of streets, a bull ring, a public water system piping a potable supply to 78 houses and strategically located street faucets, and, finally, a grid of wires feeding electricity to the street lights and all but 20 of the homes. The electric power lines were installed in 1937 and the service is extended as new houses are built. The water system was built over the years 1952 to 1958, under the sponsorship of General Cárdenas as director of the Tepalcatepec project, a multipurpose river valley scheme. Although the well, pumphouse, and storage tank are located in Huecorio, the system serves seven other nearby communities as well, and its capacity is inadequate to meet the peak demands placed upon it during the dry season.[8]

Summary of Capital Inventory

The total private capital for which we can account in Huecorio amounts to 1,233,021 pesos. (See Table 6.) This aggregate would rise by perhaps as much as 50% if more refined methods were used to tap additional information, particularly concerning consumer dur-

TABLE 6

Summary of Private Capital Values

	Pesos
Private nonresidential buildings	45,408
Private residential buildings	545,790
Agricultural capital [a]	452,785
Capital employed in manufacturing and other occupations	27,532
Inventories in stores	6,000
Consumer durables	155,506
	1,233,021
Per Capita[b]	1,477

[a] Agricultural buildings and land excluded.
[b] Total population 844, less Tzipecua (9) = 835.

ables and land values. It would rise by at least a further 25% if estimates of public investments could be accounted for. Standing alone, the aggregate capital figure tells us very little, and would have meaning only if similar studies were done in other communities or if Huecorio were to be studied again some time in the future. In the latter case, valuable data on capital accumulation and changing patterns of investment might be revealed. At present the bulk of the investment is devoted to agriculture, clearly indicating the main occupa-

[8] The system cost some 360,000 pesos, and villagers pay water rates of six pesos per month per household. See below, Chapter 6.

tional focus. Per capita investment is modest: less than $200 U.S., even if allowance is made for the data not collected. Even so, this per capita figure may be lower than that of a decade earlier, for a high rate of population growth has in all likelihood more than offset a probable low rate of capital accumulation.[9]

CAPITAL ACCUMULATION

With the exception of those animals acquired by individuals as the offspring of their own animals, all the types of capital listed in Table 7 have one important attribute in common. Their accumulation involved abstinence from consumption.[10] In Huecorio this abstinence takes the same variety of forms that one finds in a more complex economy, although the relative importance of each will be different. Lacking satisfactory quantitative data, we can only make the obvious point that as compared with, say, the larger and contemporary New England town, accumulation in Huecorio by means of taxation will be of less importance while that utilizing communal or self-employed labor will be greater.

Six distinct methods of capital accumulation can be seen in Huecorio:

(i) Voluntary saving in cash or kind. This is the form of saving most familiar to persons from Western cultures, and takes place whenever income is not spent.

(ii) Voluntary saving through self-employed labor. An individual creates some capital asset by utilizing his own skills and energy.

(iii) Voluntary saving through communal labor. Public or private projects are undertaken by a group of individuals cooperating voluntarily.[11]

[9] See below, pp. 186–89.

[10] This statement may trouble the reader when he realizes that some of the capital creation resulted from self-employed labor, as, for instance, when a man builds his own house. This is no exception to the general rule. He is either forgoing leisure, which is a form of consumption, or neglecting some other productive occupation such as farming. This choice of activity lowers the income that he can potentially enjoy.

[11] As we shall see, neither the political nor the social structure of Huecorio allows for involuntary communal labor.

TABLE 7

Classes of Capital Accumulated and Representative Examples

Category	Public	Private
Construction	Buildings: Social Center, church, school, laundry, etc. Communications: Paved or graded roads and streets Utilities: Street lighting, waterworks Economic facilities: Diversion channels for Río Guan Social facilities: Drainage ditches, public garden	Buildings, commercial: Shops, *taller,* stables Other commercial: Irrigation ditches, stone fences Buildings, noncommercial: Homes
Equipment	School desks, benches, etc. One *molino de nixtamal* [a]	Agricultural: Ploughs, saddles, axes Manufacturing: Sewing machines, *molino de nixtamal* Commercial: Scales, carts Consumer durables: Kitchenware, musical instruments, stoves
Inventories	Water in storage tank	Agricultural: Crops in field and storage Manufacturing: Furniture and garments in process Commercial: Merchants' stocks awaiting sale
Other		Animals, privately owned land
Knowledge	Library of Social Center[b]	Knowledge of farming and commerce accumulated by individuals. Literacy. Books and magazines

[a] Introduced by the *Asociación Avícola* after the team left.
[b] Public knowledge is stored outside of Huecorio but available to it in the form of libraries, technical experts, etc. Since these were not accumulated within the village they would be excluded from the table.

At the laundry in the plaza, with baby in rebozo

Work team painting interior of kindergarten

(iv) Involuntary saving through taxation. Huecorianos pay taxes to federal, state, and municipal governments, which in turn create capital directly benefiting Huecorianos.[12]

(v) Involuntary saving through inflation. Inflation may lead to capital accumulation through the redistribution of income from those with fixed money incomes to others, such as speculators, whose profits derive from rapidly rising prices. A further necessary condition is that these profits should be ploughed into capital formation.

(vi) Credit. Available from both village and external sources, credit comes from a variety of institutions.

Voluntary Savings in Cash or Kind

Except for the very poor farmers who cannot even put aside seed corn for their next year's crop, all Huecorianos engage in saving even though they themselves may not consider that they are so doing. Of the 53 individuals who were queried about their practices, only 21 said that they had saved in 1961. Nevertheless, as in all communities dedicated to agriculture, crops—or the cash from their sale —are held to permit a more even flow of consumption throughout the year, and half of those who admitted to saving verbalized this as their motivation. However, if we bear in mind that Huecorio is a net importer of corn, it is clear that from the point of view of economic development this form of saving has no significance, since it does not release resources for capital accumulation. Indeed, an analysis of individual cases reveals that only seven of the 53 persons accumulated net savings in 1961. The amounts varied from 50 pesos to 3,000 pesos, but only one farmer was included in this group. Farmers' incomes are generally too low to facilitate the accumulation of a cash surplus, although farmers as well as nonfarmers utilize accumulated crops to provide liquidity. One relatively well-to-do family, for instance, had sacks of lentils, wheat, and *frijoles* stored in a bedroom, and these were disposed of to meet the emergency of the

---

[12] We made no attempt to measure this, although undoubtedly the aggregate tax payments made by Huecorianos are less than the over-all benefits they receive from the various levels of government.

housewife's illness. The usual custom is to retain savings in the form of cash, but money will sometimes be transferred into a stock of corn, which is not only liquid but also profitable. The same purpose is achieved, at a greater risk and lesser liquidity, by other villagers who lend trading profits, in amounts as high as 2,000 pesos, at 5% a month.

Only four of the respondents were saving with the clear intent of accumulating real capital. Two of them were saving to build houses, and the others to buy agricultural equipment.

Further light on voluntary savings can be seen by examination of housing construction. Over the decade prior to 1962, houses were built on an average rate of four per year.[13] Only in one case did an individual borrow to construct a house,[14] and the general practice is to buy the materials out of savings. Since house values average about 3,433 pesos and since about half of the cost of house construction in Huecorio is usually the nonwage labor of self and relatives, it is implicit that the savings involved amount to perhaps 6,866 pesos a year, or about 8 pesos a year on a per capita basis.

Savings are, of course, devoted to other capital, such as work animals and tools, although our data do not tell us in such cases whether the savings were made prior to a purchase or subsequent to it. In the latter event, a form of credit would be involved. Nevertheless, all indications are that the volume of voluntary savings is extremely low indeed.

Such voluntary saving as does take place is concentrated among a few persons in trading, salaried employment, egg production, and migrant labor. The only known exception to this rule is one farmer who was able to save 300 pesos from an income of 6,500 pesos gained by a specialization in cash crops. Two village merchants have saved from profits, and in one case the earnings went into two *molinos de nixtamal*. Two *comerciantes* reported large savings—2,000 pesos in one case and 3,000 in another. Wage earners reported small savings ranging from 30 pesos to several hundred. One young girl who earns about 40 pesos a week as a seamstress puts from one to three pesos a

---

[13] The basis for this estimate is detailed in the section on rate of capital accumulation, below.

[14] The amount involved in that case was 300 pesos.

week in a "piggy bank" for spending money at *fiestas,* but this never aggregrates more than 30 pesos before it is claimed. A chauffeur, on the other hand, had saved 500 pesos toward building a home.

These sums are insignificant compared with the potential contributions of the *granjeros*. At the time of our visit, none had quite completed the amortization of the initial investment. Profits ranged from 2,500 to nearly 6,000 pesos, and the *granjeros* talked of investing those profits in agricultural equipment. In addition, through voluntary contributions to an *Asociación* revolving fund, the *granjeros* were already saving at an average rate of 500 pesos a year.

Before the closing of the border to migrant labor, the most important voluntary savings had come from the *braceros*. Most of the men repatriated at least half their earnings to Huecorio, and the more enterprising among them invested rather than dissipated the savings. Antonio Iturbide, for instance, returned with $600 U.S., which permitted him to open a store. Geronimo Roca bought an irrigation pump for $160 U.S., thereby tripling his productivity. Ricardo Arizpe bought a sewing machine in the United States for $62 U.S., and was able to escape from an agriculture that he had learned to detest.

The verbalized motivations for voluntary saving in cash or kind were several, although careful testing would be necessary to permit a valid ranking. Apparently the most important was the need to even out the consumption flow in the face of wide seasonal swings in income from agriculture. For most farmers, income suddenly ceases in December and returns only with the wheat harvest in April or May. Fishermen, on the other hand, have a lean time of it during the summer months, when frequent storms upset the lake waters and drive the fish to the bottom.

Liquidity, in the sense of a fund ready to meet emergencies, is also important, and one woman informant gave this as the principal reason for keeping 3,000 pesos in her home. Saving is also directed toward specific objectives such as having cash to spend at *fiestas,* for building a home, or for acquiring a productive asset. The very few persons who are able to accumulate more than 100 pesos in cash may lend to fellow Huecorianos.[15]

---

[15] See section on credit, below.

Finally, voluntary saving is sporadically prompted for social reasons. According to their means, all families are supposed to make cash donations to support such things as *fiestas* or the *Centro Social*. The individual contributions are small, ranging from the 20 centavos that might be collected from a couple on the dance floor at the Center to ten pesos from a well-to-do family toward the cost of decorating the church or hiring a band. One person, who was believed by all to have a bad conscience, sponsored a mass once a month. Although the term "voluntary" does not always fit in its strictest application to these donations, and while the burden is indeed uneven, the costs of these social activities are well spread throughout Huecorio. Other studies of Mexican villages emphasize that a very important means to status is for a man to sponsor a religious *fiesta* entirely from his own resources, perhaps pauperizing himself in the process. Economic life in Huecorio, however, is almost as secular as that of the New England village.

As far as could be ascertained, no Huecoriano deposits money in a bank.[16] Indeed, only one person out of the 46 queried on this matter saw any advantage to that practice. Large sums in bank notes—as much as 3,000 pesos in one case—are kept in the home, even though all respondents but one were aware that banks pay interest. Even though there is a bank in Pátzcuaro, the majority of persons claimed that it was just too inconvenient to make deposits there. What was meant by "inconvenient" was not always clear. In three cases the reference was specifically to liquidity. "You might need the money right away and have to take it out. It's just like playing a game." Four persons felt that the sums of money they had—500 pesos in one case—were not large enough to go through all the procedures. Another four persons felt that income opportunities were better elsewhere. Bank rates were not high enough, and one could earn better on a short-term basis speculating in corn, or in the long run by buying a cow.

Two men felt that banks were robbers that were sticky about releasing deposits and paying interest, but the general attitude to the

---

[16] A possible exception might be the *granjeros* who have contributed to the revolving fund of the *Asociación Avícola* at the rate of one peso for every bird and bag of feed purchased. This is not a true bank and the deposit cannot be drawn upon but merely borrowed against.

bank appeared to be one of indifference rather than hostility. We would speculate that, to a villager, the bank with its well-dressed officers and patrons inspires an awe and reinforces a timidity that present a barrier as formidable as a closed vault.

Voluntary Saving: Self-Employed Labor

In a group where incomes and stocks of cash are low, one would expect to find that capital creation would usually involve individuals in making their own tools, equipment, and so on. In Huecorio, however, self-employment possibilities are not fully exploited in this respect. Only in the construction of houses does one find wide use of nonwage labor. Of the 13 cases studied in which the present owners built their houses, only one was contracted out entirely. In this case a *bracero* gave his father the entire 13,000 pesos involved.

In six of the cases, the owners hired masons to lay stone foundations but finished the work themselves with the aid of male relatives. This intrafamilial reciprocal cooperation was used exclusively for the labor in the remaining six houses. No payment is involved, although the home builder will give meals to his father, brothers, and uncles who pitch in. They, in turn, anticipate similar assistance when they start building.

While the contribution to the value of the building of nonwage labor is about 50% for houses, it falls to about 12% for the next most important category, the *granjas*. In only one case was all the labor undertaken by the *granjero* himself (aided by his young son). Although the owners made some small contribution in the other ten cases, the bulk of the work was contracted out even when the *granjero* himself had the necessary skills. One example serves to explain this pattern. One skilled mason hired other masons to do the job, and he gave two reasons for doing this. First, his wages were higher than those of the masons he hired, and to absent himself from his steady job would be wasteful.[17] Second, he was able to borrow for the labor as well as

---

[17] One may recognize here an application of the principle of comparative advantage.

money costs. Since the *granja* promised a monetary return, the hazards of indebtedness raised less apprehension than would have been involved in mortgaging a house, for instance.

Another category of capital which can sometimes be accumulated by using self-employed labor is agricultural equipment. While it is perhaps unreasonable to expect villagers to make steel ploughs, wheelbarrows, or pumps, the levels of skill involved in making devices such as wooden ploughs, traces, and yokes are not high, the materials are readily available, and such equipment was indeed made in the early American farmstead. Yet few farmers made these devices. The total value of the wooden ploughs, traces, and yokes in Huecorio was 3,195 pesos, of which value only 175 pesos, or less than 5.5%, was created by the farmers themselves.

The situation with regard to agricultural tools is even more surprising. The Agricultural Survey data indicated that only one of the tools used was made at home. Admittedly all the tools listed contain some metal and there is no foundry in the village; however, wooden handles for axes, mattocks, shovels, etc., could be whittled relatively easily.

With respect to the utilization of their own labor for the creation of capital, it would appear that Huecorianos are not fully exploiting their abilities.

Voluntary Saving: Communally Employed Nonwage Labor

The satellite villages of Mexican *municipios* have neither political autonomy nor fiscal resources. Lacking the power to tax, village leaders when faced with demands for public projects must either petition higher authorities for funds or rely on voluntary cash or labor contributions from fellow villagers. In Chapter 5 we will discuss the patterns of communal cooperation, and we are concerned here only with describing this nonwage labor cooperation as it relates to capital accumulation.

Men of Huecorio are continually being called upon to donate labor time to community projects. In some instances a political or social leader will request the help of a single individual who has a needed skill. For instance, Salvador Gorozpe was called in after his regular work was finished in the afternoon to install iron bars in the window of the Social Center.[18]

More frequent, however, is the *faena,* a communal work project called to repair or construct a public facility. Although all able-bodied men are supposed to make themselves available for the *faenas,* attendance is poor and the burdens are unequally borne. On one occasion during our stay, an effort was made to dig a ditch to drain a large body of stagnant water from a street. Only 40 males turned out of a potential of 211 who were 16 or over.

One other important project of a quasi-public nature was the diversion of the Río Guan. In 1961, *ejidatarios* with land in San Pedrito, La Peñita, and La Lagunilla banded together to dig a series of channels to divert the stream and enrich the area by deposits from the floods of summer rains.

In terms of potential communal benefits, there is great scope for many public projects, but organizational difficulties in an individualistic culture without fiscal resources usually frustrate those who wish to take initiative.

Inflation as Forced Savings

As previously mentioned, two conditions are necessary for inflation to lead to capital formation. It must be associated with the transfer of income from one group which is forced to reduce consumption by paying ever higher prices, to another group which in turn must utilize this transferred income to acquire some capital asset.

Data on price movements in the Pátzcuaro region are lacking, but food cost indices for Mexico City show an annual increment of slightly more than 2% a year from 1958 to 1962.[19] This is some-

[18] The bars were installed to prevent the theft of sewing machines which had been given to the community by CREFAL. The money to buy the supplies had been raised at a dance.

[19] Specifically, the index was 142.9 in 1958 and 157.2 in 1962. (*Comercio Exterior,* Banco Nacional de Comercio Exterior, S.A., Mexico City, June, 1963.)

what less than a wild, runaway inflation, but could conceivably result in the forced savings–capital accumulation sequence.

In the context of Huecorio the situation is more difficult to analyze. Farmers and merchants might conceivably gain from secularly rising prices, and one of the storekeepers, as mentioned above, has turned his trading profits into two *molinos de nixtamal*. Superficially his case would seem to prove the point, but a difficulty remains. Were these profits the product of inflation, or merely the normal result of hard trading? The first of the two *molinos* was installed by the trader in 1949 while Mexico was still being buffeted by an inflation of war-time origin. Thus forced saving might well have had a part to play in this case. Monopolistic profits from this first mill made possible the acquisition of the second.

Credit

Credit is distinguished from voluntary savings in cash largely by the time dimension. Credit recipients do their saving after the acquisition of the asset rather than before it, and for this privilege must usually pay rather than receive interest.

When asked how they felt about borrowing money, Huecorianos universally verbalized a reluctance which, when the matter was further pursued, turned upon a sense of economic insecurity. One's ability to repay a loan was determined by the elements, which one could not control. Heavy or unseasonal rains, frosts, winds, or droughts could ruin harvests, and obligations to extinguish debts would add burdens to already difficult situations.

Of interest is the adaptation of certain types of credit to this condition. Two such customs are the practice of offering land and its crops to a creditor for a specified period, and the practice of the *Asociación Avícola* in amortizing loans from the future production of the *granja*.

Their protestations notwithstanding, slightly more than half of the Huecorianos interviewed admitted to having borrowed money. In the Social Survey, for instance, 36 persons were asked what they did when they had insufficient money to buy basic necessities. Six claimed that this problem never arose but 18 of the remainder said they borrowed small amounts to see them through.[20] Similarly, 19 of the 34 farmers interviewed had also borrowed, although not necessarily for some agricultural purpose.

Sources of credit available to people in Huecorio are both informal —from friends or moneylenders, for instance—and institutional— from banks or the *Asociación Avícola*. Although it may be more common than our data suggest, only one person reported resorting to consumer credit from stores. In any event, the four stores in the village confine themselves to cash sales.

It is infrequent that employers lend money to their employees, but this is due to the obvious fact that few Huecorianos are salaried workers or wage earners. Again, only one such case was reported, and in keeping with the institution of benevolent paternalism no interest was charged on this loan, which was for 400 pesos.

In terms of the number of transactions involved, one finds that in Huecorio the most common loans are for small amounts of less than 100 pesos, usually entered into to facilitate consumption during slack agricultural periods, although sickness or a need to acquire trading stock sometimes figure as reasons. These loans are informal, short-term, carry no interest, and are transacted within the village among relatives and friends.

Larger loans are sometimes contracted within the village, and although there was insufficient consistency to permit easy generalization about them, they frequently involved the payment of interest, the offering of security, and had as their purpose some productive endeavor. The amounts involved in the seven reported instances ranged from 150 pesos to 2,000 pesos, and the repayment periods from two months to one year. Although hearsay had it that village interest rates were as high as 10% per month, money interest was levied in only two of the cases and that was at the rate of 5% per month. However, in two cases, including one where interest was charged, land was offered as security and the lender had the right to work this land during an agricultural cycle—a practice which effectively raised the interest charges. Even these larger loans do not involve formal, signed

[20] The 12 who did not admit borrowing said that they simply reduced the amount they would eat at these times.

agreements, but are arrangements between two persons who are—at least when the agreement is reached—friends. Large loans are usually for productive purposes such as acquiring goods to trade, becoming a *bracero,* or building a stable.

The four village storekeepers also receive credit from Pátzcuaro wholesalers. Antonio Iturbide, who started his store with money earned as a *bracero,* not only will borrow large sums within Huecorio, but is advanced up to 1,200 pesos in commodities at no interest.

One final, informal credit mechanism involves the purchase of capital goods. The sewing machines used by those working in the *taller* are purchased from a *compadre* of Don Juan. Not only do the workers receive a small discount, but also, once they have made the 100-peso down payment, no interest is charged. Similarly, one Huecoriano negotiated during our visit to buy a 1947 Dodge truck with a nonfunctioning 1½-yard dump body. The price of 6,000 pesos was to be paid off without interest in 500-peso monthly installments.[21]

In general, then, one can say of the informal credit arrangements so far discussed that, perhaps because of the personal relationships between creditor and borrower, they do not involve an effort to exploit the weak position of a supplicant. The same cannot be said of the activities of certain individuals residing in Pátzcuaro known as *acaparadores.* Although the literal translation of this term is "monopolist," they are, more accurately speaking, moneylenders. One villager, discoursing on the Revolution, spoke of them in this way.

> Many of these same priests and politicians have risen again. They have offended the Revolution and continue to subjugate the *campesinos.* The rich ones always say, "Look, if you want money to go into business I cannot lend it to you. Do you want money to go to *el norte*? I will lend it to you." There is here in Pátzcuaro a fellow, an *acaparador.* He has done this many times and even so they keep going to him and he relieves them of 5% a month. Me, when I wanted to go to *el norte* I got the money together by selling some pigs and chickens.

[21] It is an interesting commentary on the relative scarcity of capital goods that the author bought a similar 1947 Dodge truck in the United States in 1956 for $75. At the current exchange rate the Dodge in Mexico sold for $480 U.S. Both trucks were alike in their general state of disrepair.

Although certain of the facts related by the informant would not appear to be correct, the general characterization of the *acaparadores* as a group that takes advantage of the weak position of the *campesino* is probably true enough. The data offered in Table XXX suggest that while the *acaparadores* do indeed lend to *braceros* they will also lend for agricultural activities. The rates of interest vary, but we found nothing to suggest why this variation exists. The *acaparador* referred to in the above quotation made the last five loans listed in the table, each one at a different rate. He has recently adopted the banking practice of discounting all or part of the interest, and this leads, of course, to a higher real rate.

There is a special activity associated with the *acaparadores* known as *el trinquete del 8 de diciembre*. The following quotation is from a special report on the *trinquete* prepared by one of the research assistants, Señor Bolívar. The information did not come from the villagers themselves, but rather from informants in Pátzcuaro. We would infer from this that the unfortunate practice does not frequently occur in Huecorio.

The word *trinquete* in Spanish, or more accurately in Mexico, is generally used to denote a person who does not act in good faith. For example, a person who takes a thing lent to him and does not return it has made a *trinquete*. By the same token, a person who takes advantage of others who have an urgent need for money by buying unharvested crops at less than the market price, is also making a *trinquete*. In other words, the expression *trinquete* signifies many things founded on bad faith which benefit a few and injure many. There was a *trinquete* in Huecorio when one man who was *jefe de la tenencia*[22] took advantage of his position and sold several pieces of land belonging to the village and then spent the money except for a little that he handed over.

The *trinquete del 8 de diciembre* is like this. As the national fiestas of Mexico and Pátzcuaro are those of December 8th, *Nuestra Señora de la Salud,* and January 12th, *Nuestra Señora, La Virgen de Guadalupe,* all good citizens or good Catholics want to buy new clothes and visit the fairs in Pátzcuaro to enjoy

[22] This incident will be amplified in Chapter 6.

these, their great days. Those people who want to attend, but have insufficient income at this time for the expenditures, have to sell their corn to the *acaparadores,* who buy it from them at a minimum price.[23] They take advantage of their necessity to exploit the poor *campesinos* in this way. *Acaparadores* work in other ways too.

We know that at times they control the prices in the market, although this is rare because the government has offices that regulate grain prices. Some villagers think that the *acaparadores* are mixed up in this too.

Last year the *acaparadores* did not want to buy wheat from local people because, they said, they had brought it from Sonora at a lower price. Is this true or just another trap to rob the people more? How did one person acquire 30,000 hectares of land? Did he lend money to *campesinos* and take title to their lands when they could not pay? [24]

It can be said that commercial banks play no role for the people of Huecorio. Although they are aware that, with security or a cosigner, one can borrow at 3% monthly from a commercial bank, it is felt that the banks do not like to lend to the poor. *"El probe toda la vida es en el suelo."* [25] Although there may be other reasons why Huecorianos are timid about entering the portals of commercial banks, it is also true that they rarely have valuable assets the clear title to which can be assigned.

The official source of agricultural credit for those with private holdings is the *Banco Agrícola y Ganadero Michoacano,* and it was clear from discussions with the manager of the Pátzcuaro office that although no Huecorianos had approached them for credit the bank's officers were most sympathetic and responsive to Huecorio's needs.

[23] The expenses take place just before the corn crop is harvested. The *acaparadores* buy the crop at half its market value while it is still in the field. It must then be delivered to them when harvested. Cash payments are not accepted by the *acaparadores,* and in the event that there is a crop failure the farmer must honor it with the following year's harvest.

[24] One can infer that, had the farmers not had the protection of the *ejido* system, the *acaparadores* would have been able to acquire their lands with the consequent retrogression to latifundia.

[25] "The poor spend their life on the land." The spelling of the noun *probe* for *pobre* is not accidental. This variation was frequently found.

The credit is supervised, and technical advice is given when needed. However, the bank's terms of reference apply only to privately held land, and the minimum area assignable as security is five hectares. Only one of the 34 farmers interviewed had private holdings above this minimum—in this case 8.5 hectares scattered over 11 different locations. This farmer had no need to call on the *Banco Agrícola,* since he could acquire credit through the *Asociación Avícola.* The *Banco Agrícola* normally supplies short-term credit for working capital but can also facilitate the purchase of tractors. For Huecorianos these are even less accessible than credit, since the minimum area for which they are thought to be advantageous under Mexican conditions is 50 hectares.

In nearby Villa Escalante there is an office of the *Banco Nacional de Credito Ejidal,* which offers credit to *ejidatarios* on the security of their crop rather than on their land, which cannot legally be mortgaged. Again, no record was found pertaining to Huecorio, and it was inferred that, since this credit is given not to individual *ejidatarios* but only to *ejidatarios* united in a society, the Huecoriano's individualism and preference for working alone had stymied the necessary cooperation. A few years previous to our investigation, 35 people had joined together to get 200 pesos apiece from the *Banco Ejidal* in order to buy animals. The bank was unwilling to extend more than 50 pesos to each farmer, and the attempt was abandoned. Societies of *ejidatarios* are not easy to establish, since, in the words of the villagers, nobody wishes to undertake the responsibility of leadership.[26] Under these conditions, even small failures are likely to stifle further efforts.

Certainly the most promising credit development has been the creation of the *Asociación Avícola,* described in Chapter 2. CREFAL is now attempting to make the association independent and self-sustaining. The credit of 100,000 pesos extended throughout the sphere of influence in 1956 had risen to 940,900 pesos outstanding in 1961. In recent years no payment arrears or defaults have taken place.

[26] For amplification of this important problem, see Chapter 6 on social structure.

The economic effects of the program in Huecorio have been noteworthy for the 11 local members. We have seen that changes have been brought about in substantial increases in income, capital accumulation in the form of *granjas,* improved agricultural techniques resulting from the application of *gallinaza* to the *milpa,* a new willingness to experiment resulting from the demonstrated fact that one can, indeed, control one's environment, and investment in new areas such as transportation and irrigation facilities. A CREFAL report[27] adds that social change has been stimulated.

> The fact that the *campesinos* have common interests within the Association, has been a great stimulus in ridding them of the traditional isolation in which they live, facilitating and reinforcing relations among neighbors in their own community and even in other communities, among which in times past there existed strong rivalries. The constant visits to the Association, the meetings and the trips of groups of *campesinos* from one community to another—have been favorable factors in diminishing hostile attitudes, permitting an interchange of ideas, experiences and opinions which have had a significant impact on their cultural elevation.

By means of contributions of one peso for each bird and sack of feed purchased by the members, the revolving credit fund built up by the *Asociación* now permits the members to branch out into new lines of endeavor. We have seen that Francisco Cruz purchased a horse and cart that permitted him to become a teamster, that two *granjeros* planned to invest in pumps to irrigate their fields, and that in 1963 the members from Huecorio acting as a group acquired a *molino de nixtamal* to break the monopoly of José Dongo. In the same year they started a furniture-making *taller* to expand local employment.

The *Asociación Avícola* is now the most important means available to Huecorianos for large amounts of cash for productive purposes, and it promises to play an increasingly important role in changing the economy of the village. This role, however, is somewhat

[27] José Manuel Luján, *Breve Reseña del Programa de Crédito Avícola Supervisado,* p. 13.

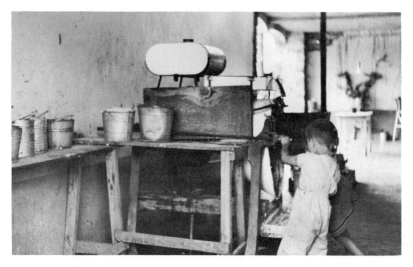

New molino de nixtamal, *introduced by the* Asociación Avícola *in 1963*

Apiculture, introduced by the Asociación Avícola *in 1964*

constrained by the very small number of individuals who avail themselves of its funds through membership in the *Asociación Avícola*.

Although it is clear that credit is used to meet a wide variety of
needs, the retail consumer credit that plays such a large role in
wealthy countries is almost nonexistent. Similarly, mortgage credit
for home construction is not used, although borrowing may take place
for home improvement. Measured in terms of the number of transactions, small informal cash loans for consumer emergencies probably comprise the most important form of credit.

RATE OF ACCUMULATION OF CAPITAL

Since we lack a base line inventory of capital goods for an earlier
year, it is impossible to determine accurately the rate of capital accumulation for Huecorio. Nevertheless, a calculation is attempted
which permits us to ascertain a minimum floor on the amount of
capital accumulated during the ten-year period preceding our investigation. We would judge that no accumulation of agricultural
tools or work animals has taken place, largely because the number
of farms seems to have been stable. The chief item in the equipment
category is the steel plough acquired in the 1930s, and the only addition during the period was the irrigation pump. Although farmers did
acquire work animals during the decade, in all probability they were
replacements for animals that died.

In Table 8 we offer estimates of accumulated capital.[28] Two aspects
of each estimate must be justified—the value itself, and the reason
why we judge this capital to have been created during the decade
under consideration.

The interest in milch cows is a relatively recent phenomenon, arising as it has from the rapidly increasing demand in the Pátzcuaro
area. Thus, this table gives about half of the 1962 total value of the
milch cows, although this may be an underestimate. The value of the

[28] Based on data derived from other tables in this chapter and in Appendix D.

TABLE 8

Estimate of Capital Accumulated in Decade

Prior to 1962 (pesos)[9]

Private	
Agricultural buildings[b]	33,408
Agricultural equipment[c]	2,000
Agricultural tools[d]	0
Work animals[d]	0
Cows[e]	60,000
Chickens[e]	37,515
Fruit trees	?[f]
Nonagricultural tools[e]	4,780
Nonagricultural equipment[e]	16,170
Store inventories[g]	1,000
Nonagricultural buildings[e]	137,320
Home improvements[h]	?[i]
Consumer durables[e]	76,932
	369,125
Public[h]	
Social Center improvement	1,459
Waterworks	?
Public washhouse	?
Children's playground	?
Public park	?

[a] For explanation of the rationale for the inclusion of the various items, see text.

[b] The *granjas* and one *corral*.

[c] The irrigation pump.

[d] The number of farmers did not change significantly during the period in question. Tools and work animals were probably replaced rather than accumulated.

[e] See text.

[f] Possibly positive but no means available for calculation.

[g] Of the one recently opened store. The inventory of this store was 3,000 pesos but the lower figure makes an allowance for the closing of another store during this decade.

[h] Insufficient data.

[i] Question mark indicates no means available for calculation.

chickens represents all those populating the *granjas,* since they were introduced since 1956. Nonagricultural tools include those of masons, carpenters, and the barber. Because virtually all of these were purchased by *braceros,* it is safe to assume their recent acquisition. The principal items in the nonagricultural equipment category are the sewing machines of the garment workers and, again, the *taller* is of recent vintage.

The nonagricultural buildings are houses, and the incremental value estimate is slightly more complicated. There were 142 occupied houses at the time of our visit, housing a total of 844 people or 5.94 persons per occupied house. In 1950 the population was 555 persons. If we apply the occupancy rate to the population difference, we estimate that over the 12-year period 48 new houses were built at an average rate of 4 per year.[29] The average house value is 3,433 pesos, which implies an increment in value over the ten-year period of 137,320 pesos.

Home improvement has also been significant, but of an indeterminate pace. According to the report of the CREFAL team working in Huecorio in 1957, they induced the installation of 15 latrines and 21 tile or cement floors in that year. These installations are representative of the home improvements that Huecorio has recently seen.

Consumer durables such as radios, phonographs, sewing machines, bicycles, beds, and kerosene and gas stoves are of recent acquisition, although since electricity came to Huecorio as early as 1937 we cannot assume that the electrical goods all were introduced during the period under consideration. Nevertheless, they were bought by returning *braceros* and were observed to be relatively new. Thus, for their increment the 50% of total value that we assumed is undoubtedly an understatement.

A certain amount of the public construction took place during this period, although values cannot be assigned except in one case.

If we concern ourselves momentarily with the private capital accumulated in the decade prior to 1962, we see that at the very least

[29] This rate of construction is roughly confirmed by the difference between the total for inhabited and uninhabited houses in 1956 of 134 and the total for 1962 of 162. This is a difference of 28 as opposed to a difference of 24 by our calculated rate.

the increment in value was 369,125 pesos, which is about 30% of the total private capital for which we were able to account. Looked at in another way, it would appear that private capital grew by perhaps 42.7% during the ten-year period. If the capital-output ratio had the highly favorable value of 1.3, then this rate of accumulation would be just sufficient to maintain the level of living of a population growing at slightly less than 3% a year. But such a favorable capital-output ratio is unlikely, and private capital accumulation alone would be insufficient to meet the needs of Huecorio's growing numbers. Public capital formation may offset this inadequacy, but the data are insufficient to be of help in the analysis.

CAPITAL UTILIZATION

The factor of production known as capital is by definition scarce in all societies, but particularly so in underdeveloped countries. Accordingly, in the stolid academic literature of economic development and exhortations of persuaders of policy, prime attention is focused on the need to allocate capital wisely through the device of economic planning. And on an *a priori* basis one might reason that this acute shortage of capital would lead one to find, even in the context of microsocieties such as that of Huecorio, a conscious and reasoned attempt to conserve and direct it to its most beneficial uses. Such, of course, is not the case.

Other authors, notably Hirschman,[30] have pointed out that a universal characteristic of underdeveloped countries is their casual attitude to the maintenance of capital. We find in Huecorio the faucets of the public water fountains damaged beyond repair, streets rotting under constant abuse, and drainage systems clogged and useless. Were this phenomenon confined only to such public utilities we would quickly reach the conclusion that we are observing a manifestation of a lack of the sense of social responsibility. But, at least until recently, houses have decayed and privately owned irrigation facilities have

[30] Albert O. Hirschman, *The Strategy of Economic Development* (New Haven, Yale University Press, 1958), Chapter 8.

degenerated. The notion and practice of maintenance are nonexistent —surely a paradox in the light of the desperate need for capital.

Although we are not satisfied that our explanation is complete, certain factors are clear. The kind of equipment which is mainly used —ploughs, spades, etc.—require only the most elementary care, and the realization of the need for greater attention is not transferred when the instrument becomes more complex and delicate. Similarly, the cash resources have been limited and have not offered surpluses which can be used for the cash outlays that maintenance often requires.

Historically (and paradoxically), the idea of conservation is not necessarily associated with a conservative, traditional society. Since one is subject to great forces beyond one's control, one does not make an effort to manipulate (hence conserve and maintain) the various elements that influence one's well-being—the weather, soil, seeds, tools, and so on.

Nor is there any attempt by some high village authority to direct the use to which capital will be put. Huecorio is *laissez-faire* in this respect, even though the sense that one is or should be master of one's own destiny is not yet manifest. A reallocation of capital and other resources is taking place away from agriculture to egg production, manufacturing, trade, and dairy farming. The reasons for the shift lie in obstacles to further crop production combined with the profitability of other occupations.

Investment in agriculture has been stifled in recent years, although this may change. Farmers expressed interest in investing in new steel ploughs, irrigation pumps, and tractors. Although several small companies in the United States still manufacture the chilled-bottom steel plough, it is not available in Mexico and Huecorianos reject the ordinary steel plough as virtually useless. Irrigation pumps have not been purchased because of the inability of the average Huecoriano to accumulate the large sum of money involved. The credit available through the *Asociación Avícola* will surely change this. Several farmers, particularly those with larger holdings, saw great advantages in tractors, but the difficulties involved with them are probably insurmountable; unless small, powerful garden tractors can be developed, animal traction will remain unchallenged.

Severe restraints, in particular those imposed by poor and inadequate land, suggest that Huecorio can never exploit a significant part of the wide range of the application of technology to agriculture that has been utilized in other parts of the world.[31] The future of its agriculture is limited and, as its people come to recognize this, they transfer their resources and energy to other pursuits.

[31] We recognize that history has a way of mocking those bold or impertinent enough to try predictions. Agronomists may devise ways to amplify many-fold the returns of minifundia, or Mexico may become so rich in capital that she can reconstitute by huge investments the poor soils of places such as Huecorio. Neither, however, is a likely possibility, and by the time these improbables occur, Huecorio is likely to have become a suburb of an expanding Pátzcuaro.

CHAPTER 5

ENTREPRENEURSHIP

A L T H O U G H economists generally agree today that the critical element determining whether or not a nonsocialist economy will develop is that factor of production that we call the entrepreneur, the definitions of entrepreneurship commonly used tend to be too confining, since they stress the leadership characteristic and ignore the general contribution of the mass of imitators who follow. For instance, to Schumpeter the entrepreneur was an innovating leader who introduced new products into the market or new methods of production, and to Hagen, the entrepreneur is the creative businessman whose main contribution is the economic innovation he introduces.[1] Common to both of these writers, and to the rest of the literature, is the implicit characterization of the entrepreneur as a business leader —rather "big time," as it were.

Our contention is that for economic development to take place entrepreneurial behavior must be quite widespread. It can be recognized in Huecorio as well as Monterrey. Differences are mainly a question of degree. An entrepreneur, then, is *one who innovates in*

---

[1] Joseph A. Schumpeter, *The Theory of Economic Development* (Cambridge, Harvard University Press, 1949). Everett E. Hagen, *On the Theory of Social Change* (Homewood, Ill., Dorsey Press, 1962).

At work in the taller.

the use of resources with a view to their continual expansion. He is
not necessarily a leader, nor the *first* to introduce an idea. What is
important is that he accepts the notion that there can be a better way
to utilize his assets, and that he generally seizes opportunities when
they show up. He may also actively seek out better methods and products. But this is not always necessary. If it were, the 11 Huecorianos
who started egg production at the instigation of CREFAL could not
be called entrepreneurs. Yet most of them are, at least in the sense
that they put into practice a very important innovation that substantially changed their economic position. In other words, innovational attitudes can be spurred and encouraged from the outside—a
very important part of the approach to economic development that
Hirschman discussed.[2]

Economic development cannot take place without capital accumulation, and therefore it is not enough to innovate and then dissipate
the profits. They must be ploughed back, at least to a large extent.
For this reason the *comerciantes* of Huecorio would not be considered
entrepreneurs. They may be shrewd and money-wise, but they are
nevertheless just traders making a living.

[2] Hirschman, *The Strategy of Economic Development,* Chapter 1.

193

CONDITIONS OF ENTREPRENEURSHIP IN HUECORIO

The entrepreneur need not necessarily be a grand or spectacular impresario. The farmer who constantly tries to increase his output by using new tools, seeds, or techniques, the tailor who finds a cheaper way to cut cloth or looks for a new market, the trader who buys a truck so he can sell a greater volume—all make some contribution to their society, small and unnoticed though their achievements might be. To overlook, ignore, reject, or suppress these contributions would be an injustice and disservice in any country. Indeed, successful economic development must have a wide base, and for this reason we shall consider the circumstances of entrepreneurship in Huecorio along with evidence of the pertinent psychological, social, political, and economic characteristics of the community.[3]

Societies bound by tradition and those undergoing change are distinguishable from each other. The important elements of the traditional society are its rigid structure and sense of fatalism. It has a recognized social hierarchy with little mobility, and the various groups are tied together by mutual obligations which may be expressed by such phenomena as paternalism and *compadrazgo*. Its stability is reinforced by the sense that the world is ungovernable—it cannot be manipulated—and this resignation to fate is supported by a fear of change. Thus, one might find that those whom one does not know— foreigners for instance—are a threat to one's little world, which

---

[3] Whereas in principle it is possible to isolate the various social science disciplines, very frequently this cannot be done in practice. Psychological characteristics must sometimes be inferred from social behavior, and social interactions become clear only by examining individual attitudes. For this reason we do not find it possible to deposit certain of our findings in psychological pigeon holes and others in the sociological classification; therefore, these two approaches are lumped conveniently, but not neatly, together. Hagen's definitive work on social change arrived while our field work was under way, and there was no opportunity to recast our investigation to fit his trenchant structure. Nevertheless, his analysis is most appropriate and we have found it a useful point of departure even though our data may not fit with precision.

offers a thin security only because it has not changed and is therefore predictable. Needless to say, elements of traditionalism exist in all societies, and since one cannot measure its degree, social scientists face great difficulty in assessing the progress a society is making toward dynamic change.

To an extent, to construct the model of the progressing society one need only reverse the signs. Rigid hierarchy is replaced by social fluidity, fatalism by experiment and analysis, isolationism by xenophilia, etc. But a new element is added—the secular, apolitical leadership of the creative entrepreneurs. Hagen argues, in a fashion more elaborate than we can do justice to, that entrepreneurs usually arise from a group which, having once had status in a society, lost it, perhaps to an invading foreigner. The psychological retreatism which would have resulted from the invasion would give way after many generations to a new, positive, and creative attitude. If the normal routes to status, such as inherited mobility or political service, were closed, this attitude would be channeled into money-making pursuits. Among other things, the new class would manifest a dissatisfaction with the old. It would wish for change, believe that change could take place, and believe that it, acting individually or collectively, could effect that change.

What can we say of Huecorio? Is it stagnant and traditional, or is it undergoing change? Is there a recognized and rigid social hierarchy?

Elements of a hierarchy can be found in any society. In Huecorio the evidence of a rigid stratification is not persuasive. Huecorianos regard themselves as rather humble, and hold a certain respect for priests, professional people, and others. But the status of those whom they respect is not ascriptive, and it is not unattainable. In other words, it is believed that upward mobility is possible, if not for oneself at least for one's children.

Farmers were asked what kind of work they would like to do if they were not farmers.[4] Except for one man who said he would like to be an artist, photographer, and sculptor, the replies showed simultaneously limited imagination and the realistic recognition that a

---

[4] The replies tabulated as follows: trader, 13; artisan, 8; laborer, 3; no change desired, 3; clerk, teacher, artist, factory worker, 1 each; don't know, 3; no answer, 3.

person mature in years would have little possibility of acquiring a sophisticated skill. Therefore, they thought principally in terms of trading and semiskilled labor.

Higher aspirations were held out for children, as can be seen in Table 9. The replies to the question, "What occupations would you

TABLE 9

Farmers' Replies to Question: "What occupations would you like your children to follow?" [a]

	Sons	Daughters
Professional (doctors, teachers, etc.)	13	10
Office work	3	4
Get an education	5	3
Aviator	1	1
Farmer	1	0
Factory work	1	3
Trader	1	2
Artisan	2	1
Get married	0	2
Fisherman	1	0
Leave Huecorio	1	0
Not farming	7	0
Whatever they want	1	1
They won't study	1	1
Unspecified	1	2

[a] Most farmers mentioned several possibilities, so that the number of answers recorded does not coincide with the number of farmers interviewed.

like your children to follow?" indicated acceptance of the view that upward mobility is possible principally through the vehicle of education. For most Huecorianos, the respect for education remains congealed in a wish, although about a dozen families have made the necessary effort to send their children to secondary school and at least two families have enabled their children to pursue higher education. It is worthy of note that seven farmers were quite explicit in their wish to get their sons out of agriculture.

A hierarchical structure is said to exist within the Mexican family, with authority cascading from the oldest male to the newborn baby, each individual obeying those who are older and ordering about those who are younger. The cult of *machismo* is reputed to be so pervasive that any male in the family can order any female about, regardless of age. Furthermore, the hierarchy is supposed to be enlarged by the extended family, within which the patriarch or matriarch holds the ultimate reins.

We found no evidence of any of these manifestations. That the eldest male is respected and obeyed may or may not be true in any given family. Some husbands hold their wives in fear and obedience through their brutality, but it was quite clear that in most cases the woman was an equal partner who would disagree or contradict her husband as much in public as in private. *Machismo* will be discussed later, but we saw no evidence in Huecorio of the predominant role it is supposed to play elsewhere in Mexico. Neither does the hierarchy of the extended family exist for Huecorianos. There is a clear preference for individual households.[5] Children and parents continue to visit back and forth among the households, but rigid parental control has broken down. Even unmarried daughters now challenge paternal authority, and some children will no longer accept their parents permanently in their homes even when they are aged. These manifestations of independence did not always exist, and older men nostalgically and pathetically appreciate younger persons "who treat us with respect."

Other vestiges of the hierarchical structure remain. When this structure exists in its purest form, clearly delineated mutual responsibilities and respect tie together the several classes. For instance, the *patrón* is supposed to embrace his beloved workers in a protective shield while they in turn reward him with an affectionate loyalty.[6] Paternalism still exists to some extent in Huecorio as a behavior pattern on the part of the more powerful or affluent. They might, for instance, provide free instruction in some skill to their employees, or arrange to obtain insecticides free of charge for the farmers, etc. It has frequently been maintained that there is a counterpart belief on the part of the villagers that they have a right to such protection.

[5] See Chapter 7 on population.
[6] All these matters will be more fully considered and supported in Chapter 6.

This allegation will be discussed in Chapter 6, but it can be said that while the expectation of paternalistic care still exists, it is weaker than one would anticipate. By the same token, villagers show loyalty to persons who befriend them, but do not do so unquestioningly. They readily identify as *egoístas* those whose attitudes are condescending, and no person who works with or for them is immune to criticism.

Fatalism, another measure of the tradition-bound society, is essentially a belief that events are predetermined and thus are not subject to human control. In the various questionnaires, 56 persons were asked about the principal problems they faced in trying to improve their life and how they thought those problems might be resolved. As Tables 10 and 11 show, most respondents felt that their family's position could be improved, although they were understandably unspecific as to how this might be done. Few persons appeared resigned to their position—*"pobre soy, pobre acabaré"* (poor I live and poor I will die)—although it is arguable that some of the 13 who did not reply were also fatalistic. Since six of the 13 giving no answer had previously said they had no problems, the total for those expressing fatalism would be a maximum of 12, or less than 20% of the sample.

In their attitude toward outsiders, Huecorianos show the entire conceivable range, but if the generally hospitable reception accorded our team is any indication, they are not to be characterized as xenophobic.

In summary it can be said that, although elements remain, Huecorio does not fit the image of a traditional society.

Does it meet the more positive criterion of a milieu favorable to the nourishment of entrepreneurial attitudes? What of social mobility? Do Huecorianos believe that they can improve their social, as distinct from economic, position? The adult Huecoriano believes that it may be difficult for him, but not for his children, to move. He has had before him the demonstration that mobility is possible as Huecorianos have moved on to become teachers, nurses, and in one case a doctor. Society may present difficulties to him, but not unscalable ramparts.

To establish beyond doubt the considerations that motivate a person is difficult, in part because motivations are complex and usually hidden. Although few reject the behavioral standards set by their fellows, it does not follow that all people are necessarily preoccupied with a desire to achieve higher and higher social status. One could, for instance, read the Huecorianos' aspirations for their children in two ways. Those persons who want their children to have a profession could conceivably wish selfishly to bask in reflected glory. They could, however, be expressing the hope that their children should be economically more fortunate than they.

The second interpretation is supported by a number of factors. One is the rather emphatic rejection of agriculture, which in Huecorio is drudgery without reward. More than anything else, Huecorianos

TABLE 10

Replies to Question: "What are the principal problems you find in trying to improve your life and that of your family?" [a]

Economic		
A lack of money	18	
A lack of employment	9	
A lack of agricultural inputs	7	
Difficulties in going to United States	1	
Fixing house	4	
		39
Pertaining to Children		
Education of children	5	
Providing inheritance for children	2	
Other	3	
		10
Pertaining to Health	2	
		2
Other		
Fatalistic	1	
No answer	1	
No problems exist	6	
		8
		59

[a] The totals for Tables 10 and 11 do not agree, since some gave more than one answer to the first question and six persons replied that they had no problems.

TABLE 11

Replies to Question: "How do you think these problems might be resolved?"

	Number of Replies	Indicating Individual Responsibility for Solution	Indicating Social Responsibility for Solution
Economic			
Work harder	7	7	
Borrow money	1	1	
Buy land or other agricultural inputs	5	5	
Improve water supply	2		2
Improve employment possibilities	5		5
Start factories	2		2
Start public works	1		1
Go to United States	4	4	
Leave Huecorio	3	3	
Control prices	1		1
Education			31
Educate children	3	3	
Get scholarships for children	1		1
Fatalistic			4
Specifically fatalistic statements	3		
Have bad weather	1		
Who knows?	1		
			5
Other			
Cooperation	1		
What would you suggest?	2		
No answer	13		16
			56

are preoccupied by economic problems, as one can see by observing Tables 10 and 12. In the latter are tabulated the replies of 52 respondents to the question, "What are the things you seek in this life?" Although the range of concerns is wide and the women express a greater concern for their families than do the men, a preoccupation with the economic is clear. Indeed, only seven of the 52 (13%) were not concerned with the economic aspects of their life.

For entrepreneurship to take root it is necessary that individuals feel that they themselves have a reasonable chance of manipulating resources to their benefit. We have seen that Huecorianos tend not to be fatalistic, and the relevant part of Table 11 would suggest some sense of individual responsibility for one's position in the world. Of the replies stipulating economic or educational solutions to individual problems, 23 can be interpreted as indicating that the respondent felt that he could improve his lot by his actions,[7] while 12 felt that they would have to rely on that external thing called "society."

In addition to this sense of individual responsibility, some persons in the village show an even clearer understanding that the environment can be manipulated. One external manifestation of this attitude is extended and logical reasoning. When persons can trace cause and effect through a number of steps and argue in either abstract or concrete terms without invoking folklore or mysticism, it is reasonable to conclude that they are at least flirting with the scientific state of mind, and having been so tempted are amenable to the persuasion that the world is an orderly and ultimately understandable place. Having this power to reason does not automatically make an individual an entrepreneur, but on the other hand economic success is not achieved by wishing or invoking gods.

We made no tests of the reasoning power of Huecorianos, and the examples we cite were serendipitous fruits of other parts of the study. Geronimo Roca had sought and found satisfactory explanations of phenomena that puzzled him. He found reasons why certain steel ploughs caked dirt, why the *ejido* deteriorated, why one should plant

---

[7] This does not mean that the individual necessarily had the resources or was indeed able to change things. All we infer is that he felt, somehow, that in some vague way, he, rather than society, was responsible for his position and its improvement.

TABLE 12

Tabulation of Replies to Question "What are the things you seek in this life?"

	Males		Females	
Economic				
Expressed in living levels	25		7	
Expressed in terms of employment	18		3	
Expressed as desire for land	3		0	
		46		10
Health				
Expressed in general terms	2		1	
Expressed as desire for long life	1		2	
		3		3
Family				
Expressed as concern for welfare of children	3		1	
Desire for education of children	3		3	
Expressed in general terms	2		1	
		8		5
Fatalism				
Expressed as resignation to present lot	2		2	
		2		2
Social Relationships				
Desire to have satisfactory relationships with other people	4		0	
		4		0
Community				
Evidence of concern for community	1		0	
		1		0
Number of replies		64		20
Number of respondents		40		12
Number of persons not expressing concern for an economic problem in their replies		3		4

before rather than after the rains had commenced, and so on. Francisco Cruz argued why lack of water in the village as a whole was his particular problem. "If there were more water," he said, "the crops would be better. If the crops were better people would have more money. With money people would fix their houses and then they would ask me to come and use my carpentry skills." These two examples are not, of course, necessarily representative, but neither do we contend that all Huecorianos are incipient entrepreneurs. We are merely suggesting that social conditions are favorable for entrepreneurship to arise.

More concrete evidence of the view that at least some Huecorianos consider that the world is controllable lies in their propensities to experiment and innovate. Few villagers have actually conducted experiments, although a number mentioned the need for experimentation before new seeds or fertilizers were introduced. Geronimo Roca did experiment with the time of planting corn, but he also felt that the ability of villagers to experiment was limited because few persons could take the implicit risks, living as they do in such dependence on their crops. Ricardo Pérez intended to experiment with an early maturing wheat, but was prevented from doing so through lack of time.

Innovations, on the other hand, have been quite widespread. The utilization of *gallinaza* from the *granjas* in a 50/50 combination with animal manure was introduced by the farmers owning the *granjas,* and the proportions were arrived at after experimentation. The diversion of the Río Guan to raise the productivity of La Lagunilla is an example of a collective innovation. Juan Mirasol's technique of planting vegetable crops that he observes are not being planted by other farmers is a successful innovation of another type. Artificial insemination, irrigation, new seeds, a pure-bred cow, *granjas,* sewing machines, *molinos de nixtamal,* a horse-drawn wagon, and a truck have all been introduced, sometimes at the instigation of outsiders but more often by the villagers themselves.

Resistance to innovation exists, sometimes for technical reasons. Hybrid seeds lose their productivity when grown in small plots surrounded by native corn, chemical fertilizers are inconvenient to spread because the plant rows are very close together or are interplanted.

Organizational difficulties are sometimes to blame. For instance, artificial insemination is not easily practiced when animals cannot be isolated. Institutions such as the *ejido* dull incentives to capitalize the soil, and the custom of fragmentation is partially responsible for keeping tractors from the village. Economic circumstances such as a lack of available credit and lack of marketing facilities also inhibit innovation.

When innovations fail to take in Huecorio, the frustrating obstacles are usually apparent, and, except where intravillage cooperation is called for, the failures do not seem to lie in any inherent flaw in the society itself. On the contrary, the number of innovations introduced in Huecorio in recent years is testimony to a more positive spirit.

We would venture the suggestion that the Huecoriano is rational rather than irrational in his behavior.[8] In addition to their willingness to experiment and innovate, they exhibit a lack of folklore in agriculture, limited efforts to use religion to influence harvests, limited interplanting of competing crops in the *milpa,* crop diversification, and considerable variation in agricultural techniques.

In some cases Huecorianos have rejected things that have seemed quite rational to outsiders. In 1954 the CREFAL team tried to persuade villagers to vaccinate their pigs at six pesos a shot. In 1962 adult animals could be sold for an average of 75 pesos, and the price eight years earlier was undoubtedly less. The modal number of pigs in a farm household was three, which meant that a farmer had to find 18 pesos in cash for an expenditure of undemonstrated value. In general, the farmers' attitudes toward animal care are as rational as circumstances will allow. This care is costly, and accordingly will be given only to the more valuable animals.

Few households have ready supplies of cash above their minimum daily needs, and this perhaps explains another pattern. One can make the generalization, subject to minor exceptions, that if an innovation involves the expenditure of cash it will not be made to non–cash-earning crops. For example, pumps and seeds will be bought for cash-

[8] One of the difficulties in ascertaining the existence of rational behavior lies in the fact that it must be determined in terms of objectives. Two persons may react to a given stimulus, yet because each has a different goal—security, prestige, excitement, cleanliness, etc.—their reactions may be different.

earning vegetables, but the innovations applied to corn were the use of *gallinaza* fertilizer and the river diversion, which did not involve cash outlays. Since few farmers produce even enough corn for their own needs, an expansion of corn production will not return a cash income to repay a debt incurred by innovating.

In some cases it might be that such an innovation would enable the farmer to produce more corn in place of supplementing his crop with purchases, thereby releasing sufficient or more than sufficient cash from other activities to cover the cost of the innovation. But this ignores the matter of timing. Cash income arrives largely in the summer from vegetable crops, just at the time an earlier accumulation of corn has been used up. The cash is needed to tide the farm family over until the next corn harvest in December. This is a difficult pattern to break, and the farmer, pressed by deadening insecurity, cannot commit himself to a risky indebtedness, particularly in view of the uncertainty surrounding the potential innovations themselves.

What of Hagen's views concerning the origin of the entrepreneurial class? There is some slim support for it in Huecorio. The village existed before the coming of the *conquistadores,* and the status of the villagers and their self-respect were destroyed by serfdom under the *haciendas* that were established. The case would seem to fit, except for the difficulty of the span of four centuries. If the theory allowed such leeway in the time dimension, all social groups could be said to have suffered status loss at some time in their history and no group could be distinguished thereby.

What of retreatism? The Tarascans of the lake region have been charged with passivity, and were not known for their overt aggression during the Revolution and the turbulence that followed. Casual observation would suggest that many individuals in the village still bear this yoke of personality while others do not. And do the people of Huecorio wish for change? About this there is no question. Although older men are conservative and women more than men sometimes show fatalism, the Huecorianos are deeply dissatisfied. They quickly express shame of the village with its unpaved, dirty streets, its lack of amenities and run-down appearance. They want more comfortable homes and an escape from energy-sapping drudgery. We would judge, then, that Huecorio is a society undergoing change, and that the social obstacles to the development of entrepreneurial attitudes are giving way.[9]

There are, of course, other social aspects of entrepreneurship not emphasized by Hagen, particularly those suggested by Max Weber's pioneering work on the Protestant ethic and the spirit that nourished capitalism.[10] Although this work was a contribution in its emphasis on noneconomic aspects of economic growth, the central role it gives to Protestantism has now been reconsidered. Were Protestantism a precondition for the rise of the entrepreneurial attitude, missionaries might have more justification for their work and the prospects for economic development in Huecorio would be dim. We did not feel it prudent to pursue a deep investigation of religious attitudes in Huecorio,[11] but our interim judgment is of a community of believers but not of fanatics. Those who were clearly innovators ranged from the only dissenter in the village to sincerely devout men. We must, however, speculate on another aspect. It was claimed by nonvillagers that the Church, in preaching resignation to one's fate, sapped people of their will to surmount difficulties. Further investigation may reveal that members of the village who are still retreatist are also especially devout.[12]

The prospect of earning profits is strong persuasion to the entrepreneur, and they provide the funds necessary for the accumulation of capital. Although Huecorianos know little about the accounting of costs, they are very much aware of profits, and upon no occasion did we hear a condemnation of profit-seeking such as Zinkin reports for India.[13] Girls buy fruit, candies, and drinks at one price and sell them for another at religious *fiestas,* and traders like the activity because of the pesos it brings in. The waking hours of the elders of the Pérez

[9] For more details on their aspirations, and the causes of the change they are undergoing, see Chapter 6.

[10] Max Weber, *The Protestant Ethic and the Spirit of Capitalism* (London, Allen and Unwin, 1948).

[11] At the time of our study, a researcher working on a nearby island found his advances rebuffed when it was believed that he had a subversive intent to convert.

[12] One such group consists of fishing families from Carián who meet both conditions. This is not, however, enough on which to build a case.

[13] Maurice Zinkin, *Development for Free Asia* (Fair Lawn, N.J. Essential Books, 1956), Chapter 6.

family are constantly devoted to the bakery, garden, *milpa,* dairy, and cows in pursuit of slim margins indeed. Antonio Iturbide leaves his *milpa* to his brother so that he can devote his time to the store, where the income is greater. Juan Mirasol has the skills and tools of a mason but does not use them, for there is more money in his vegetable garden. Not all Huecorianos pursue profits so single-mindedly—some drink, others escape from agriculture to something where they may earn even less—but profit-taking is accepted and no sanctimonious morality inhibits entrepreneurship in this respect. It is worth noting that the five individuals in Huecorio who are most respected by other villagers are all entrepreneurial types, but in only one case was the individual's economic position given as an explicit reason for his selection.[14]

Apart from social sanctions, political aspects of entrepreneurship also exist. Governments can stifle entrepreneurship with a baleful philosophy or smother it in a mass of regulation. With the exception of some aspects of *ejido* regulation, neither of these inhibiting factors has any force in Huecorio. Licensing requirements are minimal, affecting only the retail stores, and there is little opportunity for corruption. On the other hand, little is done to encourage innovation and capital accumulation. The only official stimulant is the agricultural agent, whose activities, as we have seen, are limited in their effectiveness.

The primary factors inhibiting innovation and capital accumulation are clearly economic. In agriculture these are the fragmentation and shortage of good land. The shortage cannot be overcome. The quality can be improved only by heavy capital inputs in irrigation and fertilizer, and in view of the alternative uses of financial resources there is no indication that Mexico would achieve a maximum benefit from these investments. Fragmentation and peculiarities of land tenure can be resolved by land reform, but the political and organizational difficulties would suggest that we cannot look forward to any amelioration here.

A shortage of capital to initiate changes plagues both agricultural and industrial development. In agriculture its unavailability is con-

[14] The winners of the "popularity poll" that we conducted were Ricardo Pérez, Juan Barrera, Antonio Iturbide, Francisco Cruz—and José Dongo.

nected with the legal nature and small size of individual holdings, and normal commercial channels of long- and short-term credit are not available to Huecorianos since banks can find more secure and stable risks. Innovation usually involves an initial capital investment which is large in relation to an individual's annual income, and such investments are therefore impossible out of the meager savings that a person can accumulate by working in Huecorio. Individual savings spark important innovations mainly in those cases where a man has accumulated relatively large amounts while working as a *bracero* in the United States. Sewing machines, pumps, and inventories of grain have been accumulated in this way. But *bracero* earnings are not the only permissive factor. Capital is sometimes accumulated in trading, and this may have permitted José Dongo to open his two *molinos de nixtamal.* All of these contributions to capital are overshadowed, however, by the role of the *Asociación Avícola,* which was beginning to spark profound changes through its revolving fund. The availability of supervised credit on reasonable terms is probably *the* important catalyst needed to generate widespread entrepreneurship in Huecorio.

A number of individuals in Huecorio fulfill the necessary criteria for entrepreneurship, in that they innovate and accumulate capital. Certain ones came to our attention, but undoubtedly there are others as well.

FARMERS

Only one person who was exclusively engaged in agriculture meets the criteria, although several men innovated in agriculture as well as in other fields.

Ricardo Pérez

Don Ricardo is about sixty, and heavy labor has bent his tall back and gnarled his hands. At the time of our visit all his family were together, with the exception of one son in his thirties who had gone to Uruapan in 1955 and taken over the family's trading post, an act that led to dispute, litigation, and bitterness when the others had tried to reclaim it. Visitors find Don Ricardo's household one of the most hospitable in the village, and in the clean and tidy surroundings one is cheered by the easy laughter of his daughters or a son's voice raised in song. With Don Ricardo were his wife, one son, Baltazar, four adult daughters, one of whom had with her her son of an early marriage, and, for a short while, a *peón* who had come from the *tierra caliente*. To the visitor this large and lively family seems casual and relaxed. The tension was well concealed only to reveal itself in formal interviews.

Don Ricardo, with his wife and children, had by dint of constant effort a relatively comfortable yet precarious life. At the time of our visit the net family income exceeded 11,000 pesos, and over his lifetime Don Ricardo had seen the accumulation of at least 25,000 pesos in assets, the largest shares being in animals (12,000 pesos) and buildings (8,600 pesos). Don Ricardo's contribution had been principally in devoting himself to the assiduous cultivation of about half a hectare of good land near the lake, where he grew some of the vegetables that his wife and one daughter took for sale in Apatzingán. Baltazar and the *peón* worked the balance of the 4½ hectares, which were planted principally in cereals. The other daughters sold milk, baked bread, or engaged in trading, household work, or community service.

Don Ricardo complained that he was poor, a feeling undoubtedly stemming from the constant indebtedness with which he was faced. Responsible for the indebtedness were the expenses of medical care for his wife, of the litigation in Uruapan, and of building a stable to house the Holstein cow. Other persons in the village, however, considered him wealthy, and by village standards he was. Don Ricardo was plagued from his youth by an affinity for drink—a habit that cost him many days of labor and the respect of his children, although he nevertheless gained the respect of villagers and outsiders alike by his dignity and leadership. Others said of him, "He is a man of respect and before him one feels a little less." "He is a friend and will not betray a confidence. If I tell him something I know no one else will know about it."

Don Ricardo and his family had not only accumulated productive capital, but he had innovated to some extent. Unlike other farmers, for instance, he always purchased the seeds for his garden plot from a store in Morelia where one could buy the more reliable imported varieties. At the instigation of the agricultural agent he had built a new dairy to house the Holstein, and at the urging of the same agent he intended to experiment with early wheat. Don Ricardo is one of the few persons in Huecorio who have tried chemical fertilizers. The results were poor, and they barely got their money back.

There is considerable tension within the family, and to the younger ones this presentation of Don Ricardo's innovations is far too sanguine. They had wanted to join the *Asociación Avícola,* but they say that Don Ricardo, in a demonstration of clinging to traditional patriarchy, killed the idea. "He is now finished with life and unapproachable when it comes to new ideas. He just wants things to continue as they are and save money and enjoy life." The younger children are ashamed of their father's drunkenness. This hurts Don Ricardo, and when he was asked to tell us the name of a man he admires he mentioned Antonio Iturbide because "he is younger than I am and has treated me well and with respect." Don Ricardo's wealth has been built upon a small holding of land, and he says, "We don't have much luck in business." To make up for the paucity in land and this lack of "luck," he and his wife have worked extremely hard. Don Ricardo escapes with the bottle, his wife never at all.[15]

This leads to another source of conflict. The señora complains that her sons and daughters do not like to work. "How can you make them do so?" But when one speaks of their parents' work to the children, the reaction is strong. Olga has seen her mother's constant drive and her twice-weekly trips to Apatzingán weighted down with sacks and boxes. "Trading," she says, "is a form of slavery." Don Ricardo wants Baltazar to manage the farm lands. "Why does the boy want to go away and study to be a singer?"

[15] She confided that in her youth she wanted to save for a vacation but that had never come to pass.

THE MEMBERS
OF THE ASOCIACIÓN AVÍCOLA

The members of the *Asociación Avícola* meet the criteria for entrepreneurship, and relatively detailed information was gathered for Miguel Salinas, Francisco Cruz, and Geronimo Roca.

Miguel Salinas

Miguel is probably the largest landowner in the village and inherited nearly ten hectares, 8½ of which are scattered in 11 large and small private plots. Huecorianos respect his impartiality and the faith he has in them, and a twinkle in his eye betrays his gentle sense of humor. Like Don Ricardo, he has not traveled but has a curiosity about the world, and he actively seeks advice about ways in which he can raise his productivity. During our visit he searched out counsel on starting an apiary and an orchard, and says that he would have introduced chemical fertilizers if someone could tell him what to use and how to use it. In an unusual demonstration of confidence he asked our help in measuring his fields, for he did not know how much land he had. While this was being done we visited an isolated plot on the top of a small hill, and Miguel asked us to what use the field could be put. We suggested that it might be a good location for his orchard but wondered aloud about the problem of theft. "This is no problem," he said, "I would put a fence around it and plant some trees near the fence. People would take the fruit off these trees and would leave the rest."

"Work brings all," he says. Miguel has combined this open-mindedness with hard work to build up a net worth of 38,847 pesos. About 22,000 pesos of this is in buildings, about 12,000 in animals, and the balance is in tools and household items. In addition, he had saved 2,500 pesos in six years out of an annual net income of about 13,000 pesos. Miguel's major innovations have been his membership in the *Asociación Avícola,* and the use of *gallinaza* and better potato seeds. He has tried, unsuccessfully, to improve his oxen through artificial insemination. To the time of our visit Miguel's most important accumulation of capital had been in the original *granja,* which he doubled in size when he saw its value.

Miguel is relatively young (43), but in his household there are ten persons including his mother, wife, and seven children, the oldest of whom is 15. The children are not old enough to contribute economically, but Miguel's wife and mother sell his agricultural products. Because of his relatively large holdings, Miguel must hire the services of four or five *peones* during the agricultural season. He and his family have always had sufficient; nevertheless, the thing for which he searches in this life is *"el progreso"*—to live and eat better.

Francisco Cruz

Francisco Cruz, approaching 50, is a slight and graying man of quiet and rather sad demeanor. Other villagers characterize him as friendly, cooperative, sincere, and proper. "He wants us to progress," they say, "but he does not have much energy." To Francisco the most important things in life are his family and loyalty among people. "Loyalty must depend on another person's qualities rather than on whether he is a friend, a *compadre,* or a relative. I think it is important to work hard and I want to be friends with everybody."

Francisco's family is extremely close, and it is apparent that his concern for his children is reciprocated by affection and respect. We recall, for instance, how sloe-eyed 12-year-old Josefina fondled her father's hair as we plied him with questions. Fifteen-year-old Juana went to work at Don Juan's *taller* at her father's bidding, although she says that she would rather work as a maid. Elpidio is 22 and also works at the *taller* to earn the money necessary to permit him to attend high school at night. Francisco impressed on Elpidio the hard life of the farmer in Huecorio, and the boy is studying assiduously to give reality to this father's wish that he escape it. Francisco's wife is very successful as a *comerciante,* and she used to supplement the family income by sewing, until the poor light of the candle ruined her eyesight.

The necessity of providing for his wife and children sent Francisco twice to the United States as a *bracero,* and he would like very much to return with his family. "But how is this to be done?" One needs money, passports, work, and a *patrón.*"

Although Francisco regards himself as a farmer, he works only half a hectare *a medias* and helps his father on the latter's property. Francisco toils, but without energy, as a farmer, carpenter, teamster, *granjero,* and musician. Of all these pursuits carpentry gives him the greatest pleasure, but there is not enough demand for this skill in Huecorio, and he cannot leave the village for he must attend the granja several times a day. Francisco innovated not only in introducing the *granja* but also in redesigning the roof structure to enlarge the floor area, and his idea was incorporated in the *granjas* subsequently installed. He has assumed the role of teamster for the village. To protect the goods he carries with his horse and rubber-tired cart, he made a cover from old feed sacks and waterproofed it with the wax of candles. His activities as a musician are casual, and he, Salvador Gorozpe, and others often rise well before dawn to participate in a *mañanitas.*

Hard work and ingenuity bring Francisco and his family a net income of about 12,000 pesos, and they have accumulated a net worth of about 15,000 pesos, principally in buildings but also in equipment such as the cart and three sewing machines.

Geronimo Roca

Geronimo is one of the most interesting persons in Huecorio. In appearance, residence, and to some extent attitudes, he is less of a *mestizo* and more of a Tarascan than the other entrepreneurs of whom we speak. He is young (39), tall, dark, and matches the stereotype Indian whom most Americans come to know only in two dimensions. He lives with his parents, wife, and children—11 persons in all—in Carián. In his attitudes he tends much more than the majority of Huecorianos to think of collective rather than individual solutions to problems. More than others, he acts generously and speaks for the community. When, for instance, collective action to provide tables for the community center bogged down, Geronimo bought the wood and made the tables himself. He recognizes that irrigation is most efficient if conducted on a relatively large scale, and has tried, although unsuccessfully, to persuade others to join him in the acquisition of high-capacity equipment. Having only about two hectares of land, he feels acutely the need for more and has tried to persuade others to join him in colonization. CREFAL officials were quick to appreciate his articulateness, intelligence, and concern for the community. They have labeled him a leader, but as Geronimo says, *"Un líder que no tiene gente no es líder."* [16]

His frustrating lack of success in this respect worries Geronimo, but several factors are responsible. In his advocacy of voluntary, communal solutions to village problems he fails to recognize the characteristic individualism of the *mestizo*. It is significant that in the "popularity poll" of respected villagers, 37 names appeared but Geronimo's was not among them. Why? For one thing he is an "Indian of Carián," and those people themselves recognize that other villagers look down upon them. Geronimo is an outspoken anti-cleric. He says, "I am a believer but not a fanatic," a distinction more likely to be taken by others as a criticism than as a fine point. Geronimo, perhaps mistakenly, claims too that people talk about him because "my father was a Revolutionary." We see here a detail in the larger canvas of people divided by a Revolution still remembered.[17]

Failing as he has in solving problems in a wider context, Geronimo has had to work alone with the support of his parents and wife. He reported that only three or four hours' sleep a night suffice for him. Certainly he has energy, but his intelligence in introducing innovations is equally important. He introduced a *granja* and later doubled its size. Upon his return from working in the United States he pur-

---

[16] "A leader without people is no leader."

[17] Although Huecorianos wanted the fruits of the Revolution and seemed to support it passively, they did not identify with it and may have resented the "extremists" in their midst.

chased the only machine-powered irrigation pump used in Huecorio. He has experimented with various methods of planting corn, tried artificial insemination for his oxen, and tried hybrid maize, which he found unsuitable because it grew too slowly. Geronimo has used a net income of 10,000 pesos to build up capital of 25,674 pesos, distributed as follows:

House	9,000
Granja	6,500
Animals	6,250
Tools and equipment	3,696
Household items	228

The heavy emphasis on productive capital is apparent here. Geronimo's house has only one room and *cocinita*—a tiny kitchen. The floor is of dirt and the furnishings almost nonexistent. All the other entrepreneurs have beds, chairs, radios, and other furnishings, and Geronimo's valuation of his household furnishings of 228 pesos is far less than the minimum of 1,541 pesos found in the houses of other entrepreneurs.

His affection for his children is perhaps less articulate than that of others, but in his drive to overcome his confining environment he clearly has them in mind. "I have seven children. I have just this much land and cannot divide it in seven parts. If I do not buy more land, how can I fulfill my responsibility?" Education is also recognized as an escape, and Geronimo intends that all of his children should attend secondary school. He is making the necessary sacrifice.

THE STOREKEEPERS

Antonio Iturbide

Antonio Iturbide returned to Huecorio in September, 1961 from Uruapan, where he had been a *comerciante* for a number of years. With $600 U.S. he had earned while a *bracero,* he opened a store in a house shared with his brother, which opens on the main village plaza.

He had borrowed twice in the store's 11 months of operation, and has regular lines of credit from his suppliers in Pátzcuaro. Both of the loans—one of 1,000 and the other of 200 pesos—were from village friends, and neither involved interest or liens. They were, he said, "just peanuts," in view of his weekly gross sales of 1,000 to 1,500 pesos. His selling expenses and capital accumulation are financed from these receipts. In 1962 his income was augmented by a modest 692 pesos from wheat grown in two of his fields.

The capital equipment he needs is relatively inexpensive. He had a showcase built, and has a scale and various measuring devices and storage facilities, all of which amount to only 364 pesos in value. He was about to build a new store front for 1,500 pesos, and in the 11 months of operation had doubled the size of his inventory to 3,000 pesos.

His capital accumulation is testimony to his sense of salesmanship. His innovations are unspectacular, but effective from the point of view of expanding sales. To induce customers to his store, he tries to sell *"siempre un poco más barato"* (always a little cheaper) than his competitors.

At the time of the previous year's poor corn harvest, he realized that there would be an exceptional demand for that crop, and he invested in a large quantity. This brings customers, he says, because he always has a sufficient quantity at reasonable prices. He thinks, too, that customers come to him because he has a good selection of goods and displays them for maximum sale. His personality is clearly important. To Antonio all Huecorianos are equal and he no longer has preferences. Others regard him as friendly, helpful, and respectful.

The risks involved in retailing he regards as nonexistent. When he opened up he had only to advise the *presidencia municipal,* and nobody ever comes to inspect his store. He has merely to pay a tax of 21 pesos and 60 centavos each two months to the *Comisión de Rentas,* and has never had to pay a *mordida* of any kind.

Sales vary during the week and by the seasons. They are particularly good during February when there are many *fiestas,* and poor in September when people are buying clothes in Pátzcuaro for the *fiestas patrias*. Sundays are good because people are not working, and on Fridays there is money because people are bringing it in from the Pátzcuaro market. Wednesday is the end of the "fiscal" week, and is bad. Antonio, who is understanding but not approving of his fellow Huecorianos who indulge in drink, sells alcohol illegally. He does it, he says, for otherwise they would not buy other things in his store.

Antonio's father was a fisherman and a farmer, and Antonio, now 39, started his life as a farmer too. He still owns 4½ hectares of land and is one of the few persons in the village who have added to their holdings. In 1947 he bought a hectare of good land near the lake for 600 pesos. He works only two hectares and contracts out the work of growing corn and wheat so that he can devote all his time to the store. The balance of the land is worked by his brother and brothers-in-law without the payment of rent.

Antonio learned how to run a store from his brother-in-law, who runs a business in Colonia Ibarra. "All you need," he says, "is to know how to read and write, something about groceries, and how to handle people."

The store is open from 6:00 a.m. to 9:00 p.m., and had not been closed for a full day at any time. Antonio's wife had her own store in Pátzcuaro, but there was too much competition there and now she devotes herself to keeping house and minding the store whenever business takes Antonio to Pátzcuaro. Antonio is emphatically against hiring a *tendero* to look after the store for him. "He would steal too much."

They have two children, a boy of two, and Luz who is fifteen and attends the *Colegio San Josefina* in Pátzcuaro. Like most Huecorianos, the parents respect education for they have had so little themselves. They do not ask Luz to help around the house, but let her study uninterrupted. When Luz diverts herself in some way the Señora asks if she has no homework, and if she does then it is *"¡Pues andele!"* (Get to it!)

Antonio is a man well satisfied with his life. He would be content if his two children followed it, although, like almost all other villagers, he would be even happier if they could follow some profession. "It is good to be in business. The *centavos* in the pocket give one a marvelous feeling."

José Dongo

Señor Dongo owns one of the four *tiendas,* and introduced the two *molinos de nixtamal* that operated in the village. In addition, he owns three houses, one of which is in Pátzcuaro, and an undetermined amount of land, and he has sent one son to medical school. We do not pretend, however, that the earnings from the store and *molinos* were sufficient by themselves to permit these accomplishments.

When we asked Señor Dongo to discuss his affairs with us, he said he would if we gave him a *"botella de whisky."* Since no other person in the village asked for or received any payment for co-operation, Dongo's request was denied. Both the director of CREFAL and the *presidente municipal* asked Señor Dongo to work with us, but their requests were ignored. Two team members attempted to apply the social questionnaire to Señora Dongo. "It is none of your business. I am very busy and if you want to help me you can get me a maid." We had little more success in obtaining the census data. A little girl answered our knock and—well trained—said nobody was home. But Dongo's son, whom we shall call Felipe, made the mistake of looking out the window and was trapped into answering the basic questions. The replies, particularly those pertaining to landholdings, were clearly false, but at that time we did not have the necessary background data to permit further questioning. Later, however, we obtained information from other respondents and from some documents that enabled us to piece together aspects of Señor Dongo's life, his methods, and his character. In the files of the *Comisariado Ejidal* were some 36 letters and other documents. Fourteen pertained to Señor Dongo, and ten of these had to do with his illegal acquisition of an *ejido* parcel belonging to one José María Adames.

We learn that on September 7, 1953, Señor Dongo went to the office of the Department of Agriculture in Morelia with the complaint that the people of Huecorio were interfering with his right to use a parcel of land formerly belonging to José María Adames, and that one Manuel Martínez, to whom the Huecorio *ejido* commissioner wished to cede the land, had the nerve to harvest the wheat that he, Señor Dongo, had planted. The delegate of the department wrote the commissioner recommending that he permit the plaintiff to continue in quiet and peaceful possession of the parcel. The commissioner replied that Señor Dongo held five *ejido* parcels, two more than legally permitted, and, moreover, he had no right to any land since he was a public official in Pátzcuaro. José María Adames had borrowed from Señor Dongo to buy medicine, and Señor Dongo had taken possession of the land illegally when, with the death of Señor Adames, the debt was not repaid. Señor Dongo claimed his action to be justified since a great deal of money—40 pesos—was involved. Others claimed it was only 25 pesos. Justice finally prevailed, and the parcel in question was handed over to Manuel Martínez.

Although Dongo did not regain this land, he had not exhausted his resources. On July 16, 1954, at the instigation of the villagers, Benjamin Buenrostro, *Secretario General de la Liga de Comunidades Agrario y Sindicatos Campesinos del Estado de Michoacán* wrote the *Procurador General de Justicia* in Morelia asking assistance in obtaining the release from jail of an *ejidatario* (not named) who was imprisoned in Pátzcuaro by the *Juez de la Primera Instancia*—none other than José Dongo. And on January 3, 1958 we find that the regional head of the Department of Agriculture reports that not all of the *ejidatarios* have received their titles. These were in the possession of the selfsame judge in Pátzcuaro, who would not hand them over except on receipt of a *"determinada cantidad de dinero"*—by which is meant a bribe. But justice prevailed again. Dongo was removed from his office for malfeasance.

In another instance, occurring at an earlier date, Señor Dongo found himself at odds with the community, but achieved a success that held until 1963. In 1939 a *molino de nixtamal* had been given to the *Liga Femenil de Lucha Social* of Huecorio by the Department of Agriculture, and it was operated by Juan Barrera, who paid the *Liga* from his charges of 6 centavos for each 9 liters of corn ground. But in 1949 Señor Dongo opened a much more efficient mill and that of the *Liga* lost its clients. This provoked loud squeals on the part of *ejido* officials, who claimed that their mill was adequate for the needs of Huecorio, that the competition was prejudicial to a revolutionary organization,[18] that Señor Dongo had no urgent need to live off such an industry since he had land, animals, and a store and he was inhibiting the progress of the community for personal benefit. Señor Dongo hired a lawyer to counter these complaints made to the *presidente municipal,* and, being within his rights in what is basically a free enterprise economy, he was successful. The *molino* of the *Liga* ceased to operate, and, in manner common to monopolists large and petty, Señor Dongo raised his prices. They reached 70 centavos for ten liters in 1962. In San Pedro, several miles to the west, prices were from 30 to 35 centavos. Said son Felipe, "If the people in San Pedro don't want to cover themselves for their labor, we here do. We charge this price because we have to pay for electric current and our labor is worth more." As a result, many women of Huecorio returned to grinding corn by hand in their *metates*—a most laborious procedure. However, in 1963 the members of the *Asociación Avícola* used their credit to acquire a gasoline-powered *molino,* and the monopoly was finally broken.[19]

Señor Dongo managed in 1940 to become *presidente municipal,* but was forced to step down after only half a year in office. As we have seen, he later became a minor judge of the *municipio* but again was relieved of his duties. At the time of our visit his fall from power was not known in the village, for Señor Dongo took pains to maintain the pretense of his official appointment by traveling every day to Pátzcuaro and being seen about the *presidencia municipal.* He had, however, given good cause for his dismissals both as *presidente municipal* and as judge. In one office or another he had indulged in derelictions. As *presidente* he brought prisoners from the municipal jail to cultivate his lands, and of course did not pay them. He had the prisoners tear up the paving stones in the village plaza and used these

[18] Meaning the institution of the *ejido.*

[19] A correspondent wrote, "Speaking of the *molino* in Huecorio, it seems that the price of the diesel motor was 12,000 pesos and the installation was 2,000 pesos more. It is working well and has lowered prices. For example, Don José used to charge 60 to 80 centavos for each ten liters of *nixtamal.* Now the price is only 30 to 40 centavos."

same stones to repair his house. He sold liquor illegally in his *tienda,* transforming it thereby into a *cantina.*

In view of all this, it was surprising to find that Señor Dongo tied with Don Juan Barrera for first place in the "popularity poll." Those who respected him said: "He is better instructed." "He knows how to reach the people in Pátzcuaro." "He has pull because he has worked in the *presidencia municipal.*" Others, of course, feel differently: "He has no interest in his community. He is one of those who is preoccupied only with himself. He is an egotist and there is no point in trying to get information from him because he has done so many things against the community."

That Dongo himself may not have a clear conscience is suggested by the fact that he arranged every month for a special mass to be held in Huecorio for a purpose not revealed to his fellow villagers.

But Señor Dongo is, withal, an entrepreneur.

MANUFACTURING

Juan Barrera

Don Juan Barrera and his wife, Guadalupe, own and operate the only *taller* that was in existence in Huecorio at the time of our visit.[20] It is attached to their two-story house, which with its eight rooms is one of the largest dwellings in Huecorio. The *taller* was built in 1957 as a *granja,* and the original intention was to double the capacity of the *granja* by adding a second floor to it. Don Juan ran his *granja* for nine months, but because of the cramped living and working quarters in the house itself, it was decided to abandon the *granja* and convert it into the *taller,* which use the room now shares with sleeping, entertaining, and eating. Other than the cost of the room itself, the investment of the Barreras has been only in two sewing machines —one purchased before the war for 300 pesos and the other in 1957 for 1,200 pesos—two irons, and several pairs of shears.

[20] See above, Chapter 3.

The shop is closed only at Easter, Christmas, important *fiestas,* and on Sundays, although Don Juan and Guadalupe frequently work on Sundays. The demand for their services has been so great that they have never had the time to take a formal vacation and must

The taller. *Two-story house; television antenna installed in 1963*

confine themselves to occasional visits to Morelia or Pátzcuaro, where Don Juan might follow a basketball game or they might both see a movie.

The Barreras train the workers without charge, and aid them in buying their sewing machines. The trainee is lent a machine to use and fabric to practice on, and is taught to sketch patterns, to cut, move the pedal, and sew with and without a threaded needle. They must continually practice sewing and must dismantle pieces until they reach a satisfactory standard. When a youngster wishes to learn but has no money of his own to acquire a machine, he is permitted to use machines belonging to others while he accumulates the 100 pesos necessary for a down payment. This may involve a period of two months for beginning workers, who might earn 2 pesos or less per day until their ability increases. The monthly payments average about 70 pesos, which—in view of the weekly earnings varying from 24 to 75 pesos and the costs of the machines ranging from 900 to 1,899 pesos —amount to a substantial and lengthy burden. Ricardo Arizpe avoided this by buying his machine in the United States when he was working there.

Earnings vary for a number of reasons. There are obviously differences in skill, for which experience and motivation can account. Furthermore, not all the workers are in the *taller* all day. The piece rates are determined by Vicki, who supplies the fabrics and takes the semifinished shirts, dresses, cocktail napkins, aprons, and so on, for further elaboration.

The Barreras think that Vicki pays better rates than anybody in Michoacán, and they consider themselves very well paid. Don Juan had worked previously in Uruapan, where, he recalls, he would get only 2½ pesos to make a shirt and four pesos for a dozen pairs of pants, and could never earn as much as eight pesos a day. By way of contrast, Vicki pays ten pesos for a shirt, 15 to 25 pesos for a pair of pants, and Don Juan earns about 30 pesos a day at these rates. Vicki's high schedules are, according to Don Juan, an effective inducement to produce at high quality, and articles are rarely returned to be reworked. Originally Vicki's rates were slightly less—seven pesos for a shirt, for instance—but in view of the satisfactory craftsmanship the rates were raised voluntarily, and neither the Barreras nor the workers have requested any raises. Since the workers are actually employed on their own account, the Barreras neither provide them with meals nor pay their social security. On the other hand, the workers themselves are not required to pay the Barreras for the use of the *taller,* although two assist Don Juan by contributing two pesos each a month for electricity.

The output mix in terms of types, styles, quantities, materials, and colors is determined by Vicki. On the other hand, Don Juan feels that he and Guadalupe must have certain basic responsibilities and skills. They must, for instance, oversee the operation, and this means accounting for inventories of stock and production, calculating and measuring materials, managing the operators, and caring for the machines. The expenses of the *taller* are minimal, the major item being 35 pesos for electricity and perhaps 70 *centavos* for needles each month. In the 22 years in which the Barreras have had a sewing machine, only once have repairs been necessary. Don Juan recalls he once had to replace a plate and that this cost him 13 pesos, although belts costing six pesos are needed every few years. Don Juan keeps no accounts, but like most Huecorianos has a long and accurate memory for financial transactions.

The Barreras have no problems with the *taller*. No licenses are needed, no taxes other than those on the house are paid, and there is no competition. In this latter respect, and in line with his general concern for Huecorio, Don Juan thinks it would be a good idea if other *talleres,* either similar or different, were started in Huecorio. He is open and generous, and has given training to other individuals who could well compete with him.

Don Juan had been a farmer for 23 of his 54 years, but gave up his *ejido* holdings in 1957 when the advantages of the new occupation became apparent. He also worked as a mason, painter, and carpenter —skills which he retains and exploits about his home. Guadalupe was at one time a teacher, but she did not like the constant changing from one post to another. Her skill with a sewing machine was brought to the attention of Vicki by a teacher who worked in Huecorio, and Guadalupe's ability so satisfied Vicki that when there was a need for increased production in 1957 Don Juan agreed to learn the skills from his wife. Initially the Barreras worked alone, but Vicki brought more and more materials beyond their capacity to serve, and at that point —1958—the chickens were invited to leave the *granja* to make way for more operators.

The Barreras are well pleased with their *taller*. Nevertheless, their ability to make more money is limited in their present arrangement. They could only do better by working longer hours, but as it is they frequently work until eleven at night and also on Sundays. It is conceivable that they could do better by becoming independent or by joining a cooperative, but they reject both these ideas.

The Barreras realize that they have neither the knowledge nor the resources to strike out independently. They are not designers, and could not adapt the Tarascan patterns to suit the market. They lack the capital to buy materials, pay workers, and support themselves while they build up the business. But the most important consideration is that Ralph, the husband of Vicki, knows his market and has built up a series of outlets in the United States. Without the experience and knowledge to manage all aspects of a business, Don Juan feels that he would soon fail as an independent.

A cooperative would not work either. Don Juan mentioned a cooperative that was started in Morelia in 1957, and he saw that the members fought over the profits and even wanted to shoot it out. In another case a cooperative had an engineer to run things for it, but the engineer was not honest and did not share the profits. "To operate a cooperative successfully, you need a good person to run it, because when responsibility is shared things get very disorganized."

Guadalupe was equally emphatic on these possibilities. Why make a change? Vicki did not exploit them. On the contrary, they were very fortunate. They need guidance about products, design, and markets, and under the present arrangement they can earn good money. "If Vicki fails so will we, for we are dependent."

In terms of their potential contribution to rural welfare, Don Juan's *taller* and the arrangement under which it operates are as significant as the *Asociación Avícola*. It is worth-while, therefore, to learn a little more of the background. Ralph, or Rafael as he is also known, went to Mexico for a vacation in 1949 and married Vicki, an attractive girl from the lakeside village of Erongarícuaro. He decided to stay in Mexico, and completed his studies at Mexico City College. The shop "Vicki" was started somewhat by accident after they settled in Erongarícuaro in 1952. A Frenchman had been living there and was managing a garment-making enterprise. Vicki made a blouse for him, but he refused to buy more from her since others would make them more cheaply. With this Vicki started to make garments, mainly blouses of the region, to special order. Ralph began adapting local designs to suit tourist tastes, and opened retail outlets in Pátzcuaro and Morelia. In the United States his products are found in the Pan American Shop, Fred Leighton's, and Lord and Taylor in New York, Phoenix in Washington, Camps and Amthor in San Francisco, and in many other stores. This trade has been built up without the need for credit and has been financed entirely from sales.

He does not know how many people are working for him, but the number fluctuates between 100 and 150. It is strictly the putting-out system except for Don Juan's *taller,* and that, in fact, is a modification of that system. Most of the workers are women who embroider materials in their spare time. Unfortunately, this means that production slacks off in the summer at just the time of maximum demand, but at all times Ralph has more demand than he has productive capacity.

Ralph does not seek out his workers, but they come to him voluntarily. He cannot train them but gives them small, simple things at first in order to test them out. There are few problems. The major ones are a difficulty in finding good, evenly woven cloth; the unevenness and inadequate level of production; and a certain amount of pirating of his designs. On the other hand, the quality of the work done for him is high, and he does not often have to reject pieces.

We would calculate the Barreras' family income to be quite substantial. Guadalupe and Don Juan earn from 25 to 30 pesos a day in the *taller,* and the adopted orphan who lives with them contributes about 1,500 pesos a year from the same source. In addition, Don Juan frequently provides room and board for visitors to the village, and this nets at least 500 pesos a year. In other words, the family income for the ten persons in the household is between 17,000 and 20,000 pesos annually. With this, Don Juan, Guadalupe, their daughter Sara, their daughter-in-law Luisa and her five children, and the orphan boy Oscar, live in relative comfort. Their house is large, clean, and well furnished. All sleep on beds, there are two excellent radios and a phonograph, there are good quality living room sets, and theirs is the only house in the village without a primitive charcoal and wood stove for they have instead gas- and kerosene-fired cooking equipment.

Although Don Juan is satisfied with what he and Guadalupe have done, he wants something else for his daughter Sara, for, he says, his work is a trifle *crudo*. Sara's education in a secondary school involves an expense of 75 pesos a month, and they hope that this will lead her into nursing; but Sara has had some experience as a dance teacher and hopes to follow this profession. Guadalupe's satisfaction with her life and accomplishments is slightly blurred because Huecorio, with its limitations, could not provide her son Augusto with a decent livelihood, and so he has gone to live in the United States. Thus the family cannot be together as she would like it to be.

SOME CONCLUSIONS REGARDING ENTREPRENEURSHIP IN HUECORIO

Without sophisticated psychological testing of both entrepreneurs and nonentrepreneurs, it is not easy to state with certainty and accuracy the characteristics that distinguish those whom we have identified as entrepreneurs from noninnovating Huecorianos. Certain general and imprecise statements are possible, and even to these José Dongo may give the lie. The common denominators would seem to be a willingness to work hard, a high degree of cooperation among adult members of the family, a high level of intelligence, and a broad concern for the community in which they live.

The entrepreneur candidate certainly works long hours, and intensively. Except for a small number of villagers among the very lowest economic groups, to work hard is an accustomed pattern for Huecorianos. However, were we able to measure precisely the intensity and duration of their efforts, we would likely find the entrepreneurs high on the effort scale.

The families of the entrepreneurs combine their economic efforts. One partial exception is Juan Barrera's daughter-in-law Luisa, who does not work in the *taller* but manages her children and the household with the aid of a servant. This pattern of combined effort is true of most village families, but in the more ambitious families the income-earning activities of the wife and adult children take precedence over their housekeeping functions.

A more clear-cut distinction would undoubtedly be apparent were we able to measure intelligence differentials. Our only indication in this respect is the entrepreneurs' ability and willingness to understand and explain the various phenomena of life. We were often struck by the nonentrepreneurs' fear of the questions we asked. For some of them the challenge of even a simple question was visibly painful and manifested itself in a tenseness or the convenient escape, *"¡Pues! ¿Quien sabe?"* "Well, who knows?"

The entrepreneurs also tended to look out into the world and to be interested in and concerned about it. They are the most hospitable to outsiders, and rather than fear them they make them welcome. They are concerned for their community, are recognized as leaders, and take an active role in village affairs.

An imponderable arises when one asks the question, would these people arise at any time that economic opportunities were made available, or is it necessary that social preconditions such as the destruction of the traditional society be present? Would economic opportunities be sufficient in themselves to break down the traditionalist barriers? If the latter were the case, what would have to be the nature and strength of the economic opportunities? As we shall argue later, the breakdown of the traditional structure in Huecorio began in the 1930s, and the economic opportunities became apparent in the 1950s. These facts would support, but not prove, the hypothesis of the need to establish social preconditions.

The experience of Huecorio also provides some hints of means for introducing economic change and encouraging entrepreneurship. Both the *Asociación Avícola* and the structure of the institution of the *taller* solved problems for the entrepreneurs that are beyond their present capacity. Both provided marketing facilities and finance, and both spared the entrepreneur of any need for complex business administration. Both fitted into the paternalistic *patrón* relationship that remains as a vestigial reminder of traditionalism. This is particularly apparent in the *taller,* in which Vicki's benevolent attitude toward the Barreras is matched by the Barreras' loyalty to her and a similar tie between the Barreras and those who work in the shop.

The personal nature of the relationship is necessary for its introduction and survival, but there exists perhaps some slight danger that it weakens the necessary attack on traditionalism and does not provide the entrepreneur with independent resources should the *patrón* die or fail. Similar *patrón*-worker relationships survive in Japan, well into that nation's expanding industrialization, but they are now beginning to weaken. Accordingly, one can view them as a necessary and useful step in the transition to a dynamic society.[21]

[21] See Gustav Ranis, "The Community Centered Entrepreneur in Japanese Development," *Explorations in Entrepreneurial History,* VIII, No. 2, pp. 90–98. See also John Pelzel, "The Small Industrialist in Japan," *Explorations in Entrepreneurial History,* VII, No. 2, pp. 79–93.

CHAPTER 6

POLITICAL AND SOCIAL STRUCTURE

P OLITICAL power in Mexico centers on the federal government, and radiates from Mexico City through the state governments to the *municipios,* and finally, much dissipated, to the villages dependent on the *municipios.* These stages in the hierarchy do not, however, constitute locks in a canal through which one must inevitably pass to reach a decision-maker. Although in a formal sense Huecorio is tied to the municipal seat in Pátzcuaro, its people will frequently deal directly with the state capital of Morelia, in which are located agencies of both the state and federal governments.

Both levels of government provide welfare and technical services to Huecorio, among them those of an agronomist, a veterinarian, a visiting nurse, and the teachers. The federal government has installed electricity and subsidized the public water system and home improvements. Typical of the latter are precast concrete seats for outdoor toilets, sold to a few villagers for 60 pesos—a price which represented half their actual cost. In 1957 the government sent cement to be used to construct a wall around the public garden and to lay concrete floors in private homes, but apparently a large part of this was intercepted by two villagers and the majority of village homes still have earthen floors. In 1961, the Department of Forestry of the state gov-

Band at Fiesta of Corpus Christi

ernment gave the village shade trees to be planted in the streets, but by the summer of 1962 the trees had died through neglect. Similarly, several thousand fruit trees were given without charge to villagers in the summer of 1962. Services such as these are sometimes sponsored by CREFAL students working in Huecorio, but usually are initiated by the villagers themselves. For instance, to persuade the government to provide the villagers with the precast latrines, a group of men made several visits to Morelia and Pátzcuaro to untangle a web of promises and denials. From a budget of 100,000 pesos to operate the program in the Morelia region, Huecorio finally obtained some two dozen slabs.

Huecorio is solidly held by the government party, *Partido Revolucionario Institucional,* and political partisanship does not enter into the selection of village political officials. Huecorianos do not feel politically oppressed in any way, but give their allegiance to this party on the grounds that it also controls Pátzcuaro and they have to have good relations with the *municipio* in order to get anything done.[1]

[1] The village of Tzentzenhuaro, only a stone's throw from Huecorio, is reportedly loyal to the opposition party, *Partido Acción Nacional.* What this demonstration of independence means, we cannot say.

Yet despite this allegiance and the government's programs, villagers verbalize some discontent. A few spoke of President López Mateos as López "Paseos" because of his frequent trips abroad, and there was some feeling that the "government" should do more to solve Huecorio's problems. However, as we have seen, the majority of the villagers blame village officials and local lack of cooperation, rather than outsiders, for their failure to solve their problems. Only a minority spoke critically of the venality of the government.[2] Although some villagers, particularly the *braceros,* had been subject to *mordidas,* our own observations of the officials responsible in some way for Huecorio and other villages support the position that the majority of those men and women are sincerely interested in the people's welfare and perform their duties to the best of their abilities.

The *municipio* of Pátzcuaro is administered by a *junta* of five councilmen, each elected for a three-year term. The councilmen select the *presidente municipal* from among themselves, and this responsibility is rotated through one-year terms of office. These officials and their assistants are readily accessible to the people of Huecorio, either in Pátzcuaro or during their visits to the village.[3] The ability of the *municipio* to contribute significantly to the development of the town and villages which comprise it is severely limited by the paucity of its financial resources. Revenue is inflexible, and is derived from a series of petty taxes and licenses. Among the taxes might be mentioned those on the possession and sale of animals, the sale of houses, and the posts of *comerciantes.*

[2] One of these people said, "We need an irrigation system in Huecorio, but with all the pumps, pipes, and tanks, it would cost a quarter of a million pesos. The government could help us but all that the politicians are interested in is taking bribes. We should have a Yanqui type of government here. It would be better for the *campesinos.*" The allusion to the United States system of government was intended to flatter the American members of the team. It fell flat, however, for the informant speaking these words was José Dongo, whose wanderings from the paths of ordinary morality had become quite apparent.

[3] The visits to Huecorio are not frequent. During the summer of 1962 elected municipal officials came to Huecorio only to mediate the conflict over the ditch which was to drain the accumulated water from a street. See below, pp. 259–60. The municipal police came several times in August in connection with disturbances arising from illegal sales of liquor. See above, Chapter 1, note 6.

The taxes on animals present opportunities for evasion and are difficult to collect. For instance, the annual tax on cattle is 12 pesos, but because of the local practice of pasturing animals collectively, ownership is not readily ascertained. The *municipio* counters this by automatically doubling or tripling the number of cattle an individual claims, and taxing accordingly. Needless to say, this method is less than perfect. All animals are supposed to be slaughtered in the municipal slaughterhouse, and of the sales tax of nine pesos and 60 centavos which is levied, eight pesos go to the *municipio* and the balance to the state. This, of course, is an invitation to the common practice of clandestine slaughtering. The same tax is supposed to be paid when the ownership of animals is transferred, but with this the rate of collection approaches zero.

License payments cover a variety of situations from the registration of *cantinas,* restaurants, barbershops, and public baths, to permits to hold *kermesses* and dances. The rate for the latter is 14 pesos, and were it collected the *fiestas* in Huecorio alone could, at the conservative rate of three *fiestas* a week, add over 2,000 pesos annually to the municipal treasury.

For the fiscal year 1962 the municipal budget amounted to 370,740 pesos and 60 centavos (approximately $30,140 U.S.), to meet the needs of some 30,000 people. Salaries, low as they are,[4] absorb the bulk of the budget, and only 15,000 pesos ($1,200 U.S.) is available for capital works. To institute major capital improvements the local government must depend on the uncertain largesse of higher authorities. The year 1962 was especially fortunate in this respect, for the Rio Balsas project[5] was concerned about the traffic bottleneck developing in Pátzcuaro and was widening a bridge at the entrance to the town and constructing a traffic bypass. These factors make it clear that, until its fiscal powers are enlarged, the *municipio* can do little more for its satellite villages than maintain the peace.

Although there are only four offices in Huecorio that fit into the

----

[4] The *presidente municipal* earned from his official duties only $800 U.S. Several secretaries earned only six pesos a day, and this is less than the six or seven pesos plus food earned by the *peones* of Huecorio.

[5] A multiple-purpose river valley project administered by General Cárdenas.

formal hierarchy of political authority, the officers of certain non-political organizations are in a position to influence village affairs.

The most important of those organizations is the society of *ejidatarios,* which has 12 representatives in all. The *ejido* officials proper are the *comisariado ejidal* (*ejido* commissioner), the *ejido* secretary, and the *ejido* treasurer. These three officials, especially the commissioner, are in a position to influence the course of affairs, since *ejidatarios* can be found in the majority of village homes.[6] The *ejidatarios* are also represented by a *consejo de vigilancia* consisting of a *jefe,* secretary, and treasurer, whose duties are to observe their counterparts on the commission to ensure proper performance of their duties. In view of the history of malpractice within the *ejido,* it can be concluded that the *consejo de vigilancia* does not take this responsibility seriously. Each of the six officials mentioned has a substitute who is to take over if the official is for some reason unable to perform his duties. All twelve officials are elected for three-year terms by the *ejidatarios.* Meetings of the *ejidatarios* are supposed to be held every three months, but in practice they meet only when the officials feel it is necessary.

Other nonpolitical officials are the *prioste,* sacristan, *cantores,* and *cargueros* of the church,[7] and the president of the *Sociedad de Padres de Familia,*[8] who is elected by the fathers of school children.

The one appointed public official in Huecorio is the *juez menor de tenencia* (minor village judge), who is chosen by the *Corte de Justica* in Morelia for an indeterminate term. He passes on minor infractions occurring in Huecorio, and sends the more serious cases to Pátzcuaro. In his duties he is assisted by a *suplente* and a secretary.

The most important political post is that of *jefe de tenencia,* whose duties are similar to those of a town mayor. He is assisted by a *presidente de mejores materiales,* who is supposed to be in charge of community improvements, and by *jefes de manzana,* one from each of the four *barrios.*[9] The *barrio jefes* are supposed to hear grievances and

[6] We are not suggesting that the commissioner can subject the *ejidatarios* to his will, but merely that his position lends authority to any stand he might take, and may therefore be used to persuade *ejidatarios.*

[7] See below, pp. 277–78.

[8] Corresponding to the parent-teacher associations of the U.S.

[9] The U.S. equivalent of the *barrio* would be the political ward.

take them to the proper authority, but Huecorianos do not seem to follow this procedure and usually take their problems to the highest power they can reach without recourse to formal channels. These positions are filled for one-year terms.

The right to vote in village elections is held by all persons of 21 and over, and married persons 18 and over. Women do not generally exercise this right unless encouraged or coaxed by their husbands.

The obligations of the *jefe de tenencia* comprise an impressive list of duties. He is expected to:

Report to the office of the *registro civil* all births and deaths occurring in the village;

Advise the *presidencia municipal* of any plague or sickness that might affect people, animals, trees, or crops;

Organize the people to combat fires and give immediate help to neighboring communities if fires occur in them;

Help the village teachers by building and maintaining the school and assuring the punctual attendance of the children;

Organize the villagers for community improvement;

Prevent the clandestine sale of alcoholic beverages or participation in illegal games of chance;

Demand of people driving animals through the village the documents of ownership, sending suspicious cases to the *presidencia municipal;*

When requested, make censuses and registers of voters;

Ensure that young men register for military service and attend local military instruction;

Demand from those who organize dances, *mañanitas,* etc., the permit granted by the *presidencia municipal,* and see to it that the occasion meets the conditions specified in the license;

Obey immediately and zealously all orders received from the *presidente municipal* and other legitimate authorities;

Organize the community every year at the termination of the rains to level and repair streets;

Advise the *presidencia municipal* of the arrival of any unknown armed person or group of bandits;

Avoid the destruction of forests and organize a campaign of reforestation, particularly to encircle fields with trees to avoid wind damage and to plant orchards in homesteads to improve the diet of the people;

Prevent people from using the public land on streets bordering their property;

See to it that the national flag is treated properly and that the people sing the national anthem on civic occasions, and develop among them love of country and its heroes;

Prevent all clandestine slaughter of animals, large or small;

Care for those families hurt by sickness, absence of the breadwinner, death, or other causes;

Post in public places the laws, decrees, circulars, etc. which are sent to the village to be displayed;

Prevent acts which might disturb the peace;

Demand to see the license from the *presidencia municipal* of those who sell alcoholic beverages, permit no such sale by an unlicensed person, and ensure that licensees follow the regulations set down for the sale of alcoholic beverages;

Apprehend those committing flagrantly criminal acts and deliver them immediately to the *presidencia municipal;*

See to it that the people maintain the street fronts of their houses in a clean condition, and that they pen or rope their pigs so that they neither damage the streets nor offer an unsightly appearance;

Care for the cleanliness and maintenance of the cemetery, playing fields, gardens, etc.;

Make monthly reports on his activities to the *presidencia municipal;*

Preside over all public gatherings;

Ensure that public services such as potable water, electric light, schools, transportation, etc., function efficiently, and report any irregularities;

Avoid abuses of authority;

Maintain official quarters and records in good condition;

Report, on the day following a dance, wake, etc., the names and addresses of those who commit a nuisance.[10]

It goes without saying that while these duties are appropriate, they exceed the functions actually performed by the average *jefe de tenencia*. The *jefe* in power in 1962 ignored all the obligations except that of presiding over public gatherings, and that function he per-

[10] This record of duties was adapted from a statement kindly supplied by the *presidencia municipal*.

formed ineffectually. He was a frequent and drunken disturber of the peace, and in the incident described in Chapter 1 was carried off to jail in Pátzcuaro. Community reaction to him ranged from an apathetic "Well, he isn't so bad. He hasn't stolen anything yet," to an angry "He is incompetent. We certainly made a mistake this time." When he learned of the *jefe's* behavior, a municipal official commented resignedly, "At times it is better to have a robber that does something while he steals half the money than a character like that."

The *jefe* of 1962 was not necessarily typical. Others have been more responsible, and, according to their own accounts, managed to get something done.

The position of *jefe* is not sought after. It is clear that a conscientious *jefe* must devote a considerable amount of time to his duties even if he confines himself to essentials. He will have to make frequent trips to Pátzcuaro and Morelia, and will constantly be called to consider some issue or to persuade his fellow villagers to cooperate. He has no fiscal resources with which to work, and no power other than the negative authority to bring social delinquents to justice. Neither are there any inducements to serve. He loses income when he performs his duties, and since he is unpaid this loss is not offset. He is not respected by his fellows, indeed he is often unfairly vilified; consequently, even if he does accomplish something he cannot bask in the warmth of public approbation.

The better *jefes* find themselves darkened by the cloud cast by their venal predecessors. One *jefe* took for himself money from the sale of village land. When one villager was asked why they did not act to recover the money she replied, "Oh, why bother? Another *jefe* would only steal it again." This sense of latent public disapproval surely inhibits the *jefe* from exercising leadership. If he closes the *cantinas* he will be vilified by some, and if he does not he will be vilified by others —and, given human nature, by some who would attack both action and inaction with fine impartiality. If he talks to parents about their children's truancy from school he angers them, but if he does not do so he is a *flojo* good-for-nothing to the others.

Given the social environment of Huecorio and the hazards and sacrifices entailed in leadership, its formal political structure cannot cope with the community's needs. A partial solution would necessitate payment of reasonable salaries to the officials, coupled with training and close supervisory support from above. It is obvious, however, that with the inadequate revenues available to the *municipio,* no solution is yet in sight.

Where local formal political power is absent, informal leaders can arise who can unite the people or achieve some communal goal. Such persons do exist in Huecorio, but their power is unstructured and is exerted in an *ad hoc* and usually ineffective way. Several older men receive some token of respect from their fellows, and when a public issue arises they will attempt to persuade Huecorianos to what they feel to be a desirable course of action. Prior to the attempt to drain the waters from a village street, a group was seen gathered after Mass in the churchyard. Miguel Salinas and Ricardo Pérez were arguing forcefully about the need to accomplish the project, but as it turned out they were unable to persuade the landowner through whose land the ditch was to pass.[11] Lacking any formal authority, even men with leadership qualities generally achieve very little.

One interesting ramification of the ineffectiveness of formal and informal power is the temporary assumption of leadership by men with an exceptionally high sense of responsibility. When a crisis develops or some objective must be attained, they will take responsibility into their own hands even though they have no formal right to speak for the village. Two of them, for instance, spent several days trying to get the latrines for Huecorio. In the crisis precipitated by the plague of worms which were attacking the corn crop, four men visited Morelia and Villa Escalante to obtain DDT and insecticide dusters. Needless to say, those few men can do little by themselves to allay the apathy and cynicism of the bulk of their fellows, and even with their efforts, community development is unlikely.

[11] See below, pp. 259–60.

HUECORIO: THE SOCIOLOGY
OF ITS ECONOMICS

Economists analyzing economic development recognize that more than lip service must be paid to the social variables affecting change, yet the majority recognize their limitations and choose to hit only with an occasional guerrilla skirmish. In his *On the Theory of Social Change,* Everett Hagen mounted a full-scale invasion which seems, to economists at least, to have successfully shown the flag.

In Chapter Six of his book, Hagen discusses authoritarian and innovational personalities in a formal framework, and by his own admission builds upon pioneering efforts of several sociologists. We are told that in essence human beings are motivated to act by physiological and psychological needs, which are channeled into patterns of action by a set of values. The physiological needs—to satisfy hunger, avoid pain, etc.—require no elaboration. Psychological needs are less apparent, but our crude data throw a dim light on those of the people in Heucorio.[12]

We first consider *need achievement,* which is satisfied "in the process of solving problems, in manipulating effectively by the exercise of . . . judgment and abilities a situation . . . not previously dealt with, in attempting something difficult, in facing a test of . . . capability." [13] Of course, a need such as this can be observed only in its overt ramifications. Need achievement exists in Huecorio, but it is expressed powerfully in only a few persons—a girl who wants to open an academy of the dance, a boy who wants to sing professionally, or that minority of the farmers who experiment. Highly skilled crafts-

---

[12] In this section we attempt to describe and analyze those aspects of Huecorio's microsociety that impinge upon or seem to explain its economic system. This does not pretend to be a complete and satisfactory picture of this microsociety; instead, we limit our examination to four aspects of the social matrix: the motivations and aspirations of Huecorianos; patterns of economic association; the *fiesta* and its function; and elements of social change.

[13] Hagen, p. 105.

manship does not exist in Huecorio, although a number of persons perform competently as tailors, *palmeros,* or carpenters. Since the Mexican is well known for his manipulative skill, one suspects that need achievement is not manifested more generally in Huecorio in part for lack of opportunity. It is true that most occupations or social situations in Huecorio make few demands on mental or physical abilities; but it is possible for a society to structure its demands upon situations not necessarily associated with a challenge. For example, according to Lewis the farmers of Tepoztlán took a competitive pride in ploughing furrows that were straight and true.[14] No such institutionalized effort is made in Huecorio. It is clear from instances such as this that a social group can elicit a need, or it can ignore it. The latter seems to be the case with need achievement in Huecorio.

Need autonomy "makes one prefer to be independent of control of one's judgment by others, to make one's own decisions." [15] Again, we would judge this to be weak among the majority of Huecorianos, although there are the notable exceptions—Geronimo Roca, who arrives at his own conclusions about solutions to community problems, or Juan Mirasol, the farmer who chooses his vegetable output mix on the basis of what others are *not* planting. Indeed, all those we have named as entrepreneurs would, by definition, show some degree of need autonomy. It has been possible, however, for the majority of persons in the village to avoid making decisions. The rhythm of the agricultural cycle is clear, and if they follow established practices it is safe for villagers to assume that crops will grow and can be sold. However, the growing pressure of population has begun to squeeze many persons out of traditional activities. Many can still avoid decision-making by following a vocation such as manual labor, which does not require mental effort. Others may not be able to do this, and the unaccustomed need to rely on their mental resources may well induce painful internal conflict. We would sometimes interview a man, unaccustomed to mental agility, for whom even the simplest questions produced a fear that manifested itself in a cold sweat or a nervous pressing together of the hands. A similar reaction was even more

[14] See Appendix C.
[15] Hagen, p. 106.

common among the women who slipped through our net with the convenient, *"¡Pues! ¿Quien sabe?"*

Perhaps another small piece of evidence of the weakness of need autonomy lies in the constant meetings held to discuss, but rarely resolve, village problems. The *jefatura* is open one or two evenings a week, and a group of six to 25 or so men will talk over something that is troubling them. It is possible that these meetings have, unconsciously, a largely social function. On the other hand, they could represent the need that most Huecorianos seem to have for confirmation of any decision which lies in an area outside of the family. This does not mean that Huecorianos fail to express an opinion publicly. This they do, and the difficulty of reconciling a diversity of views hampers agreement. The absence of agreement is a stumbling block to autonomous community improvement, for it leads to anxiety which is best handled by avoiding action.

Need order is "to put things in order; to achieve cleanliness, arrangement, organization, balance, neatness, tidiness and precision." [16] Judging from appearances, this need, too, is weak in Huecorio. But although cleanliness, neatness, and tidiness are observable phenomena, there is always considerable danger of ethnocentric bias on the part of an outside observer. To take a simple, hypothetical example: A field investigator coming from a region where stone walls are neatly laid might look with unconscious disdain on his subjects whose walls appeared "thrown"—like a disorganized jumble of unlaid stone. He might, however, overlook the fact that his native stone is flat or easy to cut while those of his subjects are round or flinty.

Huecorianos lack sufficient potable and portable water throughout much of the year, their incomes are still too low to permit them to have enough changes of clothing, and they work on the land—a combination of circumstances well fitted to give an impression quite the opposite of that by which need order is defined. Yet their swelling desire to live better channels available income into things that speak of at least a repressed need order. Flower pots in the patio, pottery neatly

[16] Hagen, p. 106. Quoted from Henry A. Murray and Associates, *Explorations in Personality* (New York, Oxford University Press, 1938), p. 201.

stacked in the kitchen, and people scrubbed as the opportunity arises speak of this. In other words, one gains the impression from one's observation of Huecorio that need order is not high, but in all fairness this judgment should be tempered by taking into account the natural conditions under which the people live.

Need aggression is to "attack someone or something, to overcome opposition forcefully." There are, in addition, two important variations on this major theme. *Need dominance* is to dominate others rather than attack them. *Need submission* is a suppression of need aggression in order to avoid the dangers of a conflict, and it manifests itself in acquiescence to direction received from others.

In traditional society, the widely observed cult of *machismo* neatly fits the dominance/submission pattern of male/female relationships. In Mexico *machismo* takes many forms, which seem to vary with the economic position of the male. Among the middle and upper classes of Pátzcuaro it might be manifested in the compulsive and predatory pursuit of infidelity. In nearby Huecorio, however, these games are too costly and the average male can rarely afford even the relative charms of Pátzcuaro's brothels. Girls in the village are watched with care and incur the wrath of their parents if they are so much as seen talking to males in the street. Marriages take place as the result of a boy "stealing" a girl. While a girl who is "stolen" is not required to marry the boy, her failure to do so makes it impossible for her to find an acceptable partner, since female virginity is a prerequisite for eligibility. The possibility of such an encounter severely restricts a girl's freedom of movement outside the home.

For their part, the more acculturated females consider their male counterparts to be too rough and uncouth. This developing resistance to *machismo* is not found often among older women. "Why," we asked, "do women carry such heavy loads?" "It is to make life comfortable for our husbands." "Why do women go barefoot and men wear shoes?" "Because shoes are a luxury." "Why do women sometimes enter the church on their knees while men simply walk in?" "Well, men try to solve problems in more scientific ways while women must implore the help of God." In one interview, quoted directly, the dominance/submission pattern is shown quite clearly.

When I first asked the woman if she was a *comerciante* she said "No." Her husband quickly answered "Yes." The wife gave him a look as if saying, "Wasn't I supposed to say no?" When I asked her how much she earned from it she wouldn't say, but her husband answered for her. He also spoke honestly about his *cohete* (drinking) habit. He blames it on his friends. His wife does not mind it. He comes home *cohete* and goes to bed without bothering anyone. Next day he gets up to milk the cows. His wife controls the money of the house but he gives the orders, for he is, in his own words, *"Señor de la casa."*

It can be argued that drunkenness is an expression of need aggression. If the imbiber become belligerent, dangerous, boisterous, or noisy, it would seem that he is releasing the tensions of this need. But such behavior is not common in Huecorio. Indeed, we were struck by the fact that imbibers were usually quiet, kind, respectful, and perhaps unhappy, sometimes crying openly from the sadness of it all. For the most part, the *cohetes* could retain navigational control, although sometimes in bad weather when the usual friendly lights were obscured they foundered temporarily in roadside ditches.

At the time of our visit Huecorianos were getting fed up with the continual drinking, and were pleased when the incident we have recounted resulted in a crackdown on the illegal sale of alcohol.[17] We were aware of only two men in Huecorio who did not drink. Others, of all classes, indulged in degrees ranging from the controlled to the stupendous. Women drinkers were confined to a minority of *comerciantes* from Carián and Urandén, who, returning home from the Pátzcuaro market already *alegre,* would stop to refuel in Huecorio. Huecorio's *cantinas* also served men from neighboring Tzentzenhuaro, and these two groups intensified the impact of the relatively small number of Huecorianos who were regular drinkers.[18]

A great deal of drinking is the predictable effect of the constant

[17] Only three of the 36 persons replying to a question about drunkenness did not think that it represented a serious problem in Huecorio. One of them blamed it all on "those Indians from Urandén," while the others said it all was due to six or seven "famous" drinkers from the town.

[18] We would agree with the villagers who reported that only six or seven Huecorianos were regular and "famous" drinkers.

fiestas, both religious and private. After weddings, for instance, men will roam the streets for several days in little groups loyally bound together for mutual support both physical and moral. The men are good-natured, but neglect their work and responsibilities. In one incident a man was sitting quietly on a curb savoring the fumes that remained in his bottle when he was surrounded by some women from Urandén who pestered him to buy another bottle for them. Two members of our team tried to extricate him from the difficulty and they gently led him home. Moving slowly, he protested, "I am not drunk. Just *alegre!* I had a few drinks so as not to offend anybody. To drink in friendship is in our blood. We are Mexicans. This is our *gusto.*" In the same incident, one of the girls took a bottle from a man and emptied it in the street. Rather than become angry, he picked it up, and, with dignity, returned it to the store from whence it came.

Huecorianos are convinced that the main cause of the constantly visible inebriation is the existence of the *cantinas* in the village itself. "There are too many *cantinas* here. The men would not drink if they had to go to Pátzcuaro." "Before the *tiendas* started selling alcohol, drunkenness was no problem here. The *tiendas* keep going not by selling groceries but by selling *agua caliente.*" [19] "The authorities are weak. They should close these places but they take bribes instead. Why, there are bars right in front of the school!"

Why, then, do the men drink? At least a partial explanation can be cast in terms of need submission. If one or two men are standing at the counter drinking, they easily spot their friends who pass by. When called in the friends cannot refuse and a ping-pong–like reaction of mutual buying sets in. The crux of the matter lies in the difficulty of refusing an invitation. To refuse is to insult, to reflect perhaps on one's manhood, or even to precipitate a scuffle. It is easier to avoid conflict by submitting, and once the first draught is down resistance strengthens only with a growing discomfort in the stomach. Huecorianos recognize this and add other explanations. "It is the problems they have. They don't care to be happy. One could be happy having good friendships." "Some men drink because they have difficulties at home with their family." In general, Huecorianos are a tolerant peo-

[19] Literally, "hot water," but the closest English equivalent is, of course, "firewater."

ple, but they would nevertheless prefer protection from this problem.

This dominance/submission pattern is an essential element of a traditional society, and, as argued by Hagen, is instilled early in life. Traditionally, the children of Huecorio obey their parents unquestioningly and do not even leave the house without permission. This pattern continues into adulthood. Marina Pérez, for instance, twice found herself a *novio* but in each case her parents disapproved, and now she remains a spinster in her late forties. Sara Barrera, the ambitious lass who wants to start an academy of the dance, had a *novio* who was studying in Mexico City. Her parents opposed both of her desires, and instead want her to become a kindergarten teacher and marry a *campesino*. In this way she can remain near her home under their protective wings. When José Pérez was 25 he got a contract to join a *mariachi* band playing in another part of Mexico. His parents refused permission and he did not go.

Sports offer an opportunity to release *need aggression,* and inter-village competition in basketball under the sponsorship of CREFAL has become very popular in recent years. Occasionally the rivalry becomes unfriendly, and ugly incidents occur. Nevertheless, in none of the games observed in Huecorio was there any overt display of aggression beyond that permitted by the normal rules of the game.

In sum, then, it seems that need aggression falls within the dominance/submission pattern, with perhaps more weight falling on submission than on dominance. This does not mean that acts of violence do not occur or that tension and hostility cannot be found, but these phenomena are better explained in terms of historical circumstance, ineffective social control, and social values, and will be dealt with in the discussion of individualism and cooperation.

The pattern of need dependence, succorance, and nurturance can be seen from the data we have presented. *Need dependence* is "to receive guidance from . . . others in order to avoid the risk of failure and frustration involved in making judgments and decisions oneself." [20] This characteristic was often found among the women of Huecorio who, for instance, were frightened about answering our questions for fear they would say something wrong. As we shall see in the discussion of individualism and cooperation, Huecorianos show

[20] Hagen, p. 108.

both dependence and independence, according to their momentary role. Briefly, independence characterizes *most* but not all economic activities, while dependence is found in the social and political spheres. *Need succorance*—"to have one's needs gratified by the sympathetic aid of an allied other. . . . To remain close to a devoted protector"—and *need nurturance*—"To give sympathy and gratify the needs of a helpless other" [21]—are clearly important components of family life. Need succorance, in particular, often extends beyond the family into wider social relationships. Villagers will frequently develop a loyalty to an employer, a teacher, or a politican who is in a position to offer help in time of need.

Moral and manipulative values serve to direct needs into the channels that mark patterns of social behavior. Moral values are molded by a multiplicity of pressures—parents, popular heroes, teachers, propagandists, etc. In Huecorio, we would judge that these values are instilled largely by the agency of the Church and correspond to its teachings. They need not, therefore, be elaborated upon, except to say that the preoccupation with physical sin and loyalty to the family divert attention from the wider loyalties to the state and from individual moral responsibilities toward society at large. Herein, as we shall see, we have a partial explanation for some of Huecorio's problems. However, new value determinants that have been at work in recent years—through CREFAL, political leaders such as General Cárdenas, the schoolteachers, the Americans with whom the *braceros* come in contact—are undermining old values and replacing them with new ones that are not yet explicit.

Manipulative values relate to the ranking that individuals apply to trades, occupations, mental and physical activities, political activities, and so on. "How does the individual rate, on a scale ranging from strong repugnance to strong attraction, the activities involved in work with his muscles and hands on the land, or handling objects, or with tools and machines; or work which keeps him clean or gets him dirty; killing animals; exchanging ownership of goods; studying the physical world versus studying concepts remote from the physical world; . . . and so on?" [22]

[21] Hagen, p. 110, quoted from Murray, pp. 182, 189.
[22] Hagen, p. 117.

Confining ourselves to the manipulative values relevant to economic activity, we would make the following characterization of the Huecoriano. He has no objection to manual labor or to getting dirty, but is developing a distaste for tasks that are especially arduous; he ranks farming low on the occupational scale, and vastly prefers professional pursuits while commerce fits between; he never thinks of military activities as being worthy of consideration; he is a pragmatist who rarely engages in speculative contemplation or abstraction; he is a believer in private property but will nevertheless call in higher authority for help with little hesitation; and he considers that political and religious activities are no longer important sources of prestige.

Several other possible desires motivating Huecorianos should be discussed. They are the desires for prestige and power, the satisfaction of pride, the achievement of material comfort, and the care of one's family.

If a desire for prestige is to move men to their actions, it is reasonable to assume that the prestige-giving behavior would be readily identifiable, and that prestigious individuals would have common, or at least clearly distinguishable, characteristics. In an attempt to isolate the prestige-giving patterns in Huecorio, we asked 36 persons to name the three persons in Huecorio whom they respected most. The replies, tabulated in Table 13, revealed no clear pattern except for two things. Over a third of those questioned refused to be drawn out, and usually countered with a statement to the effect that all Huecorianos are equal. This reaction may have reflected a dislike for the question, or on the other hand a prevailing but not fully accepted philosophy of egalitarianism. On the other hand, friendship figured as an important response determinant for the majority of those who replied to the question. Obviously there are reasons why friendships are formed, and intensive open-end questioning by skilled interviewers might have uncovered much about Huecorio's system of values. We were not in a position to pursue the matter more deeply, although we could see some indication that friends are bound by ties of reciprocal assistance. They say, for instance, "He lends me animals," "He invites me to parties," "We take care of each other," and so on.

There were 18 replies that specified qualities of personality as being important, but these qualities were so varied as to make generaliza-

TABLE 13

The Five Most "Respected" Individuals in Huecorio,
and General Tabulation of Respect Verbalizations

Most Respected Individuals	Number of Votes Received	Reasons Given for This Choice
Juan Barrera	4	He makes you clothes and gives easy payments. He is interested in the community and is kind to those people from outside who come to help. He is interested in Huecorio and helped me when I was *jefe*. He invites me to parties.
José Dongo	4	He is better instructed. He knows how to reach the people in Pátzcuaro. He worked in the *Presidencia Municipal*. He has pull. He is the son of my *madrina*. I don't know why.
Ricardo Pérez	3	He is a man of respect and he has money. Before him one feels a little less. I have confidence in him. If I tell him something I know that no one else will know about it. He is a friend and lends me animals.
Francisco Cruz	3	We live close and take care of each other. He is a member of the band and always cooperates when we ask him to play. He aspires to progress and is sincere and proper. But he does not have much energy.
Antonio Iturbide	3	He is the oldest in the family. He is younger than I am and treats me with respect. If you ask for favors, he helps.

Table 13 (continued)

Respect Verbalization[a]	Number of Times This Given as Reason for Choice	Some Sample Responses
Friendship	20	We have always been good friends. We are good friends. He is a neighbor and we get along well together.
Qualities of personality	18	A good person. He likes to work. He has no bad habits like drinking or smoking. Is a dignified man in his conduct and personality even though he drinks. Hard working and honest. He doesn't try to take advantage of you.
Economic	8	He has money. He lends me tools. He can lend you money when you need it.
Interest in community	6	He has done work in the community. He helped and encouraged me while I was in office.
Relationship	5	We are neighbors and cousins. He is my father-in-law.
Miscellaneous	7	He is powerful. He is intelligent.
Number of persons who refused to make a choice	13	To my way of thinking, all Huecorianos are equal. All are good. All are of Huecorio. Esteem is not possible here. We work without union. I don't like anybody. All are equal and I don't have a preference except that I don't like José Dongo, the big politician.

[a] Each of the 36 persons who responded to the popularity poll was asked to choose the three persons whom he or she respected most. Accordingly, the tabulations for friendship, qualities of personality, economic, interest in community, relationship, and miscellaneous represent an enumeration of *responses,* while the last entry is a tabulation of *persons* who gave only one response apiece.

tion impossible. Similarly, although wealth, power, interest in the community, and relationship figured in other responses, none predominated sufficiently to show any kind of pattern. This is also true of the five persons whose names appeared most frequently in the "popularity poll." Apart from their entrepreneurial traits, Juan Barrera, José Dongo, Ricardo Pérez, Francisco Cruz, and Antonio Iturbide share one characteristic—they are relatively well-to-do. But this was mentioned only once in connection with them, and there are many other men in the village who are equally affluent but who did not appear on the list at all. Wealth, apparently, is not sufficient to bring prestige, but neither is it a bar to community acceptance.

The omissions seem to be as significant as the overt reasons given. No one, for instance, mentioned the word *compadre,* although this relationship may have hidden behind what was called friendship. Similarly, no person was chosen because of the quality of his religious faith or because of his contribution to *fiestas,* although we were told by nonvillagers that supporting *fiestas* and being active in church duties—as *mayordomo* or *cantor* for instance—gave rise to prestige. Furthermore, a number of respondents made it clear that they considered supporting *fiestas* to be a nuisance and obligation rather than a privilege and honor. Another nonvillager explained that the *fiestas* associated with weddings are a source of prestige. The parents of the bride and groom spend "several" thousand pesos to hire *mariachis* and provide food and drink for the whole village. The emphasis seems false, however. The large expenditure is not to gain prestige, but rather to avoid criticism.

It is possible that the various political offices give rise to prestige, and several, but not all, of the men who had held political office were respected by their fellows. Apparently it is not the post itself that brings honor, but rather the manner in which an individual performs his duties. Political offices are not sought after, for like the religious offices they are demanding of time and money. In sum, we would conclude that Huecorianos are not motivated by a desire for prestige, although like their fellow humans throughout the world they are for the most part sensitive to the disapproval of others.

Nor does a desire for power seem to be important, for few opportunities to exert power over one's fellows exist. The local political authorities have no means of compelling compliance with their wishes and must rely on the weak force of persuasion. Pride can be a motivating force in some contexts—for instance among growing nation states, or in some circumstances in small communities. Huecorianos do not seem to be supersensitive to any real or imagined slight, and while they express an affection for their community frequently they reveal an embarrassment about its lack of cleanliness and other shortcomings.

More positively, the Huecorianos are preoccupied with two closely related aspects of their life—their economic well-being and their families. They are aware that economic conditions can be better than those under which they live, and they want to have clean, attractive houses, beds, radios, and so on. Similarly, husbands and wives are genuinely (with some exceptions, of course) concerned both for each other and for their children. Given the economic circumstances under which they live, the Huecorianos are, as individuals, guided primarily by these desires.

INDIVIDUALISM AND PATTERNS OF COOPERATION

In the promotion of economic development, considerable attention is being focused on a technique known as community development. Unfortunately the working concept is vague, for there are at least as many definitions of community development as there are experts in the field. Implicitly there seem to be two essential elements in the concept, although they are not always stated. For community development to function, the community concerned is supposed to be united in its goals and action, and the dynamic force is internal rather than constantly pushed from the outside. Huecorio by no means meets these criteria, even though cooperative associations can be found and community improvements have taken place. But the cooperation and the improvements rarely involve the entire village, and examination shows that a variety of associations exist side by side.

If we broaden our concept of cooperation from the narrow ideal of voluntary cooperative association to include all types of association directed toward some economic or social objective, we see that there are at least 12 distinct types that can be found in Huecorio.

The patterns of cooperation and work association are based on: the biological family; the extended family; the *compadre* relationship; friendship; labor or other nonmonetary exchange; a commercial transaction; vertical ties (e.g., *patrón*-worker); a special, temporary, community of interest involving a segment of the village; a special, permanent, community of interest involving a segment of the village; the contiguity of landholdings; the *ejido*; and a communal goal, permanent or temporary, involving the entire village.

One would expect in a small rural village such as Huecorio that work teams—such as those used to cultivate corn—would be comprised principally of the biological family, or, if the number of males in the family were insufficient, would make use of *compadres* or members of the extended family. One would further expect that the *compadres,* uncles, cousins, and so on who were called in to help, would be compensated by some reciprocal labor or material exchange rather than by means of a cash payment. These expectations are based upon the qualities of the ties of relationship. Mutual loyalty within the biological family is usually strong in Huecorio, and vertical and horizontal blood ties extend horizontally by godparent and godchild to unite otherwise unrelated individuals.[23] Fathers whose children are tied in this way may refer to each other as *"compadre,"* although, since this term is often used in friendship, one cannot automatically assume the relationship when one hears it used. However, we would judge that the ties of extended family and *compadrazgo* are much weaker in Huecorio than they are assumed to be in other communities. *Compadres* were rarely mentioned in any connection,[24] and one farmer emphasized that in choosing his friends or workmates qualities other than that of relationship were more important.

[23] A *madrina* (godmother) is considered to be a real relation—so much so that her sons are considered to be brothers of the *ahijado* (godchild).

[24] In one case, a *compadre* was commercially convenient for it enabled one individual to get a discount at his store. In another, a man was especially tolerant toward his drunken *compadre* who worked with him. But these latter two men were tied by what seemed to be a more important bond—they played frequently together in a band.

When we examine the composition of work teams, we see that the relationship involved is usually temporary and commercial rather than one based on relationship and labor exchange. It is clear from Table XXXI that even in the production of corn, a noncash crop, Huecorianos tend to hire nonfamily members rather than use relatives outside the immediate biological family. Two other considerations help us understand this. Only one farmer paid for the *"peón"* by switching roles and working for the *peón*. In all the other cases, a money payment was made. Furthermore, when labor is hired it comes, as often as not, from outside of Huecorio. This would seem to imply that as a rule farmers consider agriculture to be an individual commercial venture, quite separated in their minds from the other ties they have to people. It is possible, although we have nothing upon which to base this statement, that if relatives worked for each other, either for cash or in labor exchange, it would demean their relationship in some way. A cash payment might suggest a hard desire to commercialize a higher form of association, and work without payment may bring into subconscious recall the work without pay of the *encomienda*.

Friends, of course, are often tied in some kind of economic relationship, but it seems the rule that care is taken to avoid relationships that would insert a commercial wedge that might split the tie. For instance, a friendship could not survive if one person was always acting in the role of *patrón* and the other as his employee. This would imply an intolerable role conflict. On the other hand, friends could work together in harmony if they were both employed by someone else. Similarly, in order to maintain true mutual loyalty, friends who borrow money need give no security or interest, and a friend can borrow a tool or use a pump for a short period of time without making any payment, while another person could not borrow the tool and would have to pay for the use of the land. Commercialization enters only when the item considered—a *buey,* or a piece of land, or a large sum of money—has a considerable value.

Although the exchange of labor for labor does not seem to occur frequently except within the immediate biological family,[25] slightly

[25] When a father has given some of his land to a son there will be frequently a labor exchange, which in effect merely extends the work relationship that existed before the land was divided.

more complex exchanges of tools or animals can be found. In one reported case one man lent a second man a *yunta,* and in payment the second man worked on the land of the first. After he had completed this work he took the *yunta* to plough another plot which he was working *a medias.* Commercial economic transactions seem to be the rule, however. *Peones* are paid a daily wage of cash plus a noon meal, animals are rented usually by payment of a specified quantity of a crop, land is rented on a sharecropping basis (*a medias* or fifty-fifty), goods are exchanged for cash and are not bartered, servants or craftsmen are paid in cash, and so on.

Vertical relationships have a special character, with the senior partner (*patrón*) expected to provide some protection for, and be indulgent of, the junior partner in exchange in some cases for labor but often for an intangible loyalty. Don Juan's *taller* is typical of this. He is a wealthy person by village standards, and as such takes under his wing in the *taller* a number of persons whom he trains and for whom he provides facilities. Those persons, as we have seen, do not work for Don Juan. He is merely helping them because he is able to do so.

Don Juan is also charged with collecting the payments for the use of water. He is expected to be considerate of the families of slender means, and indeed, instead of demanding the 100 pesos in one lump he accepts smaller contributions as the money becomes available.

The *patrón* relationship extends beyond the village, of course. It was expected, for instance, that our research team had some obligation to Huecorio and it was natural that I be invited to buy a new basketball for the village. This traditional manifestation of need succorance, as we shall shortly see, is relied upon to solve problems that the community cannot organize itself to attack.

Huecorianos are faced with a constant flow of special, temporary goals which they are asked to meet. Examples of these are the needs to finance a *fiesta,* to repair the sewing machines of the *Centro,* to combat a plague of worms attacking the corn crop, to arrange a program for a *fiesta patria,* or to paint the kindergarten. The success with which these goals are fulfilled varies considerably.

The *fiestas* of a religious nature are a well established part of village life. For them, bands and decorations must be provided at great expense. Three bands were present at Corpus Christi, and they along with the decorations cost 3,000 pesos, which was financed by collecting 25 pesos from each household. As good Catholics the villagers support this expression of their faith, but not without grumbling about the burden.

The *fiesta patria* does not involve the expenditure of money, but is celebrated with such things as the widely popular basketball game and social dancing, and its organization is accomplished without resistance. The social dancing at the *Centro Social* offers a relatively painless means of solving other short-term problems which involve essentially a modest sum of cash. For instance, at the dance on the evening of Corpus Christi each couple was assessed 20 centavos per dance, and in this way money was made available to repair the sewing machines belonging to the Centro.

Other short-term goals involving cash or labor contributions were much less successful. We have mentioned above[26] the plague of worms which attacked the corn crop. A problem of this kind can be solved, technically speaking, by a small number of men using the appropriate equipment. We saw, however, that Huecorio failed to surmount this crisis because of difficulties of organization, a lack of sense of social responsibility on the part of some of the affected farmers, a lack of equipment, and, finally, the simultaneous occurrence of a wedding which precipitated several days of debilitating inebriation.

Huecorianos combine relatively successfully in small groups associated more or less permanently together for some common purpose. The several groups functioning in Huecorio in 1962 were a Girls' Club, the *Asociación Avícola,* and the basketball team. All were sponsored by CREFAL, but the basketball team and the *Asociación Avícola* are now carried along on their own momentum. The Girls' Club meets two or three nights a week, and its 15 or so members—married and unmarried girls in their teens and twenties—receive instruction in home economics from teachers and students from CREFAL. Attendance is never 100%, for the girls have chores to finish in their homes, and their activities are restricted because of a lack of equipment.

[26] Chapter 2, pp. 69–70.

The success of these three separate small groups seems due to two main factors. First, the goals are clear, desired, and attainable.[27] Second, the activity does not involve the social commitment of certain less enthusiastic individuals. Perhaps we might explain it this way. Although in the insect plague it was not technically necessary to have the participation of all the farmers whose crops were attacked, the fact that some did not wish to participate created resentment that they should benefit from the effort of the others. On the other hand, in the voluntary associations participation is a prerequisite to the receipt of benefits.

The contiguity of landholdings is at times another basis for association for both permanent and temporary advantage. In the insect plague crisis, the fact that unaffected and affected farmers had adjoining plots of land was insufficient to unite them to overcome the organizational difficulties. In the northern section of the *ejido*, San Pedrito farmers attempted during the 1930s to farm their lands cooperatively. The effort inevitably broke down due to disputes over the division of the crops, and thus we have a case similar to the insect plague crisis but with a slightly different twist. Although all farmers cooperated in the work to varying degrees, the suspicion arose that some would receive a reward exceeding the value merited by their effort. However, another example shows that these objections do not always arise. In 1961 the Río Guan was diverted by means of three canals dug in La Lagunilla, La Peñita, and the southern part of San Pedrito. All the landowners participated, and the question arises why the participation was universal in this effort and not in the insect plague crisis. The reasons are several: the job was done during an off season when it did not compete with other work, the organizational difficulties were slight, the benefits were more or less equally shared, and, more important, they were clear, substantial, and permanent.

The *ejido* is another potential source of cooperation, but only in a limited way. *Ejidatarios* do not cooperate as a group except for the

[27] For the Girls' Club the goals are the pleasures of making attractive garments and cooking more appealing foods. The members of the basketball team find a sort of catharsis for their surplus energy and need aggression, and the members of the *Asociación Avícola* derive satisfaction from their substantial profits.

rare one-shot efforts such as the Río Guan diversion, and in the general acceptance of the manner of rotating the fields in the crop-fallow cycle. The sequence of rotation does not vary, and the pattern is carried through by inertia and the sanction of custom. Thus cooperation does not go beyond this weak routine. According to one informant, in the early enthusiastic days of the *ejido* the drive to cooperate had more force. In addition to the 5% tax on their crop that *ejidatarios* still pay, they accepted a 10% levy to be used for community improvement. However, disagreement over the utilization of the fund angered some *ejidatarios* and they refused to contribute. The effort naturally collapsed. *Ejidatarios* could benefit by cooperating in small groups of ten to twenty to pool their resources and apply for credit from the *Banco Ejidal*. This is not done, however. The advantages are not clear, there is a fear of collective responsibility for a debt, no *ejidatario* is willing to undertake the necessary leadership which would involve considerable time and effort on his part without a correspondingly greater reward, and activities such as this are frustrated by a deeply imbedded pattern of mistrust.

Certain goals and development projects offer a diffuse benefit to the community as a whole, and it is implicit that the cooperation to achieve them must be community-wide. Typical instances of these goals are the construction, maintenance, and reconstruction of the water supply system; the construction, maintenance, and library utilization of the *Centro Social*; the transfer and maintenance of sewing machines to be placed in the *Centro Social*; the opening of a drainage ditch to clear water from a street; and the construction of an irrigation system. The difficulties associated with these projects illustrate that there is little likelihood that Huecorio can progress spontaneously and autonomously along the lines suggested by the advocates of community development.

The Water Supply System

In 1952 General Múgica suggested to General Cárdenas, who was at that time in charge of the Tepalcatepec Project in Uruapan, that the spring in Carián could be investigated and a study made as to the feasibility of providing water to Huecorio and seven nearby communities that were badly in need of it. The project was undertaken in 1954 by the federal government, at a cost of 300,000 pesos. Each household to which water was piped was supposed to make a token contribution of 100 pesos. As we have seen, many families had not met their quota by 1962.

Unfortunately, when completed the system proved to be inadequate, and during the dry season the water is directed to Huecorio for only two or three hours a day. The reason for the paucity in the dry-season supply is not clear. Most likely the water table falls to a level where the reservoir of the wellhead fills too slowly to permit the pump to draw continuously. Huecorianos had another, but erroneous, explanation. They believed that since the inlet to the main reservoir was at the bottom of the tank, the pump had to work against the pressure of all the acumulated water. The solution, they felt, would be to relocate the intake to the top of the tank, for they reasoned this would reduce the weight of the water against which the pump was working. This of course is not correct, since water pressure in a stagnant body is a function of its vertical, not its horizontal, dimension. The villagers rejected this solution to their problem, not because of any awareness of the laws of physics but because of the social aspects of executing the plan. They estimated the cost would be 15,000 pesos, and Huecorianos, although most concerned about the water shortage, were reluctant to contribute this money when the benefits would be shared by other villages. There is no mechanism to facilitate inter-village cooperation, and Huecorianos listened instead to a CREFAL student who tried to persuade them to build a completely new system for their own use. This suggestion lost momentum as soon as it was realized that each family would have to contribute at least 500 pesos— more than their annual income in some cases. The reaction to the impasse was typical. A number of Huecorianos said to us, "If you really want to help us, you should get someone to solve our water problem."

The Centro Social

The building which now houses the *Centro Social* had functioned as a community meeting hall in the years before the Revolution, but was in a state of disrepair until 1954. At that time a dynamic village leader, now dead, persuaded the state government to provide about 1,500 pesos in materials to repair the building, while the labor was undertaken by the villagers themselves. The *Centro Social* is available for community functions such as meetings and dances, for the use of clubs, and it is open every evening as a library. Each family is supposed to pay five pesos a year to maintain the *Centro*. Responsible village leaders have the task of collecting the money, but many families do not contribute. Those who do not are not permitted to borrow from the library, but this penalty has small success. The *Centro* functions only because of the willingness of a minority to take a special responsibility. For example, in order to place the sewing machines safely within it it was necessary to install a grate in the window. The money for the bars came from a dance, but one man had to donate the cement and another his labor to install the grate.[28]

The Drainage Ditch

Heavy summer rains frequently flood village streets, and on one street in particular the water accumulates into a stagnant, oozy, unsanitary mess. A drain once led from the street to the lake but it has clogged up through lack of maintenance. The *municipio* of Pátzcuaro obtained new tile for the project with the understanding that villagers would provide the labor. Accordingly, one Saturday morning 42 men left their fields and began to dig the ditch. Unfortunately, the ditch had to pass through a private plot already planted in corn. This land was owned by the *ejido* commissioner, whose brother was the *jefe* of the village. The commissioner protested vehemently against the

[28] The *Centro* had ceased to function by the time of my visit in 1964. Apparently, not enough money could be collected to pay the utility bill.

damage to his *milpa,* and it was agreed, after a discussion of alternatives, to vote on the project. The ballot was 36 to six in favor of continuance, but, despite the presence of an official from the *municipio,* the commissioner remained adamant. He clinched his opposition by a threat "to fill with lead" anybody who so much as lifted a spadeful of dirt. The workers prudently retreated, and the dangerously unsanitary water sloshed around in small ponds for the duration of the rainy season.[29]

An Irrigation Project

Villagers complain of the shortage of irrigation water during the dry season, and as we have seen, Geronimo Roca suggested a network of a pump and 12-inch pipe which he said would cost only 36,000 pesos. Farmers could easily recover this amount out of the increase in crop production, and the money could be borrowed if only 30 to 40 men would join in a society. But, he said, "nobody follows me." Perhaps Geronimo does not understand his own society. Not only are his fellows reluctant to assume a large debt, but without the kind of outside organizational and managerial leadership that characterizes the *Asociación Avícola* they cannot bind themselves permanently together. It is clear that Huecorianos are divided by the mistrust of a negative individualism.

Individualism

The essential characteristic of individualism is the minimization of firm ties binding a person to others—a desire, for some reason, to be independent. But individualism can be either positive or negative, and undoubtedly both facets can appear in the same person. When individualism is positive, one must add other characteristics to the

---

[29] The *ejido* commissioner remained respected by Huecorianos despite this incident. While they did not like his antagonism to the project, they understood the nature of his claim to his private land.

Women of Carián laundering at lake shore. Fishing canoes in background

Farmers discussing the issue of the drainage canal

desire for independence. The independence is tempered by a sense of social responsibility and acceptance of partial permanent or temporary restraints—such as the payment of taxes—for the benefit of the community at large. Neither is it constrained by a false egalitarianism under which no differences exist, but instead there is a belief in individual responsibility and the meritorious rewards for effort. Furthermore, the positive individualist is reasonably self-confident and is willing to indulge in the adventure of risk-taking. When individualism is negative there is no firm pride in accomplishment or achievement, and the person exhibits an ego- rather than group-focused image of change. Only activities which bring benefit directly to the self will be undertaken. There is as well an underlying mistrust of the motives of others and a fear that one will be cheated in any association with a person with whom one is not thoroughly familiar.

Fragments of evidence testify to the nature of the Huecoriano's individualism. There is, for instance, the pattern of residence. Married couples arrange to separate from their in-laws as soon as possible. Ninety-eight of the 142 households contain only one family, while only 44 are made up of two or more families. In the majority of the cases the multifamily households became such when a bereaved parent moved in after the death of a spouse, or they are temporary associations in which a young couple accepts shelter in the home of the husband's parents until a separate house can be built.

Furthermore, in the economic sphere persons try to avoid relying on or becoming obligated to others. They seek no advice from others, they prefer once-and-for-all money or crop payments for services rendered, and they avoid indebtedness not because of any moral implication but for fear of the consequences of default. Cooperation, especially if it implies a long-term association, is distasteful for it carries the well-founded fear that someone will take advantage of the relationship. In other words, ties beyond the immediate family are bound to be broken, so why expose oneself to the risk and disappointment?

For historical reasons, and because of a lack of their own accomplishment, Huecorianos suffer from feelings of inferiority in their dealings with others. They have at times been taken advantage of by outsiders,[30] and they are ashamed of the appearance of their village and the humble aspect they feel they present to others. Their negative individualism would seem to be a natural defense against what appears even now to be a hostile world.

Centrifugal Forces

A number of factors combine to destroy any hope that the people of Huecorio can be united easily in common purpose and effort. The four main centrifugal forces are negative individualism, the demonstrated venality of officeholders, divisive factionalism, and, finally, paternalism.

The aspect of negative individualism which is most destructive is the ego-focused image of change. The majority of villagers will not contribute to an activity unless—or in some cases even if—they derive some direct benefit. Said one, "The *pueblo* does not progress, because there is no cooperation between the people and the authorities. When the majority of the people fails to attend *faenas,* one can do nothing. *Si no no hay fuerza no se puede hacer nada."* (Nothing can be accomplished without a means of forcing cooperation.) And, as with the ditch-digging *faena,* it is possible for an individual completely to frustrate an expression of the general will. In a similar case, several individuals persisted in using scarce water from the public system to irrigate their gardens during the dry season. There is no social or political force which can be applied to bring recalcitrants into line.

The actions of some Huecorianos in positions of authority are not such as to inspire confidence. One instance of venality which rankles villagers concerns R., whose reputation for integrity was soiled when he became *jefe de tenencia.* During his tenure it was arranged to sell some small lots belonging to the village to a number of poorer families who had no property. R. pocketed the money and disappeared

---

[30] Particularly officials and others who demand *mordidas* of them. However, our experience would suggest that the majority of the government officials who deal with Huecorianos are sympathetic and generous. Those whose attitude is condescending are immediately identified as *egoistas* by a people as sensitive as the Huecorianos.

for a while.[31] Now the people joke bitterly, "Oh so you want some money! Why don't you go see R.?" This action on the part of one whom the villagers respected has embittered them and undermined their trust in any leader. They say, *"Ya no hay hombres que obren con debida honradez."* (There is nobody whom you can trust any more.)

There are many such examples of venality. José Dongo, who took stones from the plaza to fix his house; D., who as *ejido* commissioner took some vacated parcels of land for himself, gave others to his sons, and sold some for personal gain; J., who as *presidente* of the *Centro Social* took the furniture that had been given as a gift by CREFAL, and when charges were brought slipped away to *el norte*. Even the organizers of religious *fiestas* are accused of keeping for themselves the money left over. It is little wonder that Huecorianos say, "Yes we have leaders, but they lead only for personal benefit."

An even more serious centrifugal force is the division that results from various forms of factionalism. Villagers turn against each other and separate into factions for a number of reasons, the most common of which seem to be cultural antagonisms, physical violence, the *ejido,* envy, slighted pride and last, but definitely not least, women. Occasionally a family will be sundered by a disagreement over land or some other economic asset, or by children's resistance to parental control. More commonly it will be family against family, and may be started by something relatively innocent such as a fight between children. But they become a vortex sucking brothers, fathers, uncles, and *compadres,* into an antagonism that is easier to fan than to suppress.

A cultural gap exists between the Huecorianos who live in the main part of the village and the residents of Carián and Urandén. The people of the village center were rarely heard to speak of the others in a derogatory fashion, but those from the two former islands are aware of an ostracism. One said, "The people don't talk to us much." "Why?" "They just don't." Perhaps because of this, some of the more Tarascan people behave in a manner closely resembling

---

[31] This is the kind of deceit the people call a *trinquete,* and once when we used this word while interviewing R. he paled and said that it was a bad word and we should not use it.

a childish rebellion. They sometimes crash parties to stare at and embarrass the participants. On one occasion an elderly woman, one of a group of crashers, held a baby in her arms and sat drunkenly in a pool of her own urine while she quacked, "Yes, we are the ugly ducklings of Huecorio." This ostracism may explain why leadership efforts from the men of Carián are stonily ignored by other Huecorianos.

The establishment of the *ejido* in Mexico slashed a deep wound into the social structure of many villages that has not yet healed. Allied with the *hacendados,* the Church led an attack and a division developed between persons who wanted land and others who respected the words of their priests. Although the priests attending Huecorio continue to harbor this sense of injustice done and consider the *ejido* to be a monstrous robbery, we found no evidence that the villagers remained divided over it.

Feelings of envy may sometimes rise to the surface in manifestations of open dislike, but the evidence to justify those feelings is slim. In a dispute over the transference of the sewing machines from the jurisdiction of the schoolteacher to that of the *Centro Social,* some Huecorianos claim they detected a trick. Two men still floating from the effects of a wedding *fiesta* brought up the subject gratuitously when we encountered them in the street. "We want the machines to remain in the school because they are the gift to the people of Huecorio and must be cared for. The idea of taking them from the teacher is a trick of Don Juan, who will take them from the *Centro* and put them in his *taller*." The gentlemen chose to ignore the fact that the teacher would not make the machines available to be used by the people. Similarly, Huecorianos are not above making caustic and critical remarks about their fellows—remarks which seem to reveal envy and dislike. One family, for instance, sneered at another because although they were "rich" they still slept on the floor instead of beds, whereas the second family criticized the first because although they were "rich" they still continued to eat "bad food."

Slighted pride may be more important than envy in its ability to divide, but again it is difficult to obtain the necessary evidence since people do not usually reveal the true motives for their actions. The only instance that can be documented involved a request by two members of our team to use the church organ for choir practice. The sacristan was reluctant to let the girls have the key and wanted to know who would be using the instrument. Thinking that it would support their case, the girls mentioned the names of the choir members who were also active in the *Centro Social*. "Then you cannot have the key. I have many times wanted something from the *Centro Social* but they have never accommodated me." [32]

It will surely come as no surprise that women are frequently involved in the incidents that lead to discord. One team member reported a feud in the following manner:

> It all started when L.R. decided to get herself a lover. The unfortunate luck fell on the uncle of P.M., who was foolish enough to fall into the trap. In a fight over L.R. the lover killed her father. Some time later, to avenge the death of their father, J.R. and B.R. killed the lover. It could not end there, of course, so the brother of the lover killed B.R. Then C., the brother of B.R., killed the brother of the lover.[33] The dispute continued, and P., who was only a baby when his father, the lover, was killed, was plagued by the feud into adulthood. He was provoked into shooting C., and paid for this with ten years in jail.
>
> All these deaths were started by L.R., and it seems that the R. women are famous for these affairs. The latest adventure of the R. women came to a climax about six months ago with the death of their brother, J.R. This started with A.R., who wanted to take another girl's boy friend. A.R., with her sister-in-law and aunt, played a trick on the boy, tearing his clothes, taking one of his shoes, and then crying "rape!" The charge was not widely believed but the family tried to make the boy marry A.R. He wisely left for *el norte,* but the R. family continually provoked his brother L. who remained behind. J.R., the brother of the famous women, was at a dance attended by L., and to make L. dance J.R. started shooting at his feet. L., seeing himself

[32] The choir only became a reality upon the kindly intervention of one of the priests, Padre José Cortés Castro. Several Huecorianos have fine voices, and the choir functioned harmoniously for the short while that interest could be maintained.

[33] We apologize for the apparent confusion, but the use of symbols instead of names is obviously needed to protect those who managed to survive.

wounded, pulled a gun and shot J.R. in the stomach. For this death L. spent three months in prison.

The male survivors are now at peace. They feel that there have been enough killings, but the R. women are still searching for excitement and A.R. is now trying to get L.'s new boy friend. Yesterday morning in the bus one of the R. women kicked another woman in the fanny because her son had protected L. in the latest of the killings.

The institution of paternalism and its psychological counterpart, a strong need succorance, are divisive forces to the extent that they manifest the belief that one need not take the responsibility to solve one's own problems since some higher "other" has the obligation. This attitude was clearly revealed in the conversation with the two inebriated gentlemen mentioned above. "Señora Múgica should help us and visit us every week." "Why?" we asked. "Look here, *maestros!* When the general asked us for the little hill on which to build his *quinta* he offered us many things, even to buying a clock for the church. These promises were not fulfilled."

In speaking of the people of Huecorio, outsiders expressed similar views. "Those people are accustomed to receive but never to give." "CREFAL has given them too much and there is no impetus for self-improvement." Indeed, just enough material help has come from outside Huecorio to reinforce the feeling on the part of some villagers that they are entitled to aid but are not obligated to help themselves. The federal government has given agricultural dusters and a social center, while CREFAL has offered books, trees, and so on. Nevertheless, the majority of the goods and services that flow in from official sources are subsidized and require a counterpart effort.

In addition, it would seem that this passive reliance on outside help is very much less than universal. Villagers were asked how they felt village problems could be solved. It was clear that many consider that responsibility is internal rather than external, for only eight of the 40 respondents said that the government should be petitioned, while the others were evenly divided between an expressed desire for community cooperation and a need to improve the local leadership. Typical responses reflecting the several views were: "We should petition the federal government. We have no leaders here," "We should cooperate to ask the government for help. There are no leaders here. Everyone is working for himself." In speaking of the poorly paved streets, one said, "We should organize a group to do it. We need to change the *jefe*. We made a mistake this time, the leaders are not competent." Paternalism, it would seem, is not an insurmountable obstacle to autonomous change.

Binding Agents

A number of influences at work in Huecorio have the potential to offset the disruptive forces, but their power has been weak or in some cases negative.

Some informants argued that cooperation was formerly the rule rather than the exception. "In 1949, even before CREFAL, the people collaborated. They attended meetings and worked together. With their labor and money they built the public washhouse, the water trough, repaired the *jefatura* and the jail, and they paved several streets." "In years gone by Huecorio was more of a united community. People used to take more responsibility in helping the church or making a *fiesta*. When you gave a *fiesta* people who were not invited did not come. Now they have no shame. They come uninvited not only to eat but also to steal. They have stolen dishes from my house." It is not easy to distinguish these statements from nostalgia or self-aggrandizement. In the first quote a man referred to his tenure as chief, and in the second to years long past over which the pains may have dimmed and the warmer memories strengthened. However, the weakening of community cohesion is a distinct possibility stemming from the apparent breakdown of the authoritarian, traditional society.

Although the unity of their faith does not bind the people of Huecorio in their secular life, the Church can be considered a potentially dynamic force. Young Mexican priests appear to have an increasing interest in the social and economic problems of their flock, but argue that the role of the Church is primarily spiritual and that secular activities are restrained by the limited financial resources available. The respect that most Huecorianos have for their faith and its representatives puts the Church in a position in which its persuasive power, if rightly used, could heal the wounds created by the institution of the *ejido* system and offer the villagers a positive unifying spirit.

Similarly, the spirit of the Mexican Revolution holds a potential contribution. Nationalism and revolution *may* give a people a common, constructive purpose, an enthusiasm, and a feeling of responsibility to the wider group. Huecorianos are proud of their Mexico, but they are no longer imbued with the spirit of the bloody Revolution of 1910 or of the quiet but spectacular economic revolution of the 1960s. A minority talk of the Revolution but it is a talk of bitterness rather than hope. "They say that the Revolution is over but it is a lie. No! They are finishing us off, bit by bit. The prices of the things we sell go down while the prices in the shops are higher every day. We are in a revolution and for us it would be easier if they said, 'Here is a gun. Take it and fight!' Then we could defend ourselves better. The first revolutionaries labored in good faith with the cry *Tierra y Libertad*. But the big *ricos,* the landowners, after the Revolution insinuated themselves into good positions and they are always subjugating the *campesino*."

The influence of CREFAL in Huecorio has unquestionably been good. Its *Asociación Avícola* is a brilliant success, and its sponsorship of basketball games and *Centro Social* activities contributed to a richer life for the people. Perhaps the most important effect has been subtle, serendipitous, and rather long-range in its impact. Huecorianos are being exposed to people of widely different cultures who come from all over the free world, but especially of course from Latin America. Some are transient visitors but others reside in village homes for long periods. In their dealings with these people, Huecorianos gain self-confidence and their protective shells are cracked. They learn of other places and cultures, and gradually minds are opened.

CREFAL's valuable role is tarnished to some extent by a lack of close supervision of the students in the communities. Those in Huecorio in 1962 were responsible and serious, but one in particular irritated the villagers with a constant stream of half-baked ideas. While the *Centro Social* needed attention and support, this individual ignored it and was trying to arrange lights at the school, repairs to a stone fence, repairs to the church, and so on. The family quotas of five pesos a year for the *Centro Social* were never fully collected, but the student arranged other contributions including three pesos for the church and one peso for the stone wall. When asked about the money for the *Centro,* the reply was an offhand, "We'll get it later." [34] Another student succeeded, after much effort, in obtaining several thousand fruit trees for the village. He was aware that villagers should pay for them but had promised them as a gift. This had the unfortunate effect of confirming, in the minds of the Huecorianos, their right to a largesse from above.

All such visitors find that advice is painless to give and that ambitious schemes are cheap to dream. The villagers are bombarded by a constant stream of interference which is unflattering and annoying. Gratuitous advice and wild schemes inexpertly offered seal the protective shell that the same contact in another context could serve to open. Nevertheless, the general feeling that Huecorianos have for CREFAL is one of appreciation, compromised to some extent by a few personal antagonisms and an occasional misunderstanding.[35]

Teachers who reside in villages such as Huecorio are clearly in a position to stimulate and lead,[36] but the principal teacher in residence during 1962 neglected his role. There was a widespread feeling among Huecorianos that the teacher did not exercise leadership or participate in the life of the village. Some were particularly incensed that he refused to turn over to the *Centro Social* the three sewing machines that had been donated by CREFAL, and complaints about his

[34] Other of his enthusiastic schemes could be documented but this would be pointless. Those schemes and his constant references to quotas and cooperatives created a resistance to him and nullified any good effects he may otherwise have had.

[35] On one occasion a woman refused to give us information until she was assured that we were not from CREFAL. "They are always coming here and asking us questions but we never know what they do with the information," she said.

[36] This proposition needs no supporting argument, but it is of interest to hear of an example cited by General Cárdenas. During our conversations he said, "I tried to help the people of La Pacanda in 1924 but I could not reach them. In 1928 I thought I could help them again but they did not respond. In 1935 when I was President I arranged for soldiers to plant fruit trees on the island to help their economy, but they simply neglected the trees. But now there are 54 *granjas* on the island started by CREFAL and they are advancing. The passage of time and the school have given the people confidence over these years."

actions and attitudes were made to the regional representative of the Federal Department of Education. Not only did the teacher refuse to cooperate with the students from CREFAL, but deep anti-American feelings moved him in an attempt to turn the community against our project. The tone and vehemence of his effort are well illustrated in his reply to a discussion in a village meeting in which we attempted to explain our project.

What you say is lies. You speak without saying or doing anything. You and those people from CREFAL come here into our communities and say you want to find out how we live and what we want. But it is a lie—all of you—you are a bunch of liars. You come among us so you can lie about us later on. You say you are here to teach us—a pure lie. You walk with your cameras to lie more about us. Once in Santa Ana a fellow took a photograph of children playing and later said *he* was teaching us.

No, *señores,* you are professionals and doctors but you have nothing special. You only know how to lie and lie. We do not need anybody from outside to come and say they are helping us. We know all these things already and better than you do. You! You wrote in *Selecciones de Mayo*[37] a whole bunch of lies that are offensive to us. You said that we in La Pacanda before you arrived were only able to make five pesos a day, that we were not capable of doing anything—not even to talk—and now, thanks to you, now we are people and we are able to live better and eat better. We can tolerate you no more.

Don't interfere in our schools. We don't need anybody to help us. We are more capable than you. I say to you I don't want you.

The teacher sat down in an awkward silence broken only by the man next to him, who was heard to say, "We don't come here to

[37] The reference is to the edition of May, 1962 of the Spanish translation of the *Reader's Digest.* The English version was a condensation of an article by Robert S. Strother in *Latin American Reports,* Vol. IV, No. 11, published in the April, 1962 edition of the *Reader's Digest* as "The Golden Eggs of Patzcuaro." Apart from occasional lapses into the slick style that plagues American journalism, the offensive nature of the article is not clear and it seems generally to be a statement of fact. The teacher's resentment is explained not by misrepresentation of the role of CREFAL but by CREFAL's success which served to emphasize his own failures.

listen to your stupidities." A village leader rose and asked support for our spokesman, Señor Bolívar, and he was warmed by a round of applause. The teacher was replaced at the end of the school year.

Huecorio's teacher was a graduate of the University of Morelia, an institution of reputedly leftist bias. His bitter xenophobia embarrassed the people of Huecorio, whose warmer feelings toward foreigners had been molded by the presence of CREFAL and the experiences of many men in the United States. Huecorianos are perceptive judges of personality and do not let the formal patterns of respect associated with face-to-face relationships interfere with their private views of an individual. Thus the teacher may have believed that because Huecorianos greeted him politely with the title *"maestro,"* they felt the respect implied. The general sentiment was quite the contrary.[38] The teacher's bitter, negative attitude was despised, and this reaction, combined with his lack of leadership and lack of responsibility, precipitated the steps that led to his removal. The lesson is an important one. With the universal obeisance now paid to education as a key to economic development, there exists the temptation to concentrate attention on the number of teachers produced rather than to consider the qualitative aspects of their wider role in a community. As with the agricultural agents, the teachers must receive training in their community roles, and as far as possible be selected on the basis of effective personality.

Effective and self-sustaining community development, especially where there is no working political power structure, requires energetic and persuasive leadership and active cooperation on the part of the body of the populace. Neither condition exists in Huecorio. There are formal and informal organizations from which leaders might arise and through which their power might be channeled. Those groups are the political officials, the *Sociedad de Padres de Familia,* the basketball club, the *Centro Social,* and the lay religious functionaries. In addition, persons with leadership qualities might be found outside these groups. Few persons, however, are motivated to exercise more than casual, temporary leadership roles. Whenever a situation arises that

[38] This disparity between a nonvillager's self-image and the assessment made by Huecorianos was very apparent. Words such as "egotist" or "nuisance" were frequently applied, and no outsider had a status sufficient to guarantee immunity.

calls for someone to take initiative and responsibility, a handful of men such as Salvador Gorozpe, Ricardo Pérez, or Geronimo Roca will respond on an *ad hoc* basis. These exceptional men will contribute time or money in temporary situations such as installing a window in the *Centro Social,* visiting a government office to ask for help for the village, or attempting to persuade others to cooperate in a *faena.* Understandably, there is a reluctance to undertake more permanent roles, particularly that of a *jefe de tenencia,* since the effective performance of responsibilities requires a great deal of time without financial compensation. Since Huecorianos are fully occupied with earning a living, permanent leadership roles impose a heavy burden on them. "The authorities do not have time. They have to earn a living and so the official work is not done. The people do not progress because of this. In the elections the people should consider more carefully whom they choose." Furthermore, as we have seen, leadership is unrewarding. Leaders receive no respectful recognition from other Huecorianos, and if they do wish to take initiative find themselves faced with an invisible wall of noncooperation.

For their part, the villagers complain bitterly of a lack of leadership.[39] "The authorities are lax and do not take their responsibilities seriously." "We need energetic authorities. They talk but leave the serious business behind." "It is always *egoismo.* For me, yes—for the village, no." "We need to change the *jefe.* He isn't competent." "There

[39] When asked about the best ways to solve the problems of Huecorio, the majority of respondents thought in terms of improved community organization and about half of these felt that the problem lay in a lack of leadership while others recognized the need for cooperation. Replies to the question "How should the problems of Huecorio be solved?" tabulated as follows:

Improve leadership	17
Community cooperation	15
Petition the government	8
Borrow money from banks	1
Buy more lands	2
Fix the water system	5
Start a factory	2
Educate people	2
Get a good teacher	1
"Who knows?"	3
No reply	14

are no leaders here. Everybody is working for himself." Thus the much needed communal unity is stymied on the one hand by the costly and unrewarding demands placed on leaders, and on the other by the community's lack of cooperation, which stems from its negative individualism and mistrust of the motives of the leaders.[40]

Nevertheless, Huecorianos are disturbed by the conditions of the village and seem to harbor a desire to make Huecorio a comfortable and attractive place to live. Table 14 clearly indicates this. More adequate water supplies and more sanitary and presentable streets and public places would erase some of the shame that Huecorianos feel when they are visited by outsiders. This concern seems compounded by a sense of impotence—an inability of the community to solve its problems.

Recognition of a need is the first and necessary step in promoting community development. It is not, however, a sufficient condition. In a traditional society with recognized patterns of authority and effective social controls, noncooperating recalcitrants can be brought into line when community projects are initiated. In Huecorio, traditional patterns of behavior have been or are being destroyed, and no new organization and control has been established or is likely to arise autonomously. Under these circumstances, a new structure of government has to be imposed and should take the form of greater village autonomy with more effective control over resources. Furthermore, individualism should be taken as a social datum, and naïve reliance on voluntary cooperation should be eschewed. Specifically, this means that the local village officials should be given authority to levy taxes and to spend the income on desired community improvements. Tax revenues could come from several sources—in particular, from partial repatriation of the *ejido* tax and of the property taxes levied by the federal government on land and buildings, and from modest head taxes levied on households by the community itself.[41] The major difficulty lies in the well-founded suspicion of the venal nature of public officials. This could be mitigated by several measures, namely, a

[40] "The problems are for the *empleados* to take care of. It is not our responsibility to worry about them. That's why they are chosen."

[41] A small head tax would not be burdensome, and could, if the household wished, be voided by a labor donation.

TABLE 14

Tabulation of Replies to Question: "In your opinion, what are the principal problems confronting Huecorio?"

Replies	Number of Replies
Pertaining to Community Improvement	
A lack of water for domestic and/or agricultural use	20
Poorly drained and/or paved streets	12
Inadequate street lighting	7
Need for repairs to church	3
Need for improvements to park	5
Need for improvement of other public facilities: (Social Center, planting of trees, etc.)	6
Need for painting houses	1
Pertaining to Economic Improvement	
A shortage of land	3
Need to provide employment (e.g., start factory)	7
Lack of agricultural inputs	4
Pertaining to Social Problems	
Lack of unity	6
Lack of leadership	6
Drunkenness	5
Lack of recreation	1
Need for better medical service	1
Need for better education of people	1
Miscellaneous	
"Who knows?"	2
There are no problems	2
Total number of replies	92
Total number of respondents	70

modest salary payment to the officials, adequately audited bookkeeping,[42] and posting of accounts in a public place, for instance in the *jefatura*. As one perceptive villager put it, "It is important to report to the people every month on the expenditures for the village. Now

[42] Public officials would be required to keep books, give tax receipts, and accept receipts for all disbursements. Auditing could be done by officials from higher levels of government.

the people don't know how the money is spent and therefore they always complain about the perpetual quotas. They have no confidence and don't want to cooperate."

Undoubtedly this independence would sometimes be abused. Nevertheless, human beings respond to confidence, and trust that is given freely will be honored. The possibility of punishment, and the bookkeeping, auditing, and publishing procedures would simultaneously offer a subtle control. Public officials would require some education in procedures, and the position of the villages in public law would have to be enhanced. This calls for a constructive attitude on the part of national leaders and conflicts with their own desires for hegemony, but national economic development would undoubtedly be enhanced by replacing the paternalistic conception of community development with a more dynamic conception of community independence. Traditionalism is dying in Huecorio as in most rural communities, and authoritarian attitudes toward them swim against the tide.

¡Fiesta!

Fiestas, both religious and secular, constitute a very important part of the life of the people of Huecorio. Religious functions are essentially a catharsis of the deep faith of many villagers but contain elements of the primary motivation for secular *fiestas,*[43] to wit a temporary diversion from the drudgery of everyday life. In addition to the religious aspects of weddings and saints' days, a number of events in the Catholic calendar are given prominent attention in Huecorio. One of the three village priests who attend Huecorio kindly offered the following characterization of the religious year.[44]

The religious year of Huecorio begins on December 25th with the feast of Christmas. The feast begins at midnight with a High

[43] It would probably be more apt to call the secular *fiestas* parties, but this word lacks some of the colorful quality found in the secular *fiesta* of Huecorio.

[44] This is a quotation from a letter written in English, a language that Padre José Cortés Castro had taught himself to master.

Mass. After Mass at midnight *buñuelos*[45] are distributed to everyone. In the morning there is another High Mass with skyrockets and fireworks and three brass bands play music. There are Indian dances and general rejoicing. At this time a new religious leader is elected and he is, in a sense, the chief of the village. He is called the *mayordomo* or the *prioste*. The people expect much of him, and if the *fiesta* is not up to standards they will blame this *mayordomo* and he will be harshly criticized. This criticism, when it comes, is so harsh that no *mayordomo* in his right mind will warrant such abuse. Other lesser chiefs are in charge of arranging the other *fiestas* of the year. They must arrange to have the priest come to the village and are in charge of getting music, fireworks, etc.

Two sacristans in the church take care of the cult. There is also a *vaquero* who is in charge of arranging a rodeo. Also the *cantor mayor* and *cantor menor* must be elected. When these people are elected they come to the altar after the Mass and an olive crown is placed on their heads by the priests. At this time the *mayordomo* receives the symbol of his office which is a small flag on a pole. The sacristans receive the keys of the church and all the new officials receive a large candle and a tall sugar cane. The priest is also given a sugar cane. He then leads the new officials from the church, and they go in procession around the atrium of the church with fireworks and a band of music.

An important day in Huecorio is the 2nd of February (*La Candelaria,* the Blessing of the Candles), High Mass in the morning, and fireworks. Everyone brings candles and seed corn to be blessed. After Mass the priest gives a candle to everyone. The Indians do a dance called *Los Pastores.*[46] The only profane part of the *fiesta* is a rodeo, and even it is connected slightly with religious symbolism.

Another *fiesta* is called the Procession of the *Cristos.* Before the village became Christian the Indians had, every year, the procession of the idols. Vasco de Quiroga changed this to the Procession of the *Cristos* when he converted the Indians. The *fiesta* is held on a Wednesday in Lent. The procession is held after the Rosary in the night. Then people, each carrying a

[45] Fried pastries.
[46] The shepherds.

lighted candle and a crucifix, march through the streets singing hymns. It is a very beautiful procession with hundreds of candles. They pass along every street in the village. It lasts almost three hours. After this procession, everyone eats a confection made from *chilacayote* with *atole*.

Another fiesta is the Procession of the Holy Sacrament. This is held on Sunday after the ascension of Our Lord. It follows the same routine as the other *fiestas,* with High Mass in the morning and processions held in the afternoon. The people carry the saints on little platforms, upon which are also mounted little trees. Hanging on these trees are bananas, cookies, candies, and bread. This procession is held in the atrium, with at least three bands playing. Thousands of skyrockets are shot off. At this time many girls are stolen by their *novios* and get married.

The Indian people have an exaggerated veneration for the dead which is carried over from their pagan days. On the Feast of the Dead on November 2nd, the Indians place food and candles on the graves of their dead.

Procession of Most Blessed Sacrament, Corpus Christi

The most important *fiestas* celebrated in Huecorio in the year of our visit were described by the priest as follows:

January 12   *La Virgen de Guadalupe.*

January 17   *Blessing of the Animals.* The animals of the village are decorated and brought to a field to be blessed.

February 2   *La Virgen de la Candelaria, patrona* of the community. On this occasion households are assessed up to 40 pesos each to pay for the religious and secular proceedings. This is the time of carnival, and a "ball" of *petate* is paraded from house to house to collect the cash quotas. Huecorio is visited by people from neighboring communities and there are many *fiestas* in private homes.

March 19   *Fiesta de San José, patrón* of the village. A Solemn Mass, nocturnal procession, and a band playing all day in the churchyard.

March 26   *Día de la Conserva de Chilacayote.* In all the homes women prepare pastries and a sweet made of *chilacayote* and unrefined sugar. Music and a nocturnal procession.

June 10   *Día de Corpus Christi.* A Solemn Mass, a procession with bands, fireworks, and dancing. (See below.)

October 31   *Día de Difuntos.* In a house where any child has recently died an altar is set up with sweets, flowers, candles, and toys. *Atole* is eaten and rockets fired. A band plays and there is dancing.

November 2   *All Souls Day.* Villagers take *pan de difuntos* (bread of the dead) to the church and give it to those present to pray for their dead. They pray at night at the graves of their beloved ones and then return home to a feast.

December 25   *Christmas.*

The *Fiesta de Corpus Christi,* observed during our visit, is officially celebrated in the Church on the Thursday after the Feast of the Ascension, but is celebrated as a *fiesta* day in Huecorio on the following

Sunday.[47] The feast is primarily one of adoration and thanksgiving for Christ's Gift of the Blessed Sacrament—the Body and Blood of Christ under appearance of bread and wine reposing in the tabernacle on the altar.

Although the *fiesta* really begins with the celebration of Solemn High Mass, a band went playing through the streets at least an hour beforehand. The three priests arrived at about 10:30, accompanied by an organist and singers of Gregorian chant. During the Mass a young boy distributed about 30 or 40 candles, first to the women, all of whom were seated on one side of the church, and then to the men. It appears to be the custom to pray while holding candles, and later in the day when the Blessed Sacrament was exposed, the boy would light a candle and bring it to a person who was praying.

Not everyone in the village attended the Mass. Fireworks could be heard igniting in the plaza, and a band played loudly, sometimes interrupting the sermon. After the Consecration about 20 men left their benches to kneel in the sanctuary, but only six persons received Holy Communion. When the Mass was over, the priest stood near the church door and took a collection from the faithful.

Immediately following the Mass, a team of young men began a basketball game with another from nearby Colonia Ibarra. Each team was dressed in sneakers and colorful shorts and shirts which identified their village.[48] The game was vigorous, although there was a noteworthy lack of intemperate outbursts. Huecorio won. The game seemed to be played for itself rather than the stakes of prestige, money, or covert aggression.[49] Huecorianos do follow their teams closely, however, and a loss will cause in some an acute depression only alleviated by a bottle.

A Rosary was said in the late afternoon, but anticipatory arrangements began after the basketball games. Men prepared a corridor in

[47] This practice is common in many churches around the world, since it is sometimes difficult to congregate a large number of people on a working day.

[48] The costumes for the Huecorio team were financed by a movie and a *kermesse*. It was on this occasion that we were invited to purchase a good basketball. In keeping with the community development principle of self-help, we accepted half the burden.

[49] Angry outbursts did occur in a game between Huecorio and Janitzio, and for reasons unknown to us the playing was untypically rough.

the yard for the final procession. Poles were placed in the ground about ten feet apart, and between them, 12 feet above the ground, nets were stretched and pink flowers scattered upon them. The corridor followed the walls of the court and formed a hollow square, the inside of which was delineated by a fence of crisscrossed green reeds to a height of about four feet.

About 4:30 the faithful began to gather, and the women entering the church outnumbered the men. Some persons carried green branches decorated with offerings of fruits and cakes. With these offerings God is thanked for his blessings and his help is asked in time of shortage. A group of about ten men and women came from Carián. The women wore long white cotton veils, and one carried a banner representing the Virgin. Together they sang in a thin, high-pitched chorus a plaintive melody about a heaven filled with the best of earthly things. The women entered the church on their knees, while the men walked behind carrying the bountiful branches. After praying with their arms extended, they sang again and left the church, walking backwards so as to remain facing the altar. Their intense devotion was incongruous with the hubbub in the courtyard, where groups of men chatted, three bands competed simultaneously, and children chased each other and rushed in to pick up the firecrackers that crackled continuously.

The tolling of the bells announced the return of the priests, one of whom said the Rosary for the congregation packed into the church. Then the faithful were led in the procession of the Most Blessed Sacrament. A mass of people disgorged through the door, led by the priests and women carrying two fruit-laden platforms bearing glass-framed pictures of Our Lady of Guadalupe. The procession stopped at altars placed at each corner of the yard, and each time the Blessed Sacrament was placed on an altar prayers were chanted and a hymn was sung. As the people paced slowly from altar to altar, a band played solemnly. Finally the Blessed Sacrament was returned to the tabernacle, a hymn was sung, and the religious part of the *fiesta* was over. The priests doffed their robes and with a friendly *adiós* left for Pátzcuaro.

In the plaza women began to sell fruits, candies, ices, and fruit punches, a basketball game progressed, and thoughts were turned to dances and private parties to be held in the *Centro Social* and private homes. The dance at the *Centro Social* began about nine o'clock. Villagers entered quietly to sit along the walls, the men on one side and women on the other. Perhaps with their courage bolstered by a nip from a bottle of *Uruapan*[50] that was passed from man to man, girls were soon asked to dance. There were quite a few nondancers apart from the old ladies who sat watching from the sidelines and the children who darted vigorously among the couples. Swing music of 1940 vintage blared from a borrowed phonograph, and the dancing was formal and unrelaxed.[51] At midnight, the mothers, *madrinas*, and older sisters gathered the young girls to take them home, and the *fiesta* ended without incident.

Private *fiestas* are held in village homes several times a week, the most common proximate cause being the need to celebrate the day of someone's patron saint. Such *fiestas* begin with a *mañanitas* party before dawn, and are taken up again in the evening after a day's work.

Typically, all the participants rise around 4:00 a.m., in some cases having been involved until after midnight with preparations such as making floral wreaths for the celebrant. Silently a group will gather under the window of the celebrant, and when all is ready the band of trumpets, trombones, clarinets, violins, and basses will join with the singers in the strains of *las mañanitas*. The celebrant is supposed to be pleasantly surprised, and appears at the window to receive the tribute. A party begins. Furniture is pushed aside and the band plays for those energetic enough to dance. For those not intending to attend Mass a bottle of *aguardiente* is found, to make a hot weak drink of brandy, pineapple juice, and sugar, while others might sustain themselves with coffee. The predawn activities do not usually affect the Huecoriano adversely, and he breakfasts and is out to do his chores before the sun has had time to soften the morning chill.

After a full day of work, sufficient energy remains for a larger

[50] A popular brand of *aguardiente*.

[51] Huecorianos seem to have no interest in the colorful folk dances of Mexico. Few will attempt a *jarabe*, and then only after considerable pleading. Does this represent a rejection of their heritage, or is it simply less appealing than the opportunity that social dances offer to speak with or shyly touch one's partner?

evening party to celebrate a saint's day. From field notes we can ex-
tract some of the spirit of such a party as recorded while the image
was still firmly engraved.

> The party was more or less under way when we arrived. The
> chairs were arranged around the perimeter of the room, and a
> crowd of young girls was sitting awkwardly and tittering over
> the new arrivals. We scattered among them and tried to break
> the ice with conversation. The phonograph soon arrived from the
> community center and a large speaker was placed on the roof of
> the patio. Couples began dancing, and one had a scene typical
> of the romantic image that *norteamericanos* carry of life south
> of the border. The night was cool, the moon was bright, the
> patio was lined with flowers and tropical plants, and tiled roofs
> covered the porches on which many gathered to watch. An
> iconoclast might, however, have noticed that the dance floor was
> earth and scoria, that some were dancing in bare feet, that the
> dancing was rather stiff, and that the music did not consist of
> rumbas or tangos but timeworn foxtrots from the north. A
> snack consisting of a thick gruel of pork and corn braced with
> chili was served together with the thick sweet drink *atole,* some-
> what resembling hot chocolate.

Of another *fiesta* our notes recall:

> In the evening a *fiesta* at the house of José, who was celebrating
> his day. A very good *mariachi* band from another village was
> tightly wedged into one end of the porch, and a tarpaulin had
> been stretched over the ground in front to protect dancers from
> the drizzling rain. Groups of guests could be seen coming down
> the road, their way lighted by blazing torches of pitch pine.
> Couples were dancing ballroom steps in a rather staid fashion.
> Distances were "proper," and the atmosphere of decorum sur-
> prises the *gringo* brought up to think of Mexicans as wild and
> uninhibited. The general air of self-restraint was striking. Al-
> most everyone, from the little wizened Indian ladies to the group
> of rather fierce looking fellows that trooped in, behaved with
> dignity. Liquor flowed and the effects showed inevitably on one
> or two. These were older men, and they were treated with respect
> and considerate care.

Weddings are, of course, an occasion for *fiestas,* and their celebration is an excuse for the men to drink for several days. According to Padre José, "In all the Tarascan villages, it is the custom for the young men to steal their sweethearts. Afterwards, the parents of the boy must take a large basket of bread and wine to the parents of the girl, for he has offended them. About a month later the couple get married in the church, and the newly married couple dance with garlands of vegetables and little bottles of wine. Then there is an enormous feast. Everyone is invited and the people dance for three days straight." Such weddings involve the groom's parents in expenditures of as much as 3,000 pesos for the clothing, food, drink, and music.

One such wedding was observed. In the late morning a young couple had been married at the *basílica* in Pátzcuaro and walked with friends and relatives to the gate of Tzipecua, where they stopped and were met by about 50 more persons and a band which accompanied them back to the village. The music was gay but the demeanor of the principals was serious and seemingly sad. Some young people were in high spirits, however, and a number of men were already well fortified with alcohol. Two of them retired quietly to a ditch to sleep it off while the procession went slowly on. The party briefly visited the church to pray, and then was fed at the house of the bride. Later the dancing began at the house of the bridegroom's *padrino,* and eating and drinking activities oscillated from house to house during the following three days.[52]

Relief from the routine of work is provided within the village by an occasional movie at the *Centro Social* or a *kermesse,* both of which are means of raising funds for something such as repairs to the *Centro* or the purchase of basketball team uniforms. No *kermesses* took place in Huecorio during our visit, but they were regular events in Pátzcuaro. Those *kermesses* observed raised money by selling food, sponsoring dances, or holding mock weddings. Under the careful eyes of nuns or chaperones, teen-age girls watch for passing or attending males who are "invited" to "marry" them. Whatever he does is costly, for the young man finds he must either buy a mock wedding license or pay a fine to escape. Then, before he has a chance to say

[52] Needless to say, no informants could be found during this period and our research activities were temporarily halted.

"honeymoon" the man sees his fickle sweetheart disappear to ensnare another passer-by. At the *kermesse* there is a spirit of energetic fun and laughter that strikes one by its absence in the life of the village.

Elements of Social Change

Although Huecorio still retains elements of a traditional society, social change is taking place. As we have seen, the majority of the population remains low in need autonomy, need order, and need achievement; need dominance and need submission are strong; and families cling to authoritarianism. Nevertheless, the signs of transition to a more viable psychosociological environment are unmistakable.

Huecorianos manifest a mounting desire to live in more comfortable surroundings, for they now recognize that poverty, ugliness, and discomfort are not a necessary part of their lot and they aspire to a better life for themselves and, even more, for their children. This cognition is likely to stimulate the need achievement in the young Huecorianos who are not yet among the few entrepreneurs whom we observed.

Huecorianos are beginning to question the omnipotence of the natural and social environments. They are dissatisfied with Huecorio and with their poverty, and are beginning to experiment with new technologies and organizations and to ask questions about alternative methods of production and ways of life. Some have begun to reject their past. Several women have cast aside the long skirts, aprons, shapeless blouses, and braided hair that identify them as rural folk, and have adopted the modes of the cities. A few men own business suits and have generally accepted shoes, shirts, pants, and windbreakers in place of the *huaraches, calzones* (white cotton pants) and white cotton collarless shirts and jackets.

All villagers seem to have rejected the traditional dances of Mexico, and Tarascan is spoken only by the residents of Carián and Urandén although many villagers understand a little of it.

We would suspect, furthermore, that Huecorio's inability to unite and to control effectively the actions of its populace are further indications of the changes taking place. We have no firm evidence that

Huecorio was once united, although the older informants claimed that this was so. It is not possible to ascertain the weight to attach to the statements about deteriorating morality, the decline of respect, or the effective cohesion and cooperation that once existed, for in a changing world nostalgia can be an escapist comfort. But if these statements are an accurate representation of historical fact, they would be consistent with the effective social control inherent in a traditional, authoritarian society—a situation that no longer accurately characterizes Huecorio.

The breakdown of authoritarianism within the family is more evident. While the majority of children still respect and obey their parents, and wives do not overtly challenge their husbands, disputes and tensions disrupt the harmony of those families in which the youngsters are becoming open to the experiences of the outside world. One youth, after his father had berated him for leaving the house without permission, held back his anguish with the comment, "It is very sad here, is it not?" His sister, an ambitious lass in her late teens, similarly rebels against the tight control her parents try to exert, and secretly smokes and meets with the boys of whom her parents disapprove. In another family with several adult children, the father is despised for his drinking. One said, "He is finished with life and his mind is closed to new ideas." In this family the son and daughters have since left Huecorio to find new lives in Mexico City and the United States. The tensions within these two families frequently exploded into violent argument and tears. Wives, too, have begun to break away from the former pattern of unquestioned obedience to their husbands, and in one case the woman's sense of mistreatment led her to divorce.

It is impossible in a study conducted at one point in the continuum of time to measure the degree of change that is taking place, but it is reasonable to presume that these straws herald more violent winds of change. As an effective social force, traditionalism has broken down and Huecorio stands buffeted in an unsettled interregnum while a new course is being set.

It is possible to identify the forces inducing change in Huecorio, but not to rank them in terms of their power or the direction they give. Some are clearly weak and possibly without any influence.

Among these would be numbered communication media and the proximity of Pátzcuaro. Radios are constantly blaring in the homes, but they provide merely a background to everyday activities and little attention is paid to commercials or commentaries. Similarly, few persons read newspapers or magazines. Huecorianos frequently visit Pátzcuaro, but their contacts there are limited to persons of a similar station in life. They do not relate in any way to Pátzcuaro's acculturated middle class or the streams of tourists.

Because of the antagonism of the chief teacher in Huecorio, it was not possible to arrive at satisfactory conclusions about the influence of education on the social environment. We have observed that the three years or so of attendance that Huecorianos customarily experience has little momentum, and that few villagers exploit their literacy or use it to satisfy a curiosity about the world.

To be a positive element in social change, education must contain two elements in addition to training in literacy. First, the teachers must be emotionally well balanced individuals, who can stimulate both children and their elders by persuasion and the example of their own behavior. Huecorio may have enjoyed such teachers at various times in the past, but the necessary criteria were less than completely met by the bitter man who antagonized the villagers in 1962. Second, an educational system must stimulate curiosity and initiative by demonstrating to children that their environment can be manipulated. As it applies to the social environment, this might involve such things as student government and learning of the world's social, political, and economic innovators through studies of government and history. Children can also gain some sense of their ability to influence their natural environment by the use of school gardens, manipulative games and toys, and exposure to new ideas. The education offered to the children of Huecorio was, however, most conventional and conducted in poorly lit and uncomfortable surroundings, which can hardly have served to inspire them or arouse curiosity. We would judge that education, as practiced in Huecorio, has contributed little to its progress.

Adult immigrants could be another stimulant to change if they came from places where cultural practices were different and if they were articulate and recognized. Of the 140 married couples in the village 41, or approximately 29%, had at least one member who was born elsewhere. However, the majority of the migrants were women who came from nearby villages, and because of the cultural similarity of their birthplace with Huecorio, and because women rarely raise their voices on public issues, it can be concluded that such cultural heterogeneity as results from migration is of little importance. (See Table XXXII.)

Travel by Huecorianos is another matter, however. One-third of the adult males have been to the United States, and over one-half of the men have traveled to distant parts of Mexico. These men, particularly those who have crossed the border, have generally returned to Huecorio with attitudes conducive to change. They have demonstrated to themselves that they are capable of performing unaccustomed roles, they have been stimulated and excited by new experiences, they have come to question the inevitability of their customary way of life, and they have had their wants stimulated. They are, in other words, new men, and have begun to change the village in ways which we have examined. Their ability to improve the economic position of the village has been restricted by lack of complementary factors of production, by limited vocational outlets for their new enthusiasm, and by the dead weight of the community's divisive social structure. Nevertheless, their new attitudes have found expression in new occupations such as shopkeeping and egg production, and in a general willingness to try something new.

The influence of CREFAL is at least as great. Over the decade of CREFAL's existence, Huecorianos have been exposed to people of very different backgrounds and experience. Although the enthusiasm of some of the CREFAL students has been misdirected and therefore rejected, Huecorianos have been stirred up and their complacency, apathy, and defensiveness have been eroded. By showing Huecorianos alternative ways of life, CREFAL has stimulated the process of acculturation, and through its programs it has provided channels into which the new attitudes could flow. In the Girls' Club, a small group of the more acculturated girls learn new domestic arts and, perhaps more important, gain some measure of self-confidence. The *Asociación Avícola* has given some of the men an economic opportunity without which any innovational propensities they had might have withered.

As with the Girls' Club, the confidence-building aspects of this successful venture should have the long-run effect of undermining apathy.

Another stimulant to the community has been the presence nearby of Tzipecua. Until his death General Múgica took a benevolent interest in the people of Huecorio, and his widow has carried on the tradition. She always makes herself available to offer counsel and, if she can, material help. This is done graciously and with a sensitive awareness of the desirability of inducing villagers to use their own resources to solve their problems. The agricultural experiment station on Tzipecua is run jointly by Montana State College and the Mexican government, with the objective of introducing new techniques in all the villages of the region. A young veterinarian at Tzipecua visits Huecorio almost daily to care for its animals. The impact of the agricultural demonstrations had not been great by the time of our visit, since the villagers felt that the Tzipecua land was so superior to their own that its techniques could not be generalized. Subsequent to 1962, the project intended to rectify this shortcoming by conducting its experiments on village land.

Huecorio is undoubtedly moving away from an economically sterile traditionalism, and new, more creative attitudes are beginning to form. Nothing suggests that by themselves these changes will induce a momentum sufficient to propel Huecorio to wealth. Its internal resources, in particular land and capital, are inadequate to the task. Capital will, at least initially, have to come from the outside. Equally important are the needs for expert guidance, a vastly improved educational setup, and a more viable political structure. In these respects, Huecorio is no different from nation states in their efforts to strike off the shackles of poverty.

CHAPTER 7

POPULATION

T H E data available for presenting and analyzing the demographic changes in Huecorio are incomplete and unsatisfactory. In particular, published information on birth rates, death rates, and longevity are not broken down by communities, and since our visit to the village encompassed only a small part of a calendar year we were unable to derive these data for ourselves. With our information we can only draw inferences about fertility, mortality, and migration. One can ask the living about their age, place of birth, and so on, but the dead do not respond—at least to us.

In the four decades for which data are available, the population of Huecorio doubled from 429 persons in 1921 to 844 in 1962. The rate of growth has, however, varied considerably during the period. Between 1921 and 1930 the population declined by 6.76%, for reasons that are not entirely clear. The disturbances of the Revolution continued to reverberate throughout the countryside during that unsettled period, and soldiers of the various armies were stationed in Huecorio. Villagers also reported that people from mountain communities came to the lakeside villages to escape the depredations of bandits. Individuals from either of these two groups may have been included in the census of 1921, thus accounting for an inflated

The village center. School and church behind ancient portal

population figure. A low point of 400 persons was reached in 1930, and in the peaceful decade that followed the mean annual rate of increase was nearly 2.5%. The 1940s saw only a modest rise averaging about 1.1% a year, which was followed in the 1950s and early 1960s by an extraordinary jump to a mean annual rate of over 4%.

What accounted for this variation? Even though we have no adequate data on birth and mortality rates for Huecorio, we have good reason to believe that the change had nothing to do with a spectacular increase in the birth rate or a happy decline in the death rate, but resulted instead from different techniques in enumeration. In 1956 the CREFAL students in Huecorio enumerated 727 persons. This gives a mean annual rate of increase of 5.1% for the period 1950 to 1956, and of 2.6% for 1956 to 1962. The normal technique of a national census is to count the number of persons in all communities on a given day, while we and the CREFAL students found it necessary to conduct our censuses over longer periods of time—in our case, one full month. Accordingly, those conducting a national census will normally find many doors closed, or when an individual does respond some persons in the household will be away

291

for a short period of time and will not, therefore, be counted. On the other hand, our team covered every house which was occupied at some time during the month of June, and although we did not include persons such as *braceros* who were away for an extended period, such individuals were often enumerated before they left or after they returned. We would judge, then, that the yearly rate of population growth for Huecorio is closer to 2.6% than to 4%. If this is the case, then Huecorio's growth rate is little different from the national average of 2.9%.

TABLE 15

Population: Male and Female; Absolute Changes and Percentage of Change

Year	Population			Change	
	Male	Female	Total	Absolute	Percentage
1921[a]	214	215	429		
1930[b]	190	210	400	− 29	− 6.76
1940[c]	247	252	499	+ 99	+24.75
1950[d]	259	296	555	+ 56	+11.22
1962[e]	400	444	844	+289	+52.07

[a] Estados Unidos Mexicanos, Depto. de la Estadística Nacional, *Censo General de Habitantes, 30 de Nov. de 1921. Estado de Michoacán.* Talleres Gráficos de la Nación, Mexico, 1927.

[b] Estados Unidos Mexicanos, Secretaría de la Economía Nacional, Dirección General de Estadística, *Quinto Censo de Población, 15 de Mayo de 1930. Estado de Michoacán.* Samuel Catrillo P., Av. Madero 890 Orte, Morelia, Mich. México, D.F., 1935.

[c] Estados Unidos Mexicanos, *Sexto Censo de Población, 1940, Michoacán,* Secretaría de la Economía Nacional, Dirección General de Estadística, México, D.F., 1943.

[d] Estados Unidos Mexicanos, *Septimo Censo General de Poblición, 6 de junio de 1950,* Secretaría de Economía, Dirección General de Estadística, Estado de Michoacán, México, D.F., 1952.

[e] Census conducted by research project, June, 1962. (The data for the 1960 Census were not available at the time of writing.)

In spite of the absence of specific information, it is possible to infer that Huecorio has had a relatively high birth rate in recent years. This can be done by comparing the number of children in a given age group and the number of females in another age group to similar ratios for other areas. In rural India, for instance, the number of children 0 to 4 years of age was 735 for every 1,000 women of the ages 15 to 39.[1] In Huecorio there were 136 children in the age group 0 to 4 and 162 women in the group 15 to 39. This is a rate of 839 children to 1,000 women in the corresponding groups. It would appear, therefore, that the birth rate in Huecorio is significantly higher than in the rural areas of India, a country generally conceded to have a population problem.[2]

Close inspection of Table XXXIII and Chart 2 reveals two interesting phenomena. If one examines the number of persons in each age group, one sees a not unexpected downward trend as the age group rises. In other words, there are more infants of less than one year of age than, say, persons of 70 years of age. Superimposed on this trend is a five-year cycle. Generally, the number of persons whose ages are reported as falling on every fifth year is higher than in the years immediately preceding or following. This, of course, has nothing to do with fluctuating fertility or feast and famine, but reflects instead on our technique of enumeration. As a rule the census data for each family was supplied by just one member of that family —at times a juvenile—and the respondent gave the ages of the other persons as an approximation to the nearest five. This problem had been anticipated and we attempted to verify the ages in years by asking birth dates. For most persons it was even more difficult to supply this information, and we soon gave up the attempt.

The other phenomenon of interest has to do with the clear preponderance of females in Huecorio. There were 444 females in 1962 and only 400 males. Females outnumber males in 37 of the 83 age groups, the numbers are equal in 13, and males outnumber females in 33. In poor rural communities one might account for this by the

[1] Kingsley Davis, *The Population of India and Pakistan* (Princeton, Princeton University Press, 1951), p. 70.

[2] Since the data say nothing of relative infant mortalities, the statement cannot be made more affirmatively. Another factor to be considered is that only 35% of the women between 15 and 39 in Huecorio are married (one woman had 2 children illegitimately), whereas the percentage in rural India is higher. This, of course, means that once they marry, the women of Huecorio are more fertile, relatively, than the over-all figures would indicate.

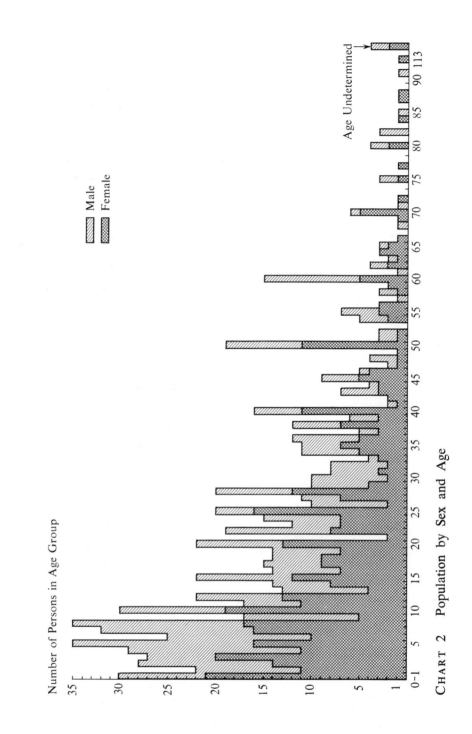

Number of Persons in Age Group

CHART 2 Population by Sex and Age

Male
Female

Age Undetermined

emigration of young males in search of work. While this factor might have had some influence, the males of the ages most likely to migrate—20 to 34 years—are only two less than the number of females.[3] Females outnumber males even in the early years, and in the age groups 0 to 19 they outnumber males in nine classes while the reverse is true in only six classes. In Huecorio, apparently, more females than males are born.

In spite of the apparently high birth rate the average number of persons per family unit is only 4.35, although the number of persons per household is naturally greater—5.93. This stems in part from the definition of a family unit as being comprised of persons in a vertical lineal relationship of no more than one stage. Households will frequently include, for instance, a grandparent living with a married child and several grandchildren. This household would comprise two family units, one of only one person and the other of three or more. There are only three households in Huecorio in which a person lives alone, but 25 family units of only one person. In most cases those persons are grandparents, although one resident *peón* and one servant are included. The modal family size is four persons, but 43.8% of the families are from five to eleven persons in size. (See Table XXXIV.)

To compile mortality rates for Huecorio was a task beyond our capabilities, and locally obtainable official data is not presented in a manner which would have permitted the identification of deaths with the residence of the deceased. Had we been in Huecorio for the entire calendar year of 1962, we might have found it possible to record all the births and deaths taking place, but even in a small community such as this the problems of communication and diplomacy would have been difficult.

Neither are infant mortality data particularly helpful in indicating any change in over-all mortality rates. (See Table XXXV.) Of the women responding to our question about the loss of infants—mothers in the age groups from 21 to 60—53% had experienced no such loss, but the higher the age group the greater the number of infant deaths experienced per mother. For those mothers 21 to 25 years of age the average number of infants lost was 0.53, while a

[3] 91 males and 93 females.

higher average of 3 was found in the 51 to 55 bracket. The association of higher infant mortalities with mothers in higher age brackets could be explained by the better maternal care that younger mothers received, but it is equally possible that younger mothers, having only begun their career, so to speak, will experience more infant mortalities as they grow in age.[4] This question can only be answered by another investigator at a later date. On the other hand, it can be said that unless conditions of health change substantially, the chances of a mother experiencing the loss of at least one child are almost three to one, and on the average she will lose two children. Nevertheless, in spite of the lack of definitive data it is reasonable to assume that both the death and infant mortality rates have fallen, and will continue to fall. Prenatal and maternal care are undoubtedly better than previously. A visiting nurse holds a weekly clinic in the village, almost all babies are now delivered in hospitals in Pátzcuaro, and milk is readily available now that cows are a popular source of income. Preventive public health in the form of malaria control and the provision of better sanitary facilities have had some unquantifiable impact. Doctors, dentists, medicines, and hospital facilities are accessible in Pátzcuaro, and the frequency with which sickness is cited as a reason for indebtedness or the sale of an asset would indicate that Huecorianos generally utilize medical services when the need arises.

The combination of an apparently high birth rate and an apparently recent decline in the death rate leads to a population in which 54% are under 20 years of age. This implies both a high dependency ratio and, within the dependent group, a high proportion of very young persons. It we assume that a person is a dependent rather than a producer from birth until his fifteenth birthday, and from 65 years on, 376 persons fall within the first group and only 31 in the second. (Table XXXIII.) These 407 persons comprise 48% of the entire population, and imply in a rough way a one-to-one ratio between productive and unproductive persons.

It is safe to assume that conditions of health will continue to improve in Huecorio, and that an increasingly large proportion of the

[4] One woman volunteered the information that children no longer die in as great numbers as they did in "former times."

youth will therefore survive to the reproductive ages. Although there are some interesting straws blowing before the shock wave of a population explosion, there is no firm indication of any significant interest on the part of Huecorianos in having fewer children. Unless adjustments are made, Huecorio will face unbearable pressures on its limited agricultural resources within the next decade. The anticipated forces could conceivably be worse were it not for a certain stability rendered by the institution of marriage. For one thing, as can be seen in Table XXXVI, marriage is not usually undertaken before the age of 21. Indeed, 61% of the males and 27% of the females in the 21 to 25 age bracket had not yet married. The respect for marriage is fortunate in another way. Females outnumber males by 11% (Table XXXIII), and were the village morality such that free and casual unions were accepted, one would undoubtedly find the unmarried women (with, of course, the cooperation of some of the men) contributing to the problem.

ADJUSTMENT TO THE PRESSURES OF POPULATION

With the continuing pressure of increasing human numbers upon a limited area of land, the people of Huecorio are and have been faced with a classic dilemma, to which they have adjusted in ways rather different from "war, famine, and pestilence." The alternative solutions available to them have been agricultural adaptation, finding nonagricultural employment in Huecorio, emigration, and, finally, reducing the birth rate. All of these steps have been taken in varying degrees, and manifest at least a subconscious recognition of the problem.

Adjustment in Agriculture

If an increase in population results in a larger number of persons employed on the land, the adjustment can take place in one of three ways, or in a combination of them. (1) The number of farms can

San Pedrito, late July. A tiny milpa *for a growing population*

remain the same but more persons will be employed on each farm. If this took place it would be indicated by an increase in the size of work teams or by alternative (3) below. We have established that work teams in Huecorio are small and apparently have not increased in size. (2) The number of farms could increase by fragmentation of existing units. Some fragmentation of private holdings has taken place, but in the 40 years covered by our population data this has been confined to an insignificant number of parcels. (3) There can be an increase in the number of persons who do not own land but who are employed full- or part-time in agriculture. This has taken place to some degree but not to the point where there will be unemployment during the agricultural season. Huecorio farmers find it necessary to import labor from other communities during the busy season.

Adjustment in the Structure of Employment

The major adjustment to the pressure upon the land has been to seek nonagricultural pursuits. Some of those pursuits are closely associated with agriculture. There is the growth of dairying—which, however, is likely to limit further the amount of land available because of the need for pasture areas. There is the *Asociación Avícola,* which provides some farmers who have insufficient land with a valuable alternative source of income. Other Huecorianos have ceased completely to work the land and have moved into related pursuits such as selling agricultural products, or into completely unrelated trades such as furniture weaving, garment making, or masonry. These alternatives have been feasible because of the special circumstances of the establishment of the *Asociación* and Vicki's, the general development of commercialism in Pátzcuaro, and improved communications with other areas. Had these factors not provided safety valves, the pressure on agriculture might have become intolerable or emigration might have been more significant.

Emigration

Emigration, both permanent and temporary, has taken place. Temporary migration is primarily a stopgap, and permits villagers to survive on their limited local resources. One-third of the men 21 years and over, have worked in the United States as *braceros,* and about the same proportion of the farmers work on farms in the *tierra caliente* during the slack season. In addition to the 65 men who have visited the United States, 85 men and 14 women have traveled outside of the state of Michoacán, and it is reasonable to assume that the majority went in search of work. Men reported visiting Ciudad Juárez, Matamoros, and Mexico City, where they worked a short while and then returned. Several women have worked as domestics in Mexico City and Guadalajara.

Some rough estimate of the volume of more permanent migration is possible. Fifty-three persons of families resident in Huecorio were living permanently elsewhere.[5] In the village itself there were 19 unoccupied houses,[6] and if we assume that each was at one time occupied by the average number of persons per village household (5.93), this would suggest that an additional 113 former Huecorianos had left the village. On the other hand, 87 persons[7] in Huecorio were born elsewhere. This suggests a net emigration of 79 persons. It is not possible to calculate the annual rate of emigration, since the years of arrival and departure are not available. Without making allowances for the reproductive contribution of the emigrants, it can be said that the population of Huecorio would have been 9% higher in 1962 than was actually the case, and to this extent migration relieved the accumulating pressure. We anticipate that its role in the future will be greater if offers of colonization are again made.

Huecorianos have at least twice been offered the opportunity to occupy land in other parts of Mexico. In 1943 General Múgica offered land in a colony in Apatzingán, but according to one informant, "it was too hot and too far away and nobody went." In 1947 the Department of Agriculture offered land in El Bado near Tehuántepec in Michoacán, but again no villager took advantage of the opportunity. Acting as an individual, Geronimo Roca asked for land and was offered 13 hectares in 1961. However, he said he could not go because of his contractual obligation to the *Asociación Avícola*. He says now, "Here, every day the population grows but the land is inadequate. The plots get smaller and the soil is destroyed or washed away. If other people joined me in asking for land and it was offered to us, I would go."

According to General Lázaro Cárdenas, with whom we discussed Huecorio and its problems, attempts to raise agricultural production within such communities as Huecorio are too expensive in terms of potential benefits, and a much more viable technique is to persuade

[5] Seven had migrated to the United States, 18 lived nearby in the Pátzcuaro region, 14 lived elsewhere in Michoacán, and 14 lived in other parts of Mexico.

[6] The number of unoccupied houses in the community as a whole was 28. Four of them were under construction and five were guest bungalows at Tzipecua.

[7] Twenty-one males and 51 females from the Pátzcuaro region, and eight males and seven females from elsewhere in Mexico.

the villagers to colonize new areas. "In Mexico," he said, "there is sufficient land for all. For example, in Sinaloa there are one million hectares of irrigable land and in the south there are two to three million hectares more. And there is even more in the river basins. The colonists get land, houses, light, schools, water, and supervised credit. They can be established after five cycles of production." We would agree with General Cárdenas that for those persons who wish to continue in agriculture, prospects in Huecorio are poor and colonization would offer a brighter future.[8] Is it likely that Huecorianos would respond to an offer of colonization were it made?

Huecorianos are acutely aware that their land is insufficient. In the 1930s they complained that their *ejido* parcels were a third the size to which they were entitled, but they had to face the fact that no nearby *hacienda* was available for repartition. In an attempt to see if Huecorianos saw any connection between their growing numbers and the limited area of land, we asked what should be done to solve this problem. As might be expected, of the 36 men who were questioned none saw the solution in terms of limiting the population growth of the village. Instead, 26 said that they should ask for new land in other parts of Mexico.[9]

There is, however, some difference between a recognition that migration will assist one and a willingness to move. When the same men were asked if they would like to live in another part of Mexico, only 13 replied affirmatively and the majority of these gave a variety of reasons for remaining. Huecorianos have deep roots which cling

[8] Statements such as this should be underwritten with figures on comparative costs and benefits, but our conclusion is based only on the observations of Huecorio itself and two *ejidos* near Apatzingán to which the General kindly took us.

[9] Replies to the question, "What should be done about the shortage of land in Huecorio?"

Reply	Males	Females
Ask for more land somewhere else	26	5
Redistribute land in Huecorio	1	0
Work harder on what we have	2	3
Increase agricultural inputs	4	3
"*¿Quien sabe?*" "Who knows?"	1	14
No answer	2	11

tenaciously to the soil and cannot be extricated without damage. They speak of Huecorio as the place where they were born and brought up, where they have their animals, land, and livelihood, where there is peace and tranquillity. A smaller number[10] worried about the organizational difficulties. Where would they find the money and how would they care for their families while they were making the adjustment? Others were repelled by the hot climate of the *tierra caliente* or a fear of hostility in the new home. "We are afraid to go somewhere else. We might not be welcome and Mexicans always carry guns. The land where you are born is dear to you so if you have enough to eat, you stay." "Life is easier for me here. I am not rich but I live well enough." "I would like to go to Apatzingán but I have property here and would have to sell it." It is still possible to survive in Huecorio, one is secure in an understood and established way of life, and a new environment would present unknown and therefore frightening adjustments.

Yet, at the end of our visit when Richard Bolívar talked to villagers about the new *ejidos* near Apatzingán, he had no difficulty in finding 28 men who said they would like to go. Clearly, one sees here an ambivalent attitude in which fears and inertia still outweigh the inducements and pressures to change. The fears and inertia can be overcome by education and by moving large groups of Huecorianos to new locations.

Migration to the United States represents a partial but difficult solution to Huecorio's difficulties. Twelve of the same 36 men expressed an interest in permanent migration. They felt that there a man can improve himself with less effort and that Mexicans are treated well. But at the same time there were obstacles which prevented their going. They mentioned, in particular, the need for a *patrón* to give them a job and for a sum of money to buy the necessary papers. Six others would go to the United States only to work temporarily, while nine did not want to go.[11] One of the latter objected to the taxes that people pay in that country, and another said the work was too hard and that when he was there before his em-

---

[10] Three, as opposed to the 18 who talked in terms of binding ties to the village.

[11] The remaining 9 did not reply.

ployers were so strict that he was not even allowed to whistle. Still another said he was too old, while the remaining six said they did not know what the United States was like so how could they say they would like to go there? Were it not for legal and financial obstacles, undoubtedly a significant number of Huecorianos would cross the border to become permanent residents, but such a solution to the difficulties of Huecorio and its people is unlikely to come to pass. Indeed, with the present termination of the *bracero* program, villagers are no longer able to look to the United States for some of the benefits they have been able to enjoy.

Adjustment of the Birth Rate

As far as can be ascertained, Huecorianos make no attempt to limit the number of children they have in the sense that a conscious effort is made to reduce the possibility of a pregnancy. The basis for this statement is the manifest lack of knowledge that exists about birth control measures.[12] The number of children that men and women claim they would like to have is on the average more than they actually have. The average number of living children per couple is in the order of 3.8,[13] whereas men expressed on the average a desire for 5.5 children and women 4.4. (See Table XXXVII.) The low actual average number of children relative to the number desired is undoubtedly accounted for by the fact that the survey included many young couples who were only beginning their families.

The difference in the number of children desired by males and females is quite significant. It speaks first of a lack of communication between husband and wife. The partners were interviewed separately, and in response to our questions said that each agreed with

[12] See below, p. 308.

[13] This figure was obtained by counting the number of children belonging to the couple interviewed who were living in the household plus the number who were not living in Huecorio. It does not, however, include children who were living elsewhere in Huecorio. When there was reason to believe that there were such children not enumerated, the data were excluded from the calculation of the average.

the other on the desired number. This was, however, merely an expression of loyalty, for in only three cases did the numbers actually agree.[14] Although our sample is small, the difference in the number of children desired by males and females would seem to be real and not accidental. The average number desired by men is 25% higher than that for women, and the range of the number desired by women

TABLE 16

Tabulation of Replies to Question: "Why do you consider the number of children you stated to be a good number?"

	Males	Females
Answers Indicating a Desire to Limit the Number of Children		
One should have the number that one can feed and care for well	20	10
One should have only a few in order to be able to educate them	2	2
Too many are difficult to control	1	6
Answers Indicating a Desire for a Large Family		
Many can help with the work	0	1
A large family is a happy one	1	0
Answers Indicating Fatalistic Attitude, Acceptance of Actual Number, or Lack of Thought on Matter		
It is God's decision	0	2
Because that is what we have	2	1
"Who knows?"	4	6
Question Not Answered	6	8
Totals	36	36

clusters from two to six while for men the clustering is between three and eight.

The reasons for the difference are not explicit, but some hint is offered in Table 16. Although one can say that of the men and women

[14] Said one husband in response to this question, "She always agrees with me. I am the chief."

who responded with some kind of meaningful answer there was a general feeling that some limits should be placed on the size of a family, the reasons given by men and women differed in one significant respect. Women in the village environment are more directly involved in the care of children than are the men, and are faced throughout the day with the chores of discipline, washing, and feeding, and although they did not state this, they are obviously more aware than men of the discomforts and pains of childbearing.

One other explanation for the difference lurks in the cult of *machismo,* which among its other odd and interesting manifestations is supposed to impel a man to great feats of impregnation to demonstrate his virility. It is said that a man, by keeping his wife pregnant, not only proves his perpetual tumescence but effectively prevents the access of others. If this were the situation in Huecorio, we would probably have found a significant number of men rather boastfully talking in terms of a dozen or more children, but among both men and women there were few who expressed a desire so extreme. (Table XXXVII.) Neither does it follow necessarily that the men who have a large number of children are motivated by *machismo.* To argue thus ignores the circumstances under which Huecorianos live. Said one man who had seven children, "We breed out of ignorance and do not know how to stop. You want your wife and you do not think of the family that may result. Or you hope it doesn't." And another, who also had seven children, chuckled when we naïvely asked, "How do you keep warm in winter?" We were, of course, trying to find out whether or not the houses were heated in any way, but instead he artfully misinterpreted us and replied, "We have each other." The simple circumstance of "bundling" is sufficient to maintain a high rate of reproduction, and so one might argue that the solution to the problem lies in central heating.

Although Huecorianos make no deliberate effort to limit births, certain circumstances effectively reduce it below the maximum physiological potential. Men labor daily at enervating physical tasks, and we may speculate that their fatigue, combined with the inevitable fading bloom of early romance, reduces desire and capacity on their part. In addition, the travels to the *tierra caliente* and the United States separate families for lengthy periods of time. It is also possible, but unlikely, that men visit the houses of prostitution in nearby Pátzcuaro and alter thereby the locus of pregnancy. Were this the case, it would provide some relief in a sense for Huecorio. However, as one woman put it in explaining the fecundity of Hue-corio women, "The husbands don't have the pesos to go to the Krem-lin[15] and women here take no precautions." We made no special investigation of this pattern of behavior, of course, but accept the señora's statement. The least desirable of the whores divest a man of more than a day's wages, and this takes no account of what he must spend on drink to arouse his courage. The young unmarried men of Huecorio do make such visits with an unverified, but probably low, frequency. Paradoxically, it might be argued that the existence of this form of release contributes to the stability of social relations for it protects to some extent the young unmarried lasses from effective persuasion.

What are the prospects for a decline in Huecorio's birth rate? Infant mortality will certainly and rapidly be reduced, and this will have the inevitable effect of raising population pressures close to an explosive level. After the survival rate increases for a number of generations, it is likely that Huecorianos will become aware that in order to have the ideal family of x children one does not need to bring into the world x plus y children, y of whom will die. But most likely this realization, articulated or not, will work too slowly to help Huecorio and its people. Only a deliberate effort on their part to reduce births will do the job, and while Huecorianos would accept the principle of family limitation they are quite ignorant as to how it is to be done.

Huecorianos are, in a general way, concerned with providing adequately for their children. This is seen in the 22 males and 12 females (73% and 42% respectively of those responding) who felt that one should have that number of children that can be educated, or fed and cared for well. (See Table 16.) Those wanting what they considered to be large families were clearly in a minority—only one male and one female. Huecorianos are not at all sanguine about their ability to care for their children, however. (See Table 17.) Only five males and six females (14% and 21%, respectively, of those responding) apparently felt that children could be adequately cared for,

15 The allusion should be obvious.

although 13 of the 64 responding were cautious enough not to make a blanket statement about the village as a whole.

However, a concern for children is one thing and a clear recognition of the relationship between fecundity and scarce resources is another. In other words, Huecorianos realize that land and capital are

TABLE 17

Tabulation of Replies to Question, "Do you think that the people of Huecorio can care for their children?"

	Males	*Females*
No	9	4
Yes (Qualified by such statements as "But not well," "They eat somehow.")	12	11
Yes (Unqualified)	5	6
Some can but others cannot	8	5
"*¿Quien sabe?*"	1	3
No answer	1	7
Totals	36	36

limited and that children are not provided for as well as they would like, but they are not fully aware that the children's future could be more adequately provided for if the number of children entering the world were reduced. The most common position would be exemplified by one who said, "That parents bring so many children into the world does not mean that they do not care about their children's futures. Before a man dies he leaves each son a house and, if he has enough, a plot of land. For instance, one man who is 75 has settled all his sons in houses and is himself living in a little one-room house on his wife's property. One of his sons has settled *his* son in a house of his own. Sometimes a father is so poor that he cannot provide for his children properly." Other Huecorianos are more apprehensive, and their views indicate a growing cognizance of the problem. "The people increase. The land does not." "We are poor. How can we have more than three?" "I have seven children but not enough land to divide into seven parts. If I cannot buy more land how can I fill my responsibility?"

Although Huecorianos generally believe in family limitation, they have no idea of how to go about it. Husbands and wives were asked the question, "Should a couple limit the number of children they have?" Of the 25 men and 23 women who gave a meaningful answer, only two men and five women were unqualifiedly against limitation. Four men and three women who answered in the negative apparently did so because they felt that family limitation was impossible. Indeed,

TABLE 18

Tabulation of Replies to Question, "Should a couple limit the number of children they have?"

	Males	Females
No (Without qualification)	2	5
No (With added rhetorical question, "How can one?")	4	3
Yes (Without qualification)	8	5
Yes (By abstinence)	3	1
Yes (With added rhetorical question, "How can one?")	8	9
"¿Quien sabe?"	5	5
No answer	6	8
Totals	36	36

from the fact that 12 men and the same number of women voluntarily added a comment to the effect, "How can one do this?" one can infer that deliberate and voluntary limitation would take place if acceptable means were available. Apparently several know, at least theoretically, of the effectiveness of abstinence, and one woman said there was an abortionist in Colonia Ibarra but that it cost too much money to avail oneself of her services. Only two women suggested that religion might have something to do with their negative attitude.[16] On the other hand, another woman volunteered, "I know some women who want only two or three children but they keep coming," and one of the more educated men of the community approached a person associated with CREFAL asking advice on con-

[16] One said, "Only God knows how many children one should have," and the other, "We are too Catholic here."

traception. He was about to marry and did not want to have more than two children.

It is, therefore, safe to say that were appropriate means made available, Huecorianos would accept and use contraception. This is not the place to discuss the alternative devices, but it goes without saying that only the so-called rhythm method is likely to slip by the opposition of the Church. Although this method is less than fully effective, Huecorianos are sufficiently educated to apply it intelligently and it might have partial success. The villagers themselves would undoubtedly accept a wider range of methods than the Church allows, but an attempt by outsiders to introduce them would necessarily be condemned from the pulpit, and this would in all likelihood lead to bitter division within Huecorio.

Huecorianos are not likely to discover new devices on their own. Until some outside agency acquires the necessary courage, tact, and skill, or the Church modifies its position, the desires of the people of Huecorio will be ignored and their problems will compound, perhaps to the point where the progress now being made will be deflated like a rent balloon.

CHAPTER 8

LEVELS AND STANDARDS OF LIVING

I N the literature of economics, a distinction is sometimes made between levels and standards of living. Levels of living refer to the real incomes of people as evidenced by the conditions of health, housing, diet, and forms of consumption that they actually experience, while standards of living should refer to the levels of living to which people aspire.[1] If, for a given people, the levels and standards coincide, it can be inferred either that they are more or less content with their way of life or that they are apathetic and cannot conceive of the possibility that their levels can be raised. It will become clear in this section that while some Huecorianos exhibit apathy there is a significant gap between the levels and the standards of living of most of the population, and they have a deep sense that their way of life is not what it could or should be.

---

[1] Needless to say, the distinction between levels and standards is not always made, and the term "standard" is often used when "level" is intended.

Better homes are important to Huecorianos. Adobe wall construction

HEALTH CONDITIONS

Since a meaningful and valid evaluation of health conditions is outside the competence of this study, we have confined ourselves to reporting the villagers' cognizance of the problem, and to commenting on some of the more obvious factors involved.

In the 36 households in which the social questionnaire was administered, the housewife was asked to state those sicknesses that occurred most commonly in her family. Of course, this reporting suffers from laxity of definition, for it is clear that the layman is unable to distinguish symptoms. Those reporting stomach pains might have incipient or mature ulcers or may have merely eaten unripe fruit. On the other hand, vitamin deficiencies, abnormal blood pressure, or intestinal parasites might persist unidentified, and even unnoticed. Even when symptoms are clear to the individual he may define them incorrectly. Only three genuine cases of malaria were found in Huecorio during the five years prior to 1962, yet three persons in the sample reported having experienced it in their families. Did our sample inadvertently include those three persons? Had some or all of the three contracted malaria prior to the five-year period? Or, since *paludismo* (malaria) is a rather common word in the familiar lexicon of Huecorio, did some respondents misname some other complaint?

All that can be said definitely from the respondents' replies is that respiratory complaints are frequent. (See Table XXXVIII.) To this can be added the statement of a CREFAL team that worked in Huecorio in 1957 that "whooping cough, diphtheria, typhoid, etc." are common. In the summer of 1962 one woman died of what was apparently tuberculosis, and a youth died of a respiratory complaint the day of his return from the *tierra caliente*. Our general impression, for what it is worth, is that the health of the people of Huecorio is not extraordinarily bad and that the unsanitary conditions under which they live are partially compensated for by a relatively balanced diet and the availability of medical services.

In examining the measures taken by Huecorianos to prevent sickness, one finds that they do little to protect themselves. Although they pay lip service to the need for cleanliness, the cognition of proper practices is not implemented. There is a general recognition that respiratory complaints result from getting wet, but little can be done to avoid this, especially during the rainy season, since the downpours are so sudden and heavy that any person who must pass from one place to another will get thoroughly soaked. The poorer Huecorianos must frequently continue to wear damp clothing, for some have an insufficient number of changes and others none at all. In their unprompted responses, only one or two villagers mentioned flies, mosquitoes, or "carelessness" as possibly causing disease, while nine of the 36 respondents resorted to the noncommital screen of "*¿Quien sabe?*" when queried.

However, when they were prompted about measures to prevent disease, respondents generally knew the "proper" answer to the question and could frequently explain the causative sequence. Villagers were asked whether they believed that diseases could be caused by garbage that was not buried or destroyed, by flies, by consuming unboiled water, by exposed human waste, by food prepared by unclean hands, and by food unprotected from dust. It is clear from Table 19 that the replies are generally correct in a formal sense. Most women remember, when prompted, that there are certain principles of preventive sanitation, and they can generally but not always offer a reasonably correct explanation of the principle. "Flies step on faeces

TABLE 19

Tabulation of Replies to Questions Pertaining to Sanitation and Disease

	Number of Respondents Replying		
Question	*Yes*	*No*	*"¿Quien sabe?"*
Do you believe that disease can be caused by:			
Garbage that is not disposed of?	32	0	4
Flies?	34	0	2
Unboiled water?	30	1	5
Human waste that is not disposed of?	34	0	2
Do you believe that:			
A woman should wash her hands before preparing food?	36	0	0
Food should be protected from dust?	36	0	0

and then on food" was a common reply, but there were some variations. "Faeces might not cause disease, but it's disgusting," or "People always leave it lying around but in times past they used to go in the lake and it would be carried away." "Yes, I know I should boil the water I get from the lake but I have never had any trouble with it." "Water carries many microbes that cause malaria." "The *Consejo de Salubridad* told us that we should boil the water but I don't do it." "People should go in a place of their own to protect other people." "Yes, I know we should use latrines but I forget the reason." "Cleanliness is a beautiful thing." "I learned in school that garbage should be buried but I don't do it." "You don't have to boil the water from the pipes because the pipes are clean and the well is covered."

It is clear that educational campaigns have had the effect of making Huecorianos aware of certain elementary principles of sanitation. There is, however, a wide gap between this vague awareness and actual practice. A few Huecorianos use household garbage as compost, but the majority throw it carelessly from the kitchen into the street or patio where it is investigated by chickens and pigs.

Flies abound and alight on waste and food alike. Little can be done to reduce their numbers in an agricultural community, and the houses are not easily sealed from their invasion. Kitchens are frequently in open sheds, doors and windows are often wide and difficult to screen, and the clay tiles used on roofs are loose-fitting and offer easy access to insects even if everything else is sealed. For the individual householder to protect himself from disease-carrying flies considerable inconvenience and expense would be involved, and this he is unlikely to undertake until he appreciates the hazard at the level of a constant and conscious awareness.

There are, of course, no flush toilets in Huecorio, but about half the homes have outside privies. Fields, hedgerows, a corner of the patio or garden otherwise suffice. The deposit is not buried and toilet paper is not used. This condition is gradually changing as the federal government encourages the construction by privies by subsidizing precast concrete seats.

Most women do indeed wash their hands before preparing food, and the more acculturated people wash before eating as well. However, food is rarely covered to protect it from dust and insects, and the virtue of the partial cleanliness is clearly offset. Only ten of the women interviewed regularly boil the water used for drinking, although several others boil it when sickness has already hit. How is the general negligence of the others to be explained? Laziness, inconvenience, lack of conviction in their rote verbalizations?

Once sickness has struck, Huecorianos generally combat it by resorting to modern techniques,[2] which include visits to clinics, hospitals, and physicians as well as drugs, injections, and so on obtainable from

[2] Specifically, of the 36 respondents, 20 rely exclusively on modern medicine, four exclusively on home remedies, ten combine the two methods, and two claim they do nothing.

drugstores. Home remedies might include brews of herbs,[3] alcohol rubs, steam inhalants, and salt baths in galvanized tubs. Exclusive use of these is found only among the poorest villagers, for there is a recognition that home remedies are not especially efficacious. Where home and modern methods are used in combination, the procedure is usually to try the home remedies first, then to try pills or injections obtainable at drugstores in Pátzcuaro or from the clinic held once a week in Huecorio, and if these are unsuccessful finally to visit a physician.

Huecorianos are not covered by the Mexican social security program, but are visited for a few hours once a week by a nurse who administers basic services and gives women health instruction and advice. In addition, Huecorio is visited every two months by a traveling team from the *Comisión Nacional de Eradicación del Paludismo* (National Commission for the Eradication of Malaria), who visit all the homes to check on the incidence of malaria. The CNEP is aided in its work in each village by informants who report suspicious cases and send blood smears to Morelia for testing. Huecorio is not in the malaria zone, and the three positive cases reported during its five years of existence involved persons who had contracted the disease while in the *tierra caliente*.

It is apparent that sanitary conditions in Huecorio leave much to be desired. Bathing is infrequent, waste is not properly disposed of, flies abound, animals freely enter living quarters, many persons still sleep on dirt floors, cooking facilities are close to the ground, water and food are easily contaminated, and for most villagers clothing is insufficient to keep warm and dry. The exhortations of teachers and government officials have had little impact on improving the situation, in part at least because of practical difficulties such as those involved in controlling flies or in providing water at sufficient volume and pressure to enable villagers to install flush toilets or showers.

Nevertheless, improvement is undoubtedly taking place. Huecorianos are beginning to accept the government subsidized toilets, men returning from the United States are now uncomfortable because

[3] One mentioned for fever was a tea made from the husk of *zapote*, lentil roots, and chile.

they had become accustomed to daily showers while there, a few women are becoming interested in cosmetics[4] and in personal hygiene.

NUTRITION

To the nonspecialist observer, the diet of the people of Huecorio would seem to compare most favorably with the patterns described for people in other peasant communities. The last column of Table 20 clearly indicates that the average diet is built around the basic subsistence crops of corn and *frijoles,* and that these are to be found at almost every meal at almost every table. Soups and broths derived from corn, beans, meat, or rice are generally consumed daily. Indeed, it is clear that some protein intake is the rule rather than the exception. Vegetables and particularly fruit consumption are much less frequent, but this would not appear to be due to their unavailability. Even when they are not being harvested in Huecorio, some fruits and vegetables will find their way from the *tierra caliente* to the Pátzcuaro market.

As pointed out above,[5] vegetables are used to provide Huecorio farmers with their meager cash income and they are therefore less frequently available for home consumption. This is true, although to a much lesser extent, of milk. A few farmers will sell all that they produce in order to supplement their cash earnings.

Fish, which is more or less readily available just for the catching, is clearly less popular than meat, and this difference appears to involve the matter of taste. For some reason, many villagers do not like its flavor. Fowl—rather scrawny farmyard chickens and very rarely turkey—tends to be reserved for special occasions, but because of its price it is not consumed in poorer households.

Milk is the most popular beverage with meals, and is preferred to *atole* which is regarded as a substitute. Coffee is not widely con-

---

[4] It is reasonable to argue that an interest in clean clothing, hair, and appearance will be generalized into a broader acceptance of cleanliness.
[5] Chapter 1, p. 40.

T A B L E 20

Patterns of Daily Family Food Consumption

| | Number of Families and Daily Frequency of Consumption | | |
| | | | |
Food Item	Once	Twice	Three Times	Not a Regular Part of Daily Diet
Frijoles	0	18	16	2
Tortillas	6	4	21	5
Soup	23	2	0	11
Caldo[a]	21	2	0	13
Meat	15	6	2	13
Milk	14	3	0	19
Fish	10	3	2	21
Bread	13	2	0	21
Vegetables	14	1	0	21
Coffee	10	3	1	22
Eggs	9	2	0	25
Cheese	7	2	0	27
Potatoes	8	0	0	28
Atole	7	1	0	28
Cinnamon tea	5	1	0	30
Chile	5	0	0	31
Chocolate	4	1	0	31
Gelatine	3	0	0	33
Fruit	3	0	0	33
Oatmeal	2	0	0	34
Squash	2	0	0	34
Noodles	2	0	0	34
Orange leaf tea	1	1	0	34
Rice	0	1	0	35
Lentils	1	0	0	35
Chicken[b]	1	0	0	35
Tacos	0	1	0	35

[a] A broth.
[b] In view of the price of chicken, we doubt that any family consumes it once a day. This reply would seem to be an error.

sumed, but whether this was a question of taste or cost was not established.

The variety apparent in Table 20 is, of course, general. For the poorer families meals are a monotonous repetition of corn, *frijoles,* soup, broth, and *atole,* perhaps amplified by fish or meat once a day. Wealthier families will consume a much larger variety of foodstuffs daily, and will frequently add sugared desserts and spiced dishes to garnish the customary pattern. Some families have set higher standards for themselves than have others. They indulge in variety, quality, and quantity, and they scoff at other well-to-do households that set lower standards.

Customarily families sit down to three meals a day, and between-meals snacks are rare for adults. These snacks, if taken, may be fruit if trees are bearing, or cookies and soft drinks purchased at a *tienda.* The early morning meal is heavy and is eaten anywhere between the hours of 6:00 and 8:00. As with "lunch" and "dinner," the most frequent components are *frijoles* and *tortillas* supplemented with milk and meat or fish. The American pattern of eggs, toast, and juice is not found at all, but two families regularly consume oatmeal. A midday meal (*comida*) is quite heavy, and soup or broth and meat or fish are standard. The *comida* takes place in midafternoon about two or three o'clock. *Cena* is a light meal—"to live longer"—at about seven, and often is nothing more than *frijoles* and *tortillas* with perhaps coffee heavily sweetened with sugar.

HOUSING

Housing conditions vary to a degree that makes simple generalization misleading. One can identify four distinct classes of home, although of course the conditions range on a continuum from hovels unfit for human occupancy to spacious, clean, and comfortable dwellings.

A minority of families—no more than five—live under conditions which are deplorable by any standards. In one such case, a family of six exists in a hut only ten by ten feet, half buried in the ground and covered with a leaking roof of resurrected tins. There is nothing here to elevate man from the basest circumstances. While some Huecorianos may experience such existence as a temporary phenomenon, for others the degradation exists not because of the niggardliness of fortune but because of what might be called defects of character.

More common are the tiny shelters of the poorer families, for whom the inadequacy of their homes is the inescapable result of their economic condition. Huecorianos have a great attachment to their homes and they try to improve them whenever the opportunity arises. A poor home of this kind is described in this excerpt from a daily report:

We went this afternoon to interview Señora Gómez, a timid little old lady whose husband was off working somewhere in *el norte*. She had filled her tiny house plot with a jungle of corn, melons, and beans to such a degree that the house was hardly visible. We greeted her as we walked to the gate in the stone wall and the tone of her *"Buenos tardes, maestros"* clearly indicated that she was less than happy that we had come to bother her.

We were not invited to enter the gate, but had we been so easily dissuaded the project would have been abandoned well before. The rains had just begun to sweep in from the east and we sloshed through the corn to the little house, set back from the alley. It was a single-room shack of *adobe* blocks, and it measured not more than 12 by 12 feet. There were, of course, no windows.

We used the light rain as an excuse to insinuate ourselves on to the porch, which was covered by an extension of the roof. The floors of the porch and the dark, unlit room were of dirt. There was neither water supply nor electricity, and there was a clear evidence in the lot that a latrine had not yet been built. A dog, with long wolf-like ears, cowered at the end of a chain. A dirty, mewing cat with a cord tied about his shoulders tried to climb to the top of the oven to escape the damp, chilling cold. Chickens were also tied by strings, but even they managed now and again to dart, clucking, into the room. The open porch and ill-fitting tiles on the roof offered us no protection from the intensifying deluge, and as the *señora* backed into the room to escape the lightning that so frightened her, we slipped in uninvited, asking questions as we went.

The oven of baked mud seemed to occupy one quarter of the available space. Clothing hung on a rack suspended from the ceiling, and wooden boxes piled in the far corner contained most of the couple's worldly possessions. Furnishing consisted of a tiny table and three or four rickety chairs. A *metate* testified to their economic condition. This was one family that could not afford to grind their corn at the *molino*.

Of a rented house in Carián we wrote:

We went there last night and after successfully negotiating the muddy road from Huecorio in pitch darkness stumbled over some stones, through a patio, and into the blinding rays of an electric light streaming through an open doorway.

The men greeted us in a most friendly way and we seated ourselves on boxes and an upturned canoe. Two *mariposa* nets were hung from the ceiling and cord for making others was neatly rolled up on a corner. The room had been decorated with pictures from calendars and newspapers pasted on the walls. Behind where I was sitting was an altar suspended by cords from the ceiling and decorated with colored paper and religious images.

There were no beds, but *petates* were rolled up out of the way along a wall. When they slept, this was all that separated the people from the bare concrete. The house was lit by a single, naked electric bulb and a radio was connected to the only wall outlet.

In one corner stood an ancient muzzle-loading flintlock. The stock was homemade, but the gun turned out to be loaded and was therefore given only a most cursory examination. On the trigger guard were two duck bands from the U.S. Fish and Wildlife Service.

Two little girls were watching everything that was going on. One was a giggly six and the other a flirtatious two.

The majority of the homes in Huecorio are older and more substantial than this. They have at least two rooms, although one of the rooms may serve the combined purposes of kitchen, living, and sleeping. (See Table XXXIX.)

When resources permit, families build a separate structure to use as a kitchen, and in it will be found pottery and glassware neatly arranged on shelves. In one home there were several pieces of aluminum cookingware which had never been used. In another glazed clay pots were placed one on top of the other in a balanced pile that reached to a height of over eight feet beside a wall. "What," I wondered, "would happen in an earthquake."

These "middle class" houses are usually constructed around a rather well-defined patio, which is normally of dirt but might be partially paved with flagstone or covered with crushed scoria. The patio is sometimes planted with a decorative shrub, but because chickens and pigs are often kept in it such attempts at decoration are fruitless. More viable are the potted flowering plants often placed on the low walls that divide the patio from the open porch that runs the length of the house.

Rooms are arranged linear fashion around the patio, each with a single door and perhaps, but not often, a glazed window facing the porch. The rooms are rarely larger than 12 by 12 feet. Only about a third of the floors are surfaced, but when they are unglazed clay tile, flagstone, cement, or wide pine boards are used. Several Huecorianos stated a strong preference for wood floors because of their "warmth." Nevertheless, the use of wood is exceptional.

"Middle class" homes tend to be the ones in which a constructed latrine is used, and most have electricity and water piped in. It is in these homes that furnishings become more apparent and elaborate. At least one bed is usually found, and there are chairs, tables, chests, wardrobes, radios, sewing machines, etc., which speak of a life emerging from poverty.[6] Certain of the furnishings, especially the sewing machines, will be given a place of honor in the center of the room; even though they rest on a dirt floor, they will be dusted and polished with affectionate pride.

Only a handful of houses in Huecorio are more elaborate than those just described, and three of them are the two-story structures to which villagers aspire. The houses of the relatively well-to-do will be distinguished by a larger number of rooms and qualitative refinements such as glazed windows in steel frames, and wooden or glazed tile floors. They may also boast gas or kerosene stoves, and noticeable accumulations of furnishings of good quality.

[6] Although the beds are frequently without springs or mattresses, they nevertheless represent an improvement over the *petate*.

Any but the meanest of the hovels will often show the feminine touch. Curtained windows, colorful pictures from calendars or magazines, photographs of family or visitors from the outside, or artificial flowers may brighten a dark interior. Almost all patios and porches will be adorned with decorative plants growing in pots of clay or tin. Most houses are uncluttered and clean, although patios might be littered with garbage and human and animal excreta. Flies are ever present, for even in the well-to-do homes there is no practical way to exclude them.

It is safe to say that housing conditions in Huecorio are unsatisfactory. The average area available per person is 60 square feet at the maximum, and even this is a misleading exaggeration since many of the rooms counted as living quarters have other functions—grain storage and cooking in particular.[7] Privacy—the ability of a person to be alone—would seem to elude the Huecoriano, although there is no reason to assume that this is a matter of importance to him.

About two-thirds of the homes still have unhygienic floors of dirt, and the wood-burning clay oven is usually raised little above this. One-third of the houses have yet to be provided with the convenience of electricity, and about the same proportion lack the reasonably potable public water. Where water is not piped into the houses, housewives may draw from nearby public faucets in the village streets. This alternative is not available to people in Carián and Urandén, and they draw from shallow open wells or from the lake. Open wells are sometimes utilized even in the village center.

Needless to say, raw sewage can enter both the lake and the wells. Only about half of the village homes have latrines, and no attempt is made to place them beyond minimum filtration distances from open wells or ditches.

During much of the year, especially at night, temperatures are uncomfortably low, yet the houses offer little protection from cold. While the thick adobe walls provide some insulation, heat escapes quickly through the loose roof tiles. The only source of artificial heat is the kitchen stove, and even this is frequently separated from the

[7] The average number of rooms per household in the sample survey is 2.3, which on the generous basis of 150 square feet per room gives an average area for a household of 345 square feet.

living quarters. There are no open fireplaces. With all this, Huecorianos are hardy and do not seem to be concerned about the cold.

In sum—housing conditions in Huecorio are cramped, cold, and
unsanitary.

LEVELS AND
PATTERNS OF INCOME

For 35 households, representative of the 140 odd in the village,
reasonably complete data are available on the productive contributions of the economically active individuals. Table 21 presents these
data in the form of an aggregate account. From various rearranged
summaries, conclusions can be drawn concerning the contributions of
the different occupations, income levels and functional distribution,
the relationships between income and household size, and, finally, the
division of income between cash and kind.

The aggregate "national income" of these 35 households was 287,-
807 pesos, which gives an average household income of 8,218 pesos
($657 U. S.). The range was wide. One household earned only 2,167
pesos ($173 U. S.), while another earned a relatively comfortable
26,152 pesos ($2,092 U. S.)—more than 12 times as much. The
average per capita income for the group as a whole was 1,313 pesos
($105 U. S.), with a minimum of only 271 pesos ($22 U. S.) and
a maximum of 4,673 pesos ($374 U. S.).

The situation is not nearly as bleak as these data might suggest,
however. Household 15 is responsible for the minimum figures, for
both household and per capita income, and the earnings of one
member were not included in the calculation. Furthermore, the conversion to U. S. dollars is misleading, and a factor of at least three
should be applied to adjust for price differences and the disparate
market baskets of the two countries. In other words, particularly
insofar as international comparisons are concerned, the data should
be regarded as a first approximation.

In Table 22 we observe the various occupations in terms of their
contributions to the "national product," the labor force of the sample,

TABLE 21

Estimates of Household and Per Capita Incomes (pesos)

Code Number	Total Household Income	Number in Household	Per Capita Income
B1	12,195	7	1,742
2	12,843	10	1,283
3	11,705	8	1,463
4	18,692	4	4,673
5	26,152	6	4,359
6	2,509	2	1,254
7	2,284	4	571
8	13,772	5	2,754
9	5,659	8	707
10	4,076	6	679
11	9,195	5	1,839
12	11,016	9	1,224
13	5,518	9	613
14	4,187	4	1,046
15	2,167	8	271
16	2,465	5	493
17	8,987	7	1,284
18	3,247	4	812
19	3,244	4	811
20	4,208	5	842
21	10,391	5	2,078
22	9,952	11	905
23	7,054	6	1,175
24	10,891	8	1,361
25	2,657	4	664
26	3,635	5	727
27	2,886	5	577
28	8,800	11	800
29	20,503	8	2,563
30	4,570	2	2,285
31	6,682	5	1,336
32	6,766	6	1,127
33	4,590	4	1,147
34	4,318	9	480
35	20,000	10	2,000

TABLE 22

Income in Cash and Kind from Various Sources
and Average Productivities (pesos)

Source	Income[a]			Number of Producers	Average Productivity
	Cash	Kind	Total		
Farming					
Crops	13,145	23,510	36,655	39	937
Fruit	2,545	3,240	5,785	27	214
Firewood	2,600	940	3,540	12	295
Eggs	25,630	2,398	28,028	17	1,649
Milk	40,577	6,732	47,309	19	2,490
Animals	3,770	1,681	5,451	21	256
Fishing	6,257	(?)	6,257	2	3,218
Unskilled labor	7,557	1,749	9,306	10	930
Migrant labor	26,500	(?)	26,500	2	13,250
Net weaving	600	(?)	600	3	200
Furniture weaving	6,170	0	6,170	3	2,057
Masonry	9,280	0	9,280	3	3,093
Carpentry	710	0	710	2	355
Baking	130	910	1,040	2	520
Garment making	26,252	(?)	26,252	10	2,625
Trading	39,056	0	39,056	21	1,859
Storekeeping	18,000	(?)	18,000	2	9,000
Music	505	(?)	505	6	84
Household service	4,520	(?)	4,520	3	1,507
Miscellaneous	12,843	0	12,843	7	1,843
Grand Totals	246,647	41,160	287,807		

[a] See below, pp. 329–30, for a discussion of the division of income between cash and kind. Question mark indicates no means available for calculation.

and their relative productivity. The five most important contributors to the "national product" are, in pesos, milk (47,309), trading (39,056), crops (36,555), eggs (28,028), and migrant labor (26,-500). It might be argued that crops and trading should be lumped together, since as a rule the traders are selling crops—usually vegetables—produced in their own households. If this were done, the combined occupations would assume first place in the scale. However, the traders also sell on their own account vegetables, milk products, fish, pottery, and other products not produced in their own household and often not produced in Huecorio. Accordingly, combining trading and crop production would inflate the role of the latter.

Casual observation of Huecorio's fields of growing crops and study of the distribution of the labor force would inevitably persuade an outsider that Huecorio is an agricultural community. By these measures it is, of course; but viewed in terms of its *economic* contribution, the production of crops slides down from its preeminent position. (This role is further denigrated when we note that it is outranked by two part-time occupations and followed by a third; in addition, the fifth ranking occupation—migrant labor—involved the activities of only two men.)

In terms of productivity[8] the greatest contributions are made by the *braceros* (13,250 pesos), storekeeping (9,000), fishing (3,128), masonry (3,093), and garment-making (2,625). One of the two *braceros* who visited the United States during the year in question claimed that he returned with some 24,000 pesos, which he used to build a house. His gross earnings would, of course, have been greater, but there is nothing necessarily inflated about his claim. Twenty-four thousand pesos amounted to $1,920 U. S., and this is a net cash return easily obtainable in a twelve-month period in the United States, even by an agricultural worker.

Of course, the fact that the *braceros* gained their income in the United States is the explanation both for their high contribution to productivity and for their abiding interest in such employment. In terms of the village economy, storekeeping is the most productive occupation. Two of the four such tradesmen are especially astute and have accumulated large assets.

In view of the fact that fishing households seem to the observer to be among the poorest of the village, the relatively high ranking of this

[8] For our purposes, average productivity in an occupation is found by dividing its net contribution to the "national product" by the number of people who make that contribution. This method is not conceptually impregnable but is called for by the limitations of the data.

occupation is unexpected. The explanation is clear, however. In few of the fishing households is any other activity pursued. (See households 27 and 34.) They have little or no land, and few additional skills. Furthermore, they live in sections isolated from the main current of village activities and have many of the characteristics associated with low social status. In other households full-time activities such as farming are supplemented by part-time pursuits such as baking or producing eggs.

Masonry ranks fourth, and is for most masons a casual trade taken up on those few occasions when a villager has a little extra cash available to fix his house. Its position on the scale is high because one of the masons had steady and well-paid employment outside the village. Garment-making ranks fifth, but would be higher were it not for several persons who follow the trade in a fashion that is essentially casual or part-time.

The most significant point in this discussion of productivity is the extremely poor showing of crop production (937 pesos). It lies ⅔ of the way down the list and is outranked by several part-time activities. This ranking would be even lower were it not for the high productivity of cash crops, which save the principal crops of corn and wheat from what would otherwise be complete disgrace. Corn and wheat dictate the rhythm of life in Huecorio and many other Mexican villages, they dominate the largest areas of land, they are the principal items of diet, and to them the outside policy-makers pay prime obeisance when they consider ways to raise the level of living. Doubling the productivity of these principal crops would still not raise agriculture to the top ranks of per capita productivity, and one is inevitably prompted to ask questions. Are we not doing a disservice to farmers when we try to raise productivity in their minifundia? Are we not, in effect, misleading them to believe that there is some hope that agriculture can offer them a better life? Are there not other, more productive activities open to them? Is it efficient and wise for a state to allocate funds and technical skills to something which seems to have so little promise?

Two other interesting and connected phenomena are observable in these income data. As can be seen in Table XL and Chart 3, the number of persons in a household has some bearing on both the total

income of the household and the per capita incomes within the household. Stated briefly, the larger the household, the higher its aggregate
income and the lower its per capita income. Observation of Chart 4
makes the reason for this quite clear. As may be expected, the
number of economically active persons in large households is greater

CHART 3

Relationships Between Household Size, Total Household Income,
and Per Capita Income

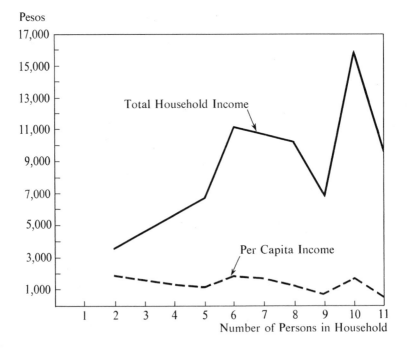

than in small households, and thus there are more producers to
create the higher total income. However, the number of producers
will decline as a proportion of the total household as the household increases in size and there are, accordingly, more dependent mouths to
feed. This phenomenon has a striking similarity to Engels' Law and
might be paraphrased: as the size of the household increases, so does
the number of producers, but at a lower rate.

The final observations to be extracted from the income data pertain to the relationships between cash income and income in kind. (See Table XLI.) The highest proportion of income in kind to total income from a given source is found in the baking of bread (87%).

CHART 4

Relationships Between Number of Persons, Number of Producers, and Percentage of Producers, in Household

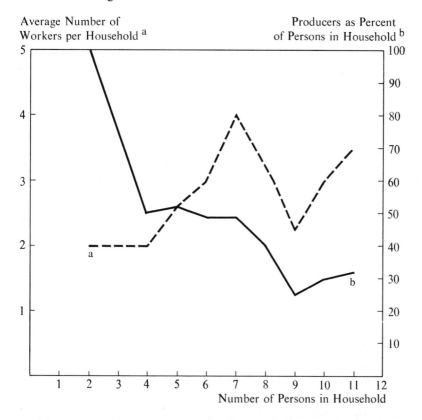

Average Number of
Workers per Household [a]

Producers as Percent
of Persons in Household [b]

Number of Persons in Household

This high ranking has very little significance, since the bread is produced by only one family in the village and their stated purpose in selling bread is not so much to make a cash profit as it is to cover out-of-pocket breadmaking expenses and thus to produce bread for their own household, "for free" as they see it. On the other hand, corn and wheat are major components of the diet of Huecorianos, and very little of those crops are sold. The cash component of the crops (36%) is almost entirely derived from vegetables. While the percentage of fruit consumed to that produced is high (56%), fruit production is casual and unimportant in Huecorio.

Some aspects of Table XLI should be explained. Unskilled farm labor working on the corn crop receives some portion of its wages in kind in the form of meals provided by the *patrón*. For certain occupations, it was understood that income in kind would exist but it did not prove feasible to calculate the level. Musicians, for instance, frequently perform at a *mañanitas* or other *fiesta* without receiving monetary compensation. They, like the other guests, are fed and given drink. *Braceros* working in the United States received in addition to a money wage, housing, medical care, food, transportation, and sometimes clothing. Garment workers make clothes for their own use, servants receive meals, and fishermen obviously eat some of the fish they catch. However, some occupations seem to involve little or no consumption of the articles produced, or exchange of commodity for commodity. Examples of these would be trading and masonry.

In sum, it can be said that the Huecorianos live in an economy that is almost entirely monetized. The only important activity characterized by subsistence is the production of crops. Of the total production that we were able to estimate, only 14.38% is consumed directly, and undoubtedly even this will fall as the economy of Huecorio advances.

LEVELS OF LIVING

In the absence of household budget data, no firm conclusion can be reached concerning patterns of consumption in Huecorio. There is no reason to believe that Huecorianos differ from the poor people of other parts of the world in the practice of devoting the major portion —perhaps as much as 75%—of their income to food. This position is supported by the obvious difficulties that Huecorianos face in accumulating cash income to be directed toward other basic needs in clothing, housing, and health, and by their verbalized desire to eat better.[9] Although about two-thirds of the homes have both electricity and water, houses remain generally overcrowded, unsanitary, and unattractive. Huecorianos are naturally concerned with their immediate surroundings, and when the opportunity occurs income will frequently be channeled into home improvement. Since most such improvements involve cash outlays that are substantial when measured against local income, they are usually associated with extraordinary cash gains such as repatriated *bracero* earnings. In one such case, a villager with whom two members of the team were boarding was busy cementing his patio and building a wash basin a few days after he had been paid his monthly rent.

Neither does his income position permit the average Huecoriano more than a meager wardrobe.[10] Some villagers do not have a change of outer garments,[11] and pants may be so patched as to make easy identification of the original material impossible. Clothing is made and

[9] See below, p. 338.

[10] Foster's description—pp. 41, 48—of the patterns of dress in Tzintzuntzan fits closely that for Huecorio and need not be elaborated upon. For women, three distinct classes of dress can be seen. The Indian women of Carián and Urandén wear the colorful ankle-length skirts and amorphous blouses characteristic of the Tarascans. The first stage in the rejection of this costume is the dress of the majority of Huecorianos. For them the skirt is raised to calf length and both it and the blouse are likely to be cut with more precision but made of a cotton material of drabber hue. Both these groups of women will always wear aprons and *rebozos,* their hair will be braided into two pigtails, and they will frequently walk unshod. Several girls have made a second transitional rejection and wear the dresses or skirts and blouses of the urban youth; to emphasize the point, they have cut their tresses and clip along in high heels, unsuited though these are to the unpaved streets of Huecorio. No men, on the other hand, will be found to use Indian garb of white cotton pants and shirt as described in Lewis, p. 201. Their workaday garments differ from those of North American farmers only to the extent that they may sometimes wear *huaraches* in place of shoes and will never feel dressed without the handsome "cowboy" type *sombrero* typical of the region. For more formal purposes older men will wear the cotton *guayabera* jacket and younger men will have windbreakers, or, if they can afford them, business suits.

[11] One man was most embarrassed when he was visited on the day his only pair of pants was being washed.

repaired with the omnipresent sewing machines, although, since they are more complicated to make, men's jackets, suits, and work pants will be store bought. These garments are the particular spoils of *bracero* visits to the United States.

Poverty has been a constant in the lives of most Huecorianos. They are aware that it surrounds them with a wall difficult to breach, and they feel oppressed and dispirited by it. We would judge that they are not a happy people, for their unrealized aspirations, not very different from those of more fortunate people in middle-class societies, seem to them to be so difficult of attainment.[12]

Some villagers disagree with our conclusions about their level of living, but it is significant that those who disagree have begun to escape and are among the relatively affluent. Said one, "There are no poor people in Huecorio. It is only a saying. Some say they are poor because they don't believe they have the resources, but the majority engage in trade, and at the very least have enough to eat without going into debt. They eat in peace for they earn enough. Or, if they must borrow, the amount is not very much. Sometimes they say they are poor perhaps because they don't have enough seeds or they can't find another job to augment their income. A fellow can go to Apatzingán to earn more—15 pesos a day—but then it is to buy clothes or to save to buy other things to live better for a while." Clearly, poverty is a relative concept.

Some Huecorianos are beginning to raise their level of living beyond the basic requirements for food, clothing, shelter and a few sticks of furniture. Houses are being improved with wooden or concrete floors, new rooms are being added, beds are becoming the rule, radios are found in half the houses, and since 1962, two television sets have been installed. It is clear that the level of living is rising as a result of increases in income from new nonagricultural pursuits such as egg

---

[12] It is, of course, presumptuous for one person to judge the state of mind of another and perhaps we overemphasize the case, for indeed we would be uncomfortable in the unfamiliar and drab environment of the Huecoriano. Yet there is something about the listless pace, the deadly seriousness of the *fiestas,* the infrequency of spontaneous song and laughter, the preoccupation with elementary existence, that convey such an impression to the visitor.

production, furniture making, trading, itinerant labor, and artisanship.

There are a few dissident voices, of course. One villager, perhaps indulging in nostalgia, claimed, "Before the Revolution and before we were given land, we lived better. We were fewer in number and we all worked on the *haciendas* and sugar mills and we ate well. Our private land was sufficient only for two *yuntas* to work and there were eight cows to provide milk for our families. We worked outside the village and came home for two or three days at a time. Now we have land but not enough work."

Some observers have criticized what they feel to be irrational practices of consumption on the part of Huecorianos. In the words of a nonvillager, "The people have money enough to eat and dress better but they spend it on booze. And they spend so much on weddings that they don't have enough left over to pay the priest." As we noted previously, one villager criticized his fellows for not consuming the more nutritious crops they produced but selling them instead for corn. In view of the village's need to import corn, this attack has little force. Certainly, however, one can find examples of impulsive expenditures. A man from Pátzcuaro did a brisk trade in Huecorio selling electric shocks from a hand-cranked dynamo. The charge, he said, was good for rheumatism and nerve ailments, and many handed over the required 50 centavos. On another occasion, a wealthier villager bought two large caged birds for 40 pesos, although undoubtedly a more "rational" use for the money could be argued.

To judge the Huecorianos "irrational" on the basis of such evidence would be unwise indeed. For one thing, rationality must be defined in terms of the objectives to which the behavior is directed. If we accept the proposition that the ultimate objective of economic activity is the fulfillment of some human want or desire, irrational behavior is hard to pinpoint. Those who received the electric shocks may have wanted some small, exciting escape from their surrounding boredom, as the drinkers find pleasure in a somewhat lengthier escape. To what extent should one person judge the objectives to be sought by another?[13]

[13] This is hardly a definitive discussion of rationality. Our sole purpose is to hint at the folly of passing judgment on Huecorianos in this respect.

INCOME ASPIRATIONS
AND THE "DEMONSTRATION EFFECT"

We have seen the evidence that Huecorianos are preoccupied with the business of making a living and that they consciously and constantly express a desire for a higher level of material well-being. Some revealing light is directed on these attitudes in Table 23. Householders were asked the seemingly guileless question, "What would you do if you had ten pesos more every week?" After this question was answered, the ante was raised to 25 pesos and then to 100.

The replies were generally realistic, but it was evident that for some the weekly increment of 100 pesos was astronomical and beyond the reach of plausibility. One woman ended the inquiry flatly by saying, "You cannot earn that here!" With others the reaction was a rich, indulgent joy. Said one man, "Oh! I'd go nuts. I'd put it in a bank and start a *taller* to help people." A woman answered, "I'd save it. I would be very content—very happy." But after a moment's reflection the mood changed, "Or even sadder from fear." Two persons, either indulging in naïveté or leg-pulling, announced that they would use the money to buy automobiles.

Perhaps the most noteworthy observations are the differences between the responses proffered by males on the one hand and females on the other, and the pronounced changes in income disposition that were evident as the hypothetical weekly increments rose. In the conventional literature of economics, income which is not consumed is, *ipso facto,* saved. For our purposes it is useful to fragment the savings category one stage further into Group II—savings, the primary purpose of which is to add to income[14]—and Group III—savings for non–income-earning functions such as liquidity or the education of children. It is clear from the table that given the choice between (I) immediate increments to consumption, (II) income-earning uses of savings, and (III) non–income-earning uses of savings, men tend to favor II while women tend to choose I.

[14] This is not necessarily synonymous with investment. Deposits in banks, even though earning interest, are not investments.

The female preference for consumption cannot be used to levy against them the charge of being spendthrift, although the weight they attach to clothing purchases may have its source in vanity. More likely, the explanation is founded on the different roles of men and women. Women more than men are faced perpetually with the reality of preparing food and mending clothing, while men find themselves constantly confronted with the frustrations of their limited productive resources.

Those men who would direct their incremental income to consumption think more in terms of improved housing. Again, a likely explanation is that the construction and maintenance of the home falls within the male province. One, speaking in a sense for the entire village said, *"Una casa mejor. Esta es todo que se piensa aquí."* (A better house. This is all we think about here.) With their dreams of brick and mortar, Huecorianos show their bonds with others who are more fortunate.

For both males and females, the pattern of hypothetical income division would change significantly as earnings rose away from consumption and toward productive endeavors. Although it does not follow that Huecorianos would indeed subscribe to the pattern that they verbalize, their attitudes are significant, particularly in view of the notion of the "Demonstration Effect" that prevails among economists. As this is stated by Nurkse in his application of the concept to economic development, "When people come into contact with superior goods or superior patterns of consumption, with new articles or new ways of meeting old wants, they are apt to feel after a while a certain restlessness and dissatisfaction. Their knowledge is extended, their imagination stimulated; new desires are aroused, the propensity to consume is shifted upward." [15]

The critical phrase is the last one. Those who succumb to the "Demonstration Effect" will, out of a given income, spend more and save less in response to the external stimulus of relative plenty. We would submit that, on the basis of the data from Huecorio, this interpretation of the "Demonstration Effect" is nothing but an exercise in ethnocentrism.[16] Indeed the people of Huecorio have been mer-

[15] Nurkse, pp. 58–59.
[16] The use of the word "superior" in the quotation above hints at this.

TABLE 23

Tabulation of Replies to Question: "What would you if you had x pesos more every week?"

Disposition of Additional Income	Amount Specified Per Week					
	Ten Pesos		Twenty-Five Pesos		One Hundred Pesos	
	Males	Females	Males	Females	Males	Females
(I) To Consumption						
Household furnishing	1	2	0	2	1	0
Home improvement	5	2	10	6	3	6
Home construction	1	1	4	1	6	1
Food	7	12	3	8	1	3
Clothing	5	6	1	12	1	6
Travel	0	1	0	1	1	3
Miscellaneous spending	4	4	2	5	2	5
Totals	23	28	20	35	15	24
Percentages	44.2	62.3	36.4	66.1	23.8	47.1
(II) To *Acquisition of Income-Earning Asset*						
Bank to earn interest to facilitate capital acquisition	4	0	8	3	13	3
Animals	5	3	8	1	8	0
Land	3	2	4	2	7	6
Farm equipment	0	0	1	0	4	1
Start a business	5	1	5	2	8	2
Totals	17	6	26	8	40	12
Percentages	32.7	13.3	47.3	15.1	63.5	23.5

(III) To *Savings* for:

No specified purpose	6	6	5	6	5	8
Children	1	0	3	1	3	1
Liquidity	5	5	1	3	0	6
Totals	12	11	9	10	8	15
Percentages	23.1	24.4	16.3	18.9	12.7	29.4
Number of replies[a]	52	45	55	53	63	51

[a] There were 41 male and 40 female respondents. Some replied with compound answers that were fitted in more than one category.

cilessly exposed to affluence. Some have seen it in the United States, others in Mexico City, and all among the tourists who flit through Pátzcuaro. But the Huecorianos are not the "perfect fools" that the proposition implies. The closeness of the margin between their income and their basic needs allows little room for increased consumption, and, more important, long contact with the realities of production gives them a thorough awareness of the relationships between production, income, and consumption. They are aware that, if they are to enjoy a better material life, they must produce more. In the words of one of the more affluent villagers, "What do you do to have a better life? First grow bigger and better crops, then you buy the radios, etc."

The "Demonstration Effect" operates in a manner exactly contrary to that ascribed to it by Nurkse—it does not raise the average propensity to consume, it lowers the marginal propensity to consume as people invest to produce to consume.[17] This interpretation is further supported by the behavior of the *braceros* and the *granjeros*. With their return to Mexico the *braceros* repatriated the bulk of their earnings. Some part of these went inevitably into consumption. For the poorer families this was a matter of survival. Other prominent consumption expenditures were for clothing and radios, but for the men at least much of the clothing was in the form of heavy-duty shoes, jackets, and work garments. Another portion of the earnings went into home improvement or construction while yet a third went toward capital in the form of sewing machines, irrigation pumps, tools, and inventories of merchandise for sale. At the time of our visit the *granjeros* were preparing to utilize the credit they had accumulated from their membership in the *Asociación Avícola*. In no case was this used for consumption but instead was invested in irrigation pumps, a horse and cart, and a woodworking *taller*.

The propensity to devote a higher proportion of income to productive pursuits at higher levels of income suggests another important behavioral principle: In peasant societies investment will be undertaken

[17] We do not mean to imply that the Huecorianos would lower the average propensity to consume out of present income. Given their low levels of income this would call for excessive hardships. Instead, the evidence suggests that the marginal propensity to consume would be low, and this would lead to a lower average propensity to consume at higher incomes.

only if the time between the decision to invest and the installation of the investment is short. To state this in another but oversimplified way, conventionally an investment decision involves two main elements, namely, the cost of the capital input and the annual flow of income. But when savings are not available immediately, a third element should be added—the time necessary to accumulate the required savings. The longer this period, the less desirable the capital project.[18]

The capital investments needed to break out of the monotonous cycle of poverty are substantial in terms of the incomes of Huecorianos. They are such things as irrigation pumps, lathes, tractors, inventories, and so on, and they involve outlays of several thousand pesos. When the amount of money that can be saved is small—let us say ten pesos a week—the time necessary to aggregate the required sum is so great that the desired object remains invisible below the time horizon. Too many temptations and emergencies lie waiting for even the most disciplined saver on his ten-peso-a-week journey toward two thousand pesos. When he gets to 40 pesos he might be offered a share in a pig, at 900 pesos his wife might fall sick, or at 1400 pesos a son's wedding might take place. However, if he could save 100 pesos a week instead of only ten, the 2000-peso pump would become visible since it would be available in five months instead of four years.

The explanation of the low rate of investment in such an environment lies, then, not so much in some inherent lack of discipline on the part of the people as in the "lumpiness" of worth-while productive investments.[19] Since Huecorianos are unlikely to receive large, steady, and unencumbered increments to their income, substantial capital creation can only be initiated with the provision of credit from the outside.

We hasten to affirm that some capital would be created at low levels of incremental income. One man, for instance, said that he would save his weekly ten pesos until he had 100 and then he would buy seeds to

[18] Economists can reduce all of these elements to a calculus by the use of discounting procedures, although they run into difficulties in the selection of the appropriate rate of discount. These are touched upon in my "Aspects of the Theory of Discounting," *Engineering Economist*, Vol. VI, No. 3 (Spring, 1961).

[19] This bears no analogy to the "big push" theory of development for it is independent of simultaneous market creation.

sell. Another said that he would buy thread to weave nets. But such investments, while of some value, have little noticeable effect on income and are insufficient to lead to a technological breakthrough.

The villagers are aware that capital accumulation would involve them in a period of abstinence until sufficient savings had been accumulated. One pointed out that the sum of ten pesos a week was too little to bother about and he would spend it, but 25 or 100 pesos would be worth banking until there was enough to buy maize to trade or a cow to produce milk. One man enunciated his thoughts in the form of a duty. Ten or 25 pesos he would save for his children, for sickness, or to buy land, but 100 pesos he would put in a bank "to make more. If an individual progresses, Mexico progresses. If the rich would put their money in a bank, the banks would lend it out to *ejidatarios* who would then be able to produce better crops. Banks now do not have enough money for loans."

Only those who clearly indicated that they would bank the money to earn interest or facilitate capital acquisition were included in Group II. Others—who were classified in Group III—sometimes indicated that savings would be deposited in a bank but either did not specify a reason or were thinking in terms of liquidity. One of the principal motivations behind the desire for liquidity was a fear of the economically devastating effects of an unexpected illness. This motive was frequently mixed with others, such as a desire to care for children in some unspecified way or to permit some indulgence in consumption. Typical replies in this category were: "I would save for sickness, new clothes, and to take a trip." "I would save for new clothes and to be able to take the children to a doctor when they are sick." "I would save for sickness but I would not put it into a bank because it is too difficult to take out."

In view of their concern with a better material way of life, do Huecorianos actively seek to achieve it or do they idly hope for some miraculous, painless salvation? Dream they do—of more and better food, warmer, drier, better-looking clothing, a comfortable home, perhaps travel or even a car. These dreams, however, are no surrogate for reality, and they serve as a spur to achievement. Most Huecorianos work hard and long hours for modest rewards, and they are constantly alert to the small economic advantages their environment might offer. But hard work and skill in petty negotiations are shoestrings for survival rather than bootstraps by which one can raise oneself. Only by the expansion of capital resources and the acquisition of new skills can the Huecoriano turn hope into reality, and these necessary conditions are coming to pass for some villagers— principally the *braceros* and the *granjeros*.

However, the villagers' hopes seem to be directed even more to the life that will be led by their children, and they make considerable efforts to provide for their education. One man had doubled the size of his *granja* and was preparing to irrigate his fields, for, he said, "I will need 300 pesos a month to put my children through secondary school. Even though the oldest is only eleven I have eight children and must plan for it." Another man had come to Huecorio from an island in the lake. He was an ardent musician and had traveled throughout Mexico acquiring his skills. His sole purpose in coming to the mainland to live in a rented house was to be nearer to people who could teach music to his boys.

Investment in skills and capital are the two means available to Huecorianos to fulfill their aspirations, and they both grasp opportunities when they show themselves and seek them out—not necessarily successfully—when they do not.

CHAPTER 9

HUECORIO AND POLICIES FOR RURAL WELFARE

H UECORIO is not the mistress of her own destiny, for the welfare of this tiny community is buffeted by influences and decisions generated in the large centers of power, particularly Mexico City and Washington.[1] This does not mean to say that an autonomous display of will and leadership arising within Huecorio cannot invoke some desirable changes, but it is clear that Huecorianos can overcome their feeling of impotence only if correct policies and practices are established by those with the means to do so.

It is, of course, easy and costless for an outsider to offer advice, especially if that outsider has neither the responsibility to carry out the programs nor the obligation to think through all the practical dif-

[1] As examples of important externally made decisions, we might cite the following. The policy of the Mexican government to stabilize corn prices at a low level will affect the earnings of farmers who sell corn on the market but not, obviously, the real income of those who grow it for subsistence. If Mexico is successful in increasing its rate of industrialization, this will provide some employment for those who leave the land; and, if the government decides to adopt a positive program of birth control, this will lower the mounting pressures on the already overworked land. Washington could aid Mexican rural communities by a new and carefully controlled program of migrant labor importation.

Señor Bolívar at work in Agricultural Survey

ficulties that might be involved. In what follows we must couch our statements in generalities, rather than details, for several reasons. First, there is hardly a facet of village life that cannot be improved in some way, but to undertake a complete accounting would lead to the presentation of many trivia and the needless exposition of the obvious. Second, studies of feasibility are likely to be complicated and call for specific technical knowledge that the writer does not have. Third, our intention is to identify the messages that Huecorio can send to other communities rather than to propose recommendations specific to Huecorio itself.

HASTENING THE PROCESS
OF SOCIAL CHANGE

Economic development cannot take place in the absence of social change, and while many of the changes in Huecorio have been beneficial, the most important fact to bear in mind is that a traditional

343

authoritarian society has broken down and no clear new morality and internal discipline has been built up to replace it. This has meant, among other things, that there is no means to insure participation in cooperative undertakings such as the *faenas*, and consequently other ways of constructing public works, maintaining the peace, controlling the abuse of water, etc., have to be found.

The people of Huecorio want a better life, to live in peace, and to be proud of their village, but they are helpless to achieve these things alone. In some way, their society and social psychology must be restructured along certain lines. An absent or latent need achievement must be aroused so that the people not only realize that their environment is malleable but also take delight in constructive achievement. Their need autonomy must be nurtured so that they feel sufficiently secure in themselves to think and act independently within the framework of the general good. Negative must be converted to positive individualism; in other words, their strong desire for self-improvement must be tempered by a sense of social responsibility. This would mean, for instance, that they would accept some burden of taxation for a diffuse and wider benefit. The vestiges of the dominance/submission syndrome, in particular paternalism, should be eliminated, since as long as it prevails the tendency to wait for higher "others" to undertake responsibility will never be overcome.

How are these things to be achieved? The principal responsibility will lie, of course, with education. It was noted that the education received by the people in Huecorio had little carry-over; that is, villagers had little curiosity and hardly ever used their literacy to read books or magazines. There are undoubtedly three main causal factors here.

First is a home environment not conducive to study because of poor lighting, a lack of privacy for children, and a lack, on the part of parents, of cognizance of how to encourage the efforts of their children.

Second is the quality of the teachers. They are frequently shifted from school to school and thus lack identification with the problems of the village. More important, however, is the fact that many do not act as models worthy of emulation, and they hardly inspire their charges. This, in turn, is due in part to the fact that many are themselves subject in their training to the mechanistic and essentially negative influence of Marxism.[2] Neither are they trained in dealing with community affairs, and their own poverty embitters them—an attitude that children cannot fail to notice.

Third, there is the question of curriculum. We could not study this in Huecorio, but were told that teaching was by rote and was not designed to encourage questions. Can the child be given the feeling that his environment is controllable? School gardens, imaginative play, simple scientific experiments, visits to other places, and meeting different kinds of people might help.

There are opportunities for adult education as well. The *Asociación Avícola* might teach its members something of simple business methods so that they could keep accounts and learn how to reduce costs and expand sales. The propensity of villagers to gather for meetings would be an opportunity for adult education, informative movies, and thought-stimulating discussion.

Through other agencies, also, new values can be instilled. The newly awakened social interest of the Church in Latin America is one of these. The younger priests, although still bound by pre-ecumenical dogma, are becoming increasingly interested in the welfare of their parishes, and villagers respond to their interest. Can those priests speak in terms not only of spiritual morality but of secular morality as well—the responsibility of a man to his family, to other men, and to society at large?

Self-confidence and curiosity can be stimulated if villagers have satisfactory contacts with people of different backgrounds. Some Huecorianos have achieved this in their travels throughout Mexico and to the United States, and by being hosts to visiting foreigners. Can such successful relationships be had with peoples elsewhere?

Paternalism, as we have remarked, is a well-known hazard, one to be avoided if communities are to mature into development. Although Huecorianos verbalize and probably accept a large measure of responsibility for their own progress, they fall easily into the need sub-

[2] Marxism is regarded as a negative influence largely because it is authoritarian in character, and this has the effect of buttressing those elements of society which are antagonistic to individual creativity and innovation. Furthermore, a Marxist in a non-Marxist society is more concerned with that society's destruction than with its evolutionary development.

mission pattern and often expect higher "others" to protect them or bail them out of difficulties. These expectations are reinforced by the well-motivated but unfortunate generosity of *patrones,* the government, or others, who by their acts of giving violate an accepted tenet of community development. Geronimo Roca expressed this situation clearly when he said:

> I ask that our condition should become improved—not in terms of luxury houses—I could forgo that for many reasons—but es-. pecially because when things come as gifts they are rarely looked after. The things that one really wants and which involve a great deal of labor to achieve are the things that one will look after better. The principal need is for good organization of the people. We must unite, organize, and work together for Huecorio.

THE NEED FOR POLITICAL AUTONOMY

Geronimo Roca's call for unity and cooperation runs counter to the individualistic character of Huecorio and other rural communities, and with the breakdown of the traditional society there is little hope to create the ideal of an autonomous, self-energizing development based only on good will. Furthermore, even for small communities the demands of contemporary technology and the complexities of a rapidly growing and changing environment cannot be handled in an *ad hoc* manner, but call instead for a strong and permanent authority. Accordingly, it would seem desirable to strengthen local government by increasing its power and the resources at its command.[3] These possibilities were discussed in Chapter 6. As we saw, officials at the local level are expected to undertake heavy responsibilities without recognition or salary, and there is clearly a need to compensate them for their economic losses. Revenue should be made available to the villages, either by means of small allocations from other levels of government, or, better, by devising taxes—head or property taxes for

[3] Of course this does not accord with the attitude of authoritarians on higher political levels who would, in all likelihood, reveal their latent paternalism by scoffing at the ability of villagers to govern themselves responsibly.

instance—which can be collected locally.[4] It is possible that villagers would prefer these known levies to the casual but constant requests that are made on them under the present system. Labor donations in lieu of cash payments should be possible under some circumstances. Venality on the part of public officials is a problem that may arise but may be mitigated by audited bookkeeping, the posting of accounts in a public place, proper recording of receipts and disbursements, educational supervision from above, and some degree of training for the local officials.

POPULATION GROWTH
AND ITS EFFECTS

Huecorio's high, but not abnormal, rate of population increase of about 3% per year has already created pressures and reactions. Since their land of good quality is distributed under inefficient minifundia, Huecorianos have come to realize that agriculture holds no promise and they have cast about for alternatives. Three of these alternatives —migration to the cities of Mexico, migration to the United States, and nonagricultural employment within Huecorio—have been partially exploited. Huecorianos are also ready to think about two other possibilities—colonization and family limitation—but they are inhibited from taking action by fear and a lack of knowledge.

Colonization of new areas in Mexico offers the only prospect for Huecorianos to achieve a respectable standard of living in agriculture, but even when offers of land are made they fail to take decisive action because of a timidity when confronted with the unknown. Their life in Huecorio, unsatisfactory though it may be, offers reasonable certainty, and they do not know anything of the land to be colonized except that it is in the *tierra caliente*—a hot, uncomfortable, and unwholesome place to live as they see it. They are uncertain too as to how they would survive economically. General Cárdenas pointed out to

[4] Collection and enforcement would undoubtedly have to be reinforced by *municipio* authorities, since the villages may not easily assume police powers with effective safeguards.

us that the farmers would get land, credit, houses, electricity, schools, and water in the new areas, and that the colonists could be established within five cycles of production. But the Huecorianos do not know this. It would seem, however, that their fears might be mitigated if they, or some of their leaders, could have the opportunity to visit some of the new communities to see the results for themselves.

Family planning is a clear and urgent need in Huecorio, and the villagers seem prepared to accept it. The present position of the Church may make it difficult to introduce, although the rhythm method may have some limited effectiveness. If the Church modifies its position, it would undoubtedly be wise to encourage villagers to think in terms of the cost of contraceptives, salpingectomies, or vasectomies vis-à-vis the costs, both economic and in terms of the health, happiness, and education of the children who would otherwise be brought into the world. Family limitation is imperative for the future well-being of the people of Huecorio, and no time can be lost in making it available.

AGRICULTURE

With regard to agriculture, there are certain facts evident in Huecorio which undoubtedly are to be commonly found in many other peasant villages. Given the existence of minifundia, fragmentation, and poor soils, there is no future in agriculture *and the farmers know it*. This means that apart from the possibilities inherent in colonization, there are two contradictory alternative policies available.

The first of these is to encourage the transformation of the inefficient minifundia into large family-size farms which could more effectively employ capital equipment, soil management techniques, and improved seeds and stock. A radical policy shift such as this would have to have certain built-in safeguards. Since the number of persons employed in these more efficient enterprises would be small, such a program would have to be accompanied by a fairly rapid increase in nonfarm employment. To avoid the rise of absentee ownership and management there would have to be watertight assurance that the owner-manager had true residence in the community. If the legal and administrative problems could be solved, the changeover could take place gradually, even under Mexico's *ejido,* if the erstwhile *ejidatarios* were given full and clear title to their land. This suggestion will undoubtedly be coolly received, and I hasten to affirm that it would lead to a debacle unless most carefully thought and carried out. Yet history would indicate that only with such a move to efficiency can agriculture support a viable economy.

The second alternative requires no meddling with land tenure but involves the recognition that agriculture cannot, by itself, decently provide for the average rural family and should therefore be a supplement to other activities. Of course, if alternative occupations did expand sufficiently a shift toward them could lead to the eventual, but more natural, adoption of the first alternative. This is not likely, and agriculture will undoubtedly remain a technological backwater.

If this second alternative is followed, there exists a battery of methods to raise the productivity of minifundia and make them less of a drag on the rest of the economy. In Huecorio, and undoubtedly elsewhere, farmers would shift their output mix to higher value crops if such crops could be grown. In that case one would make the usual recommendations about introducing fertilizers, machinery, irrigation, improved soil management, better seeds, and supervised credit. We noted in Chapter 1 that there are definite but not necessarily insurmountable obstacles to such improvements, and the suggestions that follow are designed to facilitate a breakthrough.

The technique of introducing a new method is as important as the technological improvement itself; it is here, perhaps, where the efforts fail. Extension workers are not often given training in working with tradition-bound farmers, and such knowledge is as important as the technical information they have to offer. In Huecorio, the majority of the farmers did not even know that an agronomist was working in the village. As we observed, this man stated a preference for working with individuals and he would undoubtedly have been more effective if he had taken advantage of the villagers' propensity to gather frequently to discuss village problems. At such meetings he could have delivered lectures, shown movies, and encouraged the farmers to speak about their problems.

There is a subtle psychological problem involved as well—a vestige of traditional authoritarianism, I suspect. Villagers sense that trained engineers feel superior to them and are inclined to issue their recommendations in the form of dogma. It is much more effective for the agronomist to pose questions and to encourage and guide the farmers to think their problems through. Not only does this reveal to the agronomist obstacles that would otherwise be hidden, but it gives the farmers a sense of proprietorship in the solutions so discovered. The solution now belongs to the farmer and he has a larger interest in seeing it effectively carried out.

Another means to encourage better methods would be the introduction of agricultural fairs, perhaps tied in with religious *fiestas*. Farmers could be enticed by prizes and awards based on the quality of their product, improvements in productivity, etc. This would also offer an opportunity to demonstrate new techniques and products. Another, but less costly device, would be to introduce short daily radio programs —perhaps in the early hours of the morning—from which farmers could learn about the weather, price movements, and other things of interest to them. In Huecorio radios are constantly blaring in the houses, and the broadcast industry could make some small contribution to society.

The introduction of improved equipment is important to farmers, and at a simple level there is an urgent need for better ploughs. For instance, could a country such as Mexico produce the chilled-bottom steel plough that is no longer made by the Oliver Company, and sell it not only in Mexico but elsewhere in the world? More sophisticated equipment—tractors, gang ploughs, reapers, balers, and so on—may have some role to play if the problems of small holdings and fragmentation can be overcome. Machine tractor stations which were used in the Soviet Union to supply machines to neighboring collective farms were admittedly unsuccessful in that country, but the fault may have lain with the lethargy of the collective farmers, who were not especially interested in supervising the machines, rather than with the institution of the machine tractor station itself. Could such centers be successfully established to make machines available to peasant farmers who could otherwise not afford them?

A final suggestion for agriculture has to do with a method for encouraging farmers to do away with monoculture in those situations where they would be better off planting a variety of crops but where they persist in planting a single crop, such as corn, out of a fear of losing their principal means of subsistence. If this obstacle is known to exist, it might be possible to use corn imported from outside the village—under the Food for Peace program for instance—as a guarantee against crop failure. It could be stored in the village in prefabricated bins and would be given free to the farmers if their new crops failed to bring in a certain stipulated income. If, on the other hand, the experiment with crop variation were successful, the corn would be sold to the farmers and the money would be handed over to the village for community improvement.

ALTERNATIVES AND COMPLEMENTS
TO AGRICULTURAL EMPLOYMENT

For those persons who remain in rural areas where agriculture offers limited rewards, means must be found to complement the income of those continuing in agriculture and to provide satisfactory alternative full-time employment to those who do not. For the former group it is important to bear in mind the need to avoid wasting capital. It has sometimes been suggested, for instance, that agricultural workers could be provided with factory employment during the idle season; but this may require that the cooperating capital equipment be idle during the balance of the year. In a country such as Mexico with its diverse climates and growing seasons, it might be possible for a government to facilitate the passage of farmers to the different regions where they could work as *peones* while their own lands are not under cultivation. In addition, a fuller use of a farmer's time and that of his family can be made by devices such as those introduced by CREFAL in its aviculture and apiculture programs.

For those who would leave agriculture the problem is, of course, to find satisfactory full-time employment. One course of action is to train young persons for various trades needed in rural areas. As an example we might cite the program initiated by General Cárdenas in the late 1930s to train masons. Several men in the village benefited, and because of the widespread use of masonry in the area their skills are much in demand. Other shortages exist around Huecorio today, especially of plumbers, electricians, and mechanics. A regional training center could be established to fill these needs in the villages and towns in the territory.

Another device that is gaining momentum in underdeveloped countries is the establishment of industrial parks, wherein small entrepreneurs—furniture manufacturers, garment makers, food processors and others—have access to facilities and to credit and guidance in business methods. The experience of Huecorio would suggest two important principles here.

The first is that little reliance can be placed on cooperatives, the success of the *Asociación Avícola* notwithstanding. In the individualistic climate of the Tarascan area, mutual mistrust gives cooperatives and even partnerships shaky foundations. The *Asociación Avícola* has been able to work so far largely because it has been administered by trained personnel from the outside.

The second principle is that the small enterprises should take advantage of the dominance/submission aspect of a traditional society until the entrepreneurs mature into new skills and attitudes.[5] The main reason why this should be done is that the small entrepreneur is usually devoid of basic business skills and is more of an artisan than a businessman. In addition, he has very little knowledge of markets and has no time to expand his sales. Accordingly he will perform most effectively if he is associated with some larger enterprise which will absorb all his output. If the industrial parks were established, many of the individual shops could be the stepchildren as it were of some larger enterprise, much as a bicycle assembly plant in Japan was fed its components from a large flock of small producers. A structure such

[5] Note this exception to the general desirability of doing away with the traditional society. What we are proposing is to take advantage of this weakness until new attitudes develop, at which time the dominance/submission syndrome will fade naturally away. This is what happened in Japan according to Pelzel.

as this has to be carefully nurtured and maintained, but the Japanese experience and that of Don Juan's *taller* in its relationship to Vicki shows that the scheme can work effectively.[6]

There is no need for industrialization to follow precisely the paths hacked out by Great Britain and the United States. Policy makers should examine their programs to see if the Japanese model might effectively be applied in their own environments, not only to hasten the process of growth and to bring its benefits more rapidly to rural folk but also to do these things more smoothly and less painfully by easing some of the social costs of urbanization.

PROGRAMS SPECIFIC TO HUECORIO

Our examination of Huecorio suggests a few devices which show promise but which may be specific to the unique aspects of its resources and location.

One factor that has perpetuated monoculture on much of Huecorio's land is the lack of water during the lengthy dry season. In the opinion of General Cárdenas, to provide irrigation for Huecorio would be more expensive than leading the same number of people into colonization. Little of Huecorio's land is level, and the cost of grading it and building adequate drainage ditches would undoubtedly be high. Nevertheless, the matter should be given a preliminary investigation based on three alternative methods of water supply. (i) By using a dragline, ditches could be dug to penetrate from the lake to the northern end of the *ejido* San José, and from the terminus the water could be pumped to grade level to return by gravity flow to the lake. (ii) The same end might be achieved by installing pipes from the lake to various release points. (iii) Springs might be tapped at the base of Tariácuri by drilling horizontally or at a slight incline into

[6] In Japan, the structure began to crack during the war when the small producers began to deal directly with the government and they learned business procedures—especially cost accounting and record keeping—in the process. They thus acquired the skills and independence necessary to nourish their entrepreneurial ventures.

the mountain, which is part of the watershed of the lake.[7] If vegetable production could thus be expanded sufficiently, a freezing or canning plant might be established to prepare vegetables for more distant markets such as the city of Monterrey, which at present suffers from a dearth of vegetables either fresh or processed.

The long-run deterioration of much of Huecorio's land is due to overgrazing by horses, *burros,* oxen, and cows. Many of these animals are of dubious economic value and, were it feasible, mechanization would obviate the need for them. In view of their productive contribution, one could not recommend removal of the milch cows. But can they be retained in such a way as to conserve or improve the land? One possibility might be to eliminate the unprofitable wheat phase of the wheat-corn-fallow cycle and to plant restorative crops or forage which could be taken to the animals grazing elsewhere. The small hills within the village might be fenced off and fertilized to provide pasture. As it is, the hills are grazed but their carrying capacity is negligible. On the other hand, there are alternative uses for the *cerros*—for example as orchards and, now that the forestry laws have been modified to permit it, for growing Christmas trees. One of the heaviest costs of United States Christmas tree growers is for shearing the trees, but given the low wage structure of rural Mexico such practices would be more justified.[8]

Consideration might also be given to building dikes along the village's shorefront. Three benefits would flow from this: some of the rich land could be drained and made permanently available for cultivation; shallow lagoons could be constructed for the production of wild rice; and these lagoons or other ponds could be devoted to the culture of fish under more controlled circumstances than exist in the lake.

Finally, despite the proximity of Huecorio to Pátzcuaro, where streams of tourists constantly arrive and as quickly depart, few Huecorianos reap any benefit from this traffic. One of the reasons the

[7] This technique of horizontal drilling is not common but has been used with some success in California.

[8] Since most of the *cerros* lie within the *ejido* land, there would be formidable problems involved in working out labor- and profit-sharing arrangements. We are only considering technical possibilities at this point.

tourists visit so briefly is that once they have taken the inevitable but not necessarily recommended trip to the island of Janitzio, they have little to do, especially in the evening. On the other hand, Huecorianos, under the direction of an able professor from CREFAL, have shown an aptitude and love for the theater. Under the clear March skies they put on adaptations of Mexican and Shakespearean drama. Surely these performances and enactments of folklore would have a special charm for the tourist, at the same time offering the Huecorianos an outlet for their talents and a modest source of income.

Although crude aggregate analysis might signal despair for the prospects of a decent life for Huecorio and its people, we must nevertheless be encouraged by the various innovations recently introduced from the outside. Given the Huecoriano's desperate desire for improvement, his intelligence, and his warmth to outsiders, one has the feeling that all this chemical combination now needs is a catalyst. In a sense, this book is a search for that catalyst.

CLIMATE, MINERALS, FORESTS, AND FAUNA

CLIMATE

The team was unable to gather recent climatological data, and agricultural researchers, for whom this information is even more important, had no more success. Records were apparently kept until recently by a gentleman who filed them in a safe, secure from public view. He has since died and the location of the records is unknown. The *Secretaría de la Marina,* the agency responsible for navigation on the lake,[1] also maintained records since it had a natural interest in analyzing the periodic fluctuations in the level of the lake. But the *Marina* no longer has secretariat functions in Pátzcuaro, so the records could not be located. In the Federal Department of Agriculture in Morelia a diligent search turned up the rainfall and temperature information only for January, 1944. In view of these problems we shall record some of the relevant data to be found in Foster.[2]

The main climatological influence in the Pátzcuaro region is its

[1] It is not clear whether the above cited meteorologist was employed by the *Marina.*

[2] For greater details of the basic data on climate, flora, and fauna see Foster, pp. 26, 27.

altitude, the lake level being approximately 6,700 feet according to the National Railways of Mexico data cited in Foster.[3] This location in the *tierra fría* offsets the tropical latitude of the region, giving it a mean annual temperature of 16.3°C. or 61°F.

Monthly variations for an "average" year are reported by, and adapted from, Foster as follows.[4]

| Month | Average Temperature in Degrees | |
	Centigrade	Fahrenheit
January	12.0	53.6
February	13.8	57.0
March	16.3	61.0
April	17.9	64.2
May	20.1	68.2
June	19.9	67.8
July	17.8	64.0
August	17.2	63.0
September	16.8	62.0
October	16.5	61.5
November	14.4	58.0
December	12.7	55.0

Killing frosts can occur in December, January, and February. May and early June, just before the onslaught of the rains, are dry and hot.

Foster cites the average rainfall for the period 1924 to 1940 as 1,041.2 mm. or 40.1 inches.[5]

The average monthly variation for the same period is given on page 359.

The unevenness of the distribution is evident from the table. The five months from December through April are virtually without precipitation, while a monsoon-like rainy season begins with the towering thunderheads of June. There is little respite from these late afternoon torrents until the end of September. This pattern of rainfall, in the absence of widespread effective irrigation, has obvious constraining influences on the agricultural cycle.

[3] Foster, p. 22.   [4] Foster, p. 26.   [5] Foster, p. 27.

| Month | Precipitation | |
	Millimeters	Inches
January	13.1	0.50
February	10.9	0.40
March	10.1	0.39
April	5.2	0.20
May	37.9	1.49
June	181.6	7.15
July	252.2	9.93
August	237.8	9.36
September	178.0	7.00
October	77.0	3.03
November	25.7	1.01
December	22.0	0.87

At present only a small handful of farmers utilize the possibilities of lake and subsurface water for irrigation. One has an animal-driven chain-and-bucket device that lifts water from a ditch leading from the lake. This water flows into channels serving about an acre of his and a neighbor's land. Another, more enterprising individual, purchased a gasoline-driven 2″ pump. One or two farmers laboriously heft buckets of water from stagnant drainage ditches. The success of these farmers in keeping their land perpetually under cultivation has not yet moved others to imitate them.

MINERALS

Scoria from the volcano is mined outside the village limits, and deposits possibly exist in the steep slopes of the volcano. Small deposits of clay suitable for adobe are found in Huecorio, but the practice is usually to purchase the adobe from the more abundant supplies in nearby Colonia Ibarra. Six to ten feet below the level of the old lake bed, on land that is now being used for agriculture, is a stratum of lime, but only one farmer is extracting it, and he is doing so in small amounts.

FORESTS

Within the village, the only major woodland gains an unsure toehold on the slopes of San Miguel. These pines, scorched by frequent uncontrolled fires, are difficult of access and are not of construction size. Some knotty hardwoods line the hedgerows and these are hacked at to yield firewood. A villager wrote that "most of the firewood that is consumed in Huecorio is brought from hills that are named Tererio, Sagrero, Loma de Nocutzecu, and el Pedregal. These hills are situated between the cardinal points south and west of Huecorio at a distance of approximately seven or eight kilometers."

FAUNA

Such wildlife as exists is hunted not so much as game but rather to be destroyed as predator. Raccoons ravage fruit and corn.[6] Rabbits are caught to be fattened and eaten. One farmer, before he built a large chicken coop, kept his birds in a cage on top of a high pole to protect them from coyotes. Harmless land and water snakes abound and, very rarely, rattlesnakes are reported.

Ducks winter on the lake, and a few U. S. Fish and Wildlife Service tags adorn some ancient muzzle-loaders. Herons can be seen cruising the swampy lake shore.

Among the more important fish of the lake are the native *pescado blanco,* the small *thiru,* and the large-mouth bass, locally called *trucha.*

A villager wrote that:

. . . there is a wide variety of birds here and the majority are harmful to the crops. The most important ones are the *tarengos,* the *corriones,* the *urrucas* and *tordos,* the *huitlacoche,* the *cuervo,* and the *gavilán.*

[6] Foster does not include the raccoon in his list of wildlife on page 27. We did not actually see the animals being hunted but they were reported to us as *mapache* (raccoon).

The *tarengo* eats the young seedling corn. The *corriones* come in the month of March, and these are the days when the wheat is beginning to ripen. These birds come in big flocks. The *urrucas* (magpies) and *tordos* (thrushes) also come in flocks, but in September and they eat the corn, especially that growing down by the shore. The *tordos* are distinguished by their yellow breast and black body and wings, and the *urrucas* are completely black. These birds always come at the same time. The *huitlacoche* comes in ones and twos and eats fruits, especially the white *tuna* and the peach. The *cuervo* (crow) is bigger than the others and is completely black. It eats the corn and sometimes bites off the ears and buries them to store them, but it never digs them up again. This corn usually rots, but when the rain comes it may grow. Also, this bird occasionally carries fires or lights and many times this is the way the fires get started in the mountains.[7] The *gavilán* (sparrow hawk) is small but kills the baby chickens when these are outside in the patio.

[7] This would seem to be an error and may be a reference to the crow's propensity to make off with small, brightly colored objects that catch his fancy.

ANNUAL AGRICULTURAL CYCLE

January

Dry, cold, and idle month.
Many go to *tierra caliente* to work cotton and fruit harvests.
Plough *orilla* and gardens to kill grubs and worms.
Animals turned into *ejido* following corn harvest.
Corn harvested in private holdings.
Selection of corn seed for June planting.
Collect firewood.
Odd jobs around house.
Repair fences and stone walls.
Look for work utilizing secondary skills.
Some just sit around.

Fiestas
   12th—*Nuestra Señora, La Virgen de Guadalupe.*
   17th—Blessing of animals.

February

Dry, cold, and idle.
Punctuated by very important *fiesta*.
Work in *tierra caliente*.
Odd jobs around house.
Irrigate *orilla*.
Collect firewood.

Fiestas
  1st to 5th—*La Virgen de la Candelaria, Patrona del Poblado.*

March

Dry, cold, and idle.
Work in *tierra caliente*.
Odd jobs.
Collect firewood.
Plant tomatoes in nurseries.
Distribute *abono de corral*.
Irrigate and plough *orilla* and gardens.

Fiestas
  19th—San José, *Patrón del Pueblo.*
  26th—*Día de la Conserva de Chilacayote.*

April

Dry and idle.
Irrigate and plant in *orilla* and gardens.
Plant cabbage and lettuce in nurseries.
Some ploughing for corn.
Work in *tierra caliente*.
Collect firewood.
22nd—Meeting of *ejidatarios* to decide fields to be planted in corn.

Fiesta
  17th—*Misa de Buen Temporal a San Isidro*

May

Busy month—hot and dry.
Harvest and thresh wheat.
First ploughing for corn.
Some also *cruzar* and plant.

June

Busy month—rains begin.
Prepare ground for, and plant, corn.
Plant vegetables—carrots, radishes, beets—in nurseries.
Cultivate vegetables.
Last wheat threshing.
Sell vegetables in Uruapan.

Fiesta
  Corpus Christi

July

Busy, wet month.
Cultivation of corn—*escarda* and *segunda*.
Plant and cultivate vegetables.
Sell vegetables in Uruapan.

August

Busy and wet.
Cultivate corn.
Cut grass for animals.
Plant, cultivate, and sell vegetables.
Prepare land for wheat—*barbechar* and *cruzar*.

September

Rains continue.
Cultivate and sell vegetables.
Harvest small squash.
Prepare land for wheat in La Lagunilla.

Fiesta
   16th—Mexican Independence Day.

October

Rains begin to taper off.
Plant wheat.
Harvest small squash.
Cut beans and leave to dry.
Harvest cabbage.
Daily visits to *milpa* to inspect crop.

Fiestas
   16th—*Misa de San Isidro Labrador* (for wheat).
   31st—*Día de Difuntos.*

November

Dry season begins.
Meeting of *ejidatarios* to decide on date of corn harvest.
Begin corn harvest.
Harvest *frijoles* and large squash.
Collect beans.

Fiestas
   2nd—All Souls Day.

December

Very busy month.
Harvest corn, squash, *frijoles,* and *chilacayote*.

Fiestas
   8th—*Nuestra Señora de la Salud*.
   25th—Christmas.

CORN AND WHEAT CULTIVATION

SOME COMPARISONS
BETWEEN HUECORIO, TZINTZUNTZAN,
CHÉRAN, AND TEPOZTLÁN

Corn

Tzintzuntzan.[1] Few steel ploughs are used, and Foster describes them as unpopular. This may be due to the unavailability to the Tzintzuntzeños of the earlier Oliver instrument. Foster offers an excellent description of the wooden plough, and it would appear to be identical with that used in Huecorio.

> Obviously this plough is far from a primitive instrument. The Tzintzuntzeños are perfectly familiar with steel plows, but feel that their *arado de palo* is a far more versatile tool. It does not turn over the soil, but by means of the various beams and adjustments the earth is thoroughly pulverized to depths of from 15 to 20 cm. after a complete preparation. The ingenious combination of beams makes possible just the right amount of cultivation at each stage of growth, without damaging the plants.[2]

[1] Foster, pp. 58–63.
[2] Foster, p. 61.

Corn cultivation practices vary significantly from Huecorio, in one respect in particular. Preparation in Tzintzuntzan involves three ploughings, the third of which is longitudinal with ridges 80 cm. apart. The planting is done at the time a fourth furrow of 80 cm. is made at right angles to the third. The seeds are planted *en cruz* where the third and fourth furrows intersect. This leads to a spacing of 80 cm. between plants. In Huecorio the farmers practiced a closer spacing, which would normally result in a higher productivity per hectare. One can only speculate on the reason for this difference. A possible explanation lies in the Tzintzuntzan practice of interplanting, which is reported to combine 3 corn, 1 *frijol,* and 1 squash in each *mata.* This is heavy interplanting, and the more luxuriant combination that results may require more space for effective growth.

One other minor difference is also in planting. An "ideal" team of two *yuntas* and *yunteros* plus three *peones* is used. One *yunta* makes the furrow, each of the *peones* plants a different type of seed, and the second *yunta* covers the seeds. Since this is described as an "ideal" system, one cannot be certain that it is common in Tzintzuntzan. It was neither observed nor reported in Huecorio.

Cherán.[3] The differences between practices in Cherán on the one hand and those in Tzintzuntzan and Huecorio on the other are quite great. Although some 30 steel ploughs were reported in 1941, the wooden plough was more common. In the Pátzcuaro area this plough uses *bigoteras* to spread dirt, while in Cherán a bow is inserted for the same purpose.

Seed selection involves a curious but unexplained practice. Corn seed selection is always done when the moon is crescent. Neither selection nor shelling is done after the full moon. Planting in Cherán takes place in March, much earlier than in the Pátzcuaro basin, but no explanation for this difference can be offered. Furthermore, interplanting is not practiced, apparently due to unfavorable soil and climate, and only two corn seeds are generally placed in each *mata*— a practice that may account for Cherán's lower yields. At this stage the work team consists of two *yuntas* and *yunteros* to furrow and cover the seeds and one *peón* to plant. The cultivation involves the

[3] Beals, pp. 21, 25.

escarda and *segunda,* although the segunda is longitudinal rather than crosswise. Apparently a significant amount of weeding is done by hand after these two processes. This practice may be more feasible in Cherán than in Pátzcuaro, due to the lack of clutter from interplanted *frijoles* and squash. Harvesting in the Pátzcuaro region is on a straight wage basis, whereas in Cherán the workers refuse to harvest without the right to glean the ears, which "accidentally" miss the *peón's ayate. Aguardiente* is served at the end of the harvest offering, imparting a rather festive character which is lacking in the apparently more commercially oriented Pátzcuaro area.

Tepoztlán.[4] Both wooden and steel ploughs were used extensively in 1943, and the wooden plough described is similar to that used in the Pátzcuaro region except that the moldboard used in planting consists of two plates in the form of a horizontal V, with the point to the front. The Pátzcuaro *bigoteras* stretch out from the ploughshare at right angles.

Slash-and-burn techniques are used in Tepoztlán by poorer farmers, but this is not found in Huecorio because of the lack of suitable forest terrain. In Tepoztlán plough culture preparation does not seem to involve the *cruzar,* but all furrows are longitudinal. "Corn can be planted at any time between June 1 and July 25 with a fairly good chance of getting a crop." [5] In Pátzcuaro the short but severe rainy season does not allow this latitude. Four corn seeds are dropped in each *mata* and interplanting with *frijoles* is rare, but comparative production data are not available.[6] In cultivation Lewis mentions that the *peones* who clear the field of weeds and protect the *matas* from excessive dirt work carefully. If this is indeed the case, their diligence would be envied by Pátzcuaro employers!

Other differences in cultivation involve the use of a steel plough for *escarda* and *segundo,* and the *segundo* is longitudinal rather than crosswise. The *escarda* consists of only one pass with the plough down each row rather than two as in Huecorio, but this may be due to the

[4] Lewis, pp. 132–43.
[5] Lewis, p. 136.
[6] We note here a useless but odd piece of information. In Tepoztlán "The seed is dropped in front of the left toe, and the dirt is pushed over the seeds with the right foot." In Huecorio it was observed that the pattern was reversed, the left foot being used for the *tapar.*

use of the steel plough. Religious and festive practices seem more common in Tepoztlán than in the other three communities, but they need not be detailed here. Spoilage of stored corn by worms is a serious problem in Tepoztlán, yet was never mentioned in Huecorio.

A certain competitive pride in good agricultural practices was mentioned by Lewis. Farmers try to make their rows of *matas* as straight as possible; the hilling of the last two rows of a *milpa* "serves as a symbol that the cultivation is over and is looked upon as a decoration or adornment of the work of cultivation"; and sometimes "men will compete to see who can strip two rows [of cornstalks] in the shortest time." [7] Such attitudes were neither observed nor reported in Huecorio. Deficiencies in field techniques on our part might be one explanation, but others are possible. Huecorianos may be less prideful of agricultural craftsmanship or, if it is good, may simply judge it as something necessary for a good crop and not something about which one must make a display. The only unsolicited comments about other farmers were usually disparaging.

These and other differences in corn cultivation among four communities in Mexico could constitute an exercise in analysis apart from other features of the cultures. What differences are due to natural conditions? If other things can be held equal, are some methods superior to others? Did better methods evolve as a result of accidental circumstances or of conscious design? What differences are solely cultural in origin? What roles do differential costs and marketing situations play?

Wheat[8]

In Tzintzuntzan[9] sowing takes place on September 17th, the day after Mexican Independence Day, rather than on October 4th as in Huecorio, but no explanation can be offered for this difference. Huecorianos were quite explicit in stating that the *bigotera* was removed

[7] Lewis, pp. 139, 140–41.

[8] The description of wheat cultivation in Cherán is not sufficiently detailed to permit a comparison, and there is no mention of its cultivation in Tepoztlán.

[9] Foster, pp. 64–66.

when the seeds were to be covered, but in Tzintzuntzan such a·beam is used expressly to mix the seed with the earth. A further difference lies in the Tzintzuntzeños' use of a heavy log rather than branches for the *arrastrar*.

With the evidence available it is not possible to determine in what way these different techniques affect productivity—if indeed they do —nor can we suggest reasons for the variations. But the differences are instructive on two counts.

They speak first of the cultural isolation of the Tarascan villages, each from the rest. Huecorio and Tzintzuntzan border on the same lake and are about ten miles apart over land, yet striking differences can be found in many details of their culture. There is, of course, the possibility that close investigation will reveal explanations of the differences. This cultural isolation is born not of natural barriers but of man's tendency to group hostility.

The second lesson to be derived is a warning of the hazards to be faced if one wishes to generalize from the investigation of one community to a larger frame. The differences we have just noted are observable, but many others surely lie hidden from our techniques of social research.

TABLES

The tables presented here, and those in the text, were compiled by the author from data collected by the team in the six surveys. The surveys are designated by code as follows: Census, A; Agricultural Survey, B; Social Survey, C; Survey of Shopkeepers, D; Survey of Manufacturing, E; Survey of All Other Occupations, F. Numbers within the codes do not correspond. For instance, code numbers B14, C14, and F14 refer to different persons and households.

Some fractional totals do not agree because of rounding.

Symbols: NA–Data not available.

?–Indeterminable because of lack of data.

TABLE I

Regional Land Distribution

Territory		Hills	Resi-dential	Arable	Total	Arable Land as Percent of Regional Total	Regional Total as Percent of Subtotal for Village
Ejidos							
La Lagunilla	Acres	7.1		61.5	68.5	89.6	4.81
	Has.	2.88		24.88	27.76		
La Longanesa	Acres			6.4	6.4	100.0	0.45
	Has.			2.59	2.59		
San José	Acres	149.9		197.2	347.1	56.8	24.34
	Has.	60.66		79.80	140.46		
San Miguel	Acres	287.7		127.6	415.3	30.7	29.12
	Has.	116.43		51.63	168.06		
San Pedrito	Acres	4.1		71.4	75.5	94.5	5.29
	Has.	1.66		28.89	30.55		
La Peñita	Acres	14.0		40.4	54.4	74.2	3.81
	Has.	5.66		16.35	22.01		
Ejido Total	Acres	462.8		504.5	967.3[a]	52.1	67.82
	Has.	187.29		204.14	391.43[a]		
Federal	Acres	6.4		162.5[b]	168.9[b]	96.2	11.84
(La orilla)	Has.	2.59		65.76[b]	68.35[b]		
Private	Acres	19.5	22.9	247.6	290.0	85.4	20.34
	Has.	7.89	9.27	100.20	117.36		
Total village	Acres	488.7	22.9	914.6	1,426.2	64.1	100.00
	Has.	197.77	9.27	370.10	577.14		
Tzipecua	Acres	4.1		91.6[b]	95.7[b]		
	Has.	1.66		37.07[b]	38.73[b]		
Totals	Acres	492.8	22.9	1,006.2	1,521.9		
	Has.	199.43	9.27	407.17	615.87		

[a] Possible margin of error 6%. Total *ejido* area under government survey was 369 has. Total *ejido* area by our estimate, 391.43 has. Difference probably due to inaccuracies of border delineation, particularly the southern boundary of San Miguel.

[b] Contains lake shore area, subject to great fluctuations.

TABLE II

Average Landholdings by Class of Holding, Occupational Status, and Total Population

Category	Number	Class of Land (hectares)				Total in Acres
		Ejido	Federal[a]	Private	Total[g]	
Arable area		204	66	100	370	915
Per Capita Holdings						
Primary occupation farmers[b]	98	2.09	0.67	1.02	3.77	9.34
Primary occupation farmers, *jardineros*, and *jornaleros*[c]	141	1.44	0.47	0.71	2.62	6.49
All farmers, *jardineros*, and *jornaleros*[d]	172	1.18	0.38	0.58	2.15	5.31
Total population	835	0.24	0.08	0.12	0.44	1.09
Holdings per Farm Household						
Primary occupation[e]	71	2.87	0.93	1.41	5.21[h]	12.87
All[f]	104	1.96	0.63	0.96	3.56	8.79

[a] The averages for the *federal* holdings are maxima, since the area available is a function of the level of Lake Pátzcuaro.

[b] All persons who called themselves farmers (*campesinos*) and who considered farming to be their major occupation.

[c] Farmers, gardeners, and laborers are associated with agriculture. The total excluded several gardeners who were employed at CREFAL. All these persons considered one of these trades to be their major occupation.

[d] This total includes all persons who worked in agriculture in some way. It is not consistent with that found by adding the totals for Tables 4 and X, since that figure (212) involves some double counting of persons. The method by which the total of 172 was arrived at is explained above, p. 140.

[e] All households in which at least one person considered some branch of agriculture to be his primary occupation.

[f] All households in which some person was involved in agriculture in some way.

[g] Totals are not consistent due to rounding.

[h] The total population for 1962 was 844. Nine persons were living in Tzipecua and are therefore excluded from data relating to the village proper. No allowance is made for several nonresidents who hold land in Huecorio.

TABLE III
Crop Locations, Areas Planted, Yields, and Crop Dispositions

Crop	Number of Plantings by Land Class[b]					Area Planted[c] (Has.)	Yield per Hectare (pesos) by Land Class[b]						Crop Disposition[d] (Number of Farmers)	
	1 pw	1 sw	2	3	NA		1 pw	1 sw	2	3	NA	Av.[e]	Sold	Consumed
Corn	7	17	9	10	1	22.25	3,500	1,295	752	280		1,294	2	28
Wheat	3	10	5	13	2	19.47	270[f]	502	146	140		246	9	12
Frijoles	0	9	4	12	1	12.42		702	530	248		372	1	20
Lentils	1	2	2	0	1	0.97						720	5	2
Peas	0	0	0	0	2	NA							0	2
Lima beans	0	1	0	4	0	2.71				335	*	335	0	5
Squash	3	6	2	3	3	7.12						51	8	4
Tomato	0	1	0	0	2	0.10						600	3	0
Coriander	1	0	0	0	0	0.04						5,000	1	0
Cabbage	5	1	0	0	2	3.79						571	8	0
Beet	2	1	0	0	3	NA					*		5	1
Onion	1	0	0	0	1	0.40	2,125					2,125	1	1
Lettuce	6	3	0	0	0	3.62	1,135	1,038			*	1,128	9	0
Greens[g]	1	0	0	0	0	1.00					*		1	0
Radishes	3	1	0	0	1	1.75	860	480				690	4	0
Flowers	1	3	0	0	0	0.61						700	4	0
Carrots	3	0	0	0	0	1.70	823					823	3	0
Potato	0	1	0	0	0	0.40					*		0	1
String beans	0	1	0	0	1	0.40					*		0	0
Bottle gourd	0	0	0	1	0	0.15					*		2	0
Alfalfa[h]	1	0	0	0	0	0.04							1	0
Forage[h]	2	3	0	0	0	2.92								

[a] In many cases a crop will be planted by a given farmer in fields of different classes. In these instances, his crop will be reported more than once.
[b] For definitions of the land classification symbols, see above, p. 11. The yields for all crops other than corn, wheat, and frijoles are underestimates. See pp. 30–31.
[c] For corn and wheat these are underestimates, since two areas planted were not recorded. For all other products these will be overestimates, since fields are generally planted with several different crops.
[d] In some cases some of the crop was sold and the rest was consumed. In these cases entries were made in both columns.
[e] The averages for corn, wheat, and frijoles are weighted. The remainder are simple averages.
[f] Severe losses account for these low yields.
[g] One person reported planting verdura, without specifying the type of vegetable involved.
[h] Intermediate products.

TABLE IV

Corn: Real Costs of Production per Hectare

Code No.	Seed[a]	Preparation of Seedbed Man-days	Yunta-days[b]	Planting Man-days	Yunta-days	Cultivation Man-days	Yunta-days	Harvest Man-days	Yunta-days[e]	Total Man-days	Total Man-days with Allowance for Incomplete Data[d]
B5	NA	8	8	NA	NA	40	20	6	6b	54	62
B6	6 litros	4	4	4	2	NA	NA	35	3.5b	11	36
B7	16 litros	6	6	8	4	NA	NA	18	6b	32	57
B8	44 litros	20	10	10	5	10	5	24	8b	64	64
B10	2 cuart.	6	6	7	4	9	4	10	3b	32	32
B11	12 litros	14	7	6	3	18	6	6	2h	44	44
B12	22 litros	4	2	7	2	20	7	8	2b	39	44
B14	2 cuart.	0	0	8	8	42	8	16	8b	68	39
B15	NA	18	3	12	3	36	12	5	5b	71	68
B17	26 litros	11	11	NA	NA	19	19	NA	NA	30	71
Huecorio											
Average	21 litros	9	6	8	4	25	9	14	5	44.5	52.5
Tzintzuntzan[e]	15 litros	7		7		21.6		9		44.6	
Cherán[f]	NA	20		9		13		9		51	

[a] Seed quantities were quoted either in liters or quarter-liters.

[b] A *yunta*-day is one day's labor of a team of two oxen pulling a wooden or steel plough.

[c] b = burro, h = horse. These animals are used to carry the crop from the field.

[d] Where the columns "Total Man-days" and "Total Man-days with Allowance for Incomplete Data" do not agree, the data from the farmer in question were partially lacking. Close examination of the farmer's schedule, in comparison with those for others, permitted us to make estimates of the lacunae.

[e] Foster, p. 75.

[f] Beals, p. 65.

TABLE V

Corn: Money Costs of Production per Hectare (pesos)

Stage	B8	B10	B11	B12	B14	B15	Averages[a]
			Code Number				
Seed Cost[b]	132	150	36	66	150	NA	63
Seedbed Preparation							
Labor[c]	200	60	140	40	0	180	90
Yuntas[d]	150	90	105	30	0	45	90
Planting							
Labor	100	70	60	70	80	120	80
Yuntas	75	60	45	30	120	45	60
Cultivation							
Labor	100	90	180	200	480	360	250
Yuntas	75	60	90	105	120	180	135
Harvesting							
Labor	72	100	60	80	160	50	140
Burros and horses[e]	24	9	16	6	24	15	15
Totals	928	689	732	627	1,134	995	923
Value of Output	2,072	NA	268	0[f]	1,575	NA	1,011
Profit or Loss	+1,144	?	−464	−627	+441	?	+88
Income from *frijoles*	493	203	162	0	75	150	389
Profit or Loss	+1,637	?	−302	−627	+516	?	+477

[a] From more complete data.
[b] At 3 pesos per liter.
[c] At 10 pesos per man-day.
[d] At 15 pesos per day.
[e] *Burros* and horses at 3 pesos per day.
[f] Crop reported as total loss.

TABLE VI

Wheat: Average Real and Money Costs per Hectare

Stage	Average Real Costs	Average Real Costs		Average Money Costs (pesos)	
	Huecorio	Tzintzuntzan[a]	Cherán[b]	Huecorio	Sample Farmer[c]
Seed	44 liters[d]	48 liters	NA	132	70
Seedbed Preparation					
Man-days	12	10	20	120	250[e]
Yunta-days	12	NA	NA	180	
Planting					
Man-days	7	7	2	70	
Yunta-days	7	NA	NA	105	
Harvesting					
Man-days	9	7	4.5	90	65[g]
Burros or horses[f]	6.5	NA	NA	13	
Threshing					
Man-days	5	3	NA	50	28[g]
Burros or horses[f]	10	NA	NA	20	
Totals					
Man-days	33	27	26.5+	780[g]	413[g]
Animals	35.5	NA	NA		
Value of Harvest				306	572
Profit or Loss				−474	+159

[a] Foster, p. 75.
[b] Beals, p. 67.
[c] This farmer gave all his information in money costs. He did not, however, allow for his own labor costs.
[d] At 3 pesos per liter.
[e] Costs of labor and animals. Seedbed prepration and planting not separated.
[f] At 2 pesos per day.
[g] Costs of labor and animals.

TABLE VII

Egg Production and Income (pesos)

Nonmembers of the Asociación Avícola

Code No.	Number of Hens	Reported Egg Production[a] (d = daily w = weekly)	Annual Income[b]
B3	2	1d	146
B5	8	2d	292
B7	1	1d	146
B8	7	3d	438
B10	2	2d	292
B14	6	3d	438
B15	2	3w	62
B17	2	2w	42
B21	4	2d	292
B22	1	1d	146
B26	8	3d	438

Members of the Asociación Avícola[c]

Code No.	Number of Hens	Income from Granja	Share of Profits	Total Income	Money Costs	Own Labor Costs	Total Costs	Net Income
B1	126	13,734	156	13,890	10,710	630	11,340	2,550
B2	268	29,212	360	29,572	22,780	1,340	24,120	5,452
B13	140	15,260	221	15,481	11,900	700	12,600	2,881
B19	300	32,700	0	32,700	25,500	1,500	27,000	5,700
B23	165	17,985	225	18,210	14,125	825	14,850	3,360
B24	265	28,885	360	29,245	22,525	1,325	23,850	5,395

Asociación Avícola: Average Annual Incomes and Costs of Production per Hen[d]

Costs of Production

Cost of bringing pullet into production	25.00
Feed	51.00
Medicines	3.00
Amortization of *granja* and equipment	2.00
Interest	4.00
Labor (for *granjas* of 500 hens)	5.00
Total	90.00

Income

220 eggs at 44.2 centavos each	97.00
Sale of hen	10.00
Manure	2.00
Total	109.00

[a] B7, B10, and B22 gave optimistic production figures, but the exaggerations were too small to justify adjustments.

[b] Income figures at 40 centavos per egg to allow for quality inferior to those produced in the *granjas*. It is not necessary to assume costs of production for the average egg, whose mother, if that is an appropriate term, scratches freely in house and patio and whose occasional offspring arise without human intervention.

[c] These calculations were made from data provided by the *Asociación Avícola* (below). They confirm more complicated calculations derived from the *granjeros* themselves. In addition to income received directly from the *granja*, *granjeros* are entitled to share the profits of the cooperative in proportion to the individual contributions to the *caja de ahorros y prestamos*, which is a revolving fund from which the *granjeros* may borrow. *Granjero* B19 joined the *Asociación* in 1962 and had not yet made an entitling contribution.

[d] The cost of bringing pullets into production includes their original purchase price of 11 pesos. The labor cost data included above are assumed to be directly proportional to the number of hens, although this undoubtedly understates the true situation for the smaller *granjas*. Eggs were selling at an average price of 7.96 pesos per kilo in 1962, and on the average there are 18 eggs per kilo. The hens are sold to the *Asociación* for ten pesos at the end of their productive career. The manure is the fertilizer *gallinaza* mentioned elsewhere in the text.

TABLE VIII

Milk Production and Income

Code No.	Number of Milch Cows	Daily Production (liters)	Average Daily Production (liters)	Daily Gross Income[a] (pesos)	Annual Labor Costs[b] (pesos)	Annual Gross Income (pesos)	Annual Net Income (pesos)	Disposition
B2	2	6	3	4.5	319	1,638	1,319	Home-consumed
B3	2	8	4	6	638	2,184	1,546	Sold
B5	1	3	3	4.5	319	1,638	1,319	Home-consumed
B9	1	3	3	4.5	638	1,638	1,000	Both
B10	1	1	1	1.5	319	546	227	Home-consumed
B11	{ 1	10	10	15	638	5,460	7,233	Both
	{ 1	5	5	7.5	319	2,730		
B14	4	10	2.5	4	638	1,456	818	Home-consumed
B15	2	2	1	1.5	319	546	227	Home-consumed
B19	2	6	3	4.5	638	1,638	1,000	Sold
B20	1		(4)[c]	(6)	638	2,184	1,456	Sold
B23	{ 1	1.5	1.5	2	638	728	2,683	Sold
	{ 1	5.5	5.5	8	319	2,912		
B26	{ 1	9	9	13.5	638	4,914	7,306	Sold
	{ 2	14	7	10.5	319	3,349		
B28	1	4	4	6	638	2,184	1,546	Both
B30	1	7.5	7.5	11.25	638	4,095	3,457	Sold
B31	2	2	1	1.5	319	546	227	Home-consumed
B32	1	3.5	3.5	5.5	638	2,002	1,364	Sold
B33	1	5	5	7.5	638	2,730	2,092	Both
B34	2	6	3	4.5	638	1,638	1,000	Sold
Averages			4.1				1,990	

[a] Average price, 1.5 pesos per liter.

[b] For those with one or two cows we assume one hour daily labor. Those with three or more cows and those who sell, two hours a day. The hourly rate is calculated by dividing the 7-peso daily rate by 8.

[c] No yield information given in this case, and the average yield of about 4 liters was interpolated.

Table IX

Years of Schooling: Males and Females, 21 and Over[a]

Years of Schooling		Males	Females
0		18	39
1		6	10
2		16	25
3		38	35
4		35	15
5		9	9
6		7	6
7		2	0
8		2	1
9		1	0
10		0	0
11		1	0
Higher education		4	1
Some, but number of years not known		19	19
No answer		18	29
	Totals	176	189

[a] Totals do not agree with those of the age distribution table, since included here are persons clearly over 20 but whose age could not be specified in the other table. The *patrona* of Tzipecua accounts for the single higher education entry in the right-hand column.

TABLE X

Secondary Occupations: Total Population 16 and Over

Sector	Secondary	Tertiary	Quartic
Primary Industry			
Farmer	37	5	
Chicken farmer	2	3	1
Gardener	5	1	
Farm laborer	18	1	
Woodsman	5		
Fisherman	4	1	
	71	11	1
Secondary Industry			
Carpenter	3	1	
Clothing factory worker	3		
Net weaver	5		
	11	1	
Tertiary Industry			
Mason	5		
Librarian	1		
Teamster	1		
Comerciante	28	2	1
Landlord	1		
Public official	2	1	
Practical nurse		1	
Housework	15	1	
Dance teacher	1		
Musician	2	5	2
Barber	1		
Night watchman	1		
Shopkeeper	2	1	
	60	11	3

Number of Persons With		
Two or More Occupations	Three or More Occupations	Four Occupations
142	27	4

Table XI

Wage Rates and Income: Tailors and Seamstresses (pesos)

Code No.	Hours per Day	Daily Rate	Weekly Rate as Reported by		Probable Annual Gross	Allowance for Depreciation of Equipment[a]	Net Annual Income	Hourly Rate
			Self	Employer				
F1	9	3 to 9	10 to 54[b]	50	2,500[ed]	102	2,398	93 cent.[d]
F2	7[e]	12 to 15	72 to 90[b]	75	750[df]	80	670	1 peso 78 cent.
F7	6	5 to 6	25 to 30[g]	24	1,200[eh]	126	1,174	83 cent.
F15	2[i]		15 to 20		900[e]	15	885	1 peso 50 cent.[j]

[a] Assumed rate of depreciation for machines, 10%.

[b] Based on a six-day week.

[e] Based on a 52-week year less two weeks to allow for attendance at *fiestas* and other distractions.

[d] Assumed weekly average rate as reported by employer.

[e] Works only seven hours due to need to care for animals.

[f] Normally works in the *taller* only during slack agricultural season (about 10 weeks). In 1962 was working all year in *taller*.

[g] Attends high school in Pátzcuaro and leaves *taller* early. Only works a five-day week.

[h] Will accept the employee's own lower estimate in this case, since it is almost equal to the average figure given by the employer.

[i] This is a maximum. These data are for a family working at home in which mother, father, and daughter all sew but only one machine is available. The average daily machine use would perhaps be two hours per person but it is used six hours during the day. The income is stated as 15 to 20 pesos each for mother and father and about 50 pesos a week distributed among all three. If this is the case, the parents would probably average at least 18 pesos a week each.

[j] This is based on one of the parents using the machine two hours a day for six days, and weekly earnings of 18 pesos.

TABLE XII

Comerciantes: Number of Days at Market, Net Sales, Expenses, and Income (pesos)

Code No.	Market Location	Number of Days at Market	Daily Net Sales[a]	Expenses Travel[b]	Expenses Taxes	Daily Net Profit	Annual Net Profit	% Own Products[c]	Net Contribution to Family Income Table[d]
F3	Pátzcuaro	16	2.50	0	0.40	2.10	33.60[e]	100	33.60
F4	RR Station	27	10[f]	0.20	0.40	9.40	253.80	50	—[g]
F5	Pátzcuaro & RR Station	365	12	0.40	0.40	11.20	4,088	100	0
F9	RR Station	365	5[f]	0	0.10	4.90	1,788.50	50	—[g]
F10	Pátzcuaro & Morelia	216	12.50	0.80	0.60[h]	11.10	2,397.60	80	479.50
F11	Pátzcuaro	260	8	0.40	0.50	7.10	1,846[e]	60	740
F13	Pátzcuaro	17	4	0.60	0.40	3	51[e]	0	51
F16	Uruapan	88	30	10.50[i]	1	18.50	1,628	0	1,628
F17	Huecorio & Colonia Ibarra	365	25	0	0.20	24.80	9,052	100	0
F19	Pátzcuaro	25	36	0.80	0.30	34.90	872.50	100	0
F20	Pátzcuaro	208	20	0.60	0.40	19	3,952	50	1,976
F23	Pátzcuaro	312	12.50	0.60	0.30	11.60	3,619	100	3,619
F24	Pátzcuaro & Mexico	51	40	17.00	3	20	1,020	25	765
F28	Pátzcuaro	208	10	0.60	0.40	9.00	3,536	0	3,536
	Quiroga	52	35	2.00	1.00	32.00			
F29	Uruapan	104	40	8.00	0.60	31.40	3,266	25	2,452

[a] Daily sales net of cost of purchasing products, in those cases where not of own household.

[b] These rates include transportation of goods.

[c] Percentages are approximations, estimated by examining products of household and products sold by trader.

[d] To avoid double counting in the family income table (Table 21) it was necessary to add in that table only the sales made by the trader of products not included elsewhere in the family income table. Thus, when the trader sells 100% family-produced products, nothing will be added. The exception is F3. In this case the *comerciante* reported that all the products she sold were from her garden, but these products were not mentioned by her husband when he was questioned about agricultural sales.

[e] From our knowledge of the informants these figures would seem too low. However, data are sufficient for corrections.

[f] These *comerciantes* reported gross rather than net sales. The net sales were calculated by examining the differentials between the prices paid and the prices received and applying an average ratio to calculate net sales.

ᵍ Figures not included in family income table since data insufficient on productive activities of other family members.

ʰ Average taxes paid. Amount will vary from day to day depending on quantity of goods for sale.

ⁱ Includes 50 centavos for accommodations.

ʲ Each *comerciante* was asked to give high, low, and average daily gross and net sales. In addition, data were gathered both on prices paid and prices received in some cases. This gave some idea of the appropriate ratios of net to gross daily sales. If these appeared reasonably consistent, the average daily sales figure was taken to be correct and was then reduced by daily expenses to get a rate of profit per day. This latter figure was then multiplied by the number of days worked to get total annual profits.

To ascertain the number of days worked, the respondents were not simply asked, "How many days a year do you work as a *comerciante*?" Instead, they were asked to specify the season worked, the number of days a week at the market, and the seasons not worked. Where the respondent sold home-produced products the total annual profits were compared with the income calculations for agricultural products, and this proved a valuable cross-check on both data.

Respondent F5 sells milk, fruits, and vegetables produced by her son, but not, of course, the products of his *granja*. According to estimates made from her answers, her net profits amounted to 4,088 pesos, which corresponds closely to the 4,104 pesos received from agricultural products as derived from the corresponding agricultural survey B2.

Similarly, respondent F17 reported profits of 9,052 pesos, which were reasonably close to the value of the cash sales of 8,613 pesos as calculated from the corresponding B26.

With F5, the *comerciante's* profits were not added to B2 to get family income, since the B2 figure was higher than that of F5. On the other hand, since profits reported from F17 were higher than the cash sales reported by B26, the difference between the two values of 434 pesos was added to get total family income.

The data provided by respondent F23 confirmed a suspicion that the farm income from the corresponding B34 was too low. This particular farmer has a relatively large amount of land but mentioned only growing corn, wheat, and lentils, giving a total value of 1,439 pesos. F23, who sells this farmer's products, mentioned a large range of fruits and vegetables that B34 ignored, and she said that it all came from the family farm. The possibility remains, however, that B34 was not trying to be deliberately misleading. His four sons, who live with him, are all farmers and may have grown the products he did not mention. Such a division of labor is sometimes found in the village, with some members concentrating their attention on one activity and other members on something else. In the Pérez family for instance, the father is busy with vegetables in the *orilla*, while the son specializes in wheat and corn. This specialization is not, of course, complete. Farmers will shift from one activity to another as the situation warrants. One other factor suggests that B34 thought and operated in this way. The team had good relationships with this family, and one of the sons was extremely helpful to our study. Because the products sold by F23 differ entirely from those grown by B34, all of her earnings are added to the family income table.

Where the respondent sold products all of which were purchased from others, the entire profit was, of course, added to Table 21. Those who mixed purchased acquisitions with their own family products offered a slightly more difficult situation. F10 and her daughter-in-law (not interviewed) sell the household farm products, but F10 also sells vegetables that she buys from others. About one-third of the products sold were purchased from others, but since with these she gains only the difference between the "wholesale" and retail prices, their contribution to her net profit would be no more than 20%. Thus, this 20% was added to the family income of B34. Similar reasoning applied to the proportionate allocations for F11, F20, F24, and F29.

TABLE XIII

Bread Making: Income and Costs of Production per Week (pesos)

Income		
Income from cash sales of bread		40
Imputed income from bread consumed at home		20
	Total	60[a]

Costs of Production	*Quantity*	*Cost*
White flour at 1.50 pesos per kilo	20 kilos	30.00
Whole wheat flour at 1.25 pesos per kilo	5 kilos	7.50
Brown sugar *peloncillo* at 1.30 pesos per kilo	1 kilo	1.30
Refined sugar at 1.80 pesos per kilo	1.5 kilos	2.70
Firewood		5.00
Labor: 2 persons at 1 peso per hour for 5 hours		10.00[b]
Depreciation of oven		1.00[c]
	Total	57.50
Profits from sale of bread		2.50

[a] Three hundred loaves are made each week at the rate of ten pieces per kilo. The loaves sell at the rate of two pesos per kilo but 100 are kept for the family's own use.

[b] This is an assumed rate and may be too low, especially if we consider that the lowest hourly rate for *palmeros*—not an especially demanding occupation—is 1.40 pesos. However the baking is done early on Sunday mornings and the opportunity cost is probably low. At times, three or four persons will help with the preparation of the loaves, but this does not affect the costs since the total labor time remains the same.

[c] Estimated.

TABLE XIV

Earning Rates: Various Occupations (pesos)

Occupation	Income in Kind	Earning Rates by[a]				
		Hour	Day	Week	Month	
Tailors and seamstresses	No	2.00[b]	15[c]	180		High
		0.33[b]	3[c]	24		Low
Carpenters	No		25			High
			20			Low
Palmeros	No	2.40[b]	15			High
		1.40[b]	12			Low
Librarian	No	2.00			100	
Chauffeur	Meals			50		
Masons	Meals	2.92		140		High
		2.45		120		Low
		4.37	35			Morelia
Comerciantes	No		40[d]	300		High
			2.50[d]			Low
Laborers	No		20			High
	Meal at 3 pesos daily		6 to 7			Low
	Room and board			40		
Servants	Meals				100	High
	Meals				50	Low

[a] Daily rates cannot be derived from hourly rates in this table due to variation in the number of hours worked per day. A similar lack of direct relationship applies to weekly rates.
[b] From Table XV.
[c] From Table XI.
[d] From Table XII.

TABLE XV

Piece Rates: Seamstresses, Tailors, and Palmeros (pesos)

Type of Work	Item	Time (minutes)	Piece Rate	Hourly Rate
Seamstress	Apron	90	1.50	1.00
	Blouse	180	2.50	0.83
	Potholder	90	0.50	0.33
Tailor #1	Shirt	180	6.00	2.00
Tailor #2	Small shirt	90	3.00	2.00
	Apron	120	1.50	0.75
Palmero #1	Large chair	600	12.00	2.40
	Medium chair	180	6.00	2.00
	Table	180	7.00	2.33
	Small chair	180	5.00	1.67
	Small chair	240	9.00	2.25
Palmero #2	Table	300	7.00	1.40

TABLE XVI

Level of Employment: *Comerciantes*

Code No.	Number of Days at Market per Year	Number of Hours at Market	Number of Hours Preparation per Market Day	Total Hours Worked per Year as Comerciante	Other Occupations
F3	16	6	1	112	Housework
F4	27	9	3	324	*Granjera*
F5	365	9	3	4,380	Housework
F9	365	8	1	3,285	Housework
F10	216	5	1	1,296	Housework
F11	260	7	1	2,080	Housework
F12	365	9	3	4,380	None
F13	17	5	0	85	{ Librarian { *Inyectadora*
F16	88	10	2	1,056	Farmer, Laborer
F17	365	4	2	2,190	Housework
F19	18	6	2	144	Housework
F20	208	5	2	1,456	Housework
F23	312	5	1	1,872	{ Housework { Agriculture
F24	51	8	2	510	Housework
F28	260	8	1	2,340	Housework
F29	104	6	1	728	Housework

TABLE XVII

Level of Employment: Tailors and Seamstresses

Code No.	Hours per Day	Days per Week	Weeks in Year	Total Number of Hours per Year
F1	9	6	50	2,700[a]
F2	7	6	10	420[b]
F7	6	5	50	1,500[c]
F15	3	5	50	450[d]
F15	2	6	50	600[e]
F15	1	6	50	300[f]

[a] The only full-time seamstress included in the survey.
[b] In 1961 this person worked as a tailor only during the dry season. He was fully employed on his farm the rest of the year.
[c] This person was also attending high school full time at night.
[d] Worked as seamstress for five days and as a *comerciante* for two.
[e] Worked on his own farm and as a laborer the balance of the time.
[f] A young girl 11 years of age.

TABLE XVIII

Inventory of Buildings (Excluding Tzipecua)

Public Buildings	
Church	Social Center
School	Chapel
Kindergarten	Jail
School bathhouse	Office of judge
Public laundry	Village hall (*jefatura*)

Private Nonresidential	*Total Estimated Value* (pesos)	
Four stores[a]		
Four barns	5,200	
Two mills (*molinos de nixtamal*)[b]	7,000	
One small factory (*taller*)[a]		
Eleven chicken houses (*granjas*)	31,408	
One grain warehouse (*almacén*)	1,800	
	45,408	$ 3,632 U.S.
Private Residential		
159 houses[c]	545,790	$43,663 U.S.
Totals	591,198	$47,295 U.S.

[a] Parts of houses. Values included therein.

[b] These are houses in which mills are installed. Value does not include mill.

[c] Possibly understated. Some families own two distinct houses opening off the same patio. Since the roofs are sometimes joined it was not always possible to ascertain this. Some of the houses are under construction and many are unoccupied.

TABLE XIX

Estimates of House Values

Code No.	(a) Inherited (b) Purchased (c) Built	Date Acquired or Built	Cost if Purchased or Built (pesos)	Current Estimated Value of House (pesos)	Current Estimated Value of House and Lot (pesos)	Annual Taxes (pesos)
C1	a	1934		3,000	14,000	
C2	b	1957	300	800[a]	1,000[a]	
C3	a	1935		1,000[a]	1,500[a]	
C4	c	1956	650	2,000[b]	3,000	
C5	b	1950	250	350		7
C6	a	1958		900	1,200	15
C7	c	1960–62	13,000	13,000[c]		18
C8	a	1942		800[a]	1,000[a]	181
C9	c	1962	400	500[b]	1,000	
C10	c	NA				12.50
C11	a	1942		20,000[c]		270
C12	c	1961	400	500[b]		
C13	c	1956	4,000	6,000		39
C14	c	1944		5,000		18
C15	a	1961		1,500[b]	2,000	13
C16	a	1920		4,000[a]		47.75
C17	a	1920		2,000	3,000	76
C18	c	1947	2,900	6,000[b]	14,000	45
C19	c	1962	800	800		
C20	c	1937		1,500[a]	2,000	
C21	a	1938		4,000		28
C22	c	1957	500	500[a]		22
C23	a	1948		6,500		18.80
C24	a	1952		8,000[b]	10,000	50
C25	c	1958	400	700	700	20
C26	a	1930		500[a]		
C27	a	1958		3,000		
C28	a	1910		3,000		100
C29	a	1962		1,000		32
C31	a	1948		1,500		20
C32	a	NA		10,000[c]		50
C33	a	1943		4,000		38
C34	c	1961		500		20
C35	a	1952		6,000[b]	8,000	35
C36	a	1937 & 42		15,000	15,000	35
C37	b	1938	600	6,000[b]	8,000	60

[a] These valuations would appear to be too low based on knowledge of house in question.

[b] Estimate based on proportion of current estimated value of house and lot or knowledge of house in question.

[c] These valuations would appear to be too high based on knowledge of house in question.

Tʜᴇ ... TABLE XX

Inventory and Value of Agricultural Equipment

Item	Number of Farm Households Owning Item[a]	Total Number of Items in Village	Value per Item (pesos)	Total Value (pesos)
Steel plough[b]	33	44	800	35,200
Wood plough	29	33	25	825
Trace	21	21	50	1,050
Yokes				
For ploughing	25	44	10	440
For cultivation	27	44	20	880
Saddles	6	8	200	1,600
Wheelbarrow	1	1	100	100
Chain	1	1	22	22
Pump and tubing[c]	1	1	2,000	2,000
Persian wheel	1	1	500	500

[a] A farm household is one in which at least one resident regards farming or gardening as his primary occupation. Not included were several households in which the gardener worked for CREFAL. There are 71 farm households in the village out of a total of 140 households.

[b] Most of the steel ploughs are Oliver ASBF-706.

[c] This equipment cost 2,604 pesos in 1951. The 2,000-peso estimate attempts to allow for the contrary influences of depreciation and inflation.

TABLE XXI

Inventory and Value of Agricultural Tools

Item	Number of Farm Households Owning Item[a]	Total Number Owned by Farm Households	Allowance for Ownership in Rest of Village	Total Number Owned in Village	Value per Item (pesos)	Total Value		Inherited	Purchased	Built
						Farm (pesos)	Village			
Machete	50	58	100%	116	10	580	1,160	1	27	0
Hoe	56	92	50%	138	15	1,380	2,070	0	44	0
Shovel	58	67	50%	101	10	670	1,010	2	30	0
Pickaxe	35	35	25%	43	12	420	516	0	17	0
Sickle	50	62	50%	93	7	434	651	1	30	0
Axe	44	46	50%	69	29	1,334	2,001	0	21	0
Mattock	2	2	100%	4	20	40	80	0	1	0
Goad	19	21	100%	42	5	105	210	0	10	0
Scythe	2	2	0	2	9	18	18	0	1	0
Crowbar	2	2	0	2	15	30	30	0	1	0
Pole	4	4	50%	6	20	120	120	0	4	0
Hoe	2	2	0	2	20	40	40	0	1	0
Ploughshare	8	8	0	8	20	160	160	0	4	0
Maize gleaner	12	15	25%	19	1	15	19	1	6	0
Lasso	2	6	0	6	3	18	18	0	3	0
Cable	2	2	0	2	5	10	10	0	1	0
						5,374 ($430 U.S.)	8,113 ($649 U.S.)			

[a] These data directly from Agricultural Survey. See Chapter 1.

TABLE XXII

Estimates of Number and Value of Farm Work Animals

	Oxen	Burros	Horses
Total from Agricultural Survey	46	14	18
Of which: Adults	27	13	10
Young animals	19	1	8
Young animals as percent of total	41%	7%	44%
Total from census[a]	62	60	30
Revision factor[b]	2.42	1	1.8
Revised total for village[c]	150	60	54
Of which: Adults	89	56	30
Young animals	61	4	24
Current value adult[d] (pesos)	1,500	180	300
Total value adults (pesos)	133,500	10,080	9,000
Total value young animals (pesos)	45,750	360	3,600
Grand Totals	179,250	10,440	12,600
Farm households without animals	39	47	55

[a] In the original Census conducted in June, 1962, data were collected on the animal population.

[b] It was anticipated that the data on animal holdings as collected in the original Census would not be correct since insufficient time had elapsed for confidence to be established, the investigators were gaining experience, and, of necessity, the Census interviews were conducted as expeditiously as possible. Confidence had improved by the time the Agricultural Survey was conducted, and the data collected for the farm households in this survey were compared with the data collected *for the same households* in the Census. The revision factor is the ratio of the original Census totals for these households to the Agricultural Survey totals.

[c] The Census totals were multiplied by the revision factor to arrive at an estimate of the total number of animals in the village.

[d] Current values were gathered in the Agricultural Survey. The values for young animals were established at one-half of that for adults.

TABLE XXIII

Sample Distribution of Work Animal Population
Among Farm Households[a]

Number of Animals per Farm Household	Number of Farm Households Having Specified Number of		
	Oxen	*Burros*	*Horses*
None	19	23	27
1	2	8	3
2	3	3	0
3	6	0	2
4	3	0	1
5	0	0	1
6	0	0	0
7	0	0	0
8	1	0	0

[a] Data derived from the Agricultural Survey. Tzipecua is included.

TABLE XXIV

Estimates of Number and Values of Chickens, Cows, and Pigs

	Chickens	Cows	Pigs
Total from Agricultural Survey	1,382	70	61
Young animals as percent of total		44%	33%
Total from original Census	2,772	136	143
Revision factor[a]	1.06	1.25	1.32
Revised total for village	2,938	170	189
Of which: Adults		95	127
Young animals		75	62
High quality[b]	2,501		
Corriente	437		
Current values (pesos)			
Adults		900	75
Young animals		450	35
High quality	10		
Corriente	5		
Total values			
Adults		85,500	9,525
Young animals		33,750	2,170
High quality	25,010		
Corriente	2,185		
Grand Totals (pesos)	27,195	119,250	11,695
Number of farm households without animals	24	22	38

[a] For explanation see Table XXII.
[b] These are white Leghorns distributed through the *Asociación Avícola*.

TABLE XXV

Assets of a Well-to-do Farmer (pesos)

Category	Item	Number	Farmer's Valuation	Subtotal
Equipment	Steel ploughs	2	1,600	
	Wood ploughs	2	60	
	Yokes	3	30	
	Aperos	1	70	
				1,760
Tools	*Machetes*	2	16	
	Hoes	3	45	
	Shovels	1	15	
	Goad	1	5	
	Axe	1	50	
	Sickles	2	24	
	Pickaxe	1	10	
				165
Work animals	Adult oxen	3	3,600	
	Young oxen	5	3,000	
	Horses	1	400	
				7,000
Other animals	Chickens	8	48	
	Cows	4	3,200	
	Heifers	3	1,200	
	Adult pigs	5	750	
	Young pigs	5	375	
				5,573
Fruit trees	11 varieties	30	750[a]	
				750
Agricultural buildings	Stables	1	2,000	
	Warehouses[b]	1	9,000	
				11,000
			Grand Total	26,248
Land	*Ejido*	1¼ has.		
	Private	2 has.		
	Federal	½ ha.		
		3¾ has.		

[a] Our valuation.
[b] Actually a second house used for storage.

TABLE XXVI

Assets of a Poor Farmer (pesos)

Category	Item	Number	Farmer's Valuation	Subtotal
Equipment	None			0
Tools	Shovel	1	10	
	Pickaxe	1	10	
				20
Work animals	None			0
Other animals	Chickens	1	6	
	Heifer	1	400	
				406
Fruit trees	Four varieties	1 each	100	
				100
Agricultural buildings	None			0
			Grand Total	526
Land	*Ejido*	¼ hectare		
	Private	none		
	Federal	none		

TABLE XXVII

Capital Employed in Manufacturing and Other Occupations

Occupation	Number of Persons in Trade	Average Capital Invested	Total Capital
Tailor (a)[a]	9	1,663	14,967
Tailor (b)	3	400	1,200
Storekeeper[b]	4	127	508
Fisherman	23	135	3,105
Carpenter	4	330	1,320
Mason	9	310	2,790
Comerciante	68	29	1,972
Barber	1	670	670
Miller	1	1,000	1,000
	124		27,532

[a] Nine tailors work in Don Juan's *taller* while the others work, more casually, in their homes.

[b] Six persons list their trade as storekeepers but there are only four stores.

TABLE XXVIII

Items Found in the Combined Inventories of Two Stores[a]

*Alcohol	*Arroz (rice)
*Azúcar (sugar)	Café
*Cal (lime)	*Canela (cinnamon)
*Carbonato (Alka Seltzer)	Carne (dried meat)
*Cerillos (matches)	*Cigarros (cigarettes)
*Cerveza (beer)	Clavos (nails)
Cohetes (rockets)	Cuadernos (notebooks)
*Chile	Chicle
Chupaletas (ices)	*Chocolate
Dulces (sweets)	Escobas (brooms)
Escobillas (whiskbrooms)	Fideos (noodles)
*Frijoles	*Galletas (biscuits)
Gelatina (gelatine)	*Harina (flour)
Huevos (eggs)	*Jabón (soap)
Lápices (pencils)	Leña (firewood)
*Maíz (corn)	*Maizcena (corn flour)
*Manteca (lard)	*Pan (bread)
Papel (paper)	Pasteles (pastries)
Piloncillo (unrefined sugar)	Refrescos (soft drinks)
*Sal (salt)	Sardinas (sardines)
Sobres (envelopes)	*Veladores (candlesticks)
*Velas (candles)	Verdura (greens)
Various canned fruits	

[a] The starred items are found in both stores.

TABLE XXIX

Estimates of Total Number and Value of Consumer Durables

Article	*Number*	*Number of Households Without Item*	*Percent Without Item*	*Total Value* (pesos)
Beds	195	32	22.8	23,071
Tables	181	20	14.1	2,795
Chairs	324	24	17.1	3,662
Radios	86	66	47.1	37,254
Victrolas	4	136	97.1	2,000
Closets	64	88	62.8	4,024
Irons	30	112	80.0	1,288
Sewing machines	60	72	51.4	31,520
Violins	4[a]	136	97.1	1,200
Storage boxes	119	84	60.0	3,273
Blankets	479	0	0	27,562
Petates	424	16	11.4	1,832
Bicycles	8[a]	136	97.1	8,000
Valises	44	116	82.8	1,620
Guitars	8[a]	136	97.1	400
Records	200	136	97.1	1,700
Cellos	1	139	.99.2	1,000
Double basses	1	139	99.2	1,500
Saxophones	1	139	99.2	55
Gas stoves	1	139	99.2	1,250
Kerosene stoves	1	139	99.2	500
				155,506

[a] Possible underestimates.

TABLE XXX

Loans of More Than 100 Pesos: Period, Interest, Purpose, and Security

Amount Borrowed (pesos)	Period of Loan (months)	Rate of Interest per Month	Purpose of Loan	Security Offered
Larger Intra-village Loans				
2,000	12	NA[a]	Sickness and construction of stable	Use of field
200	NA	0	Sickness	None
200	2	5%	U.S.[b]	None
150	3	0	Consumption	None
600	12	5%	Trading inventories	Use of field
1,000	4	0	Trading inventories	None
200	3	0	Trading inventories	None
Loans Made by Acaparadores				
600	3	5%	U.S.[b]	House
200	1	5%	U.S.[b]	House
500	6	5%	Build *granja*	House
200	6	2.5%	Hire agricultural labor	House
185[c]	4	4.7%	U.S.[b]	House
850[c]	3	5.8%	Buy cow	House
300	12	1.4%	Rent land	House
1,000	3	3%	Repair house	House
100	3	5%	Repair house	House

[a] Whether or not interest was charged in this case is not clear. The lender said he received 5% per month while the borrower said there was no interest paid.

[b] In the cases marked U.S. the borrower sought money to finance the first stages of his trip to work as a *bracero* in the U.S.

[c] In these two cases the *acaparador* discounted the interest fully or partially from a larger sum.

N.B. The last five cases involved loans from the same *acaparador*. The interest rate was different in each instance.

Table XXXI

Composition of Work Teams in Cultivation of Corn

	Number of Cases
Self plus hired *peon(es)*	10
Peones only	5[a]
Self plus immediate family only	4[b]
Self plus immediate family plus *peon(es)*	3
Self only	4
No information	8[c]
Total	34

[a] In these cases the farmer usually contracted out the entire job for a flat cash payment agreed to in advance.

[b] Usually father and son, but brothers in one case.

[c] Most of these cases involved persons farming *a medias*, and we did not ask of them detailed information on work team composition.

Table XXXII

Place of Birth of Spouses

	Number of Cases
Both husband and wife born in Huecorio	99
Both husband and wife born outside of Huecorio	3
Wife born elsewhere in Pátzcuaro region	27
Husband born elsewhere in Pátzcuaro region	4
Wife born elsewhere in Mexico	4
Husband born elsewhere in Mexico	3
Total	140

TABLE XXXIII

Age and Sex Distribution of Population, 1962

Age	Males	Females	Total	Higher Number
0	9	21	30	F
1	11	11	22	=
2	14	14	28	=
3	7	20	27	F
4	18	11	29	M
Subtotal	59	77	136	F
Cumulative total	59	77	136	F
10	11	19	30	F
11	6	11	17	F
12	9	13	22	F
13	9	4	13	M
14	6	8	14	F
Subtotal	41	55	96	F
Cumulative total	180	196	376	F
20	9	13	22	F
21	2	2	4	=
22	11	8	19	M
23	5	7	12	F
24	8	7	15	M
Subtotal	35	37	72	F
Cumulative total	250	277	527	F
30	8	2	10	M
31	5	3	8	M
32	6	2	8	M
33	1	3	4	F
34	6	5	11	M
Subtotal	26	15	41	M
Cumulative total	306	333	639	M
40	5	11	16	F
41	1	1	2	=
42	0	2	2	F
43	4	3	7	M
44	1	3	4	F

Age	Males	Females	Total	Higher Number
5	19	16	35	M
6	15	10	25	M
7	16	16	32	=
8	18	17	35	M
9	12	5	17	M
Subtotal	80	64	144	M
Cumulative total	139	141	280	F
15	10	12	22	F
16	7	7	14	=
17	6	9	15	F
18	5	9	14	F
19	7	7	14	=
Subtotal	35	44	79	F
Cumulative total	215	240	455	F
25	4	16	20	F
26	8	2	10	M
27	4	7	11	F
28	8	12	20	F
29	6	4	10	M
Subtotal	30	41	71	F
Cumulative total	280	318	598	F
35	4	7	11	F
36	7	5	12	M
37	2	3	5	F
38	5	7	12	F
39	3	3	6	=
Subtotal	21	25	46	F
Cumulative total	327	358	685	F
45	4	5	9	F
46	1	4	5	F
47	1	1	2	=
48	3	1	4	M
49	0	1	1	F

Left section:

				Sex
				F
Subtotal	11	20	31	
Cumulative total	338	378	716	
50	8	11	19	F
51	2	1	3	M
52	2	1	3	M
53	1	0	1	M
54	3	2	5	M
Subtotal	16	15	31	M
Cumulative total	363	405	768	
60	10	5	15	M
61	1	0	1	M
62	2	2	4	=
63	1	1	2	=
64	0	3	3	F
Subtotal	14	11	25	M
Cumulative total	384	425	809	
70	1	5	6	F
71	1	0	1	M
72	0	1	1	F
73	0	0	0	
74	0	0	0	
Subtotal	2	6	8	F
Cumulative total	388	435	823	
80	2	2	4	=
81	0	0	0	
82	3	0	3	M
83	0	0	0	
84	0	1	1	F
Subtotal	5	3	8	M
Cumulative total	396	439	835	

Right section:

				Sex
				F
Subtotal	9	12	21	
Cumulative total	347	390	737	
55	4	3	7	M
56	0	3	3	F
57	1	0	1	M
58	2	1	3	M
59	0	2	2	F
Subtotal	7	9	16	F
Cumulative total	370	414	784	
65	1	2	3	F
66	0	1	1	F
67	1	0	0	
68	1	0	1	M
69	0	1	1	F
Subtotal	2	4	6	F
Cumulative total	386	429	815	
75	2	1	3	M
76	0	0	0	
77	1	0	1	M
78	0	0	0	
79	0	0	0	
Subtotal	3	1	4	M
Cumulative total	391	436	827	
85	1	0	1	M
86	0	1	1	
87	0	1	1	F
88	0	1	1	F
89	0	0	0	
Subtotal	1	2	3	F
Cumulative total	397	441	838	
91	1	0	1	M
113	0	1	1	F
	2	2	4	= =
	3	3	6	F
	400	444	844	

Age undetermined but over 20
Subtotal
Grand Total

TABLE XXXIV

Number of Persons in Residence per Family

Number of Persons in Family	Number of Families
1	25
2	33
3	24
4	27
5	22
6	19
7	23
8	10
9	4
10	5
11	2

TABLE XXXV

Infant Mortality by Age of Mother

Age of Mother	Number of Mothers in This Age Group	Number Reporting Infant Mortality	Number Giving No Answer	Number Reporting No Infant Mortality	Total Number of Infant Mortalities per Age Group	Average Number of Infant Deaths per Mother Responding to Question[a]
21–25	28	6	0	22	15	0.53
26–30	25	10	0	15	15	0.60
31–35	16	7	0	9	15	0.93
36–40	26	14	1	11	32	1.28
41–45	13	6	1	6	15	1.25
46–50	18	12	1	5	39	2.29
51–55	6	5	0	1	18	3.00
56–60	11	4	2	5	10	1.11
61–65	8	1	6	1	3	
66–70	6	1	4	1	4	
71–75	2	0	1	1	0	
76–80	2	1	1	0	1	
81–85	1	0	1	0	0	
86–90	2	0	2	0	0	
91+	1	0	1	0	0	
Age not given	4	3	0	1		
Totals	169	70	21	78	—	

[a] Above the age group 56 to 60, the number of mothers responding to the question was not large enough to lead to meaningful averages.

TABLE XXXVI

Marital Status: Males and Females, 16 and Over

Age Group		Married	Single	Widowed	Divorced	Total
16 to 20	M	3	29			32
	F	8	37			45
21 to 25	M	12	19			31
	F	30	11			41
26 to 30	M	27	7			34
	F	23	5			28
31 to 35	M	20	2			22
	F	16	1	1	1	19
36 to 40	M	22				22
	F	24	3	2		29
41 to 45	M	10		1		11
	F	11		2		13
46 to 50	M	13		1		14
	F	14	1	2		17
51 to 55	M	10	1			11
	F	5		3		8
56 to 60	M	10		3		13
	F	7		5		12
61 to 65	M	5				5
	F	3		5		8
66 to 70	M	2				2
	F	1		6		7
71 to 75	M	3				3
	F	2				2
76 to 80	M	2		1		3
	F	1		1		2
81 to 85	M	3		1		4
	F			1		1
86 to 90	M					0
	F	1		1		2
91 to 95	M	1				1
	F					0
113	F			1		1
No age	M	2				2
given	F	1				1
Totals	M	145	58	7	0	210
	F	147	58	30	1	236

Table XXXVII

"Ideal" Number of Children Desired
by Married Males and Females

Number of Children Desired	Males	Females
0	0	1
1	0	1
2	2	4
3	4	2
4	2	2
5	8	4
6	5	4
7	3	1
8	5	1
9	0	1
10	1	1
11 or more	1	1
Does not know	3	9
No answer	2	4
Number of respondents	36	36
Average number desired	5.5[a]	4.6[a]

[a] Averages exclude the one male and one female who replied vaguely in terms of "more than ten."

Table XXXVIII

Classes of Sickness as Reported by Householders

Sickness as Defined by Householder	Number of Households in Which This Sickness Reported
Common cold	27
Fevers	16
Coughs	12
Diarrhea	7
Influenza	5
Stomach pains	4
Malaria	3
Headache	3
Sore throats	2
Measles, typhus, smallpox	1 each
Number reporting no sickness	3

TABLE XXXIX

Summary of Housing Conditions from Sample
Survey of 36 Homes

Number of Rooms Including Kitchen		Number of Homes
1		7
2		2
3		8
4		2
9		1
	Total	36
Number of Windows		
0		22
1		9
2		3
7		1
13		1
	Total	36
Type of Floor		
Dirt only		23
Wood only		2
Cement only		5
Combination dirt, cement, tile		1
Combination dirt, tile		2
Combination wood, tile		1
Combination stone, cement		2
	Total	36
Water Supply		
Water piped into patio		21
Well in patio or garden		8
No water supply in home		7
	Total	36
Number of homes in which living and kitchen facilities combined		20
Number of homes without latrine		17
Number of homes with electricity		24

TABLE XL

Relationships Between Household Size, Total Household
Income, and Per Capita Income (pesos)

Number of Persons in Household	Average Total Household Income	Average Per Capita Income
2[a]	3,539	1,769
4	5,579	1,389
5	6,654	1,331
6[a]	11,012	1,835
7[a]	10,591	1,513
8	10,185	1,273
9[a]	6,950	772
10[a]	16,417	1,642
11[a]	9,376	426

[a] The erratic nature of the figures at these family sizes is due to the small number of entries in these classes. Despite this limitation, the income comparisons between the smallest and largest families can be discerned. (See Table 21.)

TABLE XLI

Income in Kind as Percent of Total Income from Various Sources

Productive Source	Income in Kind as Percent of Total Income from This Source
Baking	87
Crops	64
Fruit	56
Animals	30
Firewood	26
Unskilled farm labor	19
Milk	14
Eggs	9

Percentages Positive but Unknown
Fishing, migrant labor, music, household service, garment making, net weaving, storekeeping.

No Income in Kind
Furniture weaving, masonry, carpentry, trading.

BIBLIOGRAPHY

Beals, Ralph. *Cherán: A Sierra Tarascan Village*. Washington, USGPO, 1946. Smithsonian Institution, Institute of Social Anthropology, Publication No. 2.

Belshaw, Michael. "Aspects of the Theory of Discounting," *Engineering Economist*, VI, No. 3 (Spring, 1961).

Davis, Kingsley. *The Population of India and Pakistan*. Princeton, Princeton University Press, 1951.

Edwards, David. *An Economic Study of Small Farming in Jamaica*. Jamaica, University College of the West Indies, Institute of Social and Economic Research, 1961.

Flores, Edmundo. *Tratado de Economía Agrícola*. Mexico, Fondo de Cultura Económica, 1961.

Foster, George M. *Empire's Children: The People of Tzintzuntzan*. Printed in Mexico City by Imprenta Nuevo Mundo, S.A., 1948. Smithsonian Institution, Institute of Social Anthropology, Publication No. 6.

Hagen, Everett. *On the Theory of Social Change*. Homewood, Ill., Dorsey Press, 1962.

Hendry, James B. *The Small World of Khanh Hau*. Chicago, Aldine Publishing Company, 1964.

Hirschman, Albert O. *The Strategy of Economic Development*. New Haven, Yale University Press, 1958.

International Bank for Reconstruction and Development. *The Economic Development of Mexico.* Baltimore, Johns Hopkins Press, 1953.

Leibenstein, Harvey. *Economic Backwardness and Economic Growth.* New York, John Wiley, 1957.

Lewis, Oscar. *Life in a Mexican Village: Tepoztlán Restudied.* Urbana, University of Illinois Press, 1951.

Luján, José Manuel. *Breve Reseña del Programa de Crédito Avícola Supervisado.* CREFAL, Pátzcuaro, 1962.

Nurkse, Ragnar. *Problems of Capital Formation in Underdeveloped Countries.* Oxford, Blackwell, 1953.

Pelzel, John. "The Small Industrialist in Japan," *Explorations in Entrepreneurial History,* VII, No. 2, December, 1954.

Ranis, Gustav. "The Community Centered Entrepreneur in Japanese Development," *Explorations in Entrepreneurial History,* VIII, No. 2, December, 1955.

Schumpeter, Joseph A. *The Theory of Economic Development.* Cambridge, Mass., Harvard University Press, 1949.

Weber, Max. *The Protestant Ethic and the Spirit of Capitalism.* London, Allen and Unwin, 1948.

Whetten, Nathan L. *Rural Mexico.* Chicago, University of Chicago Press, 1948.

Zinkin, Maurice. *Development for Free Asia.* Essential Books, Fair Lawn, N.J., 1956.

GLOSSARY

Abono de corral, cow and horse manure

Acaparador, in this context, moneylender

Aguardiente, hard liquor

A medias, a sharing of work, investment, or income in land or other productive asset

Apero, in this context, a broad cloth strap for lashing the yoke to the *yunta*

Arrastrar, to harrow

Asociación Avícola, poultry co-operative initiated by CREFAL

Atole, a drink made of corn meal, tasting somewhat like hot chocolate. Considered by Huecorianos a substitute for milk

Ayate, sack for carrying harvested corn

Barbechar, to plough

Basura, loose material

Bigotera, plate attached to plough to throw soil against growing plants

Buey, ox

Calzones, short trousers

Cañamargo, a hemp-like fodder

Canasta, a woven basket

Cantina, a bar

Centavo, unit of currency, 100 to the peso

Cerrito, small hill

Comerciante, itinerant trader, usually selling in a town or village marketplace

Comisión de Rentas, office in

Pátzcuaro where rent payments on public lands are made

Compadrazgo, the formal *compadre* relationship

Compadre, expression of kinship between father and godfather but also used frequently in sense of buddy or pal

CREFAL (*Centro Regional para la Educación Fundamental para la América Latina*), training center for rural workers supported by the Organization of American States and United Nations agencies

Criollo, in this context, local strain of seeds

Cruzar, the second ploughing in corn cultivation

Cuarto, in this context, a measure the size of a fully stretched hand

Chavalito, a sprat-like fish found in Lake Pátzcuaro

Chayote, vegetable pear

Chilacayote, bottle gourd

Chirimoya, a tropical fruit

Descanso, in this context, fallow land

Despegar, in this context, the ability of a plough to throw the soil cleanly

Dueño, owner

Ejidatario, one who has the right to the use of the *ejido*

Ejido, a system of land tenure organized after the Mexican Revolution in which the title to the land is held by the community; in Huecorio, the subdivided plots are worked individually

En seco, planting before the rains begin

Escarda, first step in the cultivation of corn

Faena, communal work project

Federal, in this context, land on the shores of Lake Pátzcuaro, owned by the federal government and rented to village farmers

Flecha, colloquialism for "bus"

Frijol, kidney bean

Gabán, jacket

Garocha, pole for controlling a *yunta*

Gallinaza, chicken manure

Granja, in this context, a chicken house

Granjero, in this context, a member of the poultry cooperative

Guitarrón, a bass guitar

Ingeniero (abb. *Ing.*), engineer; in this study, references are to agricultural engineers

Inyectadora, a person who gives injections

Jardinero, gardener

Jefe de tenencia, highest political officer at the village level

Jefatura, meeting place for public officials

Jornalero, day laborer

Kermesse, an indoor entertainment and fair, sometimes but not necessarily held on religious holidays in Mexico

Mañanitas, the birthday song

Manta de Costal, ground cloth

Mariposa, butterfly

Mata, plant or group of plants

Melga, flat, rectangular area delineated for broadcast seeding

Mezcal, alcoholic beverage made from *maguey*

Milpa, field of corn

Molino de nixtamal, mill for grinding corn

Municipio, municipality

Orejera, wooden plate to push earth away from plough

Orilla, land by the shores of Lake Pátzcuaro

Pala, paddle

Palmero, weaver of reed twines

Peso, unit of Mexican currency; in 1962 the exchange rate was 12.5 pesos to the U. S. dollar

Pequeñas propiedades, "small" private agricultural holdings

Petate, a reed mat for sleeping

Pica, pike

Piscador, knife used in harvesting corn

Plazero, tax collector at local market

Quinta, country house

Ranchero, popular song style associated with the Mexican cowboy

Rastro, slaughterhouse

Raya or *rayar,* the second ploughing in corn preparation

Recursos Hidráulicos, an agency of the federal government which is responsible for water resource development

Rejada, a spatula-like blade for cleaning the plough

Salvao or *salvado,* husks of wheat or barley

Segunda, the second cultivation of corn

Sembrador, worker who plants seed

Suplente, a substitute

Surcar, to make furrows or rows

Surco, furrow, or row

Taller, workshop or small factory

Tapanco, storage attic

Tapar, to cover seeds with dirt by foot

Tarascan, regional Indian language

Thiru, a small fish resembling a minnow

Tierra caliente, the hot country; low lying areas usually close to the coast

Tirar, in this context, to broadcast seeds

Yunta, team of draft animals

Yuntero, ploughman

Zapote, apple-shaped fruit

INDEX